LAND
WITHOUT A
CONTINENT

A Road Trip Through Mexico
and Central America

by Matt Savino

ILLUMIFY

MEDIA.COM

Published by

Illumify Media Global

www.IllumifyMedia.com

"Let's bring your book to life!"

Paperback ISBN: 978-1-959099-72-7

Cover design by Debbie Lewis

Printed in the United States of America

For my Mom & Dad

CONTENTS

PART ONE

BAJA MOMENTS

Run from what's comfortable. Forget safety.
Live where you fear to live.
Destroy your reputation. Be notorious.
I have tried prudent planning long enough.
From now on I'll be mad.

— RUMI

Chapter 1

Origins

I stop to assess the situation. I am in a cow pasture. I can see the town of Nueva Guinea, my escape route out of Nicaragua, a few hundred yards away. A line of trees runs between us, and beyond that, a steep ravine. There is no hope of four-wheeling it across. Thick woods block any vehicular escape to the left. Heading to the right only funnels me back to the intersection I just fled—as I pretended not to hear the cries of "Hey hey hey! HEY HEY HEY HEY! **HEYYYYYYYY!!!**" that rang out after me.

I am screwed. I have no idea why the local farmers sent me this way.

My only option is to turn around and face the source of the commotion I just created.

I crest the last hill, and the intersection comes into view. A bandana-clad student revolutionary stands in my path, his legs spread in a fighter's pose. He is aiming his homemade rocket launcher at my windshield.

I inch to a stop a few feet from the armed protester. A crush of humanity converges on us from the four corners of the roadblock.

My windows are rolled down, and I realize that—all things being equal —I'd really prefer they weren't. But rolling them up as the mob closes in seems like it would exude fear and send the wrong message. Within seconds, dozens of agitated men in straw cowboy hats descend on my car. Some poke their heads inside my passenger window, shouting in Spanish and flailing their arms in gesticulation.

I wanted an adventure. Well, I got one now.

Before we get into the story of how I wound up stranded in Nicaragua during the uprising of 2018, I'd like to share an imaginary quiz, as taken by me, before my trip. Feel free to play along if you'd like.

Mentally list everything you know about the following ancient civilizations:

1. The Olmecs
2. The Zapotecs
3. The Aztecs
4. The Maya

If your answer was something along the lines of:

1. Who?
2. Who?
3. Wiped out by Cortez. But Montezuma had his revenge and gave all the gringos diarrhea.
4. Disappeared. No one knows why or where they went. Aliens may have been involved. Also, the Maya calendar said the world would end in 2012. They made a movie about it with John Cusack. Or was it Jake Gyllenhaal? No, I think it was Cusack. Gyllenhaal was in that other one... *No More Tomorrows,* or something like that. Speaking of climate armageddon movies, at least it wasn't that dog *Geostorm.* Ugh. I want that hour and a half of my life back. *Geostorm* was so bad I almost forgot about *Prometheus* for a second. I know one thing I'll never think again: "Well, this movie has Gerard Butler, so it should be pretty good." Sorry, Gerard, that ship has sailed. The circle of trust is broken. At least with a Tom Cruise movie, it may not always be *Rain Man,* but you can expect a certain baseline entertainment value. I mean, even *Cocktail* was watchable and kinda fun... and um... wait... what was the question again?

Then congratulations! You paid as much attention as I did during the half-hour of history class we set aside for 3,000 years of Mesoamerican civilization. Also, it may be time to bump up your Ritalin dosage.

Our teachers could have taught us that Mesoamerica is one of only six isolated "first civilizations" in world history. I think that would have caught my attention. They could have captivated us with the century-long struggle to decipher Maya hieroglyphs—one of four, maybe five, original writing systems ever conceived by humans.

But no. Instead, we learned: "Cortez conquered the Aztecs—THE END." We memorized the grisly accomplishments of each conquistador like trading cards.

I visited a dozen ruins, any of which would be a crown jewel in the US National Parks system. In my research, I came across fascinating, heart-breaking, epic stories behind the dry interpretive signs. I even listened to Maya radio stations in the Yucatán—which would seem to indicate that the Maya did not, in fact, disappear.

I CAN PINPOINT the planting of the seed—the itch for adventure—to the first day of my first tour led by professional landscape photographer Marc Adamus. Late in the day in Glacier National Park, we found ourselves seven miles from the trailhead, at the bottom of a naturally terraced bowl, trying to shoot the sunset against a steep wedge-shaped peak. At the exact moment the sun went down, a driving sideways rain opened up on us.

Marc had been checking the weather report, which aggressively touted "zero percent chance of rain" all day. When the rain hit, our group was scattered around the bottom and sides of the bowl. No one was prepared for actual weather. Marc was wearing jeans. I had rain pants and a rain jacket in my pack as an afterthought. I think I just forgot to take them out.

Hiking down into the bowl had been a last-minute decision. The clouds looked like they could light up with spectacular sunset colors, as impending rain clouds often do. But instead, they just got darker and thicker as the light faded and the temperature dropped. Never again will I trust an over-exuberant weather report over my own eyes and common sense.

Navigating the rocky terrain hadn't been difficult in daylight. But the climb back up in darkness and driving rain quickly turned chaotic. I tried to keep track of the two headlamps above me as we wound through rocky terraces, then scrambled up and across a loose-rock scree slope. But as I was the least in shape, my companions' headlights steadily receded, then disappeared.

The slope became steeper as I worked my way up. Soon, I was on my hands and knees, fighting to arrest small slips on the loose rock before they became full-blown slides. This struggle drained the last of my flagging energy reserves, and I realized I was nowhere near the route we had forged on the way down. I didn't know it at the time, but subsequent photo analysis revealed that a slide in the wrong spot could have ended in a fifty-foot plunge.

Even without knowing I could be in mortal danger, the thought of a long slide was panic-inducing. I continued to wiggle up the scree slope—crawling on my belly like an alligator, pausing for minutes at a time to catch my breath. Finally, I spilled out onto a flat terraced area, where I collapsed onto my back, sucking wind and rain. I recovered, then clambered the rest of the way out of the bowl to reunite with the others at the rim.

No one knew what to expect on the hike back. Would the temperature continue to drop until the already precarious trail was covered with sleet, snow, or freezing rain? If the winds were this bad in the bowl, what would they be like along the ridge we had to traverse on the way back?

Fortunately, the temperature never dropped below freezing, and the winds abated. We trudged back to our cars in lousy spirits, soaked but not hypothermic. The rain shell I put on over my drenched hiking pants even created a surprisingly comfortable wetsuit effect.

According to survival expert Bear Grylls, multiple factors usually need to go wrong to create a survival situation (which seems to necessitate drinking one's own urine with astonishing frequency). We had one significant adverse condition: caught unprepared in a driving rainstorm on dicey terrain, far from the safety of our cars. But no one broke an ankle, we didn't get the worst of the wind or cold, and I didn't go sliding off into the abyss. In short, nobody had to pee in their water bottle that night.

The next day at breakfast, all dour spirits from the long hike back were gone, replaced with ebullient chatter about our rain-soaked ordeal. Everyone had their version of the story to tell. A bunch of office drones had just shared a real-life wilderness adventure, and we were **pumped**.

I can't speak for everyone else, but I was hooked. Something inside me realized on a cellular level that this was a thing I needed in my life.

Since we all enjoyed that first quiz so much, let's try another:

Q: Before Columbus sailed the ocean blue, what was the spiciest spice in the Old World?

A: Indian "long pepper," which has a bit more kick than black pepper but nothing close to the fire of chile peppers.

Okay, maybe you knew that. I sure didn't. I knew that corn and potatoes came from the New World. And I feel like I've learned and forgotten about tomatoes and chocolate several times over. But chile peppers? As in the heat component in every South/Southeast Asian dish that's ever sent me groping for a glass of milk? Those *all* come from the New World?

I can barely wrap my head around Italian food without tomatoes or France without fries. But Indian, Thai, Vietnamese, and Szechwan cuisine —with nothing spicier than black pepper? Inconceivable.

Maybe this is why the surprisingly varied dishes I gorged on in Puebla and Oaxaca weren't generally all that spicy. And when they were, the heat co-existed in pitch-perfect balance with other flavors. Mexican cooks have had an extra 10,000 years, give or take, to come to terms with the ornery chile pepper.

Jump cut six and a half years from that rainy night in Glacier to my seventh photo trip with Marc, this time in Patagonia. This trip was providing a different kind of adventure—one that wasn't speaking to my wilderness-adventurer soul or any other part of my soul.

It turns out the only rental cars to be had in this part of the world are tiny little pieces of crap. Remember the Geo Metro? Picture the base model Geo Metro—the one you'd swear only has seats because they're required by law—then knock that down a few levels of quality and amenities. I dubbed the car's design ethos: "openly hostile."

I whacked my head on the frame seventeen times before finally learning to enter the car with more care. With three to four of us and all our gear in each vehicle, the chassis scraped on any slight lip in the road. For highway driving, Marc instructed, "Just put the pedal to the floor and leave it there" —like one of those putt-putt cars at Six Flags. This produced a top speed of about eighty-five miles an hour and a cramp in my right calf.

But discomfort was only half the equation. The tires that come on these things are literally the temporary spare tires you see on cheaper cars in the US. Some marketing genius thought, "Hey, what if we just sell the car with **all** spares? No one will ever notice." That's brilliant, Larry! Big promotion for you.

Over the course of a week on Patagonian highways and backroads, we had multiple flat tires—which tended to pop like an engorged tick upon any slight brush with a curb. We almost rolled our car. We saw another rental like ours that **did** roll, and then a day later, we saw the poor girl who had been in the backseat—still gamely hiking with a bandaged nose and two black eyes, like some hapless teen in a John Hughes movie.

All things considered, I'd rather my epitaph not read: *He died doing what he loved—tumbling down Argentina's Ruta 40 in the worst car ever assembled outside the Soviet Bloc.*

As it turned out, Marc wanted to lead a more extensive Patagonian expedition the next year—a land trip followed by a ten-day boating expedition into the fjords of Southern Chile, where hardly anyone other than scientific expeditions had ever ventured.

I thought, "What if... I could somehow magically have my rugged, comfy Toyota FJ Cruiser in Patagonia, with its big sturdy tires, automatic transmission, power steering, wide wheelbase, multiple airbags, and vantage point that *doesn't* make me feel like a dog scooting its butt along the carpet?"

That night, I googled, "Can you drive from the US to South America?" Turns out you can!

There is one caveat: the Darién Gap between Panama and Colombia, seventy miles of impenetrable jungle with no roads. But fear not—there's a ferry! Oh, wait. The ferry went out of business in the '90s. But it's coming back! Well, maybe not. Further googling reveals the new ferry never materialized. But the standard solution is to find a partner and transport two cars in a shipping container from Panama to Colombia. Boom. Done.

So it was set. In one year, I'd meet Marc in Patagonia, leaning against my beloved FJ with a mile-wide grin.

At least, that was the plan.

Good news, everyone! By popular demand, we have time for one last question.

Q: What continent is Costa Rica in?

A: It depends... on *you*:

- If you answered **Central America**—not bad. But Central America is technically not a continent.
- If you answered **South America**, the most popular answer in my informal polling, well... at least you're in the general area.
- If you answered **North America**—congratulations! Maybe. See below.
- If you answered **Egypt**, I know several late-night talk show hosts who would *love* to interview you on the street.

A CONTINENT IS A CONTINENT, right? Well, not exactly. It turns out that might depend on where you were taught geography.

Spain, France, Portugal, Italy, Romania, their former colonies, and Greece for some reason, all lump North and South America together as a single continent called *The Americas*. These once Latin-speaking countries refuse to break up *Latin America*, which comprises Mexico and almost all of Central and South America.

As an aside, Latin Americans consider themselves just as *American* as people from the United States. So, throughout this book, if I use the word *American* in place of *someone from the United States*, I apologize. I try to keep that particular vernacular to a minimum. But unfortunately, "United States-ian" doesn't always roll off the tongue as good-ish as one might like.

Even in the non-Latin world, atlas makers only separated North and South America into two continents after World War II. This is why the flag of the modern Olympics, founded in 1894, has five rings—Europe, Asia, Africa, Australia/Oceania, and *The Americas*.

In my day job, computer programming, we call situations like this—which don't fit neatly into one bucket or follow clean rules—*edge cases*. Edge cases, by definition, make up a tiny fraction of your application's functionality yet demand a majority of your programming effort. We abhor edge cases. They're all work and no glory.

I can imagine the post-WWII atlas maker's plight in deciding whether Central America should officially reside in North or South America. By sheer geography, the cleanest break, and the one they ultimately chose, would seem to be the border between Panama and Colombia.

But the cleanest geographic distinction isn't always the winner. According to Western atlas makers, Europe and Asia are separated by a cultural land border that spans thousands of miles and cuts Istanbul in half. I mention *Western* atlas makers because Russia, Eastern Europe, and Japan are less than pleased with this delineation. They consider *Eurasia* to be a single continent.

They have a point. If cultural lines matter that much, why not separate Asia at the Himalayas? Or Africa at the Sahara?

Counterpoint: Russian Risk must be exceedingly dreary. Asia is already impossible to occupy in Western Risk. But at least some noob still tries to hold it while savvy veterans goad them on from the safety of South America or Australia. Trying to hold *Eurasia* would just be pointless on its face (see: History).

So, there is some precedent for the idea of lumping Central America in with South America on cultural grounds. But adding Mexico to South America was probably always going to be a bridge too far—given its 2,000-mile land border with the United States.

Once Mexico was tethered to the United States, one would assume that its cultural gravity and shared trading borders sealed Central America's fate as part of North America—a continent few associate it with, including the people who actually live there. To a Latin American, a *North American* is **always** someone from the US or Canada and **never** someone from Mexico or Central America.

This ambiguity works both ways. Culturally and geographically, the countries of Central America—Belize, Guatemala, El Salvador, Honduras, Nicaragua, Costa Rica, and Panama—feel more like a snake-shaped island to me than part of my home continent. Of all the multi-country landmasses on Earth, Central America must be the most untethered.

Hence the title: *Land without a Continent*.

Also, because **Mexico and Central America: Continental Edge Case** looked a little busy on the cover.

THERE! Nueva Guinea! Did I ever tell you about the time...?

Chapter 2

Preparations

 In preparing for battle I have always found that plans are useless, but planning is indispensable.

— Dwight D. Eisenhower

I SPENT the next few months devouring everything the internet had to offer on driving the Pan-American Highway. I learned that people who travel the world in their own vehicles call themselves *Overlanders*. I learned that the number one rule of overlanding is **don't drive at night**—mainly because of unseen hazards like potholes, unmarked speed bumps, and people and domestic animals walking along the road. And I learned that the Caesar salad was invented in Tijuana by an Italian restauranteur named Caesar (actually created by his cook, Livio). But that's neither here nor there.

The first question from anyone I let in on my plan was invariably some version of "But is it safe?"

There are some "no-go zones" in Mexico (mostly near the US border), the major cities of Guatemala, El Salvador, and Honduras, and (as of 2017) the entire country of Venezuela. However, outside of those, I was surprised to find only a handful of accounts of violent crime on the overlander forums—especially when you consider that every poster is not just relaying their own experience but also aggregating every story they hear through the traveler grapevine. It's a sad fact of life in these countries that the police take crimes against tourists seriously while leaving locals to fend for themselves.

By far, the two biggest hassles I encountered in my research were "smash and grab" break-ins of unattended cars and cops fishing for bribes. Per the internet, your best chance of success when thrust into a bribe situation goes something like this:

1. Demand that the policeman write up a paper ticket.
2. Act like you have all the time in the world, and there's *nowhere* you'd rather be than talking to *that* officer at *that* moment on the side of *that* road.

"Sure, I'd **love** to go down to the station with you to write this up. Sounds like a hoot and a half. Will there be snacks, or should I pick some up on the way?" According to the blogs, this behavior will frustrate the cop and convince him to look elsewhere for a quick buck.

However, all things considered, I imagine the incidents where this strategy *fails* are chronicled much less often. Paying a bribe is strongly frowned upon, since it creates a moral hazard for the traveler coming after you. I fretted over how I would respond to a pushy policía threatening to throw me in jail for some made-up traffic violation. I'm sorry to report that in my mental dry runs, I buckled pretty fast.

To deal with smash and grab, I installed a Tuffy locking drawer in my back cargo area, giving me an extra layer of protection for stuff like my laptop and camera equipment. Anyone breaking into my car would face a sturdy steel box that isn't coming apart without a fight. All the while, my alarm is going off, and I'm hopefully somewhere nearby to hear it. The drawer also divides the cavernous space in the back of the FJ and creates a nice shelf—perfect for my cooler and various plastic totes.

Throughout my research, I compiled a to-do list that never seemed to stop growing. Highlights included learning Spanish, finally getting certified in scuba, and buying various vehicle-related gadgets, paper maps, and a fancy 200-piece road toolkit.

I was inspired by *The Road Chose Me* blogger Dan Grec, who painted a map on the hood of his Jeep, to purchase stickers of every country in Latin America for my car. I figured as a big red-headed gringo in a silver marshmallow car that was never sold in Latin America, I'll never blend in. So, I'll go the other way and make my car appear to be on an expedition—like I have legions of fans following me, fans who might bring down extra heat on any would-be miscreants. Call it the "brightly colored poison frog" defense. Although, in my case, more like one of those frogs that *isn't* poisonous but uses the same loud color scheme to glom on to its dangerous cousin's reputation.

For Spanish, I needed some fast and heavy immersion. I found a tutor, Sabrina, who offered three-week packages, culminating in a test and cultural excursion. Sabrina was the best kind of tutor for me, as she'd call me out if I hadn't done my homework. I was intimidated by her and snapped into line real quick. I pulled my first all-nighter since college cramming for her test. Still bombed it.

I loved going to Sabrina's working-class Latino neighborhood near downtown Los Angeles, which always bustled with street life. The grocery store parking lot was filled with stalls selling tacos, crepes, Easter baskets, and whatever home goods someone was getting a bulk deal on that week. I often wistfully imagine growing up in one of those Sesame Street neighborhoods in Brooklyn or Philly—where everyone hangs out on the stoop, neighbors look out for each other's kids, and old biddies keep tabs on everyone from their windows. I imagine a kid growing up in Sabrina's neighborhood could do a lot worse.

As far as getting time off, I researched my company's sabbatical policy and was gratified to find they had one. I could take off six months, possibly up to a year, with the caveat that it wasn't guaranteed they'd hire me back. This seemed fair, since it was far from guaranteed I'd want to come back.

Then my company—let's call them Hyper-Global-Megacorp—offered a layoff to all former employees of Semi-Global-Megacorp, which they had acquired a few years earlier. The timing of the layoff coincided within two weeks of my planned launch date—but now with severance! I took it as a sign from the universe and accepted.

A month before launch day, I started classes to get dive-certified with PADI. I'd nearly completed the course twice in the past but missed the final dive for various stupid reasons, so I was one of the more experienced students in class. During our first sessions in the pool, I could tell the instructors were focusing their energies on others who were struggling a bit.

The following weekend, we met at the beach. This was my first dive in a wetsuit, which was so tight I could barely move. It was also my first dive in murky water, my first dive in cold water, and my first dive walking out through the surf.

I mistimed one wave and got knocked off my feet. I continued to crawl out to deeper water as instructed, then tried to put on my fins. Every time I reached down, my center of gravity shifted, and I pitched forward face-first into the surf. While I'm sure this looked comical, it drained a lot of energy, and I kept eating seawater. I finally got my fins on, then swam out to the dive buoy, exhausting myself even more as my clingy wetsuit fought me the whole way.

Once we all gathered at the buoy, I volunteered to go down first. I was the more experienced diver, and I would lead the way. Follow me, kids!

But I forgot to take my time. Instead of sitting a few inches under the surface to stabilize my breathing and get over the shock of cold water on my face, I started sinking, fast. I tried to equalize but didn't reach into my mask far enough to properly pop my ears. My mask flooded, my nose filled with water, my ears were in shooting pain, I started coughing up seawater—and I panicked.

I was as close as I imagine one can come to a full-blown panic attack without actually having one. If you can have 80 percent of a panic attack, I was there.

I grabbed the buoy rope to arrest my fall, then looked down to see no one below me and no bottom in sight—just a rope trailing off into the murky abyss. The twenty-five feet to the bottom might as well have been a thousand. I wanted nothing more than to shoot to the surface to gather myself. But I knew students were floating directly above me, and I didn't want to have to explain myself to the instructors.

I hung there for a few seconds, my breathing more or less out of control. An instructor swam over and gave me the thumbs-up query. I gave thumbs-up back—even though I was far from thumbs-up.

Eventually, I found it in me to start working down the rope. Embarrassment is a powerful damn motivator. I was finally able to equalize, although my mask was still half-flooded. The sea floor came into view, along with the horizontal bottom rope we were supposed to hold onto as we scooted down to make room for the other students.

I pulled my way to the far end of the rope while the surging current tossed me around like a bull rider. Once I settled into place, I could finally clear my mask.

Every neuron in my brain still wanted to rocket to the surface. I tried to will myself to calm down. But I learned that if the amygdala wants to have an anxiety attack, logic is useless. All my brain knew was that I was exhausted, having trouble getting oxygen, and literally out of my element.

My ex used to have anxiety attacks. I tried to comfort her, but I had no idea what she was going through. Now I know. That is no fun.

I tried to get my breathing under control, but I'd never felt so claustrophobic. The weight of the ocean felt like a collapsed skyscraper crushing down on me. Five minutes after descending, I was still a hair's breadth from doing something panicky and messing up the whole class. Stupid sports slogans ran through my mind, like "Fatigue makes cowards of us all" and "Everyone has a plan until they get hit in the mouth."

Thanks, brain—that's really what I need right now.

I started thinking about how we have three more of these dives, and did I really want to see this through? Maybe I'm just too old for this shit. The last time I was this far underwater, I was twenty-two and invincible. At forty-eight, I get discombobulated when I sleep on someone else's couch. Will I feel this out of whack in a few weeks when I cross the border into Mexico? They say if you don't learn to drive on snow and ice as a teenager, you never get used to it. Maybe this diving thing is similar, and by extension, my trip—

Again, brain, thank you. But can we please focus on the task at hand?

Eventually, my breathing slowed—a little. I tried to focus on the skills we needed to demonstrate, which were straightforward for the first dive. An instructor started playing with a sand dollar, then did a few somersaults and barrel rolls. I calmed down somewhat, forgetting where I was while I watched his antics. Then I remembered my surroundings, and anxiety came roaring back.

The only silver lining to all this near panic was that I was sucking so much oxygen, I knew we couldn't stay down much longer. The instructors kept signaling me for my air, and I happily signaled back, "Yep, 1,200 PSI—gotta go up at 1,000. Darn it! I wish we could stay down here all day!"

At the surface, I talked to some of the other students. From their wide-eyed looks, I could tell they'd been on a similar roller coaster. This made me feel a little better. We swam back to shore, switched tanks, relaxed for a bit, and then headed back out for the second dive.

Long story short—this time, I **didn't** get knocked senseless by a wave. I had a much **easier** time putting my fins on. I **didn't** exhaust myself swimming out. I **remembered** to equalize **early and often**. The dive went a hundred times easier, I sucked about half as much air, and I even enjoyed myself a little.

The next day went even smoother. We went down fifty feet on our last dive. Other than being very cold, I was fine, with zero anxiety. Our group had a lot of fun bonding over the two weekends. We didn't lose a single class member to attrition, which we were told never happens. I was buzzing for weeks after scuba class. To get outside my comfort zone and go from "Maybe I'm too old for this shit" to "No, actually, I love this shit" was rewarding to a degree I can't put into words.

I had no more major anxious episodes until the day before launch, when I ran into a problem. My car was stuffed with entirely too much stuff. The locking drawer, cargo area, and back seat were overflowing. This would be a nightmare to organize and root around in, not to mention taking on multiple passengers, as I planned to do for a few legs of the trip.

I brought up everything non-essential and spread it out on my living room floor, where each object gave mute testimony as to why it deserved to be part of this road trip. In looking for any redundancies I could winnow out, I went as far as emptying the small bags of camping essentials that I usually throw in my car or backpack without a second thought:

Aha! I don't need three camping lighters. One will do. Okay, maybe two. Those things are flaky. Yes, you can buy one anywhere, but not at 10 p.m. in the middle of nowhere, which is when you really need one...

[... Jeopardy music plays ...]

Holy crap! I just spent ten minutes thinking about camping lighters! I'm going backward!

My friend Rob came over in the middle of all this to regale me with a horror story about being harassed by police in Tijuana, where I would be the next day, and another fun tale of getting smash-and-grabbed in Costa Rica, which I thought was going to be the safest place on the whole trip.

Thanks, dude! That really helped ratchet down my stress level. Who needs essential oils when you have *Rob's True Crime Blotter of Latin America*.

Another friend came over during maximum explosion to find me on my living room floor, surrounded by a sea of tiny to medium-sized objects. She looked at me like she'd just walked in on Howard Hughes arranging his urine jars. Things were supposed to be coming together. Instead, my mess was only getting bigger and more disorganized.

But I kept chipping away and made some tough decisions, including my prized road toolkit, which, at the size and shape of second base, was an awkward fit anywhere I tried to put it. Ultimately, I managed to cut roughly half of the non-essential bulk.

The next day, I loaded up and was on the road by noon, only two hours later than my planned launch time. First stop: Tijuana to hang with my buddy Gramps for a night.

CHAPTER 3

The Longest Journey Starts with the First Beer

I MADE SURPRISINGLY good time from LA to the border. As I crossed into Mexico, a policewoman singled me out of a stream of cars for inspection. I assume as a solo white guy, I must have fit some kind of profile. She peeked into my car, had me open my locking trunk, then sent me on my way. I'm not sure what she was looking for, but I gave a silent thanks that my scheme to run Stinger missiles to Honduras had fallen through. Not today, *Locked Up Abroad*.

I had time to kill before meeting up with my buddy, so I headed to the Plaza Monarca shopping mall. However, I hadn't fleshed out how I was going to navigate Tijuana at rush hour.

First, I tried my fancy $400 Garmin GPS. I'd spent a very long, very maddening night back in LA trying to figure out the Garmin. I thought I'd finally cracked the code. Wrong. I was able to locate the Plaza Monarca on the device, but no combination of button-mashing, context-menu surfing, and hysterical cursing could convince it to cough up directions to said mall.

While losing this battle of wits and wills, I nearly made a wrong turn that would have dumped me in the line to return to the US. This line has no turnarounds and takes two hours during regular times. On a Thursday afternoon before the Christmas holiday? Shudder.

I spied a Costco sign, a lighthouse in the storm, and pulled into the parking lot to regroup.

I was done fighting with the Garmin, which was already looking like one of the dumber purchases of the trip. I'd heard Waze was good for

Tijuana, but Waze wanted to send me to the Plaza Monarca **via the United States**, where I was to turn around and cross **back** into Mexico.

Computers, man. Please tell me again how artificial intelligence is going to rule us all... any day now. Skynet just needs to sort out this *map* thing first:

[Sarah Connor voiceover]

"   *When the first Terminators came, they were easy to spot... They kept getting off the freeway, driving around in a big square, then getting back on at the same exit...*

[♫ scary sci-fi music plays ♫]

Next, I tried Google Maps, which seemed to be stuck downloading place names, and couldn't find the mall.

Finally, out of sheer desperation, I pulled up the bastard stepchild of navigation apps—Apple Maps—and it worked! I had a route to the mall that didn't involve a detour back through California.

Wandering the mall, it occurred to me that my plunge into Mexico was going about as smoothly as my first descent into the murky Pacific. At least I'd found a nice spot to equalize.

Later, I met up with my buddy Gramps at his condo tower in a sleepy neighborhood on the outskirts of Tijuana. He took one look at my tank-like FJ and remarked, "Yeah, that's not much of a smash-and-grab target," which I found reassuring after Rob's true crime pep talk.

It should be noted that "Gramps" is a screen name from the online poker world, where I was a marginally winning player but nothing compared to Gramps.

Gramps moved to Tijuana shortly after "Black Friday," as it's known in the poker world—the day the US Department of Justice seized the domains of the three major poker sites that still hosted US players. Other mutual friends moved to Canada to keep playing. I already had a day job by then, and it had become exceedingly clear that I don't have the emotional makeup to be a professional poker player. Screaming desk-pounding melt-downs, followed by notes from the neighbors to the effect of "There are children in this neighborhood, and you're scaring us," will eventually lead one to such life revelations.

Gramps took me on a tour of Tijuana's hipster food and craft beer scene. We stopped first at a bustling multi-bar complex, where he pointed out hundreds of bullet holes—scars from the gang wars a decade earlier that scared away American tourists, forcing the entertainment district to remake itself. Traditionally, Tijuana offered two kinds of bars: seedy cantinas catering to working-class Mexican men and Señor Frog's-type clubs for the Spring Break purple vomit crowd. A gastropub frequented by young local professionals was a recent idea, which seemed to be a hit from what I saw.

Gramps and I enjoy a beer at a bar called Donkey Punch. Gramps, an ex-lawyer, pointed out that this "kiddie table for adults" probably wouldn't be allowed in the US due to lawsuit concerns. We did almost fall off our oversized chairs a few times.

Throughout the night, Gramps, a grizzled expat by then, tried to pass on what wisdom he could to prepare me for the trip. Although I was mostly oblivious (I'm told it's my superpower), two incidents late in the night pierced my alcohol-addled fog.

Walking from bar #2 to bar #3, we passed a dreary, neglected house sunken ten feet below street level, surrounded by a dirt yard. Gramps had been looking at houses to buy in Tijuana. I made a stupid joke that I had found his dream home. He didn't reply and instead walked farther ahead of me. I sensed annoyance.

I grew up in Independence, Missouri—a.k.a. "the meth capital of the Midwest" (although it was mostly the weed capital back then)—in a neighborhood that could charitably be called blue-collar. We had ditches instead of storm sewers and plenty of house/yard situations worse than the one I made the dumb joke about. So, I've never considered myself superior to anyone. Yet even growing up as a lower-middle-class American, I know I was born rounding third base compared to most people on the planet. There's a fine line between snarky and ugly. Clearly, I needed a tune-up on that.

The second incident came at the raggedy end of the night, after way too many way-too-spicy late-night tacos. For some reason, I felt the need to dump a goopy, caramel-slathered ice cream crepe on top of it all. Gramps did not attempt to hide his annoyance that I had arranged this purchase while he was trying to hail a cab. I confirmed with the driver that it was okay to bring the crepe into his taxi. Gramps admonished me that I was not to take a single bite during the ride. My drunk dumb ass wondered what the problem was as long as the driver was okay with it.

Gramps explained, "Obviously, this guy takes pride in his clean cab. Even if he puts up with your sloppy eating, it's only because he needs the money."

Basically—*just because you **can** doesn't mean you **should***.

That one got through to my drunk lizard brain. I spent the ride back to Gramps's place cradling the drippy dessert in my lap, feeling sheepish.

I woke up on Gramps's couch with a debilitating 8.5% IPA hangover—jolted out of my stupor by what I'm convinced will go down as the brightest sunrise in Earth history. I thanked Gramps for the night out and the lessons he tried to impart on traveling respectfully in Latin America. I got the impression he doubted whether any of his wisdom had gotten through.

It did, buddy—more than you know.

Amistad Park

On my way out of Tijuana, I stopped at the somewhat ironically named Friendship Park—a binational reserve built around the spot where the United States/Mexico border trails out into the Pacific Ocean. A well-placed bluff on the approach to the park offers a commanding view of both sides of the border.

To my left, tourists and a few families milled around in Parque de Amistad, as it's known on the Mexico side—amidst palm trees, interpretive signs, and a concrete sculpture of three frolicking dolphins. Vendors offered souvenirs and shaved ice. Children played in the surf.

On their side of the border, the United States has chosen a more rustic, back-to-nature approach, offering no amenities other than sand dunes and scrub vegetation. A few beach strollers could be seen in the distance, approaching a large sign that I presume forbids them from proceeding any farther.

Between the two parks, a line of twenty-five-foot-tall steel girders, spaced less than skull-width apart, descends from the top of the bluff to the beach—in an undulating curve that's weirdly pleasing to the eye in a dystopian way. This barrier extends about fifty feet into the surf.

The border wall separating Parque de Amistad and Friendship Park

On the Mexican side, some of the girders are covered with graffiti. Others are painted with murals that only appear when viewed from an angle—depicting mostly idyllic scenes like swarms of butterflies and a father and son holding hands. A small "peace garden" ringed with pastel-painted tires butts up against a mural of lush greenery. A sign among the patches of straggly vegetation reads in Spanish, "We are strawberries. We want to be food. Don't step on us!"

The absence of authority figures on either side of the border surprised me. From past experience, Mexican federal, state, and local police generally seem to be everywhere—operating checkpoints or just milling around looking menacing and bored. Apparently, none of that was needed here.

US authorities must keep a tight watch on this easily breached stretch of the border, so their complete lack of presence felt a bit sinister. I guess it's harder to make a jailbreak when you don't know where the guards are or how many you're up against. A trapezoid-shaped mound on the US side concealed an entrance to an underground bunker, from which I assume anyone attempting to go over, under, or around the barrier would be met with an instant response.

By the way, when your Facebook friend from high school posts a meme that shows people scaling the border wall en masse, it's likely this section of girders. Activists on the Mexican side occasionally stage demonstrations in which, among other activities, they climb to the top of the girders. No one actually attempts to cross. US border authorities are notified in advance for obvious reasons.

Before Covid, on Saturdays and Sundays from 10 a.m. to 2 p.m., Border Patrol agents allowed pedestrians access to a mesh fence that separates the two parks. Visitors on the US side could meet and even touch fingertips with loved ones in Mexico, whom they may not have been able to hug for years or decades. As of 2022, access has not been restored, and a new border wall in the works will likely put a permanent end to all visitation at Friendship Park.

ENSENADA

My hangover and the cumulative effect of several days of packing and moving stuff into storage began to take its toll. I decided to bail on the day and find someplace in nearby Ensenada to lay flat for a while.

I found what I thought was an extremely cheap hotel—touting rooms for 240 pesos (about $12) in big purple LED letters. When I inquired with the woman in the office, that price somehow went up to 750 pesos. Stranger still—she told me I'd have to move my car to a nearby guarded lot by 10 p.m. None of this made any sense to me. But lots of things don't make sense to me, especially in Latin America. I was tired, my back hurt, and the place seemed nice enough, so I took the room.

Gramps later informed me that I had stayed at what's known as a "Love Hotel." Two hundred forty pesos was the *four-hour* rate.

Love Hotels cater to a mix of people having clandestine affairs, young couples who still live with their parents, and clients enjoying the services of one or more prostitutes. In Ensenada, I'm guessing that milieu skews heavily toward the third group. However, I am told that in places farther from the gringo tourist track, Valentine's Day is the busiest day of the year for Love Hotels, which I find oddly sweet.

Gramps expressed hope that my sheets were clean. They were. I think. I didn't get out the black light.

Had I known I was staying in a Love Hotel, I would have at least peeked out to see who was coming and going, as it were. Instead, I slept through the entirety of the evening's festivities.

I woke up feeling approximately 10,000 times better, ready for one of the most anticipated foodie highlights of the trip.

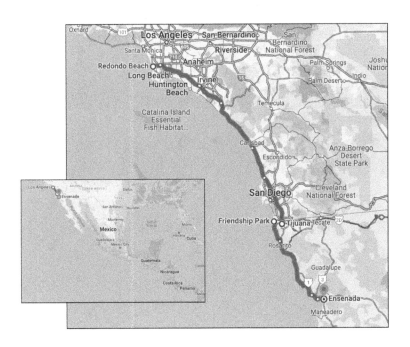

CHAPTER 4

MIKE'S SKY RANCHO

CONDITIONED to the LA food hipster scene, I was prepared to see people queued up around the block for La Guerrerense—the family-run eatery whose ceviche tostadas have won street food competitions as far-flung as Singapore, leading some foodies to dub it "the best food cart in the world." However, there was no line to order, just a dozen patrons standing around the oversized food stall, nibbling off small plates. Caught flat-footed with no time to peruse the menu, I picked the top three things.

A mixed seafood ceviche tostada from La Guerrerense

First, I tried their signature tostada: tuna ceviche topped with shrimp, octopus, sea snail, scallops, mussels, and clams. The seafood came layered on a bed of chunky salsa, topped with avocado slices—a delicious blend of creaminess, acidity, crunch, and salt. I didn't know I liked sea snail, but apparently I do! The second tostada came topped with crab salad. It was tasty but so heavy I could hardly finish the third tostada, a fish-only version of the first. If I go again, I may try to actually read the menu before ordering.

LA BUFADORA

Heading south out of Ensenada on Mexico-1, the countryside opens up to long views of farmland and rolling dirt-colored hills. I passed the coastal resort where my friend Beth got married, marking my previous deepest foray into Baja.

Despite exploring the American and Canadian West as a hobby for most of my adult life, I'd somehow never ventured more than fifty miles down the 800-mile-long Baja Peninsula. At long last, I had a reason to pull my copy of the iconic *Baja Adventure Book* off the shelf, from whence it had silently mocked me for the better part of two decades. I could have bought a newer guidebook, but I figured Baja's natural wonders probably hadn't changed much, and any establishments touted in the book that were still in business must be doing something right.

At one stoplight—which seemed to stay red for an unnecessarily long time—the intersection filled with stilt walkers, fire twirlers, and a juggler riding a unicycle. I gave the performers a few pesos and paid a vendor $1 for a quart of plump Castelvetrano olives, which turned out to be perfect road-trip snacking food.

A bit further south, I left the highway to explore the La Bufadora peninsula, a horn-shaped landmass that juts into the Pacific Ocean. Sometimes I have a plan, and sometimes I just like to pick a spot on the map and go. I followed the main road to the tip of the horn, where it came to a dead end at a mass of parked cars and tourist amenities. I parked and followed the crowd down a concrete path lined with food stalls and vendors selling traditional Mexican bric-a-brac. I talked a vendor down from $30 to $25 on a wool blanket—pleased with my negotiating skills for once.

La Bufadora means blowhole, which turned out to be the attraction we had all come to see. At the end of the path, a few dozen people clustered behind a concrete wall overlooking the craggy coastline. Every minute or so, a plume of seawater would spurt through a small hole in the rocks, occasionally shooting high enough to douse the shrieking crowd.

I noticed a squirrel on a nearby ledge who seemed to enjoy the sporadic shower. I thought, "That's the first completely drenched squirrel I've ever seen. I've seen some damp squirrels, but never one that looks like it just got out of the tub." It felt like a weird traveler's omen. Good or bad, I wasn't sure.

On the way back from the blowhole, the same vendor offered me an identical blanket for $8. Sigh. My negotiating skills were as sharp as ever. At least I've made progress from the guy who once walked into an audio store and proclaimed to the salesman, "I am **serious** about buying a car stereo today!" I was not a bright teenager.

The sun was getting low, so I scoped out a nearby campground that offered a panoramic view of the Pacific Ocean. The grounds were empty, with a denuded landscape that reminded me of the final scene in *The Lorax*. Something creeped me out about the place. Then again, I often get weird anxiety when I'm in new territory. So I never know if I should trust my spidey sense in these spots or if I'm just being irrationally fretful.

I pressed on to a campground I'd seen earlier, which *was* mentioned in the *Baja Adventure Book*—the La Jolla Campground. It seemed well-kept and wasn't completely deserted. They even gave out free tamales, which solved my problem of what to eat for dinner.

I got a beer from the cooler and sat back in my little camping chair to take in the sunset. I reflected on my first real day of the trip (I didn't count sleeping it off at a Love Hotel). I ate sea snail at the best food cart in the world. I bought a bucket of my favorite olives for $1 while a guy rode around on a unicycle juggling bowling pins. I stumbled onto a blowhole, got free tamales, and saw a wet squirrel. I decided it was a pretty good day.

As the last color of sunset faded, the lights of Ensenada began to twinkle across All Saints Bay—reflecting off moss-covered rocks and sea life exposed at low tide. Wrapped up snug in my new wool blanket, I had a euphoric moment. I was really doing this. My first campout of the trip—my first night past Ensenada—uncharted territory.

Then my chair let out an audible **CRACK** and collapsed underneath me.

I probably should have known better than to buy the lightest camping chair I could find. But it will fit so much better in my car, I thought. It will be so much easier to wrangle than my big heavy camping chair, I thought. I weigh 255 pounds, I never thought.

I sat on my cooler for a while. But without back support, the magic was gone.

I found myself wondering if this was going to be my trip—camped out alone, waiting for the sun to go down, wondering what to do with myself from 6 p.m. onward. I'm not the most introverted person in the world, but I'm also not the most gregarious, especially when my new turf anxiety is kicking in. I've found traveling alone can be very rewarding—in that it forces me to get outside my comfort zone and meet people. But the operative word here is "forces," which implies a period of boredom and/or loneliness that's *worse* than the terrifying prospect of saying hi to someone and getting rejected.

The next morning, I fretted for a few minutes, then walked over and said hi to the couple camped beside me. I was curious about the cargo carrier attached to the roof of their van—how much it cost and how big of a pain it would be to install on my FJ. It had become evident that even with all my paring down before the trip, I still had too much crap floating around in my car—including stuff I rarely needed to access, like an air pump, oil filters, and cold weather gear for Patagonia.

The couple, who introduced themselves as Kelly and Mike, explained that they work in construction in British Columbia and travel "someplace warm" for the winter every year. They were headed to Southern Baja in an older model white Ford van decked out for overlanding, with a bed in the back and cooking setup. Mike told me I could get a similar cargo carrier at AutoZone in Ensenada—which hadn't even occurred to me. Mike and Kelly were incredibly friendly and fascinated by my trip. We exchanged contact information and left open the chance to meet up somewhere down the peninsula.

I backtracked thirty miles to AutoZone, where I picked up a rooftop cargo carrier for $300. They helped me install it, which was a big plus.

Then I elbowed through both Ensenada Walmarts on Christmas Eve, searching in vain for a new camping chair. The closest thing I could find was a folding tripod stool—like you might see whisked onto a basketball court for the coach to sit on during a timeout. It would have to do until I could find something better.

My next plan was to camp in the mountains of Sierra de San Pedro Mártir National Park, where I might even see snow! In Mexico! But first, I wanted to wander a bit and see some countryside. So, I decided to take the long way, cutting across the peninsula to the east, then south to the park, which I figured should put me near a place called Mike's Sky Rancho around sundown. Mike's was one of only a few establishments highlighted in bold yellow on my paper map. I needed to know what the yellow was all about.

Mike's sits on the Baja 500 off-road race route and is very popular with 4x4 enthusiasts. I imagined a raucous scene at the bar, full of off-roaders reveling in the mandatory "review and summarize" phase that follows all group vehicle activities. Maybe I'd even get invited to some light four-wheeling on Christmas Day.

MIKE'S SKY RANCHO

I pulled up to Mike's just after sunset. I could just make out the outline of mountains all around me, but no other cars were in sight. So much for 4x4 revelry. I got out and walked toward the deserted grounds, unsure if the place was even open. I saw some movement in the back of the compound, which was encouraging at first—but turned a little spooky when no one came out to greet me right away.

Eventually, a man about my age who spoke zero English emerged. We managed to establish that yes, there were rooms available, and no, there was no wifi (he looked at me like I was a little crazy on that one). After a few minutes, a younger man named José, who spoke decent English, appeared.

José explained they had rooms available, or I could camp in the yard for free. Mike's sits at 4,000 feet. The temperature had already dropped to near-freezing with a stiff wind. I opted for the room. There was also an option for dinner and breakfast. I *could* fire up my little camping stove and eat the boil-in-bag freeze-dried meals I affectionately call "REI Rations." But something told me I should take the dinner and breakfast option. It was Christmas Eve, after all.

José led me to a row of rooms situated along a rise overlooking the compound. He explained that dinner would be ready at 7 p.m. and that I needed to run the shower for twenty minutes to get warm water. He emphasized this many times—twenty minutes. I decided to skip the shower rather than waste all that water. I puttered around the chilly room and tried unsuccessfully to get the heater working.

José appeared at my room at 6:30. He helped me get the heater fired up, then queried me about dinner:

José: Do you want carne... eh... I mean, steak... or pozole?
Me: Yes, please.
José: [blank stare]
Me: (slowly realizing I needed to choose) Uhhh... what was the second thing?
José: Pozole is our traditional family Christmas dinner.
Me: Oh!... Yes, pozole, of course. I'd be honored. Thank you!

With that, a big smile spread across José's face. I'll never know if he was happy because the gringo who showed up unannounced at sundown on Christmas Eve didn't appear to be a psychopath—or because he didn't have to thaw out a steak.

Until that moment, I hadn't considered that I would completely miss my own family's traditional Christmas Eve gathering. In this remote outpost, I couldn't even call in to be passed around the party, exchanging warm, awkward hellos with one uncle, aunt, or cousin after another.

I sat back on the bed and got more than a little emotional. There may even have been a few tears. Small, manly tears, of course. More of a welling, really. Probably fumes from the heater.

My entire goal had been to achieve escape velocity from Southern California and launch myself into the boonies of Baja *before* the holidays. Well, here I was out in the boonies, and I had stumbled—Mr. Magoo-style—into an invitation to share Christmas Eve pozole with a local family.

When it was time for dinner, I walked down from my bedroom across the grounds—past a very cold-looking pool, into a kitchen that smelled of soupy pork heaven. Is there a prettier sight on earth than somebody's mama stirring local comfort food that's been simmering in a giant stockpot all day? No, of course not. It was a rhetorical question.

José's aunt tended the pozole, a traditional stew that dates to pre-Columbian times, made with meat (usually pork) and hominy—dried maize soaked in lye, then rinsed until the kernels puff up to twice their normal size—or "giant corn" as I've always called it.

In the dining room, the family had set up a long table—with bowls of lime, onions, and shredded cabbage, plates of tortillas, and 2-liter bottles of Coca-Cola. A twinkling Christmas tree dominated one corner of the common area. Like my room, Baja racing stickers covered every flat surface.

I took my place at one end of the table while José, the patriarch, sat at the other. A dozen family members of all ages filled in on both sides. Mamá served everyone, ensuring the perfect amount of meat, hominy, and liquid from the proper level of the sauce column went into each bowl. The broth was velvety and rich, with those little orange grease bubbles that permanently stain Tupperware and always make me happy. The pork was like succulent roast beef or oxtail—with a deep, savory finish. Hominy kernels acted as mini-dumplings, soaking up the juicy goodness. Shredded raw cabbage added bite.

We made conversation as best we could, given only José and the kids spoke any English. I lost track of all the family relations. I learned that José is Mike's son and now owns the resort. "Big Mike" was something of a wheeler-dealer in Tijuana in the '60s who decided to build a mountain getaway. Mike's Sky Rancho became the beloved hangout that still thrives today.

Me with my second bowl of pozole and a niñita photo-bomb

I noticed Mamá eyeing my bowl as it got lower. I know that no verbal compliment beats an enthusiastic request for seconds. The proof is in the second order of pudding, as they say. I was happy to oblige. However, I hadn't calculated how much the giant hominy kernels would expand in my stomach. In retrospect, half a bowl would have been the discretionary part of valor. Instead, I wound up with a very full bowl, which I finished, suppressing the sharp pain in my stomach as it expanded to Kobayashi proportions.

After dinner, it was time for fireworks. The girls got little twirly things —which, even as the "safe" option, still had a tendency to spin out of control and careen into one's face. The men and boys got M-80s—roughly 1/16th of a stick of dynamite. I'd heard legends about these beasts, long illegal in the States, from my uncles and stepdad. The little bombs lived up to the hype, exploding with a force I could feel in my chest cavity.

I asked José if M-80s ever got the quick fuse, like the much smaller Black Cat and Thunder Bomb firecrackers of my youth. "Oh yeah," he said, "it happens."

This troubled me, since I felt like an anaconda that just swallowed a goat, and my reflexes weren't exactly peaking. Losing a finger seemed like a suboptimal way to start the trip.

I lit and threw **one**, content to watch after that. The men and boys got a big kick out of throwing the M-80s into a 55-gallon drum and then running for cover from the earth-shaking boom. Now and then, one wouldn't go off, which made approaching the drum a nervous affair.

An M-80—that'll leave a mark

An hour and a few pounds of vaporized dynamite later, I declined an offer to drink with the men that almost certainly would have lasted long into the night. From my experience, when there's a language barrier as wide as the one we faced, late-night drunken bonding can only achieve so much. Also, I didn't want waves of nausea and regret to sully the memory of a magical Christmas Eve.

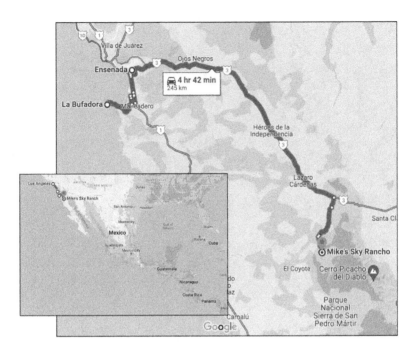

CHAPTER 5

MEDITATIONS ON MT. STUPID

I TRUNDLED down to the common area on Christmas morning, taking in my first daytime view of the resort. Sunlight poured through towering Italian Cypress bushes, casting striped shadows across the pool and hacienda-style buildings. The cold, clear air and stark mountain ridges surrounding the campus did indeed give one the feeling of being at a rancho in the sky.

Mike's Sky Rancho on Christmas Morning

On a table outside the kitchen, empty bottles of Jack Daniels and Hendrick's Gin shimmered in the Baja sun—validating my decision to bow out of the late-night men's council.

The family had gathered in the dining area, where José sat me down to a hearty breakfast of eggs, papas (fries), bacon, and refried beans. After breakfast, I thanked Mamá and the rest of the family for a Christmas Eve I'll never forget. My toddler Spanish exhausted itself at "muchas muchas gracias," so I did the thing where you make a fist and bump it against your heart a few times.

I asked José about my plan to continue south to the town of El Coyote and then on to the national park. He looked over at my FJ and offered, "That road is no good. But you should be okay. Just go slow."

A few more effusive thank yous to José and I was off on my first 4x4 adventure of the trip. The *Baja Adventure Book* beamed at me from the passenger seat, finally not ashamed to be in my presence.

The Road to El Coyote

The first half-mile was a little bumpy, but nothing out of line. I came to one of the only fishing streams on the parched Baja peninsula, where I started to veer right, following what appeared to be the shallower path. Then I caught myself and thought—no, let's do our due diligence. I got out to look, and boy, was I glad I did. The path on the right led to a deep pool. From *outside* the car, I could see tire tracks exiting the stream on the *left*. I crossed the steam without incident, pleased with myself for not just plowing ahead like I usually do.

Just beyond the stream, I passed some cows who looked at me like, "What the hell are you doing out here, gringo?"

Then the fun started.

I creaked and bounced up a steep hill on the most uneven, crater-pocked road I'd ever driven. I seemed to have finally reached the frisky part of the Baja 500. I crested the hill to see another steep descent and a similar climb back up, on a road that looked like it hadn't been graded since the '60s.

I bounced and lurched my way down the road, which was really more of a V-shaped track, looking out for sharp rocks that could puncture my oil pan or transmission. I regretted not purchasing skid plates—armor for the sensitive bits of the car's underbelly. I also regretted not having a power winch in case I got stuck. Then again, there were no trees to tie off to.

As you may have guessed by now, I don't know much about recreational 4x4ing. I have a rule that any new hobby must involve exercise. But I do know that many things can and do go wrong, and **nobody** goes four-wheeling without a buddy to pull them out.

I lurched and bounced along another nerve-wracking ride to the top of the next hill, then looked out upon an accordion of more of the same, stretching far into the distance.

"Just go slow"—HAH! Thanks for that pearl of wisdom, José. I'd have been tempted to really air it out—*Dukes of Hazzard*-style.

I checked the route on Google Maps, which, since the hiccup in Tijuana, had proven to be the most reliable map narrator in this part of the world. I still had thirteen miles of accordion driving to El Coyote, then another twelve to the national park.

The funniest part is that I could have been in a Prius, and Google Maps Lady—as she will be forever known—still would have happily sent me down this V-shaped gully cosplaying as a road. I realized I'd need to keep a closer eye on her, especially in cities, where a wrong turn could land me in a dodgy neighborhood.

I got out of the car to survey the land and have a little conversation with myself.

What kind of adventure did I want this trip to be? A 4x4 adventure? A foodie adventure? A hiking/backpacking adventure? Well, here was a 4x4 adventure staring me in the face. Was I really going to back down to my first challenge? I know what 24-year-old Matt would have done. But I also know that 48-year-old Matt wouldn't be alive to ponder this decision if he'd kept thinking like 24-year-old Matt.

In keeping with my YOLO (**Y**ou **O**nly **L**ive **O**nce) just-follow-the-crooked-roads spirit, I hadn't researched El Coyote. I'd already seen that towns on the map in rural Baja could be nothing but a few houses with no signs of life. If my car crapped out early, I'd just walk back to Mike's. But what if I made it almost to El Coyote and *then* had a problem? Would I be reduced to knocking on doors, trying to explain myself to people who couldn't speak a word of English and would be understandably spooked? What if I rolled my car and my trip was over before it started?

If there's one thing I've learned from the *Baja Adventure Book*, it's that if you get stuck and have to be rescued, you will receive a non-stop firehose of shit—from your first plea for help to the last "Adios, amigo!" And that's just your rescuers. God forbid there be any bystanders with nothing better to do that day. Busting the balls of stranded gringos seems to be something of a national pastime in Mexico. No one will be in the tiniest hurry to help you, as they shouldn't.

And, oh yeah, it's Christmas Day.

Ultimately, the plodding tortoise of potential unpleasant outcomes overtook the idle hare of my lust for adventure. I decided to turn around and go the long way. I realized that hardcore 4x4ing in Mexico—with no buddies to help, no cell coverage, no AAA, and no idea what the next town was like—might not be the smartest idea.

The net result of my level-headed decision (or cowardice, depending on your point of view) was a relaxing, scenic 120-mile detour that led me back to the outskirts of Sierra de San Pedro Mártir Parque Nacional by late afternoon.

Near the park entrance, two cars full of families had pulled over next to a sign reading, "NO MOLESTAR LOS CONDORES." Three California condors with numbers attached to their wings congregated near the sign, which I assume was a feeding station. I'd never seen a condor up close, and I can

The "road" from Mike's Sky Rancho to El Coyote

confirm they are indeed quite large. Imagine Mr. Burns from *The Simpsons*, the size of a large toddler, wearing a feather boa. The condors didn't pay much attention to me, as they were more interested in the beef jerky being tossed at them by a Mexican Clark Griswold. I'm not sure if jerky counts as *molestar*, but the condors seemed okay with it.

I arrived at the park gates and paid for a camping spot. Setting up my tent, I realized I'd left my new wool blanket at Mike's. Great. Now I had a camping chair **and** a blanket to look for. Unlike the camping chair, however, I assumed procuring one of Mexico's most popular tourist items would be a simple matter.

The next day, I took a pleasant hike amid rolling golden hills and cypress trees. I found a small patch of snow in the shade that hadn't melted yet. So I can officially say I've seen snow in Mexico.

The scenery, while lovely, looked the same in every direction, with no discernible landmarks. I started to worry about getting lost in the park, which was deserted the day after Christmas. I had no cell coverage, and I had screwed up loading the topographic map into my Garmin GPS. The Garmin had already proven worthless as a driver's navigation aid, and now, as a hiking device, it was bulky and untrustworthy. I supposed, in a pinch, I could throw it at a rabid coyote and run the other way. Other than that? Useless.

After the hike, I made my way back out to Mex Hwy 1, where I found a cheap place to spend the night that I'm reasonably sure wasn't a Love Hotel. At least it didn't have a big purple LED sign. Either way, I was the only guest. There were no comings and goings.

I got a message from Kelly and Mike, the Canadian couple I had met at La Bufadora. They were camped nearby, at Punta San Jacinto—a surf spot everyone calls *Shipwrecks*. I told them I'd come check it out in the morning.

SHIPWRECKS

After a few fits and starts with Google Maps, I found the two sand tracks that lead to Shipwrecks. Soon, the eponymous shipwreck came into view— a gnarled mass of rusted steel ribs jutting out of the surf against a hazy sky. A couple dozen vacation homes in various stages of construction lined the beach. Past the last house, I spotted Mike and Kelly's van.

We exchanged greetings and chatted for a bit. Kelly and Mike sat in their camping chairs. I got out my basketball-timeout folding stool from Walmart. As we talked, Mike strummed his guitar, and my stool slowly burrowed into the sand until my butt was barely above ground level— much to all of our amusement.

When it seemed like they weren't too weirded out by the random single guy glomming into them, I asked if they'd mind if I camped next to them. They enthusiastically did not mind. We made plans to caravan across the "gas desert" of Central Baja the next day. Then Mike went out to surf while Kelly tried to teach me a few yoga moves.

Later, a gentleman named Dale showed up in his double-cab Ford pickup to give Mike a tour of the surf spots. I tagged along.

Dale explained that he comes down from San Diego "Whenever the boooool-shit gets too much to deal with back home." Good to know. Then he informed us, "I've been married for forty-five years. My wife don't give a fuck what I do." Also good to know.

Mike expressed a passing interest in buying a plot of land and asked Dale about safety. According to Dale, the only hazards were late-night campsite thefts perpetrated on groups who were too cheap to pay $5 a night to camp within the compound fence.

Dale also talked about water reliability issues and various hassles with the local landowner. A few years earlier, the residents were given a choice between a fence and electricity. They chose the fence. Electricity was on the slate for the next round of improvements.

In the delightful book *God and Mr. Gomez*, Los Angeles Times columnist Jack Smith chronicles similar quandaries that arose during the design and construction of his dream Baja vacation home—on a site just up the coast from Shipwrecks. The problems Jack describes in getting power, fresh water, and timely construction in the late 1960s could just as easily have been Dale's description of vacation home life at Shipwrecks.

To keep Americans from buying up all the beachfront property, Mexico forbids non-citizens from owning land within fifty kilometers of the coast and a hundred kilometers of an international border. In Jack Smith's time, the only option was to lease property from a Mexican owner, for no more than ten years, and then *hope* the owner agrees to renew the lease. Repeat in perpetuity.

This leap of faith caused Jack a great deal of consternation, leading to a series of entertaining exchanges with Romulo Gomez, the builder and actual owner of the vacation house:

> *"When the house is finished," I said, "if it ever is, how will we know it's ours? You aren't going to give us a deed?"*
>
> *He laughed, a gentle laugh that expressed not ridicule but a nice appreciation of my humor. "You know, Jack, I can give you no deed. You are not Mexican. It is against the law. Do you want for you and me to break the law?"*
>
> *"Of course not, Romulo. You know that. It's just that I want to know, well, you keep saying the house will be ours."*
>
> *"Of course, it is your house."*
>
> *"How will I know that—when the time is ripe?"*
>
> *He spread his hands in a gesture that was at once humble and majestic. "I'll give you the key."*

Dale dropped us back at our campsite and invited us to a party at his place "anytime after dark when the fire is going—the more the merrier."

I walked along the beach, checking out the vacation homes of all sizes and styles—from simple corrugated metal boxes to a two-story pueblo to a tiki-themed "surf hostel" that had been abandoned to the elements. Homes tended to get bigger and fancier as I walked down the beach. Finally, I reached a lightly fenced yard with a large barking dog that deterred me from further exploration. According to Dale, the maxim for building a vacation home in Mexico is "Don't spend more than you can afford to lose." Either the people at the end of the beach could afford to lose a lot, or they trusted the landowner a lot.

Later, Kelly, Mike, and I had a few beers and watched the sunset. We waffled back and forth on going to Dale's party, eventually landing on "Let's check it out for a bit." On our way out of camp, a French guy asked for help getting his van unstuck from a patch of loose sand. I recruited some extra pushing power from a group of surfers camped nearby. After we got the van unstuck, I invited the surfers to Dale's party. They were young and cool, so I wanted to show them that I was the cool guy with the low-down on the Shipwrecks party scene.

They said they might check it out.

Cool.

We showed up at Dale's fireside soiree—to find Dale playing guitar, his son-in-law struggling to stay awake, and his daughter standing in the doorway looking perturbed that actual guests had arrived. Dale was a very good guitar player, and I was impressed with his song selection. We heard the first third of dozens of songs ranging from AC/DC to Joni Mitchell to 867-5309—all played in one continuous medley, with zero breaks for conversation.

I started triangulating the soonest we could leave without being rude. It occurred to me that if I were the only one to go, via some excuse, I could shorten that time quite a bit.

Mike and Kelly sat on the other side of the fire pit, so I communicated to them through a series of pointing gestures and sheepish facial expressions that I might head back, assuming, you know, they were enjoying the show and wanted to stay. And why wouldn't they? By this point, Dale's daughter had gone to bed and her husband was slumped over in his chair. Dale played on, undeterred. Kelly gave me a death glare that said in no uncertain terms, "Don't you dare leave. We're in this together." We lasted thirty song snippets—or about forty-five minutes. I kept a nervous watch on the beach the entire time, terrified the surfer kids would appear. I'd instantly fall from grace as *the cool guy who knows where the parties are* **to** *the lame old guy who roped them into this fiasco.* Thankfully, they never showed up.

On the walk back, I stopped at the surfer kids' camp to warn them about Dale's rager. They had settled in and clearly had no intention of going. They offered me a beer and something else that got passed around. After a bit of small talk, they returned to their previous conversation, which was full of technical surf jargon and possibly some wind-surfing jargon. I was utterly lost.

It's always fun to find out how much thought goes into a hobby like surfing, given my first impression that all surf analysis must begin and end with Jeff Spicoli's: "All I need are some tasty waves, a cool buzz, and I'm fine."

In poker, novice players generally aren't aware of the level of study needed to play the game at a high level. When I started playing, I didn't even appreciate that poker **could** be that complicated. Then I read my first real poker book and realized I knew absolutely nothing.

So, I *should* know by now that a serious hobby/sport/lifestyle like surfing *must* be more complicated than my outsider preconceptions. Yet I still assume otherwise—until I have that eye-opening moment where I realize I'm riding the first crest of the Dunning–Kruger curve—a.k.a. Mount Stupid.

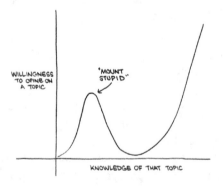

Yes I am aware of recent studies that cast doubt on the Dunning–Kruger phenomenon, but let's just go with Mt. Stupid for now. It feels right.

As I stumbled back to my camp, I reasoned that there must be some strong pull in human nature that makes us want to believe things are simpler than they actually are. A wise person once said, "Every day, I get a little stupider." It took five minutes of surf jargon to unveil a new dark passageway in my cave of ignorance.

Then my inner monologue took a turn for the meta, and I thought about how I don't get these insights as much in everyday life. I need to be outside my comfort zone—in some unfamiliar place—to wake up my senses and rattle my brain out of its habituated torpor.

There's a physiological basis to this, one I know deep enough in my bones that I don't need a Malcolm Gladwell book to confirm it.

If *hunter-gatherer you* walks through an unfamiliar patch of brush, your Stone Age counterpart's senses will be on alert for any potential threat. Once you pass through that same brush a few dozen times and the leopard attack never comes—your brain stops bombarding you with anxious feelings and sensory alerts. This frees up the rational mind to make important breakthroughs—like realizing that Spaulding, Judge Smails' feckless nephew in *Caddyshack*, was named after a golf ball.

Where was I? Oh yeah, imagine looking over the precipice of a thousand-foot cliff versus standing on a curb watching cars whiz by at forty-five miles an hour. In both cases, one slip could mean instant death. But your brain isn't hardwired to fear cars, so you don't get that weird urge to jump into traffic and fluttery twinge in your duodenum.

Other than falling off a roof, I've never felt more alive than when I was hiking and camping in grizzly bear country. When you aren't the top predator anymore, your brain will let you know it. Regular life feels like sleepwalking by comparison. I sure as hell wasn't stressing over Vicki being a little brusque with me in the weekly planning meeting. I don't have time for your passive-aggressive nonsense right now, Vicki. I've got bears to worry about.

It's an imperfect system, prone to false signals on both ends, but one that has clearly imparted an evolutionary advantage. Fight or flight first; let the rational brain sort it out later.

Of course, you could be in Bangkok, where you're probably safer from violent crime than your gritty hipster neighborhood in a major US city. But your amygdala doesn't know that. It just knows it's being bombarded with unfamiliar sights, sounds, and smells.

You can work this system to your advantage by exposing yourself to new places, or heights, or similar triggers in a relatively safe way. As long as you've done your homework and aren't on the bleeding edge—travel, bungee jumping, scuba diving, skydiving, motorsports, mountain climbing, public speaking, playing with spiders I suppose—are all ways to trick your brain into feeling alive to a degree far out of proportion to the actual risk involved.

This is the upside of my new turf anxiety. Travel and adventure get my brain fluid flowing in the same way that Philosophy 101, psychedelic benders with my friends, and meaning-of-life Chautauquas with my dad did in my formative years. Those inner journeys opened me up and forged me into the person I am today. As I get older, I've learned through trial and error to seek out experiences that reignite those bellows.

Wow. All that from one toke. See, this is why I don't smoke weed.

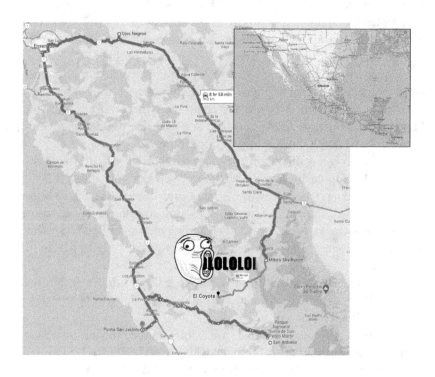

CHAPTER 6

IF I RAN THE ARBORETUM

I AWOKE at dawn to the buzz of a five-pound bumblebee circling my tent. The French guy whose van we had pushed out of the sand was flying his drone. He wanted to ensure we didn't oversleep on our big travel day. Thoughtful. Then he took off without paying the $5 camping fee.

Safe travels, sir.

Mike, Kelly, and I packed up and headed out to Mex Hwy 1, also known as the Carretera Transpeninsular. Before the Transpeninsular was completed in 1974, the drive between Northern and Southern Baja could take up to a month and require several major car repairs along the way. After "driving" the "road" from Mike's Sky Rancho to El Coyote, I can see why.

A road in some form has spanned the peninsula since Spanish priests established the Camino Real (Royal Road) to connect their ever-growing string of missions along the continent's western edge. At its peak in the early 1800s, the Camino Real stretched 1,500 miles—from the southern tip of Baja (Lower) California—to Solano, north of present-day San Francisco, in what was then known as Alta (Upper) California.

The Spanish didn't establish a foothold in Baja until 1697, almost two centuries *after* Cortés had subjugated Central Mexico, which gives a rough approximation of where saving souls ranked on their priority list versus plundering gold. Where the conquistadors weren't interested, the education-minded Jesuits filled in as colonizers, followed by the poverty-focused Franciscans, and finally, the theological Dominicans.

Jesuit priests brought ex-soldiers and other settlers from Mexico to run the ranchos that surrounded and supported their missions. These ranchers learned to squeeze a tenuous living out of the hostile landscape and came to see themselves as *Californios,* with little concern for Mexican politics across the Gulf.

While their Alta Californio compatriots living in what would become San Diego, Los Angeles, and San Francisco eventually found themselves amidst the mother of all population booms, the Baja Californio lifestyle remained frozen in time for centuries. Visiting a Baja rancho in the 1960s, before the completion of the highway, would have felt little different from a trip to a US pioneer homestead in the 1800s. Even today, electricity and running water remain a luxury for many ranchos, and some can only be reached by donkey.

We pulled over in the town of Lázaro Cárdenas to do laundry and pick up groceries. I checked around for a camping chair and/or wool blanket. No one spoke much English in these parts, so I tried various translations of "blanket"—to which I was presented a tablecloth, a bed sham, and a reasonably stylish wrap-around shawl—but no blanket. I began to suspect that Mexicans don't actually *use* the wool blankets; they just sell them to tourists.

We stopped to fill up in El Rosario, home of the last gas station before the notorious stretch of the Transpeninsular known as the "gas desert." I felt slightly Road Warrior-ish as I filled the sand-colored military jerry cans strapped to my roof.

If one does run out of gas in the gas desert, the only option is to find a donkey cart selling jars of pink liquid euphemistically labeled "gas." Whether this concoction will get you to Guerrero Negro or destroy your engine block is up to the gods that day.

Past Rosario, the road turns inland, opening up to rolling foothills draped with endless varieties of cacti. I'm used to the American Southwest, where you go to one place to see Joshua trees, another place to see saguaro cacti, yet another to see organ pipe cacti, etc. Not in Central Baja. It's the Walmart Supercenter of cactus viewing.

We rolled through miles of garden wonderland packed with, among other flora: giant cardón cacti, which look similar to the iconic saguaros of the American West; ocotillos—spindly branches that look like a dead bundle of sticks half the year but produce blazing red bottle-brush blooms in spring; a variety of chollas—with their barbed spines that slice through clothing and embed into flesh; several species of iconic organ pipe cactus—

including the "old man" variety, sporting his mop-top of gray hair; barrel cactus; prickly pear; and striking elephant trees—their pot-belly trunks sprouting gnarled, white-bark branches with dark creases at the knuckles.

But the star of the show was the cirio, also known as the boojum tree. The cartoon boojum tree on the cover of this book is not an exaggeration. In fact, it's relatively tame by boojum standards.

Picture a fifty-foot carrot ripped from the ground and placed upside down so the narrow tip is pointed to the sky. Give the carrot white bark with little green thorny branches dotted along an oddly regular grid pattern —like cheap hair plugs. Now imagine the carrot is made of taffy. The pointy top stretches upward, then curls back on itself, then maybe loops back up to the sky again, often splitting into multiple branches like a trident. And finally, cap each branch tip with a hovering fairy crown of fluffy, orange flowers.

Fun fact: *It is a breach of travel writer law to describe a boojum tree without mentioning Dr. Seuss or using the word "Seussian." There, I fulfilled the contract, doubly in fact.*

Boojum trees near Cataviña

With sunset looming, we pulled into Campo Santa Ynez, a rest stop in a tiny blip of a town called Cataviña. I set up my tent, then Mike, Kelly, and I walked a few hundred feet from camp to a thicket of cacti as varied as the scene from the road. We wandered around in this madman's cactus garden, taking sunset shots and always taking care to avoid the evil chollas. It felt like an arboretum, except all the plants were on top of one another. It would seem nature doesn't care about making room for interpretive signs. If I were in charge of this arboretum, I would tell the landscape architect to spread things out a little to—*you know*—make the scene look more *natural*.

We got up at dawn the next day and continued south, finally experiencing the car-eating potholes we'd been warned about, enhanced by the post-dawn sun's annoying tendency to park itself directly on the highway. Mike and I had some white-knuckle bobbing and weaving through that minefield.

We stopped at the turnoff for Bahía de los Ángeles (Bay of the Angels) on the Sea of Cortez to say goodbye for the time being. I headed east to explore the bay while Kelly and Mike continued south on the Transpeninsular to Bahía Concepción—where we tentatively planned to meet up again in a few days.

A bit later, I popped over a hill to a view of the two-lane blacktop meandering its way down a thousand vertical feet to a deep blue bay. Several brown chaparral-covered islands rose from Bahía de los Ángeles. The massive island Ángel de la Guarda (Guardian Angel), with its 4,000-foot-tall mountain range, watched over the whole scene.

The approach to Bahía de Los Ángeles

BAHÍA DE LOS ÁNGELES

I pulled into town, found a motel, then headed out to explore. Dune buggies and dirt bikes whizzed down the town's main drag. A massive two-story, octagon-shaped building with a wraparound deck sat decaying on the beach. Like the tiki surf hostel at Shipwrecks, the octagon seemed to be someone's ambitious Baja fever dream that ended with a whimper. I identified a few spots along the highway that looked great for sunset shots of cacti and boojum trees, then found an outdoor restaurant for lunch.

A couple who were bicycling across the "Baja Divide" sat next to me. Everything that would normally go into a multi-night backpack—clothing, tents, sleeping bags, cookware—was strapped to any spot on their bikes it could bear purchase. I decided these long-haul mountain bikers earned the Baja toughness award. Sit-down bikers—who carry all that gear, bake in the sun, and are so low to the ground that drivers can overlook them—come in a close second. But ultimately, they stay on the pavement, whereas mountain bikers spend all day plowing through cacti, rattlesnakes, and untold desert hazards.

I went back out at sunset and took some lovely shots of the cactus garden I had scouted earlier. But I kept getting stuck with cholla "babies"—the little sections they shed onto the ground—because just sitting on the plant waiting for an animal to brush by isn't evil enough. Under a microscope, the spines look like Christmas trees, with barbs all the way down—so they slide in effortlessly but don't come out without tearing off hunks of flesh. This allows the chollas to hitch a ride on anything with four legs in order to spread their lineage across the landscape.

If a cholla section does lodge itself into some part of your body, whatever you do, resist the urge to grab it. Coach yourself on this beforehand so you don't panic in the moment. At Joshua Tree, I saw a college kid pass out from the pain of having cholla spines yanked out of her palm with a Leatherman tool. Before that moment, I didn't realize someone's eyes could literally roll back into their head. I thought it was just an expression, like "I coughed up a lung." Wait... Nope, I refuse to google, "Can one actually cough up a lung?" I don't want to know.

The young lady regained consciousness as the last spine came out. Her friends wanted to rush her to the hospital. She thought the plant was actively trying to kill her. I tried to reassure her that while painful, the spines weren't poisonous. She asked how long it would hurt. Based on personal experience, I guessed about two hours. This, apparently, was the wrong answer. Her reply came in the form of a scream that woke the park's ancestors. In retrospect, I probably should have undersold that one.

Teddy bear cholla—no hugging!

I decided I was pushing my luck with the chollas in the post-sunset gloom and called it a wrap.

Back in town, the dining options were limited. The main restaurant was packed, and hungry patrons had spilled over to the taco stand next door. The woman running the stand told me my tacos might take a while.

"No problema," I replied, thinking, "I'm on Baja time" for the first time in my life.

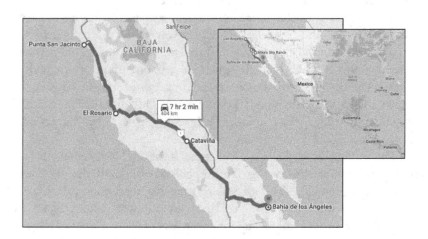

CHAPTER 7

GOD'S NAME IS WATERMELON

ILL-EQUIPPED for any of the sporting activities Bahía de Los Ángeles had to offer, I got back on the road. Not long after I had rejoined the Transpeninsular, the boojum trees disappeared and gnarled yucca plants, which I dubbed Joshua tree cousins, took over as the headliner.

I filled up in Guerrero Negro, where I tried some fish tacos from a nearby roadside stand. Maybe it was the setting, maybe it was my steadily unwinding Baja mood, but those tacos were sublime—fried delicate and crisp, topped with yellow slaw and the famous Baja cream sauce.

Back on the road, I spotted a guy selling random bric-a-brac—including camping chairs. Hooray! No more sitting on a basketball timeout stool. Here I began to understand a key concept that would serve me well throughout the trip: "You may not find it at Walmart, if there even is a Walmart, but it's probably for sale somewhere."

Midway down the peninsula, Baja fans out to its widest point. To the west, a horn-shaped sub-peninsula juts out into the Pacific Ocean. My generally accurate paper map depicted a potentially fun back-road shortcut (at least by distance) that skirted around a bay, then reconnected with the main road to the western tip of the horn.

Not long after leaving the highway, I came to the entrance for Parque Natural de Ballenas Gris, famous for whale watching. I parked and walked out to the end of a pier that extended over a shallow lagoon. I saw no whales, but I did see swarms of cabbagehead jellies that looked like indigo-blue bowling balls happily swimming along in the lime-green water.

I got back in the FJ and continued working my way around the bay, but I couldn't find the shortcut my paper map had touted. So I let Google Maps Lady treat me to another adventure, and once again, she did not disappoint.

She directed me onto a rail-straight access road that cut across a lagoon of industrial salt ponds. The dirt track rose about eight inches above the salty muck and seemed wide enough for me to turn around if I had to.

I remembered a story in the *Baja Adventure Book*, where the author, Walt Peterson, and a friend were traversing a similar, but narrower, raised causeway when they encountered a truck coming the other way:

> *I slowed down and stopped, but the other driver kept coming until his bumper was only inches from ours. Three Mexicans, very large and rough-looking and not exactly exuding empathy and good humor, got out and in unison suggested in unmistakable terms that it was going to be us who pulled off to the side of the road. We could see the tequila bottles on the floor of the cab and a shotgun in the rack in the rear window and quickly came to appreciate their logic; after all it was their country.*

Ultimately, Walt had to reverse for over an hour, with the angry locals bearing down on him the whole way. I can't imagine how his neck felt the next day.

As it turned out, I did have to reverse course. About a half-mile into the raised track, I came to a giant mound of dirt that blocked all passage. I gingerly executed a twenty-nine-point turn, repeatedly getting out to make sure one of my tires wasn't about to slip into the muck.

Executing a very methodical turnaround in the salt ponds

After that failed attempt, Google wanted to send me down an even narrower raised track, where turning around would be impossible should an obstacle or another vehicle present itself.

I stopped to weigh my options. If I did somehow get stuck, I'd have to explain why I, as a random gringo tourist, thought the route was **ever** a good idea. Would they accept "But Google Maps Lady told me it was okay?" Doubtful.

On the other hand, was I really going to turn around and wuss out **again?** Barely a week into my trip, and I'd already have two failures on my record. What kind of spirit of adventure was that?

I figured, what's the worst that could happen? Maybe someone will have to procure a bulldozer to pull me out of the morass... probably after a couple of days of waiting around... as my car slowly rusts away in the salty abyss. At least I'll brighten the day of a few salt-pond workers with a good laugh at my expense. And, of course, I'll get a good story out of it. My grandkids will **LOVE** the bulldozer story. Tell us again, Grandpa!

And so I sat there, lost in a variety of disaster daydreams, when an older gentleman shuffled out of a tiny shed to my left. I had noticed the dilapidated structure when I pulled up, but I assumed it was some long-abandoned outpost. As it turned out, I happened to stop precisely where one would stop if one needed clearance from someone in the shed to proceed.

Despite the old guy's lack of English and my still abysmal Spanish—we established that the raised track Google was trying to send me down was "no bueno."

And with that, my attempt to find a backroad shortcut to the tip of the horn officially ended. More than anything, I was relieved the elderly watchman had decided for me. No wussing out here. Road is no bueno. Old man says no. Sorry, grandkids.

On my way back to the main highway, I wondered how often that old guy gets clueless motorists like me to break up the monotony in his day. Perhaps he's a lot less lonely since the advent of Google Maps.

NOTE: When you see long, straight roads crisscrossing a shallow, multi-hued body of water like this, those probably aren't for you, no matter what Google Maps Lady says.

By the time I got back on the highway, I realized I'd never reach the tip of the horn by nightfall. After my salt-pond adventure, I was in no mood to violate the first rule of overlanding. So, I picked Bahía Asunción, a town along the southern edge of the horn that looked reachable before sunset.

The stars of the show on the drive to Asunción were the gnarled elephant trees. A few regal specimens fanned out in all directions—covering the area of a small house while never reaching more than ten feet off the ground.

Massive elephant tree on the way to Bahía Asunción

BAHÍA ASUNCIÓN

A well-placed sign on the way into Bahía Asunción read, "The La Bufadora Inn—Sherri and Juan welcome you! Just drive to the end of the point." Great! I always drive to the end of the point anyway.

I came around a curve and saw the little hotel perched on a postcard-worthy spot overlooking the cobalt-blue Pacific. I met the owner, Sherri, who told me they don't get many walk-ins, but she had a room available. I checked in and went out for a sunset walk along the coastline.

I found the blowhole from which the La Bufadora Inn gets its name. It was smaller than the massive blowhole on the La Bufadora peninsula up north but still spectacular with its shimmering spray backlit by the setting sun. I walked along the edge of the bluff to a lookout tower at the end of the point, which I learned is manned by guards who watch for abalone poachers. The scene reminded me of Big Sur on the (Alta) California coast —with deep blue surf, punctured by rust-colored rocks, lapping against golden-hued bluffs.

I thought about a numinous moment that washed over Jack Smith on one of his trips to oversee the construction of his Baja dream home:

> *After a quarter mile the pebble beach changes character. The pebbles vanish; the beach becomes a smooth flat sand, but it is strewn with great sculptured lava boulders that have tumbled*

down from the cliffs. The tide was out, and the boulders were pitted with tide pools, some of them perfect oval bowls, like bathroom washbasins, each with its sea anemones, lavender and palest green, and its clutch of polished colored pebbles, magnificent and bright in the trapped sea water.

Each bowl seemed exquisite beyond contriving. I wondered if I could move a single pebble without destroying such perfection, utterly upsetting the arrangement. Arrangement? That was hardly the word. Each pool was a phenomenon beyond the art of human hand and eye.

What then could account for such beauty? It must be chance; nothing more. Random chance. I remember having read only recently some scientist's theory that man and the universe were simply results of cosmic chance.

I lay back in the arms of a great sculptured sandstone chair in the cliff, a natural golden throne, my head against an antimacassar of bright green sea moss. I turned my face to the sun and shut my eyes, listening to the lullaby of the surf.

I don't know how long I had lain there in the clasp of the stately sea throne, like Triton napping, when it suddenly occurred to me that I knew God's name. It came to me all at once, whole and final. His name was **Random Chance***.*

On his way back to the house, Jack wrestled with whether or not to share his revelation about God's name:

Glowing with this light, I stirred myself and began to walk back over the beach toward the house. As I drew near the green tent I saw the younger stranger had moved down closer to the surf. His legs were crossed as before, in the lotus position, and the guitar lay across them, but he was not playing. He was simply looking out to sea. He had a full mustache and gentle eyes behind metal-rimmed glasses.

"It's a nice day," he said, as I came near.

"Yes. It is. It really is."

I didn't tell him about my revelation. I wasn't sure if it was the kind of revelation that would be true for anyone else. Besides, he was obviously a meditative man. He could find out God's name for himself.

Still, Jack gamely tried to relate his epiphany to Mr. Gomez, the land's owner and builder of his vacation home, with predictable results:

When I got back to the house, though, I told Gomez. As I knew he was not without fantasies and revelations of his own.

"What do you think of it?" I asked.

"Jack," he said, "when you sit in the Mexican sun, you have to wear a Mexican sombrero."

I made my way back to the inn, where I met the rest of the guests: Carol and her husband Bill, whose primary diversion seemed to be going out in a tiny boat to catch yellowtail; an Irish girl and a Swiss guy, both on motorcycles, who had met somewhere along the way; and Sherri's two friends who seemed to be staying long term. We stayed up drinking and swapping traveler stories well into the night. The following morning, I enjoyed a delicious, if moderately hungover, breakfast in a cinematic setting overlooking the surf.

Sherri and the group suggested I stay that night for New Year's Eve, which was very tempting. However, it would set me back a day and, more importantly, guarantee a long day of hungover driving—because what am I going to do, *not* drink myself stupid on New Year's Eve? So, I passed on the New Year's festivities, bade my goodbyes, and got back on the road.

When traveling alone, I never know if I'm going to walk into a built-in social scene like Sherri's or have to entertain myself like in Bahía de Los Ángeles. Someone should publish a guidebook: *Mexico and Central America for the Moderately Outgoing Solo Traveler.*

The *Baja Adventure Book* describes the next stretch of the highway as "the most boring on the peninsula." Yet I was still enthralled by the rolling foothills with endless fields of cacti. In fact, the cover of this book is derived from a shot I took along this stretch. It's also home to the town of San

Ignacio, the jumping-off point to visit the cave paintings of the San Francisco mountains.

Yawn—just another view from the boring stretch of the Transpeninsular

While the great civilizations of Mesoamerica thrived a few hundred miles away across the Gulf, an unknown culture created some of the world's most significant cave art, then vanished. Generations of nomadic hunters added to and layered over vast murals depicting animal hunts and other scenes—some of them hundreds of feet long, on cave ceilings as high as thirty feet off the ground. Whether these artists left the region or stayed and lost all ancestral knowledge of the cave paintings is unknown. The Cochimí, who inhabited Central Baja when the Spanish arrived, believed the petroglyphs had been created by a race of giants.

The cave paintings aren't accessible without a guide, and since it was New Year's Eve, that would be out of the question for a few days. I pressed on, following the highway back to the peninsula's eastern coast, through a gritty mining town called Santa Rosalia, and then on to the colonial town of Mulegé.

BAHÍA CONCEPCIÓN

I made my way just past Mulegé to a small beach along Bahía Concepción, the largest sheltered bay in Baja. As I wound down the road to the hidden beach, I spotted Mike's van at the far end of a crescent-shaped cove sheltering a lush mangrove lagoon. Most of the other vehicles were RVs, many from British Columbia. Gringos in this part of Baja tend to be seasonal snowbirds, since the drive is too long for weekend warriors like Dale.

I looked forward to sleeping in my tent again. Beds are overrated. Mike, Kelly, and I had an early New Year's toast and were all asleep by 9 p.m. I wasn't even awoken by fireworks at midnight. We may have found the only quiet spot in all of Mexico for New Year's Eve. I *almost* felt guilty for missing out on the Mexican New Year's Eve fireworks experience.

One great thing about being a light sleeper is that a sunrise flooding my tent with blazing color usually wakes me up. Thus, I was rousted on New Year's Day by one of the most spectacular sunrises I've ever seen. Horizontal ribbons of orange, red, and purple set fire to the sky over Bahía Concepción—the whole scene mirrored in the glassy smooth water.

Sunrise over Bahía Concepción

I soon became aware of odd rhythmic breathing noises. At first, I wondered if Mike and Kelly were having sunrise sex in the van. But the sound was definitely coming from the direction of the water.

Scanning the cove, I spotted a few minor disturbances in the water about fifty yards offshore. Every few seconds, a pod of dolphins would break the surface to breathe. The morning was so quiet I could make out the percussive release of pressurized watery air expelling through their blowholes, followed by the *whoosh* of fresh air being sucked in—not unlike the sounds of scuba diving. I'd seen dolphins in the wild before, but this was the first time I'd ever **heard** dolphins.

Mike and Kelly got up a few minutes later to catch the last of the sunrise. Kelly offered me some local watermelon that was like none I'd ever tasted. The mostly seedless fruit was a dense, deep red and intensely rich. Imagine the very first pull of a Slurpee—also known as Icee, Slushy, or Koolee, depending on where you grew up—when it's still velvety smooth and bursting with flavor. By comparison, every other watermelon I'd ever tasted was the tail end of the Slurpee, when it's mostly ice with little flavor left.

Munching on luxury watermelon, we watched the pod of dolphins crisscross the cove. A few feet away, an indigo-hued heron scanned the shoreline for a meal. Other shorebirds snatched shellfish from the exposed tidal pools, climbed to a few hundred feet, then dropped the shells onto the rocks and swooped down to collect their treat.

We just needed David Attenborough to narrate the scene.

I didn't have any revelations about God's name that morning. But looking back, it was the first time on the trip I thought to myself, "Where else on earth would you rather be than right here, right now?"

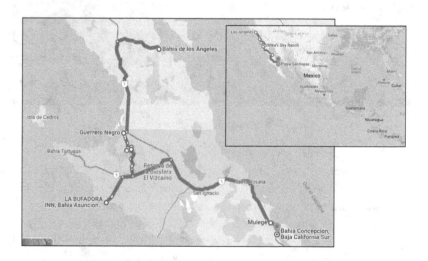

CHAPTER 8

THE BEST THINGS IN LIFE

Mongol General: Hao! Dai ye! We won again! This is good, but what is best in life?
Mongol Soldier: The open steppe, fleet horse, falcons at your wrist, and the wind in your hair.
Mongol General: Wrong! Conan! What is best in life?
Conan the Barbarian: To crush your enemies. See them driven before you. And to hear the lamentations of their women.
Mongol General: That is good! That is good.

FOLLOWING THE EARLY-MORNING NATURE SHOW, Kelly, Mike, and I forayed into Mulegé, where I finally found a Mexican blanket to replace the one I left behind at Mike's Sky Rancho. The new blanket wasn't quite as warm, but at least my five-hundred-mile scavenger hunt for one of the most ubiquitous Mexican tourist items was finally over.

The next day, I said goodbye to Kelly and Mike again. They had plans to camp at a surf beach on the western side of Baja's southern tip (generally referred to as "The Cape"). I needed to arrange a ferry passage across the Sea of Cortez. Then, I planned to spend a few days exploring the eastern Cape and the central mountains, before finally meeting up with my new friends one last time.

Just south of Mulegé, I passed through the colonial town of Loreto, the site of the first permanent European settlement along the western edge of North America. When the Jesuits landed on the peninsula in 1697, they found only a few scattered tribes in dismal shape. As it had played out else-where in the New World, Old World diseases spread among indigenous populations and preceded the colonizers. By the time the mission at Loreto was established, Baja's pre-contact indigenous population of up to half a million people, belonging to a half-dozen distinct ethnic groups, had been reduced to around thirty thousand.

A century and a half of Spanish conversion and betterment later, that number was effectively zero. The Cochimí and Guaycura of Central Baja and the Pericú of the Cape had been wiped out—their language, their culture, and most of their people. Anything left of their bloodline melted into the local settler population. Today, only a few hundred speakers of the peninsula's pre-contact languages remain, mainly in the mountains of Northern Baja.

Past Loreto, the Transpeninsular continues to hug the Sea of Cortez for a few miles, then turns inland through a long stretch of flat farmland—the first actual boring drive of the trip. I reached the outskirts of La Paz, the largest city in southern Baja, stopping first at the ferry building to procure a ticket to Mazatlán.

On my way into the city, I spotted a modern-looking hotel called City Express, with an @ symbol in the logo that seemed to promise decent inter-net. While paying for my room, I noticed the 1 p.m. checkout time and thought, "Who the hell would sleep in until 1 p.m.? That's like half the day gone."

I freshened up, then headed out to explore La Paz. The city has a lovely paved esplanade along the waterfront—which I learned from Kelly is called a *malecón*. Mexican families strolled up and down the malecón, pushing their kids in big plastic cars or watching them wobble along on roller skates. La Paz seemed to have a healthy mix of Mexican and American tourists, unlike the two Cabos, which might as well be Florida.

Hernán Cortés (yes, **that** Cortés) made three failed attempts to estab-lish a colony near La Paz, on land he believed to be an island. Baja's canyon-ridden terrain, lack of food and water, and hostile native population quickly reduced each colony to a struggle for survival, resulting in one of Baja's nicknames: *The Indomitable Peninsula*.

A Spanish writer dubbed the site of Cortés' failures *California*—the name of a mythical island "West of the Indies" populated by black female warriors, as chronicled in the contemporary adventure novel *Sergas de Esplandián*. This led a generation of explorers to believe that the "island" of *California* was populated by Amazon warriors living in cities of gold, ruled over by a Queen named Calafia. The line between fact and fiction was a bit blurry in those days. Yet such was Baja's indomitability that no explorer made inroads far enough to confirm or deny the legend.

The peninsula's only exploitable resource, charcoal-gray metallic pearls, could be harvested without going ashore. So after Cortés' failed colony, the Spanish ignored the peninsula for nearly two centuries, viewing it mainly as an impediment to their trade routes to the Philippines—earning Baja its other nickname: *The Forgotten Peninsula.*

Speaking of impediments, beware that 1 p.m. checkout time. Something hibernatory happens to me when I have that much time: "It's 9:30; I guess I better head down for the free breakfast before the kitchen closes." Back in the room: "I have plenty of time; how about I just surf the internet for a bit?" Then, a little after 10:30, when I'd typically be forced to shower and pack up to stay ahead of the dreaded housekeeper *tap tap tap*, the shame spiral kicks in: "Well, now that I've already blown half the day, I might as well just lie here in the AC and get it all out of my system. Surf away, loser."

I finally emerged into the Baja sun like a dazed vampire, heading north with no real plan except to work clockwise around the bulb-shaped cape, foraying into the mountains when a road looked fun. I checked out a beach but quickly packed it in when severe winds blasted me with stinging sand.

A little after dark, I rolled into the town of La Ventana, which I'd heard was hugely popular with windsurfers. As I passed a few upscale resorts and trendy-looking outdoor restaurants, I sensed this was not the place for a cheap hotel room. I pulled over and checked booking.com. Nothing listed for under $200 a night. I wasn't nuts about the idea of camping in unscouted territory in a potential windstorm, but I wasn't going to drive back to La Paz in the dark or shell out $200+ for a hotel room.

I drove through town, hungry, fretting, mulling my options. I pulled over at a hot dog stand and ordered a loaded, bacon-wrapped hot dog, solving one of my problems.

A local snowbird told me there was a free campsite just outside town, and the wind wouldn't pick up again until 11 a.m. I thought, "Well, that's nice of the wind to be so regular. No wonder this town is so popular with windsurfers." Camping suddenly sounded a lot less disagreeable.

I finished the hot dog and drove past town and across the arroyo (a dry flood channel, ubiquitous in Baja) as instructed. A few palapas stood on the beach in various stages of disintegration. I still wasn't sure about the situation. What if the expat was wrong about the wind? Was it safe out here—

this far from town? The drive out seemed a little sketchy. What if I get stuck in the sand? But I got over my anxiety, pitched my tent, drank a beer, and passed out.

The next morning, I awoke to another gorgeous sunrise blasting into my tent. This one was less purple and more blazing red-orange. The sun poked above the horizon, shooting off flat rays in all directions like a Peter Max poster.

I thought, "What in the hell were you fretting about last night? This is the best place on earth, and you almost missed it. If there were a City Express in La Ventana, you'd have slept through the whole thing."

I considered my plan to treat myself to a few nights at the Hyatt in Cabo and realized I didn't want that. I wanted more of *this*.

And then it hit me. I had my Jack Smith "God's name is Random Chance" epiphany, and I wasn't even out in the Mexican sun too long without a sombrero. I was having my second Baja Moment. But this time, it came with a message I could actually verbalize!

Here goes:
...
*The best things in life really **are** free.*
...
Take a minute if you need it.

Okay, maybe it sounds trite. But in that moment, I realized there was nowhere on earth—not a $250 hotel room in La Ventana, not a Four Seasons penthouse, not Justin Bieber's yacht—that I would rather be than that camping spot just past the arroyo outside of La Ventana, waking up to another insane Baja sunrise. I couldn't be any happier, and it cost ***nothing***.

Nature, laughter, friendship, family, love, sex—what else is there in life? All free. And what tastes better than a $2 fish taco or a cheap basket of strawberries from the side of the road?

I like a few creature comforts, and I know I've been fortunate to be born in the right time and place to enable my wanderlust. Yet my most soul-satisfying experiences almost always come in nature, and rarely have I had to spend much to get there.

While I gravitate to spiritual people, I don't consider myself a spiritual person in the traditional sense. I have a degree in physics. If I have to bet, I put my money on things that are measurable, repeatable, and falsifiable. But at the same time, I believe in something bigger than myself. I marvel at the impossibility of life and the infinite beauty of nature. Sometimes, I look up at the moon in the afternoon sky and think what a miracle it is that I'm alive and sentient to appreciate it all.

And if you go back to the moment before the Big Bang, then we're **all** philosophers. Two trillion galaxies in the observable universe, each with hundreds of billions of stars revolving around a supermassive black hole— all spawned from an infinitesimally tiny speck of near-infinite energy that just spontaneously sprang into existence. The most fundamental question we can ever ask: "Why is there something instead of nothing?" is apparently a paradox we can never understand.

If you want to chalk that up to God, be my guest. I'm not sure what else one would call a timeless, incomprehensible source of infinite energy that creates universes out of nothing. Let there be light.

Taking in that sunrise, the revelation hit me like a wrecking ball: my oddball spiritual vision of the world is my answer to the Mongol General. In that instant, I went from *thinking* to *knowing* that what's left of my life should be structured around finding more of these moments.

(Then Covid hit, and I spent four years writing this book. But soon!)

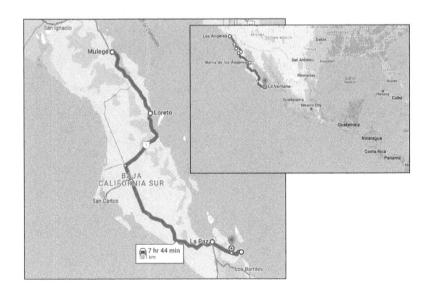

CHAPTER 9

JUST TRY IT

I'M AN ANNOYING DINING COMPANION. While I **am** listening to what you're saying... for the most part... I'm also a satellite dish for every conversation within earshot and every server, host, manager, and busser in my field of vision. As a former waiter, I can instantly spot who's in the weeds, who's hoping to get sent home, who's boffing the manager, etc. It's best to sit me facing a wall in a sufficiently loud restaurant where I can't pick out individual conversations.

For my 45th birthday, my girlfriend graciously treated me to the fanciest meal I've ever eaten. We were seated painfully close, as chichi hipster restaurants tend to do, to a *Seeking Arrangement* couple on their first date. He seemed to be about 55; she was in her late 20s to early 30s. She asked about his boat. He wondered if she had read *Infinite Jest*, as he had apparently instructed. She said she was struggling with it. I respected her honesty. The food was exquisite. Yet my enduring memory of the meal is getting sucked into their conversation, despite my best efforts to tune it out.

I'm told there are humans who can gaze into the eyes of the person across from them and tune everything else out. I don't understand these people. If they're around my age, I assume they grew up without cable TV. I think something about flipping channels every few seconds really fries the adolescent brain.

However, all the traits that make me a terrible dining companion produce a world-class people watcher. This morning, my satellite dish was tuned to a conversation in a coffee shop in La Ventana. Two young local women were having a pleasant conversation when a much older American expat/snowbird sat down next to them. I gathered that one of the women does massage, and he was a frequent client. I'm no body language expert, but it seemed to me the women would have preferred to just continue their one-on-one conversation.

It seemed his status as a paying customer, possibly combined with being a relatively affluent American, made him feel entitled to butt in. At one point, he actually told her she should smile more.

Dude.

Then he asked something that I couldn't make out. She blurted out, "None of your business," followed a second later with, "Just kidding." I was impressed because "none of your business" seemed to stop the guy in his tracks, whereas "just kidding" rescued the moment from turning truly awkward.

Like Southerners in the US, Latinos seem naturally adept at navigating social discourse. As someone who's never had a conversation I couldn't steer into cringy, awkward silence, this skill fascinates me. In my limited experience, innate social poise seems common to speakers of all the Romance languages. The French, Spanish, Italians, even Romanians seem more comfortable in their own skin than the rest of us. Perhaps the structure of our native tongue wires our behavior patterns somehow. Or maybe the Romans were just really gregarious.

I pulled myself away from the morning's entertainment and returned to the road, where Google Maps Lady was in her bag again. To get me back to the coast headed south, she found a feisty-looking road that was red on my paper map for some reason. By contrast, the hell road from Mike's Sky Rancho was gray. I wasn't sure if red meant better than gray or worse. The ink seemed more solid, at least.

It quickly became apparent that red was just as bad as gray. Either that or a recent chubasco—as the hurricanes that blow through Southern Baja every five to ten years are known—had rearranged the road. The drive started rough and got worse, then hugged a cliff face for a quarter mile and then got rough again. I thought about turning around, but the prospect of an ocean view egged me on, along with not wanting to go 0-2-1 versus Baja roads. (I counted the old man at the salt ponds as a tie.)

In a rare flat spot, I drove through a puddle guarded by a legion of extremely aggressive red-and-yellow-striped wasps, which I have since identified as *Executioner Paper Wasps*. Yikes. The wasps crawled all over my car, probing for a way in. I was thankful not to be on foot, bicycle, or even motorcycle.

Baja is still pretty wild in its wildest places. The remote parts of the peninsula remind me of Alaska, in the sense that nature is still winning. You get an inkling of what an ordeal it must have been for early pioneers to tame the land.

After another half hour of bouncing and lurching along, desert scrub finally gave way to an expansive view of the deep blue Sea of Cortez. The rust-colored road continued south, carving into the steep cardón-covered coastline, following inlets in an undulating curve that led to wispy clouds on the horizon.

Maybe it was the work to get there, but at that moment, I decided it was the most scenic drive I'd ever done. I got out and gaped at the view for a few minutes—until a red wasp showed up to herd me back into my car.

A deserted section of Baja's East Cape

I continued along the coast, mindful not to get distracted by the view lest I drive off the edge. Eventually, I passed a few houses and a beach with human beings. I headed inland toward the mountains, using my general strategy of following the most crooked road on the map. At one point, I drove through a town that I doubt attracts many gringo tourists. The local kids all stopped their soccer game to gawk at my FJ.

SAN JOSÉ DEL CABO

I pulled into San José del Cabo around 3 p.m. After a few weeks of rural Baja's exceedingly languid pace, the traffic and hustle of Cabo jarred me. The frazzled clerk at my hotel, who was busy helping several other people, apologized because I'd been standing at the reception desk unattended for all of *thirty seconds*.

It must be a considerable challenge for people who grew up in the relaxed pace of Baja to adapt to demanding gringo service. Of course, if you just flew in from New York or LA—you'd never notice a change from your usual pace of life—just another busy hotel lobby scene.

That night, I headed back out on foot to explore the town. My first order of business was to get something in my stomach. I wandered past a few fancy restaurants, a Cheesecake Factory, and a Chili's.

I wasn't feeling any of the restaurant options, and I couldn't find any street food. Then, I spotted a group who looked like off-duty service workers, so I followed them up a side street. A food cart soon appeared. Hooray! Always follow the service workers. They have to eat, too. And what they're having is usually tastier and more interesting than the overpriced garlic prawns the gringos are fussing over.

The food cart had corn dogs, which I figured should at least tide me over until I could find some tacos. Everyone in line seemed to be ordering a crazy-looking mess of stuff overflowing out of a Tostitos bag that had been cut open the long way. People walked away balancing the bag in their hands like a small puppy. That much food seemed like it would bog me down for all the walking I had planned. I wanted to stay light on my feet.

But my curiosity started to kick in. The ingredients included pepino, cueritos, cacahuate, reilito, ciamoto, jícama, and other things I couldn't translate. I could see peanuts and cucumber going into the mix, but I didn't recognize anything else.

I asked the guy ahead of me what the fuss was about. He told me the concoction is called Tostilocos, and he was clearly a fan. Even after his spiel, I expressed trepidation over the sheer amount of food. He shot back, "Just try it."

Well then. I figured I had to after that.

I received my puppy-sized bag and dug in with the provided plastic fork. I expected something with rich, heavy sauce and dense meat and cheese. But it was light and flavorful, in a watery tomato-based sauce that I realized must be Clamato (not "ciamato" like I initially read). The crunchy peanuts and salty tortilla chips perfectly balanced out the cucumber and fleshy jicama. Rielitos, pieces of tamarind candy that taste like Boston Baked Beans, added a chewy/sweet component. And of course, this being Mexico, they threw in some pork rinds—which were chewy, not fried.

I set back out with a new spring in my step—excited to have discovered this unlikely local gem amid corporate restaurant hell. I made a deal with myself that if anyone says "Just try it" for the rest of the trip, I must comply. There's a lot of meaning loaded into those three little words—much like "change your life." When I hear those words, my ears perk up. You say these lug nuts will change my life? Okay, I guess I'm buying the lug nuts.

Tostilocos

I tried to hug the waterfront as per my usual strategy. But in this area, pricey hotels seemed to have monopolized every stretch of water. So, I headed inland and uphill toward San José's Old Town.

I passed a casual restaurant with an oversized banner boasting "SAN JOSÉ DEL CABO'S BEST FISH TACOS!" which... if you think about it... is really just another way of saying, "Just try it."

Would you claim to have the best fish tacos, in the birthplace of fish tacos, and **not** tell people to *Just try it*? Of course not. So, it would seem I was obligated to stop at this place. What kind of a person would make a code for themselves, then break it twenty-five minutes later? Not a person I want to know.

The standard taco presentation in these parts is a tortilla with a bare piece of fried or grilled fish, which you dress at a condiments bar. I'm still learning what works for me and what doesn't. There's a yellow-orangish slaw that I like, and of course, the signature Baja cream sauce. Then there's a green avocado-based sauce I haven't quite figured out yet. They also offer a pinkish sauce, chunky pico de gallo, onions, hot sauce, and limes. Oh yeah, and avocado slices—gotta have those.

I usually go for all of it, resulting in an overstuffed taco that's impossible to eat with anything resembling dignity. My strategy is to shove each taco into my face so fast that it doesn't have time to fall apart in my hands. This method is hit or miss. Mostly miss. To limit the blast radius and hide my shame, I hunch over my plate and surround my food with my arms. This leaves only a narrow window into my feeding frenzy, which I try to aim away from other diners—especially little kids, who have a tendency to stare with mouths agape, then burst into tears.

Typical over-stuffed fish taco à la Matt

My plan to stay light on my feet wasn't going exactly as planned. I was thankful for more walking ahead to jostle my full stomach.

I soon climbed a cobblestoned hill to find a town square lined with restaurants and shops and bustling with people and all the requisite vendors selling glowing whirligigs and whatnots. I stopped to watch a troop of little kids breakdancing. Nearby, I noticed thirty people waiting in a line that led to a woman pulling tamales out of a steamy hold, then dressing them with a dark sauce.

I thought, "Wow, those must be some amazing tamales. And if you think about it... what is a line that long, surrounded by scores of other food vendors and dining options, if not a sign that says, *Hey, these tamales are freaking good. You should probably try them?*"

Once again, the gauntlet had been thrown down. All hopes for a light, frisky evening had vanished. Honor-bound by code, I walked to the back of the tamale line. I may be sweaty, bloated, and flatulent when the night is through—but at least I'll have my pride.

I did have one ace in the hole. I know I said earlier that I believe in the laws of physics. But I also believe that beer actually *creates* room in my stomach. Don't @ me with your "actually liquids don't compress" and other sciencey mumbo jumbo. I know my body.

Waiting in line, I struck up a conversation with Peter, an American tourist, and José, who was from the area. José billed himself as "the Anthony Bourdain of Cabo." I immediately hit it off with these guys.

The tamales were delicious, but I struggled to get them down, even with the help of magic beer. My stomach started to feel like the trash compactor scene in *Star Wars* was going on down there.

José told us there was an art walk that night, so we checked out some galleries. This was serious Mexican art for serious buyers—not cheap. We continued to wander, talking about food, Mexican culture, and some of the boorish behavior on display in and around Cabo. I officially apologized on behalf of America, and José accepted. So, Americans, you're all off the hook. Just watch it from now on.

After more wandering, José and Peter said they were getting hungry.

Oh no.

And then it came, "You have to try La Lupita! They have the best tacos in town!"

C'mon, man.

The self-professed Anthony Bourdain of Cabo not only told me I had to try it, but that it was the best in town. A throng of people waiting outside the restaurant backed up his claim.

WHY IS MY HONOR CODE BEING PUT TO THIS MAXIMUM TEST MERE HOURS AFTER ITS INCEPTION???

But, like Abraham on the rock, I got a reprieve. The place was **too** good. Even José, with all his local pull, couldn't get us a table. I feigned disappointment when, in fact, I was deeply relieved. We stumbled around a bit more, then called it a night.

CHAPTER 10

ENDLESS SUMMER

NEEDING to burn off some calories from the night before, I got an early start and headed into the mountains in search of a hiking trail. Serendipitously, my road dead-ended at a wilderness park called Rancho Ecológico Sol de Mayo. I paid the entrance fee and hiked a half mile to one of the only waterfalls in parched Baja.

I continued on the trail, up a few steep hills, then another half-mile to a forested area. Walking through the forest, something felt strange, but I couldn't put my finger on it. Finally, it dawned on me that brown and yellow leaves lay all over the ground—in the tropics. Deciduous trees in various stages of losing their leaves mingled with the usual cardón cactus, fan palms, and other dry tropical scrub, making the scene even weirder.

It turns out this forest is a tiny holdout from a previous ice age. Over time, its trees have adapted to Baja's warming climate by shedding their leaves in the dry season instead of winter. Baja's biological diversity never ceases to amaze.

On the hike back, my left heel started to hurt. I realized that if a two-mile hike on soft dirt was going to aggravate me like this, that could be a big problem for the upcoming Patagonia expedition.

Back in the hotel, *Dr. Internet* convinced me I had something called "Policeman's Heel"—basically a chronically bruised heel. The best treatment is rest. When rest isn't possible, tape the heel to keep the fleshy part from flattening out.

I bought some clear plastic medical tape at a nearby pharmacy and did my best to match what I'd seen online. My tape job looked about as close to the picture as those **NAILED IT** memes in which someone shows off their disastrous attempt at baking a Sonic the Hedgehog cake.

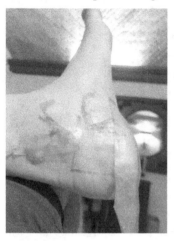

NAILED IT!

SAN PEDRITO

After three days of hotel life, I was eager to get back to camping. I made my way to San Pedrito Beach, where I pulled up next to Mike and Kelly's white van with the black surfboard carrier for the fourth time. By now, it felt like coming home.

San Pedrito's campground sits on a patch of high ground, where you can camp for $10 a night with access to an outhouse. Or, you can camp in the arroyo for $5 a night, but you have to do your business in the arroyo—behind the campers and away from the beach. Grungy-looking RVs, surf vans, and trucks filled both sites. One plot in the arroyo had three late '80s Chevy Astro vans side by side, all lovingly decked out with modifications like popup tents. I guess Astrovanning is a thing.

The beach seemed to be hopping with what, in a past life, I might have called "dirt hippies," but in this context were basically "grungy surfers." Not that they were unattractive. Of all the Baja beaches I'd seen, this one had the best-looking surfer dudes and dudettes strutting around. If tatted-up surf hotties are your thing, San Pedrito is the place.

Or *was* the place. While change comes very slowly to Central Baja, Southern Baja is constantly evolving. A beach will be empty one year, then a few campers show up. In a few years, someone builds a little bar/restaurant, and maybe five years later, a sprawling resort appears—ruining the beach from the point of view of grungy surfers, overlanders, and anyone who doesn't want to spend more than $10 a night.

The following day, we headed to Cerritos Beach, where I was excited to try surfing for the first time. Cerritos, I was told, is much better for beginners than the San Pedrito break, which crashes onto a bed of sharp volcanic rocks.

Cerritos is also the poster child in this area for the final stage of development. According to Mike, the beach scene started as a surfer hangout. Then, a few restaurants appeared. Within ten years, two large resorts and a slew of high-priced condos dominated the beach. Cerritos had nothing like the community feel of San Pedrito.

Mike surfed for a bit while Kelley and I lounged. When Mike came in from surfing, he gave me a few pointers on paddling into the wave and standing up on the board, then sent me out to try.

As soon as I put my weight on Mike's 5'5" board, the nose sank six inches underwater. I had to extend my neck and hold my shoulders up to keep my head above water. I'm obviously no surfing expert, but I don't think that's how it's supposed to work.

I paddled hard into my first wave, which dragged along a few feet until it passed over me and spit me out. On my second attempt, I got up on my knees, which pushed the board farther underwater. I considered the ramifications of this increasing submersion toward my ultimate goal of standing up on the board. Again, I know literally nothing about surfing, but I can't recall any surf videos where the protagonist shreds a wave in water up to their knees.

I tried to catch a dozen more waves, which all ended in similar fashion. I came in and told Mike, "I think I might be too big for this board." He agreed with my assessment. While Mike went out for another set, I found a rental place and procured a padded, seven-foot beginner board.

My first attempt with the longer board went much better. I also realized the water was so shallow where the waves were breaking, I could push off the bottom and **then** start paddling like crazy. This was beginner surfer heaven.

After a few failed starts, I attained a decent push-off, paddled as hard as I could, then... silence. At first, I thought I missed the wave. Then I realized I was on it!

I'd never caught a wave like that with a boogie board, so I had no idea what to expect. I'd caught some waves body surfing, but that's a very different experience: First, water invades your nostrils and ear canals, but these are mere distractions while the wave executes its true goal of giving you a wedgie.

But *this* was like that fog-of-war crescendo moment in every action movie this century—where the scene goes silent as maximum chaos swirls around our hero. I was floating above the water in complete stillness.

Wow! I caught a wave on a surfboard. What a feeling!

I kept at it. I could get to my knees and then pull my feet under me. But as soon as I tried to stand up, the board would shoot off to one side. It was frustrating, but I still loved it.

In retrospect, I probably should have just enjoyed riding on my knees and saved standing up for lesson two. I think I was egged on by the '60s documentary *Endless Summer*, in which two innocuously charming California kids travel the world surfing, sometimes on beaches that had never seen a surfboard. On one beach in Africa, the protagonists are flabbergasted when a young local man stands up on the board on his first try. I wanted to be that guy—pure strength and balance. I was not that guy. But I still had a blast.

The ending of one of my better rides

Back at camp, we played frisbee with some surfers camped next door. The way my lower back felt after a couple of hours of surfing, I now understood the surfer bros' chest-forward, arm-waggling strut.

After several days of observing surfers in their natural habitat, I formulated a theory that male surfers signal their alpha status by the amount of butt crack showing above their drooping board shorts. A one-inch buttcrack must give way to a two-inch buttcrack. If two two-inch buttcracks meet, they must fight to establish dominance—at least until a three-inch buttcrack, also known as a "beachmaster," arrives to break up the fight and send them on their way.

As sundown approached, people began to emerge from their campsites and migrate toward the beach. Mike, Kelley, and I followed.

Everyone spread out in little groups along a sandy berm to watch surfers finish their last sets of the day—backdropped by bright orange striated clouds layered with lavender sky. One by one, the surfers picked up their boards and headed in, gingerly picking their way over the sharp rocks. As the sky darkened, silhouettes of the last few surfers sawed the points of their boards back and forth against an intense band of blood red just above the horizon.

I looked up and down the beach. Not only was I having another of what I was starting to recognize as Baja moments, I knew in my *bones* that every soul up and down that berm was having the same moment. We may never be able to explain this experience to anyone back home, but at least we all knew that we all knew. We had a big group secret, one we couldn't divulge if we tried.

I feel like the attitude of gringos who want a place like San Pedrito to remain pristine, to not turn into another Cerritos, is tone-deaf at best. The economic development that leads to a better life for local residents never enters the discussion, or worse, is hand-waved away with a deeply offensive attitude that locals might be happier staying poor.

There is an argument that some forms of development hurt local residents more than they help—take diamond mining as an extreme example. So, if you want to argue that resorts, condos, and gringo-owned curio shops don't make life better for locals, then yes, that seems like a discussion worth having. But as with most aspects of the modern world, a few beer-buzzed amateur economists in fold-up camping chairs probably aren't going to tease out any useful conclusions.

The fact remains that foreigners camping at San Pedrito almost universally have much more economic opportunity waiting for us back home, even if we may be currently broke or "slumming it" on a $10-a-night beach ($5 if we're willing to poop in the arroyo). Bumming around in poorer parts of the world is a choice, not a life we were born into. There is no flip side to this equation. The kids who stopped their soccer game to gawk when I drove through their tiny ranch town aren't spending a summer bumming around Europe or America—where, ironically, we've already destroyed or developed most of our pristine places, **specifically to create economic opportunity**.

Having said all that—sitting there on that sandy berm, taking in another breathtaking Baja sunset with my new confidantes, I understood the impulse to resist development. It's a natural outcrop of not wanting to lose ***this.*** This moment. This shared secret.

BAJA REDUX

The next day, I said goodbye to my new old friends for the fourth and final time of the trip. Kelly and Mike are simply two of the most genuine, open, kind people I've ever met. I can't imagine my Baja experience without them introducing me to surf culture and leading me to hidden beaches on all sides of the peninsula.

But it wasn't the last time we'd see each other. Two years later, I returned to Baja to meet up with them on their now seasonal migration from Canada. I made it to Mulegé in two days, stopping, of course, for fish tacos in Guerrero Negro. Once again, I spotted their white van parked on the beach at Baja Concepción.

We gorged on ceviche, drank warm Modelo Lights, and got caught up late into the afternoon. I asked if they'd ever found that killer watermelon again. Sadly, they'd found none that came close, and not for a lack of trying. Maybe it really was heaven-sent.

As the sun disappeared and the last light faded from the moonless sky, the Milky Way came into view, cutting straight over our heads and continuing to the horizon, where it met its mirror image rising from the glassy bay. I've seen some bright stars, but nothing quite like that night. If you'd lived your life indoors and knew nothing about the universe, you would have sworn the stars were a fuzzy carpet of luminous pinholes a few hundred feet off the ground—like a giant planetarium.

I imagined Baja's mysterious petroglyph artists looking up at the same night sky. They were adroit engineers—able to create vast murals on high cave ceilings. Maybe they thought if they could just build a tall enough scaffold, they could reach up and grab one of the stars.

As we pondered the night sky, music floated over from the camp next door. We heard beach standards like America, Santana, and Fleetwood Mac, and songs that were either original or very obscure—all played and sung to perfection (it turned out the guitarist had toured with Santana). Dozens of our fellow campers wandered over to enjoy the music.

We contemplated walking over to join the group seated around the fire. But after six or seven rounds of "Okay, next song we'll go over," it dawned on us that we had the perfect vantage point to let the music wash over us while we gazed up at the Milky Way.

I said, "You know, I don't think anything could possibly be better than right here, right now, on this exact square meter of beach." Mike agreed with my assessment.

I hadn't come to Baja seeking more "Where else on earth would you rather be?" moments. By that time, they were just a fleeting memory if I thought of them at all. Yet here I was, having another one, viscerally connecting with myself across those two years.

I realized the flowery ramblings in my blog weren't just another Baja fever dream. The revelations I'd had weren't just an artifact of my trip into the unknown. They're a feature of this bony finger of forgotten land— where food and water are precious, but heartbreaking beauty is as abundant as oxygen.

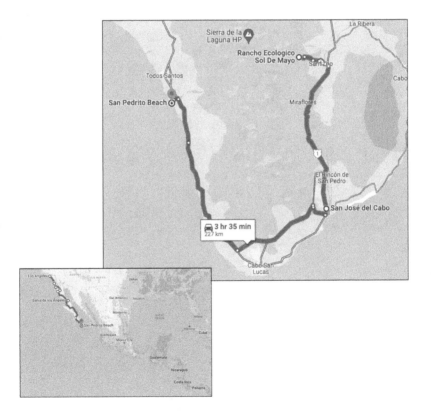

Part Two

Devouring Mexico

I've seen zero evidence of any nation other than Mexico even remotely having the slightest clue what Mexican food is about or even come close to reproducing it. It is perhaps the most misunderstood country and cuisine on Earth.

— Anthony Bourdain

CHAPTER 11

TRAIL MAGIC

WAITING in La Paz for my ferry to the mainland, I had time to sample not one but two fish taco places. I'm proud to report that, with incremental progress in dressing my own tacos, I'm down to four beard-cleaning napkins and zero crying children.

The ferry to Mazatlán costs $110 for the car with two options for the human(s) that accompany it: a private cabin for $40, or for $15, one can ride out the nine-hour overnight trip in the main dining/lounging area. I opted for the cabin, which turned out to be a nicely appointed room with a shower and even a tiny deck to take in the sunset as we pulled out of the harbor.

The controls for the heat, radio, and everything else were in Korean. I tried not to dwell on the recent Korean ferry disasters nor why a Korean ferry company might want to unload an older boat to a more regulatorily lax country like Mexico.

Since pulling up to the ferry terminal, my new turf anxiety had risen to levels not seen since the beginning of the trip. I was leaving sleepy, pastoral, island-vibe Baja for mainland Mexico—land of cartels and serious crime. I tried to tell myself to relax, but once again, my rational brain was having an argument with my mammalian anxiety response. I think the best the rational mind can hope for in these situations is a stalemate.

This time, the stalemate took the form of me fantasizing that the four young men and one young woman seated at a table in the lounge were low-level foot soldiers in a cartel. I based this on nothing other than their new

Euro-style jeans (which everyone in Latin America wears) and the cajones they had to stack two cases of Tecate on the table between them—like they were daring some hapless ferry employee to try to put the kibosh on the fun night they had planned.

More than once on the trip, I was told by a local that the only way a gringo tourist can get in trouble with the cartels is to a) try to sell drugs on their turf or b) hit on one of their girlfriends.

—Hold on, taking notes—

Okay, got it. This will put a real damper on the trip, but I guess I can stay in my lane.

Each time I came out to the lounge area to get a snack, the "cartel guys" had made another impressive dent in their Tecates. I noticed that even though they moved around the room in different permutations, the men always sat in a corner with their backs to the wall. Score one for maybe I'm not so crazy.

Just after dawn, I made my way to a rooftop viewing deck to watch us pull into Mazatlán. I couldn't see much in the smoggy haze except a rocky cone-shaped island that seemed to guard the harbor. On the way back to my room, I noticed the cartel guys had polished off all their Tecates. Judging by their animated state of inebriation, it seemed unlikely they had slept.

When it was time to disembark, a ferry employee announced two lines —one for drivers and one for everyone else. I got into the driver's line, followed immediately by the cartel guys, still chugging the last of their beers. My first thought was—holy crap, I do not want to be on the road with these guys. My second thought was—why are **all** of them driving? Is this some Bizarro Uber drunken car transport service?

I made it all the way to the exit before realizing I had somehow gotten into the **non-driver** line. I had to work my way back up through several levels of boat, wedging past people in narrow stairwells the whole way. All the same, I've never been so relieved to find out I was in the wrong line.

Back on the road, the first thing I noticed was the change in ecosystem. I went to sleep in Arizona and woke up in Vietnam. Streams and lush greenery replaced the cacti and succulent flora of Baja. At times, trees formed an interlocking arched canopy over the road, letting in sporadic beams of sunlight like a fairy-tale illustration.

I found navigating the mainland to be a whole new level of disorientation from Baja. Rarely did my paper map agree with Google Maps on any of the key pieces of information: the name of the road I was on, the name of the road I wanted to be on, or the name of a town in the direction I wanted to go.

Google Maps Lady tried to help, barking out turn-by-turn directions. But her hilariously garbled Spanish just added to the fog of confusion. When a street sign was available to break the deadlock between my paper map and Google—the sign invariably showed a third set of road and town names.

Eventually, through trial and a great deal of error, I learned that of all available sources of input, the Google Maps **display** was by far the most reliable. Of course, this meant ignoring street signs and Google Maps Lady and instead looking down at my phone as I approached a chaotic intersection or roundabout.

I had no more time for crooked roads if I wanted to make San Miguel de Allende by nightfall. So I hopped on the Autopista de Cuota, Mexico's toll highway system. Within an hour, I'd gone through another ecosystem change, this time from Vietnam to California's Central Valley. Brown scrub replaced lush overgrowth. Smoke from burning crops cast a drab haze, limiting the view in all directions. I just needed an all-smothering waft of *Eau de cowshit* to complete the Central Valley experience.

As the day wore on, the tolls started to add up. Every stop cost $2 to $5. I didn't keep track, but by the end of the day, I was sure I'd spent at least $80, possibly over $100. I can't see many Mexican nationals shelling out $80 to buzz across their country—an activity we take as a birthright in the States. Once, I accidentally exited the Autopista and had to take the Libre (free) road, where I got stuck behind a caravan of trucks going 20 mph. If I'd spent the whole trip on the Libre roads, I might still be out there somewhere.

Mexican drivers have an interesting way of signaling that it's okay to pass on a two-lane highway. They turn on their *left* blinker. It's your job to figure out if they're telling you it's safe to pass or if they're actually turning left. Choose wisely.

I found Mexican drivers much more aware and generally more polite than their counterparts in the States. The only thing that will *always* piss off a Mexican driver is forcing them to slow down and lose momentum when overtaking, especially on a hill. I suspect it has to do with making them burn more gas, but that's just a working theory.

SAN MIGUEL DE ALLENDE

I pulled into the outskirts of San Miguel de Allende just before sunset, planning to check out the town and hopefully find a place to stay. This proved to be a bad idea.

I went to pass a slow truck like I'd been doing all day. In the twilight and my fatigue from ten hours of driving, I didn't see a bicyclist coming the other way. He waved his hands frantically, eventually snapping me out of my stupor. I slammed on my brakes and got back behind the truck. The bicyclist's next move would have been to take his chances in the steep drainage culvert beside the road.

I drove on, rattled by how close I came to injuring that guy or worse. I could see the town from where I was. There was no reason to pass. I vowed never again to drive so long that I lose my senses at the end of the day, when I need them the most.

I drove through the suburbs and into the heart of town. Colonial-era houses in dark yellow, burnt orange, brick red, and the odd green or muted pink lined the cobblestone streets. At one point, I drove down a one-way street so narrow I could have high-fived someone through their kitchen window.

Street parking was San Francisco levels of non-existent. I saw a few parking lots, but they were behind an overhang that was too low for my cargo carrier. I finally spotted a parking lot with no overhang and pulled in to get my bearings. Getting out of my car, I was greeted by two large, snarling dogs straining at the ends of their chains. I appreciated the adrenaline boost, as my nerves weren't quite frayed enough yet.

As it turned out, the parking lot was for a hostel. Hooray! I was done driving for the night. I came in the back and approached the front desk. No one greeted me. A hallway and a set of stairs led off into darkness. I peeked out the door facing the street to see if anyone was out front. This set off a nerve-rattlingly loud alarm that made me realize I needed a drink. Still, no one came.

So, I sat and waited. After a few minutes, I opened the front door to trigger the alarm again. No one came. I waited some more, then repeated the process. Still, no one came.

I ventured upstairs to see if I could find anyone. I could barely see my way around in the gloom of the last bit of twilight. Much of the space was unfinished, strewn with hanging wires and construction detritus. I spotted three closed doors at the end of a dark hallway but no sign of movement.

I started thinking about what a drag it might be to stay at this place, given the cold, gloomy vibe. Naturally, the dismal torture-porn movie *Hostel* crossed my mind. But the parking was sooooo sweet, even with the scary dogs. I very much did not want to get back into my car. I checked online anyway to see what else might be out there. I found a resort hotel just outside of town, with parking, for $60 a night. I took one last look at my surroundings... and got the heck out of there.

The following day, I taped up my heel and headed back into town. The colorful architecture was even more stunning in daylight. Every crooked, narrow cobblestone street opened up to a new row of colorful restored houses, trimmed in baroque or neoclassical style (if you're into that sort of thing). If a door or window was worth having, it was worth accessorizing with an elaborately carved stone alcove and twisted wrought iron.

A bustling street in San Miguel de Allende

San Miguel de Allende, known to locals as San Miguel or just SMA, began as a Spanish colonial outpost in the 1500s. The city thrived for 300 years but fell into ruin by the turn of the century. In the 1930s, a group of American and Canadian artists fell in love with the beauty and potential of San Miguel and set about restoring homes. Their efforts brought in more writers and artists who helped locals rebuild the town into the jewel it is today.

Fliers for art talks, art classes, writing workshops, architecture walks, and the like plastered shop windows. I got the impression one could spend months in San Miguel and sign up for a new enriching activity every day. Countless small art galleries offered works priced far out of my range. Many expats even looked like artists—down to their paint-splattered clothes.

I passed a fancy hat store and stopped in for a look. Many local men sported a Panama hat or a wide-brimmed straw hat. My grubby hiking hat instantly identified me as a tourist. I thought, "I could use a nice hat to be a man about town—in San Miguel and farther down the road."

Man about town in my $140 hat

I asked the girl behind the counter if she had any hats for cabeza grande (big head). Only one of them fit me, but I liked it. I was ready to haggle. But the girl was adamant that there would be no bargaining. Her body language made it abundantly clear that she'd rather I just leave so she could get back to her iPhone. At $140, the hat was the opposite of cheap, ludicrous even. Then again, it's nearly impossible to find hats that fit me in this part of the world. So, I bought it.

I remain a master negotiator.

Naturally, I posted a shot of my stylish new look on social media, which prompted a friend to reply with this riff from Indiana Jones and the Last Crusade:

> *Savino's got friends in every town and village from here to the Sudan. He speaks a dozen languages, knows every local custom. He'll blend in, disappear. You'll never see him again. With any luck, he's got the Grail already.*

While I was initially pleased with my purchase, within an hour, I had dented it beyond repair. No problem, I told myself; a small dent adds character. After a week of bouncing around in my car, my $140 hat was utterly trashed. On top of that, Panama hats weren't popular anywhere else I went, including Panama. Dumbest purchase of the trip. But hey, if they ever revive *Hee Haw*, I've got the hat for it.

In the late afternoon, I found my way up some hidden steps to a spot above town, where I watched the sunset. I went down a different way and wound up at a town square buzzing with people and dominated by a centuries-old Gothic cathedral. I watched a father repeatedly underhand-serve a cigar-shaped balloon forty feet into the air, whereupon his kids would race all over the square, trying to catch it before it hit the ground. Those kids could have played that game until their dad's arm fell off.

I noticed lots of folks enjoying a corn-lime-cheese parfait treat served in a Styrofoam cup. It didn't look very tasty, but then again, neither did Tostilocos. So, I figured I should *just try it.*

Aaaaaand you win some; you lose some. It *looked* like corn floating in runny mayonnaise and lime juice and, funny enough, that's exactly what it tasted like.

Despite my time crunch to get to Puebla, I liked San Miguel enough to spend an extra day. I could have stayed another week, and I don't say that about many places.

Sunset in San Miguel de Allende

On my extra day, I drove to an arboretum outside of town, where I was relieved to see the various cacti adequately spaced with plenty of breathing room. The arboretum also featured several large art sculptures and an old water wheel built in the 1500s. According to the interpretive signs, San Miguel de Allende would cease to exist without water diverted in from the surrounding countryside. As a resident of Los Angeles, I can relate.

My resort hotel quoted me $160 to stay one more night, which was silly because it was still mostly empty. Needing a new place to sleep, I headed into town to look for hostels.

I was even prepared to stay at the creepy hostel. It had that sweet, sweet parking, and by that point, my curiosity had pushed out my trepidation. But I could never find the place again, despite intense searching on the ground and in online hostel guides and booking sites. It's almost like it was never really there at all. Oooooohhh.

I finally stumbled onto a nice non-dungeon hostel with parking nearby. As the rather attractive parking attendant directed me into a tight spot, I thought to myself, "I bet she'll be surprised at how well a gringo navigates

this ridiculously tight parking lot. I'm a Mexican driver now. I got this—"
CRRRRRUNCH!

In my efforts to impress the parking attendant, I clipped my side mirror on a tree, taking out a chunk of the housing. I slumped out of my car in shame.

The next morning, the hostel served me a lovely breakfast and my first taste of real chilaquiles, a Mexican breakfast staple of fried tortilla chips drizzled with runny sour cream and either a red or green sauce. So simple, perfect, and delicious.

I loved San Miguel, but my time there went how I initially feared much of my trip would go: just me walking around looking at things and people-watching—not meeting or connecting with anyone. I'm fine doing that for a few days, but my introversion has its limits. I start wistfully peeking through restaurant windows at all the shiny, happy people cavorting inside. After San Miguel, I looked for places with built-in socialization, like bustling hostels and overlander campgrounds.

Teotihuacán

On the drive to Puebla, I passed the turnoff for Teotihuacán, one of the great cities of ancient Mesoamerica. What's left of Teotihuacán's city center —dozens of monumental buildings and one of the world's largest ancient pyramids—rests on an open plain on the outskirts of Mexico City. In Teotihuacán's heyday, from around 200 to 600 of the Common Era (CE), an estimated 150,000 to 400,000 people lived in the city's sprawling residential compounds, dwarfing any capital of Europe at the time, and making it one of the largest cities in the world.

Teotihuacán was the Ancient Rome or modern New York City of its day—a multicultural supercity focused on trade, artisanal exports, and mercantilism. The city's most popular exported goods featured prized green obsidian that could only be found in nearby mines. Teotihuacán had a middle class and distinct residential sectors, some of which focused on producing a single craft. Pottery and other home goods from ethnic Zapotecs, Maya, and the successors of the Olmecs have been found clustered in neighborhoods—similar to a Chinatown or Little Italy in a modern US metropolis.

We don't know what Teotihuacános called themselves, what they called their giant city, or even what language they spoke because Teotihuacán had no writing—not even advanced pictographs like the Zapotecs and the

Aztecs. Teotihuacán's rulers and priests would have been aware of more complex writing systems from interactions with contemporary Maya and Zapotecs. Yet, for some reason, they chose not to develop their own.

The most vital clues to Teotihuacán's palace intrigue come from the city's vast influence, extending from Western Mexico to the Caribbean, as documented by civilizations that did have writing, like the Maya. Teotihuacán appears to have installed a puppet ruler as far away as Tikal in Guatemala and helped found a dynasty at Copán in Honduras, despite a thousand-mile march over rugged terrain and dense jungle to reach those great Maya kingdoms. Images of Tlaloc, Teotihuacán's emblematic goggle-eyed rain god, appear in contemporary civilizations scattered throughout Mesoamerica.

Teotihuacán's ceremonial city center burned in 650 CE—whether destroyed by a rival or internal dissent is unknown. People continued to live in the residential compounds for a few generations, but most of the unique vestiges of Teotihuacán culture quickly disappear from the archaeological record.

Due to its constant occupation, the size of the monuments, and the open setting on the outskirts of Mexico City, Teotihuacán has been called "perhaps the least lost prehistoric city in the world." Imagine one of the wonders of the ancient world—just hanging out in a suburb of a major city in the United States: "Oh, you wanna see those old ruins? Yeah, you're gonna need to take the 10 out to Diamond Bar. It's right behind the Dave and Buster's. You can't miss it."

I toured Teotihuacán on a previous trip to Mexico City and climbed the Pyramid of the Sun flanked by legions of rambunctious, uniformed school kids. I would have loved to check out Teotihuacán a second time, but my extra day in San Miguel de Allende yanked all the slack out of my schedule, so I pressed on.

School kids explore Teotihuacán. The Pyramid of the Sun sits in the distance.

PUEBLA

Reaching the outskirts of Puebla, I stopped for a red light at a roundabout intersection. A girl of maybe eleven sat on the curb a few feet from me, clipping her mother's toenails. Based on their shabby clothes, I assumed they were taking a break from panhandling or maybe selling gum or trinkets. In her singular focus on helping her mother, the young girl had a look of innocence and devotion that belied their shitty situation. I wondered if she had any hope of getting an education—to make a better life for herself and her mother. I wanted to believe the purity of that little girl's spirit could somehow overcome it all.

    I arrived at Livit Spanish School, my home and classroom for the next two weeks. Scott, the school's owner, came out to greet me. He looked at my car and asked how I was able to get a Temporary Import Permit without a front license plate.

    Wait—what?

    My front plate was gone. But the license plate holder was still there, along with the screws and even the little plastic caps over the screws. I thought—what kind of thief steals the license plate but puts the plate holder and screws back in?

Scott explained that cops in Mexico sometimes take a license plate as collateral for paying a parking ticket. Oh yeah… I'd gotten a parking ticket in San Miguel and forgotten all about it. I would have happily paid the fine, but I got the ticket on Saturday and had to leave on Sunday. There was no link to pay online.

Overlander guides strongly advise against driving without a front plate in Mexico and Central America, where cops look for any excuse to pull you over. I could also run into trouble at border crossings and in trying to ship my car from Panama to Columbia.

So, I tried a Hail Mary. I posted in the Facebook Pan-American Travelers group, asking if anyone was in San Miguel and on their way to Puebla. That night, a fellow overlander from Argentina named Bruno, traveling with his partner Moira, responded that he was in San Miguel, had plans to be in Puebla in a week, and could retrieve my plate for me.

I emailed copies of my registration to Bruno. He and Moira were kind enough to print up copies of my documents, make the pilgrimage into the heart of crazy, crowded old town San Miguel (where the police station is inconveniently located), and pay the fine for me. The cost for all that trouble? 151 pesos—about $7.50.

I told Bruno muchas muchas gracias and muchas cervezas on me.

There's a famous phenomenon among Appalachian Trail Hikers called "Trail Magic"—miraculous day-saving coincidences that seem to happen more often than they should. Assuming this worked out, I'd just experienced my first Trail Magic.

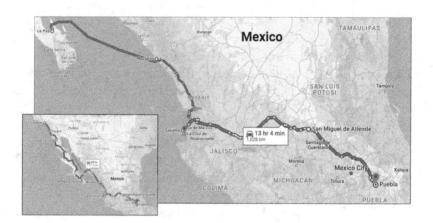

CHAPTER 12

PUEBLA: CITY OF FOODIES

I MOVED into my studio apartment on the Livit Spanish School grounds, then set out to find something to eat. I peeked inside a large indoor market and spotted a taco stand along the back wall. That'll do. Then I noticed a line of people snaking along the wall to my right.

The line led to an oversized food stall, where twenty uniformed workers whirled around in a chaotic food service ballet. Front-line workers formed an assembly line, churning out some type of sandwich. Helpers scurried behind them—handling side items, restocking supplies, and prepping a mountain of crusty buns with stringy cheese and avocado slices.

I looked back at the forlorn lineless taco stand. On the one hand, I could eat right now. My gnawing hunger agreed with that sentiment. On the other hand, this place was feeding a hundred people an hour. I assumed that so many Poblanos (Poblano can describe people, things, or food from Puebla) must know something.

Bun prep at Cemitas las Poblanitas

My curiosity won out. I walked toward what I thought was the end of the line, only to find more line winding through two dining rooms and out into the street. By the time I reached the actual end of the line, I felt pot committed. I took my place behind a local couple who explained that we were all waiting for a cemita—**not** to be confused with a torta, which, at least in Puebla, refers to a different kind of Mexican sandwich served on a softer bun.

When it was my turn to order, I planned to follow my usual protocol of pointing to some popular item that everyone else was having. But the ordering process and money exchange took place in a dark, walled-off booth that made me feel like I should be confessing my sins. This was not the kind of place that had a picture menu or any patience for clueless tourists gunking up the works. I stammered something unintelligible, prompting the order-taker to reply with a question I couldn't understand. So, I just said, "Sí?"—hoping it was a yes or no question. Apparently, it was.

I caught up with the local couple, who looked at my ticket and explained that I had managed to order the cemita with pork milanese and jamón (ham).

Me with my cemita, attempting my DAYUM!!!! face

The sandwich was delightfully tasty and so big I could barely finish it. A companion stall next door sold quarts, and only quarts, of aguas frescas (a juice drink) and horchata (a sweet milk drink that tastes like rice pudding with cinnamon). Thus, my original plan for two tacos turned into a massive cemita laden with avocado, cheese, ham, and breaded pork steak—washed down with a quart of horchata.

I regret nothing.

From 9 a.m. to 1 p.m. every weekday, I attended a beginner Spanish class taught by Scott's wife, Maru, along with two retired American women and a young guy who managed migrant workers at a dairy farm in Wisconsin. After class, the whole school sat down to lunch, prepared by Maru's mother. Five others were taking the intermediate class, including an American man traveling with his eleven-year-old daughter, who had the advanced class all to herself. Only Spanish was allowed at the lunch table. I struggled mightily with this while the eleven-year-old happily chattered away.

Every lunch was something special. We had a rich, tasty red mole (pronounced MOH-lay), a chocolate-based sauce flavored with chiles that's more savory than sweet, and some of the best pollo asado (grilled chicken) tacos I've ever had. Even on a day when we packed food for a field trip, the sandwiches wrapped in cellophane were delicious. I began to realize that Poblanos simply do not mess around when it comes to food.

One day, we had soup with a side of the same stringy cheese I'd enjoyed on my cemita. I asked Maru about this rich, salty, velvety cheese that I instantly couldn't get enough of. She told me it's called Oaxaca (pronounced wah-HAH-kah) cheese. I examined the cheese and how it peels off in strips. Then it came to me that I've probably been eating the crappy Americanized version of Oaxaca cheese all my life—in the form of string cheese.

If you're still on the fence about Oaxaca cheese (I mean, how good can string cheese possibly be?) then consider this—the cities of Puebla and Oaxaca have a fierce food rivalry. Puebla has one style of mole, and Oaxaca has a very different style. You're as likely to hear the average Poblano sing the praises of Oaxaca's mole as getting me to root for the Denver Broncos. Yet, in my first few days in Puebla, I stumbled upon two beloved local dishes featuring Oaxaca cheese. That's how good it is. Oaxaca cheese transcends tribal rivalries.

At lunch, when I was close to finishing my first helping, I'd look around the table to gauge how much progress everyone else was making. I'd attempt some quick mental math based on how much food was left in the communal serving dishes—trying to calculate when I could safely go in for a big plate of seconds without coming off like a feral pig. But then I realized that Maru's mom and her helper hadn't eaten yet, and this isn't America, where we throw out perfectly good food. So, I had to fight my instincts and tell myself that it is not incumbent on me to finish every bit of unclaimed food in my field of vision.

Of course, I still went for a healthy plate of seconds. After all, there is no greater compliment to the chef. I just didn't go in for thirds... as often. I did notice the communal portions seemed to grow after a few days of my presence at the school. So I felt compelled to keep shoveling food into my face at the same high volume, lest I insult someone.

One night, a group of my fellow students wanted to check out Lucha Libre, Mexico's iconic masked wrestling. Everything I knew about Lucha Libre came from the movie *Nacho Libre*, which I had seen in Spanish with a cadre of Mexican hotel staff who never stopped convulsing with laughter.

I assumed Lucha Libre, wildly popular in Puebla, would be a toned-down version of American pro wrestling with masks. I wasn't as enthusiastic as the rest of the group, but I figured it would be a cultural experience if nothing else.

We entered the already-buzzing arena, which, in age and appearance, could have been home to a mid-sized 1950s college basketball team. We took our seats about ten rows back. We'd heard that if we sat any closer, we could be drenched with blood, sweat, or some other fluid of indeterminate origin. Also, a wrestler could land on us.

The show was immediately more entertaining than I expected. Even the opening acts were a lot of fun. Bodies flew all over the place. Beer flowed early and often. Vendors fought over who got to serve our group. The crowd was really into it—especially the rabid fans in the cheap balcony seats.

The undercard acts tended to be small and doughy—like Jack Black in *Nacho Libre*. But as we moved up to the main attractions, the wrestlers got bigger and more buff. There were evident good guys and bad guys and the standard blind refs who never seemed to notice bad behavior, which drove the crowd into fits of apoplectic rage. **BOOOOO!!!!**

Lucha Libre—a wrestler flies out of the ring

I was blown away by the athletic moves these guys made. One wrestler would throw another out of the ring, at least ten feet down to the floorboards. The wrestler would bounce, **BOOM**, and jump back into the ring.

The headliner act featured three huge good guys knocking out three gigantic bad guys and then jumping on top of them to form a meat mountain. As a final flourish, a dwarf on the good guy team launched himself from the top rope to land on the pile—like the cherry on a parfait. The crowd went bananas.

One day, we went out for lunch to an open-air restaurant specializing in tacos placeros—thin strips of ultra-tender beef with potatoes, onions, and avocado. Before ordering, I debated if I should get one or two.

"Why would you order two now when one will just get cold? Order the second one after you're done with the first," Scott offered.

This is when it fully hit home with me how seriously Poblanos take food. As a native of Kansas City, I know this lingo. When it comes to American BBQ and its more accessible cousin—backyard grilling, every Kansas Citian is a foodie. However, Poblanos seem to be this intense about *everything*. The whole city is full of foodies who put everything they eat through the same scrutiny.

After class, each student was paired with a local guide who led them to various sites around Puebla, speaking only in Spanish. Four hours of language class seems to be where my brain turns to mush; however, after a nice lunch, walking around the city conversing in Spanish seems to tap into a different, less-exhausted brain lobe.

Every other student at the school got a local high school kid as their guide. Scott told me they were one guide short, so he would fill in and be my guide. We toured the city, discussing the history and culture of Puebla and life in Mexico in general. Here's a fun tidbit I learned from Scott: notaries in Mexico are akin to low-grade lawyers, and they make more money on average than doctors. Nothing gets done without a notary.

A trip to La Pasita bar is imperative for learning Spanish

Scott and I consumed a few alcoholic beverages—in the interest of learning Spanish, of course. We stopped at a hundred-year-old bar called La Pasita, which features a beloved local drink of the same name, served in dozens of variations. The classic version is a vanilla liqueur, served in a shot glass with raisins and a chunk of rubbery cheese. It's actually much tastier than it sounds.

We also tried one of the world's

oldest alcoholic drinks, a low-grade beer made from cactus called pulque. Scott and I were the only two in the music-blasting pulque joint not currently in high school. This is not a bad plan in my opinion: Let the kids have something with 1-2% alcohol to get their legs under them.

I told Scott about the girl I saw clipping her mother's toenails at the roundabout on my way into town. I asked if he thought she had any chance to attain an education. He didn't completely rule it out, but he wasn't optimistic. He said she'd probably have to stay out of school to help her mother. Heartbreaking. That little girl deserves better.

As we walked around Puebla, Scott would occasionally grab me before I could fall into a cavernous hole in the sidewalk. But I always saw it coming. I only *seem* to be meandering along in an oblivious fog. I told Scott, "No miro, pero veo" (I don't look, but I see). Okay, I didn't actually say that. My Spanish could never come up with something that clever on the fly. But I did think of it later!

Scott has a thick Hispanic accent, which I was curious about, given his English-sounding surname. Apparently, he found the accent effective when teaching English as a second language in Colorado—sort of like how, when I'm in Italy, I slip into the borderline offensive Italian accent my Dad used for comedic effect throughout my childhood. It works wonders. In Scott's case, however, the affected accent seems to have stuck. He told me he couldn't shed it now if he tried. I had no idea that could happen. Next, you're going to tell me if I get hit in the face while my eyes are crossed, they **could** stay crossed forever. Yikes.

One night, I stumbled upon another cuisine unique to Puebla called Tacos Árabes. Lebanese Christians have been moving to Puebla since the late 19th century and have adapted and hybridized some of their traditional food with Mexican cuisine. Much like the Mexican staple *al pastor*, which is also Lebanese in origin, the meat for Tacos Árabes is layered onto a rotating spit and slow-cooked. The conglomeration is then shaved off the spit and served with onions and sauce in a rolled-up pan árabe—a unique local flatbread that tastes like a cross between a tortilla and pita.

Maybe it's because I'd eaten so much traditional Mexican food that a change of cuisine hit the spot or because I "discovered" this place on my own, but it was one of my favorite meals in Mexico. The proprietor took an immediate liking to me. I felt like I had a new Lebanese-Mexican mama by my second trip. She ribbed me in a light-hearted way that I've experienced in family-run Middle Eastern restaurants in my neighborhood. It seems to be their way of letting you know you're always welcome.

On Thursday, the school went on an excursion to a four-hundred-year-old colonial mansion called Chautla Hacienda. A painting in the entry room caught my eye. In it, the Aztec leader Moctezuma (pronounced maak·tuh·ZOO·muh, "Montezuma" is a Spanish bastardization) offers Hernán Cortés a massive tribute of gold and jewelry. In the lower right corner of the painting, two of Cortés' men ogle the pile of booty. This vignette depicts the moment Moctezuma became certain that these strange white men weren't gods, as some Aztec legends had foretold. Moctezuma knew gods would never be so lustful over mere gold.

Of all the historical moments I'd like to have been a fly on the wall for, the moment Cortés and his small army of conquistadors first set eyes on the Aztec capital, Tenochtitlan, might be at the top of the list.

The painting at Chautla Hacienda depicts Cortés' men ogling Moctezuma's tribute

TENOCHTITLAN

From the mountains outside the city, Cortés and his men would have seen the Valley of Mexico, with the vast, shallow Lake Texcoco at its heart, ringed by settlements along its shores. In the center of the lake, they would have beheld a gleaming city of 200,000 people—a New World Venice built on an artificial island twice the size of Manhattan—crisscrossed by a network of major and minor canals and arrow-straight, eighty-foot-wide causeways shooting out to the lakeshore. A temple complex of pyramids and other monumental structures, painted in brilliant red and white, would have dominated the island's center.

Tenochtitlan would have been like nothing Cortés and his men had ever seen. The legends were *true* this time!

What a moment in human history. Never before had two advanced civilizations, developed in total isolation, come into first contact. It was a once-in-the-history-of-the-planet chance for cultural exchange.

Cultural curiosity, however, was low on the conquistadors' priority list.

*Artist Tomas Filsinger's rendering of Lake Texcoco, as
Cortés might have first seen it*

The story of Tenochtitlan (not to be confused with Teotihuacán, the much older city with still-standing giant pyramids) begins around 1250 CE when a wandering tribe known as the Mexica arrived in the already crowded valley that now bears their name. Having no wealth and nothing to trade, the Mexica were known around the Valley as lizard-eaters, the lowest of the low. In exchange for permission to settle on dismal patches of unused farmland, the Mexica worked as mercenaries, performing dangerous and dirty jobs for their host kingdoms.

But the Mexica proved to be lousy houseguests. As the story goes, when the king of Culhuacán bequeathed one of his daughters for their band to worship as something of a goddess queen, a Mexica high priest showed up at her coronation ceremony wearing her flayed skin as a robe.

Like all Mesoamerican civilizations at the time, the Mexica believed that gods demanded tribute to remain in their good graces. Tributes could range from tobacco to turkeys to human beings. The more significant the tribute, the greater the impact. No tribute was more impactful tribute than the life of someone with royal blood.

Perhaps the Mexica saw their ephemeral queen's sacrifice as a chance to grow their power and vault their social standing into the big league of Valley civilizations. If so, the gamble paid off in a roundabout way—which could be why this gruesome legend endured for centuries and remained prominent in their foundation story.

Culhuacán's King, as one would expect, flew into a rage and exiled the

Mexica from his lands. The Mexica were on the move again, this time guided by a high priest's vision that they should settle wherever they found an eagle perched on a cactus with a snake in its beak. According to their origin story, they found exactly that—on a small island in the middle of Lake Texcoco. This iconic symbol is recorded in endless Mexica art and has persisted into modern times. Take a look at the flag of Mexico. That fuzzy stuff in the middle? It's an eagle, holding a snake, perched on a cactus.

The Mexica's genius was to create new land around the island. They drove posts into the lake bottom, wove branches and reeds around the posts to form a corral, and then filled it with layers of grass and lake muck. This formed a roughly ten-by-one-hundred-foot rectangle of a spongy new land called a *chinampa*, which could stand independently or become part of an ever-expanding grid. The Valley's high-altitude tropical climate, rich lake mud, and a limitless water supply created ideal growing conditions, yielding up to seven harvests a year.

Diorama of farming Chinampas in Tenochtitlan

The Mexica continued to expand their island city, refine their culture, build alliances, and consolidate power. A century later, the now-powerful tribe allied with two other groups living on the shores of Lake Texcoco— the Texcoco and the Tlacopan. This triple alliance became known to history as *The Aztecs*.

And now you know... ... the rest of the story. I'm Paul Harvey... ... ... goooood day. (Boomer joke, never mind.)

Now the most powerful force in the region, the Mexica/Aztecs first set about conquering old enemies. They worked around the lake until they finally vanquished Culhuacán, ending that kingdom's centuries-long dominance in the region. Their sacrifice of the king's daughter had indeed set events in motion that led to the Mexica's rise to power and the defeat of Culhuacán. It just took a few generations.

Unlike the Spanish, Aztec domination didn't mean you had to worship their gods or be ruled by their vassals. It just meant you had to pay tribute —in the form of food or desirable trade items two to four times a year.

Foreign leaders from outside the Aztec sphere of influence were brought to Tenochtitlan's ceremonial plaza, a sprawling complex centered around a massive temple. The leaders were made aware of the empire's power and shown displays of human sacrifice. The leaders were then "invited" to join the Aztec tribute system, with the directive that if they resisted domination and had to be defeated in battle, their tribute would be that much higher. (Much like my philosophy with food: When defeat is inevitable, just give in and save your energy for a winnable fight.)

Tenochtitlan's Ceremonial Center with a causeway leading to Templo Mayor

The Aztecs were brutal, but they were also enthusiastic lovers of the arts. In the two centuries following their ouster from Culhuacán, the erstwhile lizard-eaters transformed themselves into a highly cultured civilization. They celebrated poets, singers, dancers, and acrobats. Tenochtitlan had an opera house, a zoo, an arboretum, an aquarium, and a museum with antiquities from previous ages. At a time when the capitals of Europe flowed with sewage, legions of groundskeepers and gardeners kept Tenochtitlan green and beautiful. Aztecs bathed frequently and were fastidiously clean. Every boy trained as a warrior, and elite male children attended finishing school, where they trained as officers and learned arts, mathematics, and astronomy.

The iconic 12-foot diameter Aztec Sun Stone, also known as the Calendar Stone—buried by the Spanish, then rediscovered in 1790

Lake Texcoco's water was brackish—fine for crops but not drinkable. So, Aztec engineers created aqueducts out of clay half-pipes that ran for miles over the lake. They also built a levy to make their portion of the lake less brackish. The whole setup provided an endlessly expanding resource of fertile, defensible soil.

This was the lay of the land when Columbus landed in the Caribbean in 1492 and when Cortés and his band of conquistadors disembarked on the Gulf coast near present-day Veracruz in 1519. The Aztecs were the dominant power in the region, with all the amassed wealth that comes from lording over some 450 tribute states. You don't get that status without rubbing people the wrong way. The Aztecs had intentionally left a nearby rival state known as Tlaxcala outside their tribute system to serve as a perpetual supply of fresh captives for sacrifice. This decision would haunt them in ways they never could have imagined.

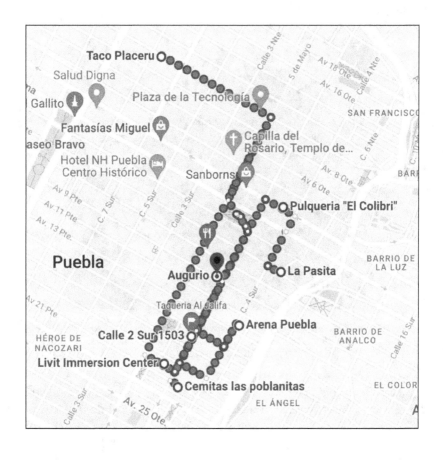

CHAPTER 13

DEVASTATING NEWS

THROUGHOUT THE WEEK at Livit Spanish, I kept in contact with my old friend Dan, who was in the midst of riding the Pan-Am Highway with three friends on BMW adventure bikes. By crazy happenstance, their legs through Mexico and Central America lined up with my trip.

Dan and his buddies are commercial airline pilots, advanced enough in their careers to secure an alternating schedule of one month on and one month off. They'd ride for a month, find a place to store their bikes, then fly back to work. A month later, they'd start up again where they left off. I marvel at how small the world must seem to them.

I spent some time coordinating with Dan in the months leading up to my launch date. I wanted his opinion on items needed for my trip. Mostly, I got roped into helping him with his abysmal website, which had him in fits. Dan was attempting to post videos and other content from their ride under the banner "End of All Roads." The fruit of his labor—the vehicle for his dreams of overlander stardom—had broken images, blog posts that looked like they were laid out by a drunken chimpanzee, and was unreadable on a mobile device.

I told Dan I could help him get the site into shape, but once I was on the road, I'd have no time to be his webmaster. Keeping up with my own blog would keep me busy enough. I offered to teach him the basics like image resizing, laying out blog pages, publishing, etc., but he kept complaining that he wasn't technical.

I said, "Dude. You fly 747s. I think you can wrap your head around WordPress."

Luckily, his buddy and fellow rider Brian stepped up to the plate. I worked with Brian over the phone a few times. He was a quick study with a great attitude for learning the ins and outs of the website. We instantly bonded, mostly through ribbing Dan over his state of perpetual hysteria about the site. I felt better knowing the site was in Brian's hands.

After a few delays, the guys were scheduled to arrive in Puebla sometime during my second week. As they got closer, Dan sent me daily status updates, generally around 6 p.m. when they were done riding for the day. They planned to cross into Mexico at Laredo, spend a few days in San Miguel de Allende, and then work their way down to Puebla.

I had scouted plenty of places to eat and a few fun-looking bars. Of course, I would take them for cemitas and Tacos Árabes. I told Dan he should be ready to eat at least four times a day because I'd found a ton of fantastic food, and they needed to try **ALL** of it. Dan, not a small guy, assured me he was up to the challenge. Maybe we'd even have time to check out Lucha Libre.

On the day Dan and his friends planned to cross into Mexico, I finished class and bummed around Puebla for a while before turning in early. I thought it was a little strange that I didn't hear from Dan around dusk as usual. I knew they wouldn't ride at night in Mexico. Eventually, I dozed off.

Around midnight, I heard my phone buzz. It was a message from Dan saying his best friend had just died in his arms.

I immediately called Dan. He told me Brian had gone off the road and crashed into a rock wall about two hours into Mexico. They were now in Zacatecas—the nearest big city to the crash site.

Dan said it was a beautiful day, and the road was perfectly smooth, but Brian and another rider, Bob, were experiencing problems with their new tires. It sounded to Dan like the tire started into a wobble that it couldn't recover from, eventually forcing Brian off the road. Tragically, a rock bluff sat just a few feet from the road's edge.

They waited two hours for the ambulance to arrive—all the while being interrogated by the Mexican Highway Police. Even if the ambulance had arrived promptly, Dan doesn't think it would have made a difference for Brian.

I offered to drive up and help however I could—as I know Dan's Spanish is non-existent. Dan told me they met a helpful cab driver who was shuttling them around and translating for them. They had spent most of the night just searching for the morgue where the ambulance delivered Brian's body. Dan said they were taken care of with their new cab driver friend, Roy—who by all accounts was a godsend.

Over the next few days, Dan kept me posted on the utter hell they were going through. Brian's family members were on their way to Zacatecas. Of course, their ride was off for the foreseeable future.

Ultimately, it took about two weeks to get everything settled and have Brian's body shipped back to the States. When he arrived at the Houston airport, a hundred airline employees in full uniform lined up in a silent salute. I imagine that meant a lot to Brian's family.

I only conversed with Brian a few times, but from the outpouring of poignant testimonials by his friends and family, it was clear he was a special person who touched countless lives.

His friends and family agreed on one thing: Brian lived every moment to the fullest. He didn't get cheated during his tragically short time on this earth.

R.I.P. Brian Johnson

CHAPTER 14

BRUSHES WITH HISTORY

I SPENT the next day wandering Puebla in a daze, heartsick over the sheer hell Dan and his friends were going through in Zacatecas.

By a weird coincidence, my old friend Nicholas happened to be a few hours away in Mexico City, staying with his Mexican-born girlfriend at her mom's house. I'd have welcomed the company and someone to talk to, but I know Nicholas. Saturday night would be club-hopping until the stupid hours, which I have little proclivity for in the best of times. So I passed.

Sunday morning, I received a message from Bruno and Moira, the trail angels in possession of my front license plate. Their car was having problems, and it looked like they'd be stuck in Mexico City for a while. I messaged Nicholas to tell him I was coming to Mexico City after all.

He replied, "If you plan to spend the night, you'll probably need to get a hotel room. This place is like a museum. I don't think I'm allowed to have guests here."

I have to admit this had me a little miffed. What the hell does "like a museum" even mean? Just say she can't have guests, dude. It's fine.

MEXICO CITY

Google Maps Lady and I went through the looking glass trying to navigate Mexico City until I reached the final boss of Google Maps—a chaotic triple-decker expressway with different exits shooting off all three levels. Google Maps Lady had no idea which level I was on but still always assumed wrong. She would shout out confusing directions in tortured Spanish, then change her mind mid-sentence. Re-calculating... Re-calculating... Ultimately, I had to shut her down and use the Force.

The address Nicholas provided led me to a neighborhood of cobblestone streets and old mansions. I pulled up to an iron gate flanked by a fifteen-foot-high stone wall, double-checked that I had the correct address, then buzzed as instructed.

After a minute, the gate slowly swung open to reveal an older gentleman wearing black slacks and a white t-shirt. He guided me up a long driveway that wound through various jumbo topiary sculptures, ending at a structure I want to call a carriage house for no justifiable reason. My only frame of reference for this place was the one episode of Downton Abbey I'd seen. Okay, it was just a preview that came on after NOVA. But I got the gist.

Nicholas came outside to greet me and guide me into the house. We entered the kitchen, where I met Nicholas's girlfriend Camila, her mother, and another relative. Camila then led me into the main living area.

I immediately apologized to Nicholas in my mind for being annoyed at his "like a museum" comment. The scene just needed a velvet rope to keep my grubby mitts off the antique furniture.

The entry from the kitchen opened up to a sort of vestibule. Again, I'm not 100% sure what a vestibule is, but it sounds right. On the far end, a delicately carved wooden staircase led upstairs. In the center of the room, a thousand-piece chandelier hovered above a claw-footed table.

Camila was a gracious tour guide, leading me through rooms lined with floor-to-ceiling Renaissance-style portraits of her family scions from generations past. She pointed out one double-wide painting and told me it was her great-great-something-er-other-grandfather, holding court with Emperor Maximilian and his bride Carlota.

Wait, Mexico had an emperor?

This is where YOLO traveling with no context falls down a bit. Knowing what I know now, I could have exchanged witticisms with Camila about her family's connection to Mexico's imported emperor, a Habsburg no less, installed by Napoleon II. Our discussion would have likely been brief, however, as Mexico's dynasty of one lasted only three years before Maximilian had a one-night stand with a firing squad. All in all, not a bad run for a mid-19th-century Mexican head of state.

*A painting of Mexico's Emperor Maximilian, his empress Carlota, and
other royal courtesans who have no idea what to do with their hands*

Camila noticed my interest in the furniture and began explaining the
pedigrees of various pieces, but my blank stare made it clear I wouldn't
know a Chippendale console table from a Chippendale dancer.

Whenever I see a room or piece of furniture that's clearly too nice for
everyday use, I like to blurt out, "That's for when the Pope comes over!"—a
joke I picked up from some '90s comedian riffing on his Italian-American
upbringing. I suddenly realized I was in a house where my dumb little joke
could conceivably be real. When the Pope comes to Mexico City, I could see
him visiting this house. I chuckled at the idea of stumbling back from the
bars and crashing on the same couch the Pope sat on.

Nicholas was getting antsy with the grand tour and started prodding us
to get going. We took an Uber to meet Bruno and Moira. Along the way,
Camila grilled me about these people. "You haven't even met them? Why
are they driving around Mexico if they're from Argentina? How do you
know they're not scammers?"

I've experienced this phenomenon before—someone who grew up in
Latin America assumes that people from the States may be too trusting and
lacking in street smarts. And to be fair, we probably are. On the other hand,
what kind of scammers would drive into San Miguel de Allende, find parking, pay my fine, and retrieve my license plate for me? I was willing to roll
the dice that I'd wake up with both kidneys.

We found Bruno and Moira in a little park hosting an art fair. They produced my front license plate, which, given the context, was the sexiest piece of sheet metal I'd ever seen.

We headed to an outdoor food court, where I bought Bruno and Moira lunch and a bottle of mescal in gratitude. As our little group got to know each other, Camila relaxed about my trail angels. Moira has a master's degree in anthropology, which also happens to be a subject of great interest to Camila. They slipped into Spanish while Nicholas and I caught up.

After a brief shopping spree and some appetizers at a restaurant that was too fancy for overlander budgets, we landed at a place to everyone's liking that served chicken wings, hot dogs, and mescal shots. We hung out until midnight, sharing and laughing—one of the most soul-satisfying random gatherings I've ever been part of.

Back to Puebla

During lunch at Livit Spanish, one of my classmates asked if my motorcycle friends had arrived yet. I didn't want to drop something so heavy around the eleven-year-old, so I just said my friends were delayed. I'm usually not that private about my emotions—or anything really—but for once, I just didn't want to talk about it. Everyone would be curious about how it happened, and the whole thing felt too lurid to talk about so soon.

I tried more of Puebla's tasty food, including a "mole tamal" recommended by my teacher, Maru. Fun fact to annoy your friends with: There's no such thing as a "tamale." The singular of "tamales" is "tamal." The tamal was delicious—maybe my favorite mole dish ever. It seems I need mole slathered over some carbs to push my tastebuds over the top. Then I got cocky and ordered a green mole with what turned out to be fish. It was okay, but I wanted another mole tamal.

On the way back from the restaurant, I heard some American-accented English wafting from a bar, so I stopped in and said hi to the two strangers speaking my native tongue. I learned they ran a non-profit called Sacred Agave, which aims to sell mescal from local villages to bars and liquor stores in the US, with all proceeds repatriated back to the villages.

They told me about all the variables and processes that go into mescal's wide range of flavors. Tequila comes from only one kind of agave, whereas mescal is distilled from a variety of species. More variables go into every step: when the agave hearts are harvested, how they're crushed into mash, and how long they're smoked. A difference of just a few hours can create a significant divergence in taste. A batch of mescal can even take on the flavor of a nearby chile pepper patch. I love that the village distiller is known as the *maestro.*

Livit's class excursion that week started at a farmer's market, but not the kind where farmers come in to sell produce to city dwellers. This was a market *for* farmers. Scott asked us to please spend a little to support the local economy, so I tried on a pair of jeans in a pickup-mounted chicken coop that doubled as a changing room, and they fit!

Doing a shot with the Sacred Agave guys. It's blurry, so you know it's good.

After the market, we checked out an old stone church and former convent. And when I say old, I mean 1548. I had to double and triple-check my Roman numeral translation, then confirm with Scott to make sure. As an American, this date is just gibberish to me. It seems impossible not to brush up against history in this part of Mexico. The church's carved Catholic icons seemed to have an Aztec-looking flair. I assume this was an attempt by the priests to relate to the local people they were trying to convert—the guitar-playing youth pastor of its day.

On the drive back to Livit Spanish, we passed the Great Pyramid of Cholula, by most accounts antiquity's second largest pyramid behind only the Great Pyramid of Giza. I'd have thought nothing of the church sitting atop a broad, oddly conical hill if Scott hadn't pointed it out. In 1519, the city of Cholula was the site of one of the worst massacres in the history of New World colonialism—a subject of intense scholarly debate to this day.

CHOLULA MASSACRE

While the conquistador Hernán Cortés was still on the coast gathering allies and intel for his planned march to the Aztec capital, Tenochtitlan, a local Maya chieftain presented him with a tribute of gold, precious gifts, and twenty enslaved women. One of the women, Malintzin, was once heir to the throne of an ethnic group called the Olmeca-Xicalanca. Malintzin had been sent out of the kingdom when her mother bore a son. She spoke Maya, as well as Nahuatl, the language of the Aztecs. Cortés' party included a Spanish priest who had been shipwrecked on the Yucatán coast, lived among the Maya for eight years, and picked up their language. So, with the addition of Malintzin, Cortés now had a method to translate Spanish to Maya to Nahuatl and thus communicate with the Aztecs.

Cortés immediately realized Malintzin's value and made her his mistress. Malintzin knew the ways of Mesoamerican royalty and was likely instrumental in helping Cortés negotiate with various groups for logistical support and warriors. She also helped Cortés ally with the Aztecs' sworn enemies, the Tlaxcalans.

In August 1519, Cortés set out for Tenochtitlan with 700 conquistadors outfitted with body armor and crossbows, 15 horses, 15 cannons, and 2,000 indigenous porters. As extra motivation for his men, Cortés famously burned his boats—one of the few tidbits from high school history that seems to have borne purchase in the folds of my memory.

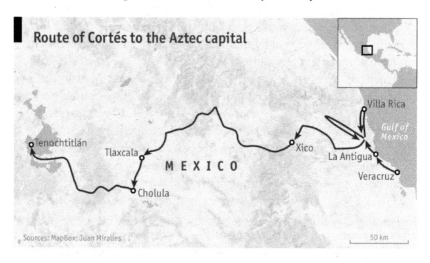

Route of Cortés to the Aztec capital

Villa Rica
Gulf of Mexico
Tenochtitlán   Tlaxcala   Xico
MEXICO   La Antigua
Veracruz
Cholula

Sources: MapBox; Juan Miralles

50 km

For unclear reasons, Cortés took a less direct route to Tenochtitlan through the city of Cholula. At the time, Cholula was nominally allied with the Aztecs and home to forty thousand people, with another hundred thousand in the surrounding area. The city was centered around a massive temple revered by the Aztecs and recognized by all the regional cultures as the home of the feathered serpent god Quetzalcoatl. Nobles from throughout the region made a pilgrimage to Cholula's temple for a nose-piercing ceremony that officially recognized them as a type of lord called a *tecuhtli*. Legend had it that if the Temple of Quetzalcoatl was ever attacked, it would unleash a devastating flood to wash away the aggressors.

The Great Pyramid of Cholula lay just outside the city. Construction on the pyramid began in the year 200 Before the Common Era (BCE), continuing over the centuries through ten distinct phases of varying styles and materials—including adobe bricks, stone, and finally, packed earth. The pyramid had been in disuse for several centuries by the time Cortés arrived.

Backed by a thousand Tlaxcalan warriors, Cortés marched into Cholula, where he and his men were received warmly. The Cholulans showered the conquistadors with gifts and held a grand reception in the town's ceremonial center. As enemies of Cholula's ruling class, the Tlaxcalans were required to camp outside the city.

According to later Spanish and Tlaxcalan accounts, the hospitality began to dry up after a few days. The Spanish claimed to have seen ominous signs that the Cholulans were preparing an ambush, and Cortés heard rumors that as many as 20,000 Aztec warriors were hiding in a ravine just outside the city. Cortés' men claimed the Cholulans had dug trenches to stop cavalry charges and piled rocks on building roofs to fling down onto the conquistadors. They also claimed that local citizens seemed nervous, and women and children were seen leaving the city.

This is when Malintzin stepped in and played a crucial role. Cholula was once the highland capital of Malintzin's band, the Olmeca-Xicalanca, who were aligned with the Tlaxcalans. But by this time, the Olmeca-Xicalanca were relegated to a minority group within the city. According to most Spanish accounts and some indigenous accounts, Malintzin told Cortés she had been informed of an impending ambush, as his men had suspected. To add emphasis, it was made clear that the Cholulans planned to sacrifice and eat every conquistador. One of Cortés' men described a recipe for "conquistador stew" as evidence of the fate that awaited them.

In response to this news, Cortés gathered over a thousand unarmed Cholulan nobles in the ceremonial center, sealed off the exits, and began slaughtering them. Several conquistadors later testified that the massacre lasted only a few hours. Other indigenous survivors claimed the massacre lasted up to five days. This should give an idea of the general level of divergence in these retellings. The Spanish claimed that most women and children had left the city, and the few who remained were spared. Indigenous eyewitnesses reported that this was far from the case.

Once they were satisfied that the Temple of Quetzalcoatl *would not* unleash a flood to drown the Spanish as foretold, the Tlaxcalans entered the city to join in the mayhem. During the fight, Tlaxcalan warriors wore twisted grass on their heads so conquistadors could distinguish them from

Cholulans. Malintzin means "Lady Grass" in Nahuatl—prompting some scholars to speculate that the Tlaxcalans were fighting for her.

A famous pictograph by a Tlaxcalan artist shows Malintzin seemingly directing the attack—while a group of Cholulans, presumably informants, are sequestered and spared. In the pictograph, a noble leaps from the top of the Temple of Quetzalcoatl rather than be killed in battle.

Malintzin depicted possibly directing action during the massacre of Cholula

As a result of the massacre, the balance of power in the city shifted to the ethnic groups aligned with the Tlaxcalans—a boon for Malintzin's people. Her role as mistress and eventual wife of Cortés would further cement her elite status as a mother capable of producing heirs—in a royal inter-marriage pattern as familiar to Mesoamericans as it was to Europeans.

Whether or not Moctezuma instigated the slaughter by planning an ambush outside Cholula, the immediate result gained Cortés several crucial advantages: he now had a Spanish-controlled city near Tenochtitlan; he delivered a massive win to his current allies, the Tlaxcalans; and he demonstrated his power to Moctezuma—whom he hoped to dominate without an all-out war. It seems reasonable to be suspicious of the conquistadors' version of events when it describes their enemy conveniently giving them an excuse to launch such a strategically beneficial attack.

Modern excavations of mass graves in Cholula have turned up 650 bodies, buried in the Spanish style—on their backs with heads pointed east. Indigenous burials were always in the seated position, facing north. So, the people in these graves, including women, some pregnant, and children as young as infants, were likely victims of the massacre. However, some estimates put the number of remaining non-exhumed burials as high as 27,000 —which is too many for the massacre alone by anyone's account. Scholars assume the mass graves are a mix of massacre victims and casualties of the impending Old World disease plagues.

The Cholula massacre remains a contentious issue in Mexican politics. In 1980, the mayor of Cholula called the massacre a myth. Later, however, the city later erected a mural depicting the slaughter. Archaeologists haven't exhumed any graves since the 1990s, and no one seems to have much appetite to reopen the investigation.

Malintzin went on to be known as La Malinche, modern Mexico's Eve, a noble heir of a Spanish colonial crown instead of her people. La Malinche remains a polarizing figure to this day. Mexicans even have a derogatory term—Malinchismo—to describe people who sell their bodies and souls for foreign ideals.

Cortés would go on to conquer the Aztecs (as we all learned in that half-hour of high school history), but not without first losing over half his men and barely escaping with his own life. His second attempt, the siege of Tenochtitlan, would be aided by 2,000 Tlaxcalan warriors and a raging smallpox epidemic. The Tlaxcalans only lasted two years as allies of the Spanish before they, too, were subjugated.

In a pattern that would repeat countless times throughout Mesoamerica, Cortés destroyed Tenochtitlan's Templo Mayor and used the raw materials to build a church. The ceremonial center of Tenochtitlan was then buried under the Zocalo (main square) and other colonial buildings in what would become the heart of Mexico City. Over time, Lake Texcoco was drained to create more land.

The base of Templo Mayor was rediscovered in the 1970s, spurring ongoing excavations. History is unearthed with every dig around old Mexico City.

At the time of the Conquest, the Valley of Mexico supported an estimated 25 million inhabitants. Under colonial oppression and Old World diseases, that number plummeted to under a million. The Valley wouldn't reach its pre-Columbian population again until the 1960s.

The full painting from Hacienda de Chautla depicts Moctezuma showering Cortés with gifts. Malintzin and the shipwrecked priest serve as translators.

We finished class on Friday at Livit Spanish and had another magnificent lunch. Given everything that had happened, more than a little part of me wanted to stay there among friends for a few more weeks. I hadn't planned anything for this part of the trip, since I assumed I'd be traveling with four other guys with their own agenda. But I figured it was time to press on. So, I loaded up my car, said my goodbyes, and headed south toward Oaxaca.

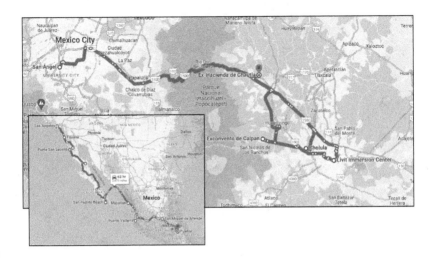

CHAPTER 15

FOR EVERYTHING GOOD, FOR EVERYTHING BAD

BY THE TIME I finally rolled into the outskirts of Oaxaca City, I was well into breaking the first rule of overlanding. I found a cheap motel, wedged my car into the tiny courtyard, paid for a room, and then asked the proprietor where I could find something to eat. He told me to walk down the dark street, turn right, go three blocks, then make another right. I had to take a leap of faith that he wouldn't send me off into danger. Then I rounded the corner and saw two women pushing baby strollers. Fears alleviated.

I followed the directions to an open-air kitchen where a matronly cook hovered over a grill loaded with sizzling steak and smelling of heaven. A table beside the grill offered pitchers of aguas frescas and bowls of peppers, cilantro, limes, and onions. Is there a more mouthwatering sight than fresh garnishes in non-matching plastic bowls laid out on a shiny tablecloth? No, there is not—not in Mexico anyway.

Inside, several patrons nibbled on crispy quesadillas stuffed with steak and cheese. Yes, please. I pointed at one of the gooey delights, "Uno por favor." My kind of ordering.

My anticipation mounted as I watched several fistfuls of Oaxaca cheese go into my quesadilla. The only downside was that this wasn't the kind of place that served beer—always welcome after a driving day—or a non-driving day. I sipped my Coke while my quesadilla acquired the crispness Mamá deemed acceptable to serve. Mamá did well. It was the crispiest, gooiest, most delicious quesadilla I've ever had the pleasure of devouring—

at a literal hole in the wall, with no sign or menu, down a dark side street in a nondescript neighborhood of Oaxaca City.

EL TULE

In the morning, I headed to a town outside the city, officially named Santa Maria del Tule, but always just referred to as *El Tule*. For months, I'd been reading about a campground called "Overlander Oasis," which seemed like a must-stop for anyone coming through Central Mexico.

I called first, as the website instructed. A woman answered.

"Oh, when were you looking to stay?"

"Well, actually, I'm about 10 minutes away."

"Oh... well... I guess we can accommodate you for a few nights."

I got the impression they didn't do many walkups. I pulled up to the front gate, where I was greeted by the proprietors, Leann and her husband, Calvin. "Is this the legendary Overlander Oasis?" I asked—hoping to signal that I was in the know.

We talked through the gate for a minute while, I assume, they sized me up for any signs of criminal insanity. Apparently, I passed, and they opened the gate. I parked in a corner and pitched my tent behind my car. I was camped next to a luxe converted RV mounted on a Land Cruiser chassis with a big label on the windshield that read "Alemania," the Spanish word for Germany.

After settling in, I walked over to Calvin and Leann's kitchen and living room, which was open to the elements on one end. An old Greyhound bus served as their sleeping quarters. Leann made me feel at home as she gave me a rundown of available activities in El Tule and Oaxaca City.

I mentioned the ordeal with my front license plate and how my trail angels had come to the rescue. Calvin blurted out, "Oh, that was you?" Hah! My fame precedes me.

Fully briefed, I walked the four blocks from Overlander Oasis into town. Like most Mexican towns, El Tule has a big central square, in this case, an acre-sized grassy park centered around a church. The church grounds house "El Árbol del Tule"—possibly the most famous tree in Mexico. The gargantuan 1,500-year-old Montezuma cypress is billed as "the world's girthiest tree." As a lifelong fan of the word *girthy*, who never misses a chance to use *girthy* in conversation, I felt this was relevant to my interests.

El Árbol del Tule—the world's girthiest tree

Speaking of girthy, El Tule has several grand public sculptures composed of geometric forms. If a metallic, neon-colored longhorn bull with dodecahedron testicles is on your bucket list, you need to get to El Tule.

Girthy.

I wandered the shops along the edge of the park, still out of sorts thinking about the awful tragedy Dan and his friends were dealing with. I tasted some local mescals and found a $10 bottle of a style called Minero, which I thoroughly enjoyed.

I bought five souvenir shot glasses, one for me and each of the End of All Roads guys, including Brian. I sent Dan a picture of the bottle and glasses, with a note that it would be waiting for them whenever they caught up to me. At this point, they were still vowing to continue the ride, but it seemed impossible to know how anyone would feel in a month or two. I just wanted them to know I was thinking about them.

Sculpture of a (confirmed) bull in El Tule

I came around a corner to see a woman tending what looked and smelled like thin-crust pizzas, cooking over coals on a traditional rounded pan known as a *comal*. The "pizzas" were topped with avocados, tomatoes, and shredded meat on a base of dark brown stuff that I assumed was mole sauce. Loads of Oaxaca cheese glistened away while the comal crisped the dough from underneath. I wasn't even that hungry. But there is no universe in which I just stroll past a scene like this. I know it. You know it. No point fighting it.

When my mystery Mexican pizza arrived, it exceeded my anticipation. The brown stuff turned out to be a black bean paste, which made a perfect base for the rest of the toppings. The meat, I'm 93% certain, was a type of spicy shredded pork known as *cecina*. Cool tomatoes and creamy avocados perfectly balanced the hot, crackly crust and salty cheese. I almost ordered another, even though I was stuffed.

In my hopeless naïveté, I wondered if I had just discovered some one-off local delicacy invented by this woman. I later learned I'd stumbled upon a beloved Oaxacan street food called a *tlayuda*.

I thought, "How on earth has a Disneyfied version of this delicacy not made it to the States?" One of the great joys of traveling in Mexico is discovering stuff like, "Oh look, Gorditas are a real thing and not just something Taco Bell made up!" How do we have tacos, burritos, enchiladas, tostadas, nachos, fajitas, taquitos, tamales, chalupas, gorditas, flautas, and chimichangas—but not tlayudas? Is it because of the name? It's not that hard—just start with teh-luh—fast. Tehluh-ayuda. See? Easy. Get on it, America. I want tlayudas. The people demand tlayudas!

Tlayudas cooking on a comal—best street food of the trip

Eventually, my heel, which still wasn't improving despite my heroic taping efforts, told me it was time to hobble back to the campground. I met some new arrivals: Stretch, a 6'8" retired tugboat captain from Alaska, and his partner Lucinda. They had driven from Northern California in a plain white van converted for sleeping and basic travel comforts.

We chatted for a bit; then Stretch asked where I was headed next. I replied, "I'm not really sure. To be honest, I'm feeling a little disoriented right now..."

Realizing mid-sentence that my statement deserved more explanation, I followed with, "I expected to be traveling with four guys on motorcycles. But one of them went off the road near Zacatecas and died."

I certainly didn't intend to just blurt that out to the first person I met in Oaxaca. It took days before I told my classmates at Livit Spanish. Typically, I'd be reticent to share such a recent tragedy with someone I just met, lest they suspect I was working some scam angle or just seeking attention. One certainly meets a few weirdos on the road. But much like when I first met Kelly and Mike, something just clicked with Stretch.

Stretch didn't ask for any details or give me a hint of side-eye. Instead, he invited me into his campsite and declared, "You know what? Oaxacans have a saying: *For everything good, mescal. For everything bad, mescal.*"

You will hear this saying **a lot** if you spend time in Oaxaca doing touristy things. This was my first time. It resonated.

Stretch procured a bottle of local mescal from his van's handy built-in wet bar. The three of us made a toast to Brian.

I did my best to suppress my usual "kid who just took a spoonful of nasty medicine" face, which happens when I drink any liquor. I'm a giant wuss when it comes to hard alcohol. I wouldn't last a day in the Old West. I love mescal, but I still make the face—at least on the first sip. It helps that you don't shoot mescal like tequila. Mescal is for sipping, always. The effects of each sip seem to diminish my medicine face accordingly.

After trying a couple of Stretch's finds, I brought over the bottle of Minero I had bought in town. We swapped traveler stories over more toasts and taste samplings. I professed my love for Alaska and recounted everything I'd seen and done on my road trip around the state.

I don't remember much else we discussed—except that the conversation flowed as freely as the mescal, and we seemed to have similar views about life and the world. I'm always keen to meet and hear stories from people a few years older than me who I think are "doing it right." I figure I'll be there soon enough, and I need a template.

The next morning, I woke up feeling more or less okay, considering how much I drank the night before. After the "for everything good, for everything bad..." saying, mescal boosters will also tell you that it's impossible to get a hangover from mescal. While I haven't always woken up bright-eyed and bushy-tailed following a mescal night, I can't say I've had a debilitating hangover. Then again, there's something civilized about sipping mescal that seems to preclude going overboard.

I borrowed an Overlander Oasis bicycle and rode it to Oaxaca City, following an old railroad grade enjoying a second life as a bike path. While I appreciated the downhill ride, I was acutely aware this would be reversed on the return trip to El Tule.

I found a place to rack the bike and wandered Oaxaca City. In the main square, groups of protesters chanted and held signs with long screeds of Spanish. I recognized the word *Zapatistas*—an indigenous Maya separatist movement.

I came across an accident at a busy intersection where a sports car had somehow become wedged into the side of an armored truck. In Mexico, when there's an accident, nobody moves until the cops arrive to sort it out, which can take a LONG time. It doesn't matter how much this snarls traffic. I'm told that if the cars move, cops won't assign blame, and the insurance companies won't pay. The interesting aspect to me is the attitude of "traffic can wait." Nothing ever seems hurried in Mexico unless demanding gringos are involved.

I had lunch at a restaurant whose feature dish was a mole tostada, which was, of course, fantastic. I feel like I barely scratched the surface of the innovative dishes to be had in Puebla and Oaxaca. I also found a travel company offering a van tour of the area, and I arranged for them to pick me up in El Tule the following morning.

On the way back to my bike, I stumbled upon what seemed to be *the* big market, with endless stalls laid out in a grid that took up an entire city block. Each stall sold some spice or food item, aesthetically laid out in baskets or stacked into pyramids—like I'd seen on travel shows.

Oaxaca has been a food mecca for millennia, starting with the domestication of maize, which fueled a massive population boom and made the great civilizations of Mesoamerica possible. Scientists puzzle over how the original Americans domesticated maize's closest known wild relative—a grass with an "ear" the size of a kidney bean—into hundreds of varieties of what we up north know as corn. Indigenous Americans became experts at keeping soil productive for centuries. Beans, squash, and maize, known together as the "three sisters," complement each other and replenish the soil. Maize also provides a stalk for the bean vines to climb, and ground-level squash leaves preserve moisture and block weeds.

Oaxaca has an array of micro-climates to grow different types of food: mountains, jungles, arid plains, and sea-level marshes. Pre-Columbian Oaxaca Valley civilizations ate **far** better in terms of nutrition and variety than their contemporaries in Europe. Give all this a few millennia to simmer into a rich food culture, toss in a few chile peppers, and you have the garden of culinary delights that is Central Mexico.

I came to a stall with baskets full of toasted crickets known as *chapulines,* ranging in color from bright red to dark brown, depending on the seasoning. I consider myself a somewhat adventurous eater, but I'm no Andrew Zimmern. I tend to shy away from stuff like eyeballs, sphincters, and feathered chicken fetuses. However, I've always been a little curious about bugs.

Of course, there's no way to buy just one chapulin, and I didn't want to insult the vendor by gagging on a free sample. So, I bought the smallest unit purchasable—about fifty chili-flavored crickets. I hoped I could resist temptation and make 'em last a few days.

The uphill ride back was as brutal as expected. I could smell mescal from the previous night oozing out of my pores.

Back in El Tule, I wandered along a row of restaurants. Each had placed a cooking device on the sidewalk—simultaneously preparing and advertising the evening's meal. One restaurant cooked tortillas on a large comal. Another roasted giant green chiles on coals. More restaurants offered simmered pork shoulders in a dark red sauce, and stewed shredded chicken. The intoxicating sights and smells went on and on and on. I wondered if every medium-sized town in the state of Oaxaca has a murderer's row like this or if El Tule was special.

I woke early the following morning and walked up to the girthy tree, where I had arranged to meet the van tour. While I waited, I watched school kids circumnavigate the tree, each with a small group of tourists in tow. Using a laser pointer, the kids would highlight various animals that could supposedly be seen in the whorls and knots of the old tree—occasionally eliciting a big "ahhhhh" from the audience, and other times a puzzled group "ehhh?" The elephant was spot on. I wasn't so sure about the monkey or the jaguar.

Even though I can do all the same stuff in my car, I still enjoy van tours. It's nice to let someone else worry about the driving and be free to soak in the view. I've also had good luck meeting other travelers, sometimes spending time with them after the tour. The best part is that I have a local guide to query about all the confusing things I've seen in the previous days.

Our first stop was a traditional textile weaver. We learned how the various dyes are made and watched a weaving demonstration. I boggled at the machinery, trying to grasp how the tangled topology of threads formed a piece of fabric. I bought a blanket. I usually try to support these places if they have something reasonably priced.

Next, we stopped at a mescal distillery, where a guide explained each step of the traditional process. Some species of agave can live up to seventy years. At some predetermined time that only the agave knows, the plant shoots a flowering stalk up to thirty feet in the air, then dies. Mescal-producing agaves are harvested as soon as the stalk begins to grow. It seems a little sad to cut off the agave's reproductive appendage just as it's about to fulfill its life's purpose. But the idea is to capture all the sugars the plant has stored up for this big moment. Once the agave hearts are harvested, they're thrown into a pit with hot rocks, covered and smoked for several days, then mashed and distilled into the final product.

After the mescal distillery, we arrived at the tour's highlight, an ancient Zapotec city known as Mitla. Zapotec culture first appears in the historical record around 1500 BCE, making them one of the founding Mesoamerican civilizations. Zapotecs began to dominate the Oaxaca Valley by 200 BCE. Mitla became a power center around 800 CE and was still an important city when Cortés arrived in the Oaxaca Valley in 1522.

Approaching the most prominent building, known as the Palace, I was struck by its imposing austerity—like a modern concrete prison or an old brick warehouse. The sharp vertices of its walls jutted out against the sky, which was suitably dramatic on the day I visited.

Intricate geometric patterns known as *stepped-frets* cover the Palace's three-story-high walls. Many frets form a distinctive square spiral known as a Xicalcoliuhqui (pronounced like... eh, never mind). At first glance, one would assume the intricate frets were created by pouring plaster into a mold. One would be wrong. On closer inspection, each block has been hand-carved and fitted into the wall without mortar. This construction has survived for more than five hundred years with minimal degradation.

"The Palace" at Mitla

I've seen echoes of the patterns at Mitla in some of Frank Lloyd Wright's famous Los Angeles houses and his son's studio. Dubbed *Mayan Revival Architecture*, the style drew ideas from all over Mesoamerica and was a popular motif in the US in the first half of the 20th century.

Frank Lloyd Wright's Ennis House—a.k.a. "The Blade Runner House"

Zapotecs and Mixtecs buried their elites at Mitla, which they called Mictlan, meaning "Place of the Dead." A priest-historian named Francisco de Burgoa recounted a sacrifice witnessed by his predecessors that culminated in a Zapotec high priest flinging the victim's body into a seemingly bottomless pit. Zapotec priests said the pit was a passageway to the Underworld, extending some thirty leagues (one hundred miles) underground.

According to Burgoa, who had a bit of flair for the dramatic, local Spanish priests believed the pit could be a portal to hell and wanted no part of it. Other colonists were skeptical and sought to prove it was just an ordinary tunnel.

As Burgoa tells it:

> *There were people, zealous prelates anxious for knowledge, who, in order to convince these ignorant people of their error, went into this cave accompanied by a large number of people bearing lighted torches and firebrands, and descended several large steps. And they soon came upon many great buttresses which formed a kind of street. They had prudently brought a quantity of rope with them to use as guiding-lines so that they might not lose themselves in this confusing labyrinth. And the putrefaction and the bad odour and the dampness of the earth were very great, and there was also a cold wind which blew out their torches. And after they had gone a short distance, fearing to be overpowered by the stench, or to step on poisonous reptiles, of which some had been seen, they resolved to go out again, and to completely wall up this back door of hell.*

And that was the end to any further curiosity about the passage to the Underworld from the zealous prelates anxious for knowledge.

Burgoa recounts that the entrance was permanently sealed. Some historians speculate the Spanish accomplished this by covering the portal with a church, which still stands today adjacent to the ruins. There's some fodder for your next supernatural thriller.

Another passage from Burgoa caught my attention:

> *Many who were oppressed by diseases or hardships begged this infamous priest to accept them as living sacrifices and allow them to enter through that portal and roam about in the dark*

interior of the mountain, to seek the feasting-places of their forefathers.

I wonder how the average Mesoamerican felt about the prospect of being sacrificed. Were they *really* as sanguine about being flayed alive as portrayed in some Mesoamerican writings? We know that victims caught in battle weren't happy about their fate. But others, like the man described by Burgoa, supposedly believed it would lead to something better for their families in this life or themselves in another life.

The human survival instinct is pretty strong, even in the face of cult-level devotion. Some of the Jonestown flock willingly drank the Kool-Aid; others had to be coerced.

Countering that, humans are classified as "hyper-social" creatures, meaning we often put the good of our family or tribe over our own, and even over our own lives on rare occasions. If you're born into the idea that there's something better waiting for you on the other side and human sacrifice is a part of everyday life, maybe that hyper-social behavior kicks in. Still, I'd like to believe there were plenty of skeptics who only gave lip service to the whole sacrifice thing to stay out of trouble.

We followed the path to the courtyard-facing wall of the Palace, which has a feature I've rarely seen on ruins—color. Brick-red plaster has survived in the cold, dry climate for half a millennium. Steps cut into the wall lead to the open-air "Hall of Columns," which opens to an inner courtyard with more intricate patterns. The place put me in such a contemplative mood, I could have hung around for a few more hours. However, one downside of van tours is that you're always on the go. We wrapped it up and headed back to town.

When I returned to Overlander Oasis, Calvin and Leann were hosting a party for the whole camp. I had many mescal shots with Stretch and Lucinda. I attempted to exalt the virtues of mescal to the German couple camped next to me. They tried, but they just weren't into it.

The Overlander Oasis party wound down by 11 p.m., but a giant outdoor wedding a few blocks away serenaded us with the latest reggaeton hits until 3 a.m. On Saturday nights in Mexico, there is no such thing as noise pollution. The message seems to be: "You might as well be at this party because you ain't sleeping through it."

Unfortunately, I wasn't invited to the wedding, and I needed my sleep for the driving day ahead. I planned to head south, then park my butt and heel in the warm sand of the Oaxaca Coast for a few days.

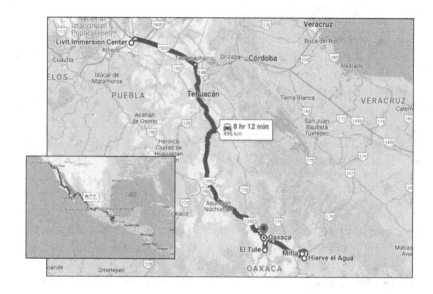

Chapter 16

Bizarre Foods

I woke up groggy, broke down my tent, and said goodbye to Leann, Calvin, Stretch, and Lucinda. Before leaving town, I wanted to pick up more bottles of the Minero mescal I had discovered. Unfortunately, that shop was closed.,

While killing time waiting for the shop to open, I decided to try one of the chapulines:

Crunchy start...

A bit of chili-flavored mushiness...

No weird finish...

Not that bad, actually.

Then, I spent several minutes picking wings out of my teeth—from **one** cricket. I can't imagine a whole bag. Maybe your teeth become saturated with wings at some point, and after that, it doesn't matter how many chapulines you eat. The original "once you pop, you might as well not stop" snack.

Still pulling wings out of my teeth, I wandered past a *queseria*. Had I just stumbled onto the source, the motherlode, the wellspring, of Oaxaca cheese? I had! As the shopkeeper pulled a cooler out from under the counter, my anticipation mounted like it was the glowing briefcase in *Pulp Fiction*.

She opened the cooler lid to reveal a soccer ball made from a thick ribbon of cheese wrapped tightly around itself. I'm not saying I've ever been on a drug deal, but this is what I imagine a major drug deal would feel like: the anticipation, the reveal, the glory of the thing. I ordered a half-kilo of the primo stuff. She peeled off a few layers and presented me with a loose, softball-sized hunk.

A half-kilo of Oaxaca cheese

Walking back to my car, I decided I could see myself settling in El Tule over anywhere else I'd been on the trip thus far. It's not too hot. It's close to a major city but not right in the hustle and bustle. It felt authentic but relaxed.

I had one more stop before hitting the highway: the Zapotec ruins of Monte Albán, situated on a hilltop outside Oaxaca City. I'd known the name "Monte Albán" as the only "mezcal" available in the midwestern United States during my formative (read: binge-drinking) years. Somehow, this lousy corporate brand has managed to taint one of the world's finest liquors *and* one of Mesoamerica's great cities. Impressive.

On the way to the site, I had to stop for road construction. While I waited, two workers spoke to each other in what I assume was Zapotec because it wasn't Spanish. It occurred to me that this might be the first time I'd ever heard an indigenous American language used in casual conversation.

In case you're puzzling over why the Zapotecs would give one of their great cities a Spanish name like Monte Albán—they didn't. They probably called the site Dani Baá, meaning "Holy Mountain." But the colonizer's name stuck, as it often does.

Sometimes, the wrong name comes from another indigenous culture—as in the case of the "Anasazi," who built the elaborate Great Houses that still stand in Chaco Canyon, Mesa Verde, and elsewhere in the Southwestern United States. *Anasazi* is a Navajo word that means "Ancient Enemy." Apparently, the Navajo weren't fans. To remove the negative stigma, the term *Anasazi* is slowly being phased out in favor of *Ancestral Puebloans.*

Imagine if your family moved away, then years later, someone asked your grumpy ex-neighbor about the history of your vacant house: "Oh, those assholes? They moved out years ago."

Centuries pass, and your family's house becomes a historical monument known as "The Asshole House," offering guided tours:

> *We believe this room is where the Assholes spent most of their time...*

> *Charred remnants in this outdoor cooking pit reveal the Assholes subsisted on a diet of pig ribs and granulated cow meat...*

> *An essential pastime of the Assholes seems to have been bouncing a round ball on this paved surface, then attempting to launch it through that circular hoop. We believe an Asshole from the losing team was sacrificed after the game...*

Even the Zapotecs, who have never gone away and are still over a million strong, don't call themselves Zapotecs. They use *Be'ena'a* ("The People") or *Be'ena Za'a* ("Cloud People"). *Zapotec* is a Spanish derivation of *Tzapotecatl*—a Nahuatl word from the Aztecs that means "People of the Place of Soft Fruit." Which is better than "Ancient Assholes," I guess.

I didn't get a guide for Monte Albán, as I only had a few hours. In retrospect, giving myself so little time was a mistake. Monte Albán turned out to be enormous, and other than the excellent museum, the site isn't overflowing with interpretative signage. I could easily have spent the better part of a day, including an hour of being guided around.

The entrance to the site spills the visitor out onto a sunken grassy courtyard the size of six soccer pitches, ringed with small pyramids and other ceremonial buildings. As far as dramatic entrances to ruins I've visited, I'd put Monte Albán's sunken plaza and expansive views second only to Machu Picchu. In its day, the entire plaza would have been plastered with white stucco, which must have been quite a sight.

As the first civilization to inhabit the Oaxaca Valley, the Zapotecs excelled at massive public works projects, including irrigation networks that maximized the Valley's rich soil and arid climate. Planned from its inception, Zapotec engineers spent decades first leveling the hilltop that would become Monte Albán and then carving out its sunken courtyards. Scholars debate whether the hilltop location at the confluence of three arms of the Oaxaca Valley had more to do with defense or trade access. At its height from around 300 BCE to 500 CE, more than 30,000 people lived in and around Monte Albán.

Monte Albán's Upper Plaza

In one corner of the plaza sits an arrangement of large stones, each carved with the likeness of a person, usually naked, sometimes disemboweled, and often in an exaggerated rubbery pose that doesn't look flattering or comfortable. The Spanish thought the figures looked like dancers and named them "Los Danzantes." Scholars believe many of the stones could be trophies representing individuals captured in battle. If so, this would make the Danzantes the oldest known depictions of violence in Mesoamerican public art. Previous Mesoamerican civilizations certainly fought battles against one another, but the Zapotecs seem to have been the first to memorialize warfare.

A similar stone from an older Zapotec site depicts a disemboweled warrior with a small pictograph—the oldest of its kind ever found. The pictograph translates to "1-Earthquake," the unlucky man's name, and also a specific day on the multi-cycle calendar shared throughout Mesoamerica.

Because of poor *1-Earthquake*, scholars know the Mesoamerican calendar is at least 2,670 years old.

The Zapotec power model resembled the Roman Empire more than most Mesoamerican civilizations. Zapotecs extended their influence through infiltration and infrastructure. They preferred diplomacy whenever possible, including arranged marriages to build alliances, and they were slower to resort to hostilities than most of their neighbors.

Before ascending the throne, a Zapotec prince was required to meet five obligations, all of them judged on style and execution:

A disemboweled 1-Earthquake

1. Take captives for sacrifice.
2. Sacrifice his own blood.
3. Build a new public works facility.
4. Commission a monument to one of his ancestors.
5. Seek support and approval of others in power.

Pretty forward-thinking for its day, no? How many disastrous chapters in world history could have been averted if a few inbred, syphilitic, nitwit princeling failsons had been quietly shunted aside using this method?

Unfortunately, I don't think it's true.

The Zapotec five obligations come from a popular book on Mesoamerica—a very popular *series of books*, in fact. I scoured the internet and found nothing about any five obligations. I poured over every Zapotec-related source in the book's bibliography and found nothing. I even emailed the publisher, as no author is listed. No reply.

This plunged me into an existential crisis over my research for this book. We all know the internet is hot garbage, but how was I supposed to know which **published books** I could trust and which I couldn't? I guess having no author listed was a red flag. But was that the **only** red flag I needed to look out for? Okay, in retrospect, when the audiobook narrator continually pronounced Palenque (correctly pronounced puh-**len**-kay) like "pah-len-**kewww**"—with an elongated French *"euuu"* sound—that was probably another red flag.

Then, I stumbled onto an engaging lecture series on Mesoamerica offered by *The Great Courses*. I liked the series so much that I took a shot in the dark and reached out to the instructor for fact-checking help. This being the early days of Covid and the unwelcome boost of free time it gave many of us, he agreed to come on board!

Dr. Edwin Barnhart—of the Maya Exploration Center

Say hello to Professor Edwin Barnhart of the Maya Exploration Center. If I get something wrong, you can send your nasty emails to him. He says he loves those.

I wholeheartedly recommend Dr. Barnhart's 48-part lecture series, **_Maya to Aztec: Ancient Mesoamerica Revealed_**. If you're unsure, he also has an 8-part series on the ancient Yucatán Maya, which convinced me to go in on the full Mesoamerica course. Professor Barnhart's love of the contemporary Maya still living and thriving in the Yucatán is infectious.

FYI: *(earmuffs Ed) Sometimes Great Courses runs deals up to 70 percent off the list price.*

Scholars like Dr. Barnhart divide Monte Albán's construction into five phases. The later phases show Teotihuacán's influence and feature more walls and other defensive structures—a sign the Zapotecs were getting into skirmishes with their neighbors. Toward the end of Monte Albán's reign, the Zapotecs began to lose territory to their nemesis: the Mixtecs. Eventually, the Zapotecs abandoned Monte Albán and moved south to Mitla and several other cities. To add insult, the Mixtecs occupied Monte Albán and began burying their elites in reused Zapotec tombs, one of which became the richest tomb ever unearthed in Mesoamerica.

By the time Cortés arrived, the Mixtecs and the Zapotecs were paying tribute to the Aztecs. Hoping to return their empire to its former glory, the Zapotecs aligned with the conquistadors, who for their part were comfortable navigating the Zapotecs' Machiavellian-style diplomacy. The two groups formed a hopeful alliance that lasted several decades. But we know how this story always ends. As soon as the Spanish had the rest of the Valley under control, they proceeded to colonize, convert, and exploit the Zapotecs. The last of the Zapotec empire crumbled.

In 1867, Benito Juarez, Mexico's full-blooded-Zapotec, five-term President, obtained a tiny measure of retribution against European invaders when he ended the short reign and life of the Habsburg Emperor Maximilian.

After Monte Albán, I headed south with my softball of cheese, which turned out to be the perfect road trip nibble food. Every bite was an odyssey of flavor, languidly working its way across the various taste buds—salty, cool, savory, creamy. Okay, I know there's no "creamy" taste bud. Or at least there wasn't, before Oaxaca cheese.

I made my way to Miahuatlán, the last big town before the mountains. To call the town gritty would be, well, accurate. There were no tourist amenities and not a gringo in sight. Most businesses seemed to be centered around farming. I passed on a couple of love hotels on the way into town and then pulled into the courtyard of the grandest-looking hotel on the main street, securing a room for 147 pesos (about $7.50)—the cheapest hotel room of the trip.

Laden with the usual assortment of remotes and a key attached to some large, unpocketable object—in this case, a flyswatter—I headed to my room. The parking lot attendant, a young woman who exuded severe boredom, told me I needed to move my car. I re-parked as instructed, then looked down at the bag of chapulines on my passenger seat. I wondered if she might like them.

I presented her with my gift, which she seemed genuinely happy to receive, for a brief moment, before reverting to her natural state of extreme indifference.

I was curious what a young Oaxacan would think of the chapulines. I wondered if maybe they're like fruitcake in the US. When I was a kid, fruitcake was still a nominally cherished item. Then, one day, a comedian made fun of them, and it's like the whole nation let out a collective sigh of relief,

"Ohhhhhh! Thank you! Those things are terrible! Maybe this will filter down to my aunt, and she'll stop sending them every Christmas!"

I wondered if maybe chapulines show up on the dinner table for traditional festivities, but at the end of the night, abuela quietly sloughs most of them into the trash.

However, based on my sample size of (1) their ability to crack a wan smile from a bored parking lot attendant and (2) my former coworker from Oaxaca who says he likes them—I conclude chapulines are statistically proven to be **not** like fruitcake. Oaxacans actually like them.

You question my science on this? Okay. Find me two people in the US who like fruitcake. I'll wait...

You found two people? Congrats. Now divide two by the number of people you had to ask before you found those two weirdos, then tell me the statistical likelihood of stumbling onto them as the **first** two people you randomly asked about fruitcake.

I stand by my analysis.

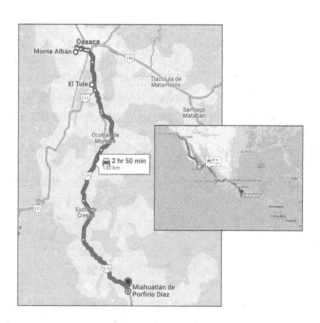

Chapter 17

Good Truck

It may have been the cheapest hotel room, but it was far from the worst. The heater worked. The walls and floors were clean and relatively well-finished. I even had a pleasant hot shower in the morning, which is more than I can say for my $89 hotel room in Mexico City.

I headed up into the mountains that mark the southern edge of the Oaxaca Valley. Once over the mountains, I planned to park my sore foot on a nice sandy beach along the Oaxaca coast for a few days. No hiking. No walking around town. Just soft, warm beach sand. The tape wasn't helping, so I figured I'd try rest.

The drive took me through winding mountain roads and steep gorges, first climbing a few thousand feet, then descending toward the Pacific Ocean. I passed rickety houses clinging to the sides of plunging ravines. I wonder how often the residents of these houses drop something off their little porch or open-air kitchen only to watch it bounce down into the canyon five hundred feet below? Do they make their kids retrieve the object just to teach them a lesson? Clearly, any game with a ball is out of the question.

The highway came out of the mountains to the town of Santa Maria Huatulco, which seemed to be the central city in the region. Getting out of the car, I was blasted with heat and humidity for the first time since Mazatlán. Absence did not make the heart grow fonder.

I wandered a bit then plopped down at an outdoor taco stand. A young brother and sister had an adorable little power struggle over who got to bring the big red-headed gringo his food. The girl won. I'm guessing they don't often serve people who look like me. I ordered two more tacos so the boy could deliver them. It's the least I could do.

I drove the remaining stretch south toward the Pacific Ocean, ending at a rocky point near a beach called Playa San Agustín. Nearby, a few fishermen stood barefoot on jagged sandstone formations, casting their lines over cauldrons of churning, blue-green surf. Black vultures and pelicans loitered nearby, hoping for a morsel of fishing detritus.

Fishermen work the coast near Playa San Agustín

PLAYA SAN AUGUSTÍN

I checked out a row of rustic restaurants and hotels lining the beach. As I read the sign to a place called Capi's, a spry bearded man in his 60s popped out of the closed gate. He introduced himself as Frans, explained that this was the only place on the beach with WiFi, and told me it had a nice restaurant. Sold.

It was still morning, and I wanted to explore the area, so I told Frans I'd be back.

Heading west along the beach toward the city of Puerto Escondido, I passed through a few towns that seemed like built-up expat/tourist enclaves. One fun-looking town, Mazunta, flowed with dreadlocked hippies. I stopped in Puerto Escondido at a very crowded beach, where I enjoyed a few cold beers and some fish tacos. Unfortunately, the tacos turned out to be crispy rolled taquitos with gray mystery meat. I realized I needed to stop trying to make fish tacos happen outside of Baja.

The beach at Puerto Escondido was crowded and seemed to have something of an Eastern European vibe, with lots of middle-aged gringos in speedos. Is a Russian still a gringo? I'm not sure. It was too late in the day to drive back to Playa San Agustín, so I headed to Mazunte.

MAZUNTE

I located my hostel, where I was told to park next door in a convenience store parking lot. The kid who worked at the store came out to help guide me. As I swung my car into the spot, I thought, "Come on, kid, I've been out on the road for months; I'm a pro at this now—"

CRRRUUNCH!

Damn it! I hit something on the passenger side.

If you're keeping score, this is now the second time I crunched into something while pulling into a parking spot too fast, and the **exact** thought running through my mind both times was, "I'm going to show this parking attendant how awesome I am at parking in Mexico."

Not content with just crunching my bumper, embarrassed and frustrated, I slammed the car into reverse and hit the gas—**kerrr-POP!**

Well, that sounded worse than the initial crunch.

It turns out I had hooked the bumper around a bend in the tree, which I couldn't see from the car. This weird bend was probably why the kid was out there to guide me. When I reversed, the tree ripped the entire bumper housing off the passenger side, where it was now dangling freely.

The kid and I pushed the bumper back on, but I knew it wouldn't just pop back into place. We got the housing relatively stable, where it could at least drive. But there was no way it would last for thousands of miles. I picked up a brownie-sized piece of black plastic that looked important and put it in my glove box.

The guy who worked at the hostel had seen the whole thing go down.

"You gotta go see Munentec," he told me. "He's a wizard. He can fix anything."

Okay, you have my attention.

"He's really hard to find. He doesn't have a sign. Just a hood up in his yard. And if you go too far down the road, other guys will say they're Munentec, but they suck. You don't want them working on your car."

I'd heard tales of the extraordinary skills of Mexican mechanics. I guess I was about to put the legends to the test, assuming I could find Munentec and not wind up with one of his imposters.

I mulled over all the worst-case scenarios of how much pain my dumb screw-up would cause. I could get stuck in some boring town like Veracruz, waiting weeks for a part to arrive at the local Toyota dealer. Would my bumper even make the drive to Veracruz? I supposed I could tie it on with coat hangers. I planned to meet a friend in Tulum in two weeks. This could be a significant issue.

I don't think my worst-case-scenario obsession is healthy or optimal. But at least if the worst thing imaginable ever does happen, I've probably already walked through it in my mind a few dozen times.

I checked out the beach around dusk—just in time to provide fodder for throngs of mosquitos. I was told Mazunta had a nude beach just around the bend from town. Like San Pedrito in Baja, the hippies in Mazunta were of the extremely attractive variety. But I wasn't going to battle mosquitos just to be the creepy old guy looking at naked hippies. One or the other.

As far as me getting naked, the public and I have a deal: I won't get naked around them, and they don't have to see me naked. All parties continue to report a high degree of satisfaction with this arrangement and see no reason to re-open negotiations at this time.

I did briefly talk to a couple of locals on the beach. One of them told me Mazunta, along with Palenque, was a very magical place. This was my second time hearing about Palenque from a Mexican local, so I put Palenque on my must-see list, knowing little except that it was some kind of ruin. YOLO traveling at its finest.

The next morning, I got another rave review about Munentec from the hostel employee working the morning shift and even more confusing directions on how to find his shop. I set off on my quest, discovering that people have wildly varying definitions of "about a mile"—which, in this case, turned out to be about three miles. I finally found a hood propped up on some scaffolding as described, surrounded by body parts and cars in various stages of undress.

I parked and got out. Two squat guys in flip-flops and cargo shorts stopped what they were working on and approached. One of the guys introduced himself as Munentec. I showed them what I had done. Munentec and his assistant immediately went to work—scurrying around my bumper like beavers.

The pair got the bumper off my car, then removed a chunk of black plastic bolted to the frame that was broken off on one end. I remembered the plastic piece I had picked up in the parking lot. I retrieved it from my glove box and handed it to Munentec. It was a perfect match.

This is where I thought, "We're gonna have to wait for a part, aren't we?" Every day, I'd come in and ask, "Is the part in yet?" Munentec would tell me, "No señor, maybe tomorrow." Ugh.

But the look in Munentec's eyes suggested he had a plan. I tentatively offered, "Superglue?"

"Superglue," he replied.

Yes! Hooray for Superglue! I doubt this solution would fly at a dealership body shop, but I didn't care. If it was good enough for the wizard Munentec, it was good enough for me.

Munentec retreated into his shop, where he applied a caulking gun full of black goo to the two broken pieces. He then pulled out a hair dryer to dry the glue.

While Munentec dried the bracket, his assistant used the same black goo to repair the chip I had knocked out of my side mirror in San Miguel de Allende. When he was done, the mirror looked as good as new. My stepdad was a mechanic. I grew up around repair

Munentec and his assistant work on my bumper

shops. I've never seen this magic black goo before.

Munentec and his buddy finished up and got my bumper firmly back in place. He explained that he had no breakaway clips, which had saved the bumper from suffering more damage, so he had to bolt the housing back on. He told me this would be more secure. Just don't do what I did again, or there would be a lot more damage.

No more hooking my bumper around a tree and then gunning it in reverse. Got it.

Once everything was back together, I asked Munentec, "Cuanto cuesta?" In another context, I might be worried that a mechanic would try to gouge me, since we hadn't agreed to anything upfront. But that would have been so far out of character from everything I'd experienced in Mexico thus far, it would have surprised me.

Munentec pondered for a second, then replied, "Quinientos pesos," or about $25, for a job that would have cost $1,200 back in the States. I thanked Munentec and his assistant profusely. As a final gesture, Munentec patted my car's hood and said, "Good truck."

Less than an hour after pulling into Munentec's driveway, I was back on the road, headed to Playa San Agustín. I thought, "Wow. That went better than I could have possibly imagined." Sometimes, I think the universe likes to make me look stupid for worrying so much. Better that than the reverse, I guess.

I patted my FJ's dashboard, "Good truck."

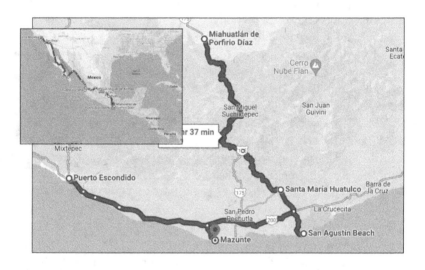

CHAPTER 18

OF PLANS AND MEN

I ARRIVED BACK in Playa San Agustín by mid-afternoon and pulled up to Capi's place. Capi, the owner, told me that Frans and his wife were out running errands. Inside the compound, several well-placed palapas and a line of natural wood fencing framed the ivory sand and blue-green surf—creating a perfect rustic beach snapshot. I thought, "Well, this is just a little piece of paradise, isn't it?"

Before I set up my tent, Capi insisted on showing me the showers and bathroom. I followed him to be polite, thinking, "I've seen bathrooms bef—ohhhh my." Spotless new tile ran along the floor and up the walls. Stainless steel fixtures glinted under the skylight. I'd be thrilled to have this bathroom in a $300 hotel room. My bathroom in Mazunte was a rickety outhouse with a toilet bowl.

I set up my tent, bought a couple of beers from Capi, then went out to swim and relax on the beach. But there was a purpose to my relaxing. In less than two weeks, I was scheduled to meet up with my friend and her friend in Tulum, where I knew they'd want to hang out on the beach. I didn't want the glare from my blazing white torso to make them go snowblind. That's no fun for anyone's vacation.

While I am a ginger, I'm also a quarter Italian, which I'm convinced gives me a faint layer of tan underneath the burn and betwixt the freckles. My friends don't see it, but I know it's there.

So my plan—and I cannot emphasize this enough: I HAD A PLAN—

was to lay out without sunscreen, rotating my body ninety degrees every twenty minutes. My friend has a theory that you have to get that first burn of the summer out of the way, then you can get some color. I'm not sure of the bro science behind this, but it feels right. So that was the plan: a controlled burn, then maybe a little more sun, with sunscreen, in a week or so.

After some time, I estimated I had achieved sufficient sun on all four quadrants of my torso, so I packed it up and took refuge under Capi's main palapa. Out of beers, I drank vodka with OJ from my cooler and watched the late afternoon sun move across the sky. I seemed to be a little pink in places, but nothing felt too burnt. However, the alcohol, the sun, and my empty stomach were working in three-part harmony to give me a feeling-no-pain buzz. So, it was hard to judge.

About an hour before sunset, Frans and his wife arrived in their pickup. I was so excited to see him that I ran to the back gate, yelling, "Frans!" They expected to return to an empty compound. Instead, they got a crazy-eyed, drunken pink gringo, whom Frans had met for all of a minute the day before, running and yelling at them from the beach. Frans and his wife Anneke were still very gracious and even fed me. We sat around their camp-site, swapping traveler stories into the night.

As I started to sober up, the pain began to creep in. I realized my controlled burn might have escaped containment.

In the morning, I awoke feeling quite warm and quite in pain. I made my way to the bathroom to get a look in the mirror. Yep, I was a full-blown lobster—except for my sides. Despite my attempts to get sun all around, I still had a well-defined white stripe running down each side. I looked like a Neapolitan ice cream bar without the chocolate: strawberry-vanilla-strawberry.

Anneke was the first to see me in the morning. She immediately questioned me in a very stern tone. What exactly was I thinking to get myself so burnt? Yes, I know I am a redhead, and I burn easily. Yes, I know I overdid it. But I had a plan. Yes, really. The plan just was not executed properly.

She continued to be dubious about my plan, so I told her there was a girl involved, which was true. I did *not* tell her that while my friend is indeed gorgeous, there was zero chance of anything happening between us, and, in actuality, I just didn't want to be embarrassingly white on the beach.

Because that would make me look stupid.

As I hoped, the introduction of *a girl* to my otherwise inexplicable behavior satisfied Anneke and brought a halt to my interrogation. "Man doing something stupid for girl" is a universally accepted trope.

Soon, Capi showed up with his family. He asked if I would like some breakfast. Absolutely! He said they have huevos... frijoles... I asked if they had chilaquiles. For some reason, he took great delight in this question and replied enthusiastically, "Sí!" Breakfast was delicious.

Breakfast in paradise

Throughout the day, Frans and Anneke's efforts to corral or otherwise scold their little terrier, Don Taco, kept me entertained. Taco was constantly escaping the fenced compound or getting into some other mischief. Several times an hour, one of them would repeatedly yell "Tah-co! Tah-co! Tah-co!" in a Dutch accent. Don Taco was very sweet, but he seemed to get into a lot of trouble.

The second night of my sunburn was much worse. I was a lot less drunk and in so much pain I could hardly sleep. The next day, I again stayed true to my goal of doing nothing, except when I accompanied Frans to see a plot of beach he'd recently purchased. He planned to open an over-lander compound with his killer draw: WiFi. No restaurant, no cabañas— just WiFi, camping, and communion with other overlanders.

Note: *As of the writing of this book, Don Taco Overlander Beach Camp is* *in full operation on Playa San Agustín and getting rave reviews on iOverlander.*

Later that day, a Canadian couple showed up in a mini-RV. Capi managed to squeeze them into the compound. The driver got out, looked around, and said, "Well, this is just a little piece of paradise, isn't it?"

Yes, I concur.

That night, we all hung around the fire in Frans' camp, swapping more traveler stories. I learned that Frans and Anneke speak a dozen languages between them. Frans had a seemingly endless well of crazy tales, including one about leading a team of motorcycles across the Himalayas for an audience with the Dalai Lama. I started dubbing him *The Most Interesting Man in the World*.

My pain abated by the third night of the big burn. However, I seemed to have eaten something that didn't agree with me. I woke up at midnight, compelled to rush to the bathroom, where I heaved up a few offerings to Tlaloc, the rain god. I took solace in the fact that I had the nicest bathroom in Oaxaca to throw up in. Amazingly, that would be the only time I threw up the entire trip.

The next day, still feeling pretty low, I parked myself in a beach chair to catch up on some reading. Sand fleas kept nipping me under the main palapa, so I moved to one of the smaller palapas, which had a few dime-sized holes that I deemed non-consequential.

Capi now had a full campground, with families occupying both cabañas. Frans repeatedly clashed with one of the dads over feeding the local stray dogs and letting a dog into the compound, which caused problems with Don Taco. The subject of Frans' ire had sandy blond hair and fair, freckled skin covered in tattoos. His partner was Latina. The kids looked like they were probably from a previous marriage.

Watching this family interact, I made up a whole backstory that he was a dirtbag Long Beach meth dealer on the run from the law. Somehow, he'd hooked up with this single mom, who knew he was no good but couldn't help loving him anyway. He did seem good with the kids, so maybe he wasn't all bad. She was sure he had a good heart, but it wasn't going to end well for her. These things never do.

Sometime in the afternoon, I went to the bathroom, looked in the mirror, and thought, "Crap! Am I getting **more** sun?" The little holes in the palapa and the ambient sun reflecting off the sand must have added up. I put on my shirt and put sunscreen on my face, but the damage was done. I was sunburned. Again.

A little later, I rose to get out of my beach chair for the last time of my stay at Capi's—**CRAAAACK**. I had broken one of Capi's fancy plastic Adirondack beach chairs. Great. I'm sunburned, sick, and my fat butt just broke another chair on this trip. I told Capi I had broken his chair. He smiled and shrugged it off, even though I could tell he wasn't thrilled that it was one of his nice Adirondacks and not one of the cheaper stackable chairs.

Frans and Anneke returned from running errands. Anneke took one look at me, **"DID YOU GET MORE SUN?!??"** She was fuming.

I tried to defend myself, "It was an accident. Really! You see, that palapa has little holes, and you wouldn't think—"

Frans, blissfully unaware of the previous sunburn drama, interrupted, "Why are you getting more sun?"

Before I could reply, Anneke turned to him and said, "There's a **gurrelll**," derisively drawing out the last part of "girl" to emphasize her point. Frans nodded in full understanding and went back to not paying attention.

"No, it wasn't the girl this time." I pleaded my case with Anneke, "It was an **accident!**"

Despite my protestations, she had trouble comprehending how anyone could be so stupid as to *accidentally* get a second sunburn while still recovering from the first sunburn.

Even as she shook her head at me in disgust, I found it oddly comforting to have a stern Dutch mother scolding me for irresponsible behavior.

When we sat around the fire that night, Anneke handed me a liter-sized bottle of aloe vera gel and said, "Just keep rubbing this on all night." I complied. Within minutes, the gel would fully absorb into my skin, no matter how generously I applied it. I wondered—where does it all go? Were my blood and internal organs now coursing with aloe vera? Was there a saturation point where I would start oozing gel out of my pores?

I wasn't feeling up for a late night of drinking and traveler stories, so I retired to my tent early, very worried about how much pain I was going to be in the next day. As I reached my tent, one of Capi's other guests emerged from the darkness, startling me.

It was the dirtbag Long Beach meth dealer. Turns out he was actually from France, and his English was as bad as my Spanish. He still managed to communicate that he had some medical-grade burn gel, which, as a fellow ginger, he felt I needed. I must have been beaming red across the compound like Rudolph the Red-Nosed Reindeer. He continued, "Put eet on, ehh, how you say... theek?" I slathered it on my face, chest, and stomach.

I sometimes make up ludicrous stories when I people-watch. Usually, they're harmless. However, in this case, my imagination prevented me from making an interesting connection. Normally, I'd try to meet someone sharing the same beach with me for a few days. But my nonsense backstory, combined with Frans' disapproval, led me to avoid the guy. Then, out of the blue, he went far out of his way to perform this completely selfless act, telling me to slather on his expensive medical-grade burn cream, "how you say... theek?"

I couldn't have felt like more of an ass.

Much like my resolve to never repeat the driving mistake outside of San Miguel de Allende, I vowed never again on the trip to judge a book by its cover. I would give people the benefit of the doubt until they proved otherwise. I have a knack, some say a gift, for making terrible first impressions. Why would I hold someone else to a standard I rarely attain?

The burn cream seemed to work, too. I slept well and wasn't in pain when I woke up the following day. I was ready to press on. Four nights at a beach resort is pretty much my maximum. I wanted to see Palenque, and I had a hard deadline to meet my friend at the Cancún airport in a week.

Before leaving, I ordered my usual breakfast. As always, Capi's face lit up when I asked for chilaquiles. He looked over and smiled at his wife—as if to share the moment with her. I have no idea why Capi and his family got such a thrill out of hearing me say *chilaquiles*, but I was happy to bring them joy.

I said my goodbyes to Capi and his family, shook hands with Frans, and hugged Anneke. I know very little about the Netherlands, but I'm going to guess Dutch mothers have a reputation for putting up with zero nonsense.

I thanked the ~~Long Beach meth dealer~~ generously kind French guy again. He gave me some pointers for things to do around Palenque.

My *hope* for the day was to make the 8-hour drive to the colonial town of San Cristóbal de las Casas. Local Oaxacans, however, had other plans for me.

MEXICO HIGHWAY 200

I'd been on the road for two hours and was about thirty miles from the town of Salina Cruz when traffic on the two-lane highway came to a stop. I couldn't see the front of the line, but it looked to be a quarter of a mile minimum. I assumed the stoppage could have one of three causes: construction, a wreck, or a roadblock.

Roadblocks are a primary method of protest throughout Latin America. They can be initiated by teachers, farmers, indigenous villagers, or anyone unhappy with their local, state, or national government. Calvin at Overlander Oasis told me about a major roadblock that essentially shut down Oaxaca City for months. The authorities finally broke it up with bulldozers, killing a teacher.

The overlander forums are rife with horror stories about roadblocks. One couple described how locals hit their truck with hammers and "threw a railroad tie under their tires." Further investigation suggested the couple actually tried to drive *over* the railroad tie to get around the roadblock, thus initiating the hammer attack. More stories like this led me to conclude that any evasive maneuver to get around a roadblock angers the locals and never ends well for the overlander. A motorcycle rider had a story about bribing his way through a roadblock for $5, but I never came across any story of someone in a car bribing their way through.

So, I was content to sit in my air-conditioned vehicle, still not sure of the exact nature of the stoppage, but not curious enough to endure the long walk in sweltering heat on my gimpy heel to find out. At one point, a gringo walked past my car toward the front of the line—his gait full of purpose. He returned fifteen minutes later—slumped and dejected. It seemed his request to speak to the manager of the stoppage did not go well. That was all I needed to see. Whatever was going on up there—no one was paying or talking their way through.

I happened to stop next to a little dirt side road set amidst a clump of shade trees. This created a natural gathering place for people wanting to escape the heat. At first, I cursed my luck, as getting out to pee with all this activity nearby would be a challenge. Eventually, however, I came to enjoy my view of the hubbub. It's rare when traveling that one can be a fly on the wall and observe locals for hours.

A vendor selling Jell-O treats showed up at the shady spot, followed by another selling what looked like bags of sugar water. The vendors started talking to a guy who had pulled his car out of line. They all seemed to know each other, suggesting the stoppage was planned, which would rule out a wreck. Given how long we'd been waiting, I also put road construction at a low probability.

A car marked "SEMEN" in bold stencil pulled into the shade spot. I wondered what semen meant in Spanish, so I looked it up. Oh. Semen means semen. Then I noticed a big metal milk jug in his back seat. He didn't seem to be in any urgency, so I figured he must be empty or have plenty of dry ice to keep his semen cold. If anyone could beg their way through a roadblock, you'd think it would be a guy with perishable animal semen.

A truck full of heavily armed military guys drove up to the front, then returned fully loaded. I couldn't imagine what that was about, but no one seemed tense.

Later, a truck pulled up to the crowded rest stop. The passenger pulled out a garden hoe and used it to clear a substantial amount of brush— creating a new shaded parking space. I figured he has squatter's rights now, since he improved the land.

Finally, I had to leave my little bubble to pee. I walked over to the side road where I passed a young guy coming from a clump of trees. I asked him, "Baño, allí?" (Bathroom, over there?) He chuckled and replied, "Sí!"

And that, ladies and gentlemen, was my first ever joke in Spanish.

On the way back, I tried to ask the semen guy when he thought it would be over. We didn't communicate very well. But I picked up that he thought it would be a few more hours.

By dark, we still hadn't moved. We had one false alarm when a truck started its engine and turned on its headlights. That triggered a chain reaction of headlights up and down the line. Everyone started revving their engines like the Indy 500. Then, nothing happened, and everyone shut down again.

About an hour later, the same thing happened, but this time, it wasn't a false alarm. Finally, we started moving. When I got up to the front, I saw that the blockage was at a bridge over a stream—which makes sense as a location to put up an effective roadblock. As far as I could tell, the closest detour around this bridge would have involved driving almost back to Oaxaca City. Even if I'd known I was going to sit there for seven hours, the detour still would have taken longer.

A school bus sat off to the side, which I assumed had been used to block the bridge. Dozens of people of all different ages stood on both sides of the road, whooping and hollering and pumping their arms in jubilation as we drove through. I guess this was a happy occasion. We just removed the roadblock we created! Hooray!

I found a City Express hotel in Salina Cruz. I was excited to talk about the roadblock with the hotel desk clerk. I had so many questions. Did he know what the protest was about? Were they teachers? Was it on the news? Did he even know there was a big roadblock thirty miles away?

Finally, the clerk paused his typing and looked up at me like a perturbed uncle, who's just trying to read his paper whilst being pestered by an inquisitive but dimwitted nephew, and said, "It's Oaxaca."

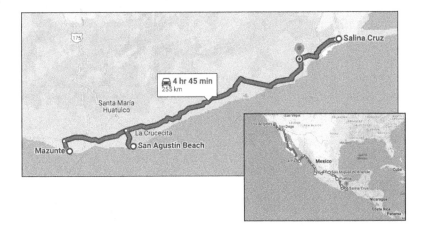

CHAPTER 19

THE ROAD BEST NOT TRAVELED

IF THE CITY EXPRESS 1 p.m. checkout time became a concern at La Paz, I had to look in the mirror and admit I had a problem at Salina Cruz.

Sleeping in and dicking around on the internet until 1 p.m. had me on schedule to arrive in San Cristóbal de las Casas at dusk. I didn't want a repeat of the San Miguel de Allende near-disaster, so I pulled up in the next closest city, Tuxtla, and checked in to... another City Express. I figured if I was going through the stages of addiction, I might as well hit rock bottom and get it over with.

The next day, I made it onto the road before noon. Recovery is about progress, not perfection.

The City Express Do Not Disturb placard

SAN CRISTÓBAL DE LAS CASAS

I pulled into San Cristóbal and found a hotel that was cheaper than City Express and actually had some character. Then, I set out to explore San Cristóbal, a charming colonial town that reminded me of San Miguel de Allende.

I tried some traditional hot chocolate, which was quite tasty and hit the spot on a chilly night. Although, it seems I got the dumbed-down version for gringos, because mine was semi-sweet with hints of cinnamon. The original Mesoamerican hot chocolate was not sweet and was flavored with chilis. Cacao beans, the source of chocolate, served as currency throughout Mesoamerica and were more valuable than gold. When Columbus raided a Maya trading canoe off the coast of modern-day Honduras, he noted that a man took great care to pick up every spilled cacao bean.

During colonial times, indigenous tribes sought refuge from Spanish tyranny in the jungled mountains east of San Cristóbal. By the second half of the 20th century, these tribes felt utterly left behind by the economic boom known as the "Mexican Miracle." Indigenous villagers weren't even allowed within San Cristóbal's city limits until the 1950s. The Mexican government didn't want their idyllic colonial city marred by the sight of protests and poverty-stricken villagers.

In 1980, a group of indigenous Maya formed the revolutionary Ejército Zapatista de Liberación Nacional (EZLN)—taking the name *Zapatista* from the revolutionary Emiliano Zapata, who, in 1919, along with Pancho Villa, ended the 31-year reign of de facto dictator Portofino Diaz.

On January 1st, 1994, the day Mexico, the US, and Canada signed the North American Free Trade Agreement (NAFTA), the Zapatistas kicked off their revolution by taking over government buildings in San Cristóbal and five other towns in the state of Chiapas. They let indigenous prisoners out of jail, destroyed land titles, and announced that their revolution would soon march all the way to Mexico City.

In the words of their mysterious ski-masked leader, known only as Subcomandante Marcos:

> *For hundreds of years we have been asking for and believing in promises that were never kept. We were always told to be patient and to wait for better times. They told us to be prudent, that the future would be different. But we see now that this isn't true. Everything is the same or worse now than when our grandparents and parents lived. Our people are still dying from hunger and curable diseases, and live with ignorance, illiteracy and lack of culture. And we realize that if we don't fight, our children can expect the same.*

Mexican President Carlos Salinas retaliated with extreme force, even bombing the hopelessly outgunned Zapatistas. Images of dead indigenous villagers caused an uproar in the international human rights community. Eventually, the Mexican government reached a détente with the Zapatistas —allowing them a degree of self-governance. Today, the EZLN retains its semi-autonomy and has some representation with the Mexican government.

Based on the graffiti I saw around San Cristóbal, the matter seems far from settled. On the side of a doorway, someone had spray-painted: "Alto al terrorismo de estado (stop state terrorism) F.N.L.S." The FNLS, or Front Line Defenders, is a human rights organization that features pictures of disappeared young men on their website. On the other side of the same doorway, someone had painted: "Fuera bandas paramilitares" (paramilitary gangs get out) and nearby: "policía fuera" (police get out).

Free of the City Express succubus, I got an early start on my drive through the jungle to Palenque. I'd heard some reports about roadblocks— including the incident with the overlanders who had their car beaten with hammers—on the Ocosingo road, the only direct route from San Cristóbal to Palenque. Many guides suggested going through Villahermosa to the north, 150 miles out of the way. But I found no reports of theft, violent crime, or cartel activity in the region, and the scenery was supposed to be breathtaking. So, I decided to take the risk. I'm just a sucker for crooked roads.

The decision not to go through Villahermosa and Tabasco meant this was as close as I would get to the heartland of the Olmecs—Mesoamerica's "mother culture." You may notice the carved Olmec head on the cover of this book. These giant stone heads, presumably of Olmec kings, stand up to eleven feet tall and can weigh up to forty tons.

You may say, "But Matt, can you really put an Olmec head on the cover of your book when you didn't even visit an Olmec site?" That is a very fair and valid question. However, in my defense—those things are freaking cool.

An Olmec Head

Back in the 19th and early 20th centuries, when it was fashionable to deny that the great New World civilizations could have sprung up on their own, some hypothesized, due to a vague similarity in features, that the Olmec heads were created by an African culture which somehow migrated across the Atlantic. Apparently, none of the proponents of this theory thought to check out the people who still occupy the Olmec heartland today. It turns out they look very similar!

Your Majesty!

Besides giant heads and several large stone altars, the Olmecs built most of their monuments out of earth. By 900 BCE, they had constructed a 110-foot-tall pyramid, the tallest in Mesoamerica at the time. The pyramid still stands today, despite being abandoned to the elements for over two millennia, at a site called La Venta near Villahermosa.

Elements of Olmec civilization can be traced to roughly 3,000 BCE, which puts the Olmec heartland on the map as one of six places on Earth where civilization sprang up more or less in isolation. The others being: Ancient Egypt, the Shang Culture of China, the Sumerian Culture of Northern Iraq, the Northern Coastal Culture of Peru, and the Civilizations of the Indus Valley—spanning parts of present-day India, Pakistan, and Afghanistan.

For anthropologists and archaeologists, the benchmark of "civilization" isn't the size of the villages but the emergence of social classes and public architecture. For these scholars, civilization is born when a group of egalitarian villages—where everyone has more or less the same status—makes the leap to "elite" versus "commoner" burials and starts producing public art that exalts and validates the elites.

In return for losing equal status, commoners get to help build grand public works projects as directed by the elites. This seems like a poor trade-off. But commoners do get greater food security, protection from hostile outsiders (albeit sometimes at the cost of their sons), and fun distractions like ballgames, acrobats, and religious spectacle. Clearly, no parallels can be drawn with modern society.

Many foundational components of Mesoamerican society initially seemed to have originated with the Olmecs, including ceramic figurines and pottery styles, the comal, the Mesoamerican ballgame, and the long count calendar—the genesis of Mesoamerican writing. However, as older sites from contemporary Mesoamerican civilizations are excavated, the concept of the Olmecs as a singular mother culture has been thrown into doubt.

An Olmec site yielded the world's oldest rubber balls, dating to around 1,600 BCE. The Olmecs added sulfur from morning glory flowers to natural latex produced by rubber trees, then heated the mixture to create pliable strips of durable rubber—a process Henry Firestone patented several thousand years later as *vulcanization.*

The oldest ball *court,* however, was found at a proto-Maya site along the Mexico/Guatemala Pacific coast. So it's unclear which came first—the ball or the ball court, or if the ballgame originated with the Olmecs.

Many Mesoamerican religious principles seem to have begun during the height of Olmec influence, such as using caves to communicate with the dead, ancestor worship, the practice of burying the dead under the houses of their descendants, the idea of a "Sustenance Mountain" which seems connected to the domestication of maize, the veneration of twins and dwarves, and depictions of humans transforming into animals—a common theme in shamanic rituals of neolithic societies around the world.

Artifacts and carved altars from Olmec sites depict "were-jaguars"—

people who transform into jaguars. Amusing to me anyway, a "were-duck" has also been found.

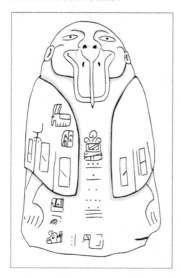

Tremble before the were-duck!

There are even baby were-jaguars, which may indicate that certain babies are considered born into the shaman role. The Olmecs also seem to have a fascination with chubby babies that never really took off in the rest of Mesoamerica. No depiction or evidence of human sacrifice has ever been found at an Olmec site, although some depictions of ritual self-harm, as practiced by elites throughout Mesoamerica, do appear.

Olmec civilization had a 2,000-year run spread across three major city centers before disappearing around 200 CE. Scholars now posit that many ideas initially attributed to the Olmecs may have come from the Maya to the southeast, the Zapotecs to the southwest, the Tlateloco, Texcoco, and other emerging cultures to the west. Whatever the source, the Olmecs were at the cross-roads of a vibrant cluster of connected proto-civilizations that stretched throughout modern Mexico and Central America.

The Precious Moments figurines of 1000 BCE

THE OCOSINGO ROAD

The drive northeast out of San Cristóbal took me into lush green mountains with sweeping views of steep gorges and rustic houses clinging to the rim. The only annoyances were endless topes (speed bumps, pronounced like "TOH-pay"). Locals put these up to slow traffic and sometimes try to sell things to the drivers when they slow down. I'd been dealing with topes since Baja, but these were the least forgiving and most frequent I'd encountered. I had to come to a near stop to keep from jarring my FJ to pieces. Doing the drive in a camper van would have been an epic ordeal. Come to think of it, a barely connected bumper would have been a disaster.

As I approached the town of Oxchuc, I drove past a burnt-out Bimbo van blocking the opposite side of the road. Bimbo is Mexico's answer to Wonder Bread and Hostess combined. I wondered why anyone would leave the skeleton of a van frame on the road like that. Around the next bend, I had my answer. A line of white taxi vans blocked the opposite side of the road, funneling traffic down one long chute, which I followed until I came to a stop. It was another roadblock. I couldn't say I wasn't warned.

A burned-out Bimbo truck outside of Oxchuc, Chiapas

As I crept forward, I was encouraged that the line seemed to keep moving. When I got close enough, I could see a few guys approaching the cars ahead of me, apparently asking for money. This was great news. I'd much rather deal with a toll roadblock than a sit-for-eight-hours roadblock. The only problem was I'd done the cardinal dumb thing you shouldn't do in sketchy cash situations. I only had about 60 pesos in change. My next smallest bill was 500 pesos—about $25.

When I got to the front of the line, a clean-cut man in jeans and a sweater approached my car, taking on a very apologetic tone: "Lo siento señor, el peaje es cien pesos, por favor. También, disculpe las molestias."

I didn't know what "el peaje" or "disculpe las molestias" meant, but I understood "sorry señor" and "cien (100) pesos."

I figured either this guy is the most polite, well-dressed highway robber of all time, or I'm in some quasi-official toll situation in Zapatista country.

Either way, my options were to a) pay the toll or b) pull over and wait some indeterminate time.

I sheepishly handed over my 500 Peso note and said, "Cambio, por favor?"

My toll-taker's eyes lit up as he proclaimed, "Sí!" whereupon he sprinted over to a group of five other men sitting behind a long plastic folding table—like you might see at a church picnic. One guy had a bull-horn; another had most of his face covered. The oldest guy sat in the middle, overseeing a metal cash box. My toll-taker approached the money man to get my change, then sprinted back to my car, again apologizing several times for the inconvenience.

My toll-taker gets change from the town toll committee

To get out of town, I had to weave around piles of rocks blocking the road. The roadblock stories from the forums, good and bad, made a lot more sense after seeing the inner workings of this one. It became clear that even if you see some way to force your way around the main roadblock, they'll just stop you at one of these secondary roadblocks. Except now they'll be pissed—which is understandable, given you probably put people in danger with your little stunt.

I'd only gone a few bends in the road when I came to some rocks covering too much of the road to weave around. This time, instead of one toll-taker, three men dressed in ill-fitting, shabby clothes—who seemed like they may have already been imbibing on this fine morning—shuffled up to my car. Let's call them Larry, Moe, and Curly. All three of them stuck their heads in my window. The leader, Moe, shook my hand and patted me on the shoulder—which could have been perceived as threatening. But these guys were so goofy, I couldn't find it in me to be nervous.

Moe made it clear they were just asking for anything I could spare, "voluntario." He repeated this several times, accompanied by an exaggerated pleading look. For some reason, it seemed very important for him to emphasize that this was voluntary. I gave them forty pesos, which seemed to make them happy. They moved their little pile of rocks and allowed me to proceed.

I kicked myself for not getting a picture of the comical trio, as I'm sure they'd have been happy to mug for the camera. I don't think I have photojournalist in my blood. I could watch E.T. probe Bigfoot in my backyard and never think to pull out my phone.

I hoped that was the last of the roadblocks. Thirty minutes later, a pickup truck full of armed, masked military guys labeled "Polícia Regional" passed me, heading the opposite way. I assumed they must be on the same team as the group taking tolls back in Oxchuc.

I came around another bend to see three women holding a string across the road, laden with little trinkets to ensure I saw it. I stopped for the women. One had a bunch of tiny bananas, which looked ripe enough. Fine. I'll support the local economy and buy some tiny bananas. Twenty pesos, the last of my change, good value. Okay, thanks ladies, Buenos días!

But they didn't budge. Wait, that wasn't enough? They managed to communicate that the lady holding the string expected to get paid, too, for the service of holding the string, apparently. My patience started to run out. I put the car in gear and crept forward. The string lady looked perturbed but finally let go.

Looking back, I'm annoyed at myself for losing my cool. I pissed off some locals on their extremely dicey home turf. I should have just paid the string lady.

My next move was even dumber.

A few minutes later, I came up to another string roadblock. This one was operated by three kids who already had a car stopped. The kids didn't see me approach until it was too late. As they dropped the string to let the first car go, I pulled up behind it and barreled through before they could pick up the string again.

Ha! You snooze, you lose, kids!

Then I thought about what I had just seen. One of the girls saw me coming, bent down to grab the string, stumbled a little, caught herself, and then thought better of it.

I still shudder at the image of her stumbling a few feet from my tire as I sped past. I could have injured or killed that little girl over a few pesos. I probably wouldn't have had to live with the guilt for long, though, as I would have been killed by an angry mob.

It didn't fully hit me how badly things could have gone until about three months after my trip when news came out that two European cyclists had gone missing along this same stretch of road. Their bodies were eventually discovered at the bottom of a ravine near two wrecked bikes. The initial police report determined it was an accident—until they took a closer look and found a bullet hole through one cyclist's skull. As of the writing of this book, there have been no arrests. Reports of robberies and more cars getting smashed up on the Ocosingo Road have come out, but no more murders.

Shaken from the experience with the kids, I resolved not to run any more roadblocks of any kind, ever. Thankfully, that was the last one of the drive.

I'm glad I got to see the gorgeous scenery. But if I ever need to get myself between San Cristóbal and Palenque again, I think I'll take the road more traveled.

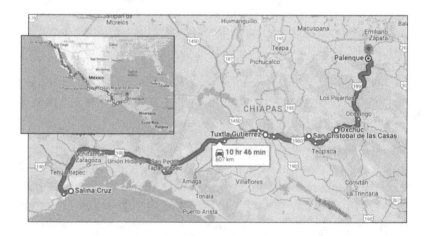

PART THREE

MAYA HOMELAND

Architecture, sculpture, and painting, all the arts which embellish life, had flourished in this overgrown forest; orators, warriors, and statesmen, beauty, ambition, and glory, had lived and passed away, and none knew that such things had been, or could tell of their past existence.

— JOHN LLOYD STEPHENS, *INCIDENTS OF TRAVEL IN CENTRAL AMERICA, CHIAPAS, AND YUCATAN*

CHAPTER 20

ANCIENT ALIENS AND GOLDEN MEANS

THE BIG REVEAL of the Palenque ruins couldn't be a stronger contrast to arid, hilltop Monte Albán. A dozen black-and-white stone structures nuzzle against a jungle backdrop that seems poised to reclaim the site the moment groundskeepers turn their backs. A raised platform supports a seventy-five-foot tower and a complex of structures known as the Palace. The Temple of the Inscriptions, one of the iconic pyramids in the Maya world, looms directly across from the Palace—as if locked in some eternal standoff.

The Temple of the Inscriptions (left) and the Palace (right)

I learned my lesson from Monte Albán and opted for a guide this time. My guide, Fabio, led me along an overgrown path, explaining that only 30 of the 1,500 or so buildings at Palenque have been excavated, and the site gets twelve *feet* of rainfall a year. As we navigated the underbrush, I found it easy to imagine I was a nineteenth-century explorer, hacking my way through the jungle into the unknown. I also got to hear Fabio speak Maya with his compatriots, which was easily worth the price of admission. Imagine touring the Pyramids of Egypt while your guide speaks a derivation of the same language the Pharaohs spoke.

Palenque, which the Maya called Bàak', was a prominent Maya city-state in the first millennium CE. Situated on the western edge of the Maya world, Palenque served as a vital trading conduit between the civilizations of Central Mexico and the Maya kingdoms of the Yucatán peninsula and Petén jungle. Palenque's inscriptions, carved onto monuments and large stone tablets called stelae, contain some of the most detailed accounts of Maya politics, warfare, and mythology ever found and are responsible for much of our current knowledge about the ancient Maya world.

In 1952, Mexican archaeologist Alberto Ruz Lhuillier discovered the lavish tomb of King K'inich Janaab' Pakal, hidden deep within the Temple of the Inscriptions. Pakal's tomb spawned a fascination with the Maya similar to the frenzy over King Tut's tomb in 1922.

Pakal's tomb appeared again in popular culture when it was featured in the 1968 Book *Chariots of the Gods*, which earns the dubious distinction of kicking off the ancient aliens craze. The author proposed that Pakal was an ancient astronaut—based on the as-yet undeciphered inscriptions carved into his elaborate sarcophagus—and likened Pakal's pose to that of the Mercury astronauts.

Aliens, Africans, Atlantians—no theory was too fanciful, as long as it didn't include the ancestors of people who still lived among the ruins and occupied the bottom rung of post-colonial society. The idea that their lineage could have built the great cities of Mesoamerica was a bridge too far.

When scholars finally cracked the code of Maya hieroglyphs in the early 1970s, the sarcophagus and countless other writings made clear that while Pakal was a great king who reigned for 68 years—which seems to put him among the longest-tenured monarchs in world history—he was still a man with human parents. He did not arrive from space. It's comical to imagine aliens capable of interstellar travel zipping around the galaxy in something as cramped as the original Mercury capsule.

*King Pakal working the spaceship controls, as depicted on
his sarcophagus lid*

The fixation on aliens blended into a general fascination with Maya mythology and spirituality known as "Mayanism," which produced the original claim that the ancient Maya predicted the world would end on December 21st, 2012. If you're reading this, you're most likely aware that the world did *not* end in 2012—possibly thanks to John Cusack. We're still looking into it.

Were the Maya wrong? Well, it depends on whom you ask. Most scholars think the Maya never predicted any kind of cataclysm. What *is* known is that in 2012, the Maya "long count" calendar, which they likely inherited from the Olmecs, essentially does a big odometer reset to 13.0.0.0.0. The 13 in the first digit represents a b'ak'tun—the calendar's largest unit—equal to 144,000 days or 394.26 years. Thirteen b'ak'tuns is roughly 5,125 years.

In Maya mythology, the previous world, which existed before the Maya, ended after **its** 13th b'ak'tun, on August 11th, 3,114 BCE. Thirteen b'ak'tuns from that Maya genesis date is December 21st, 2012. It boggles my mind that we know these things to such precision from a bunch of carved stone tablets and the very few sacred Maya codices (books) that the Spanish didn't burn.

What scholars find precious little evidence for, however, is the idea that the ancient Maya thought *their* world was going to end in 2012. For the Maya, the end of a b'ak'tun was a time for regrowth and change, not necessarily an apocalypse. Modern Maya still use one of the three ancient calendars—but not the long count calendar. So, they were nonplussed by the 2012 hullabaloo.

Fabio and I climbed up to the Palace courtyard, then followed a vaulted passageway that burrowed deep into the raised platform. The naturalistic depictions of jaguars, snakes, warriors adorned with fancy headdresses, and curved glyphs along the walls felt familiar, like something from the recesses of my childhood.

Fabio showed me how Palenque had the equivalent of flush toilets—powered by a large aqueduct that still runs through the site. As something of a climax to the tour, he squatted over the little hole in the platform where the Maya did their business. The aqueduct and running toilets reminded me of a tour of Pompeii—minus the part where the guide pantomimes the act of pooping. That's a Palenque value-add.

Fabio demonstrating that you better have good aim to use Palenque's flush toilets

After the toilet grand finale, I was left to my own devices. I pondered a steep, zigzagged stairway winding uphill to a building that resembled a giant stone house. The entrance had a high vaulted portico and what looked like chimneys on the roof. I dubbed it the Hansel and Gretel house.

Historians know this structure as the Temple of the Foliated Cross, part of three buildings arranged in a triangle symbolizing the sacred hearthstones of the comal. Archeologists are particularly enamored with these buildings for their cutting-edge architecture, some of the finest in the Maya world. The Temple of the Foliated Cross was built using an innovative double-vault construction technique.

The Hansel and Gretel House—a.k.a. the Temple of the Foliated Cross

The Cross Group and other buildings at Palenque make liberal use of the golden mean and other sacred geometry ratios—like the square root of 2, 3, and 5—which show up in ancient buildings and appear in nature.

The golden mean, or golden ratio, is essentially the ratio of the sides of a rectangle—such that if you remove a square out of the rectangle, you get a new rectangle of the same proportions, albeit smaller and rotated ninety degrees.

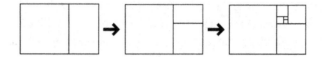

The remaining rectangle can be divided into a square and another similar rectangle; repeat to infinity. Nature uses this mathematical trick to create spiral seashells and flowers.

No mention of a unit of measure has ever been discovered in Maya writing, nor do their buildings seem to conform to a standard measure. According to Dr. Barnhart (hereafter known as *Fact-checker Ed*), it's possible the Maya had no fundamental unit of measure and instead used ratios in their construction. Some studies suggest people find buildings that make use of these ratios more visually appealing. All I know is that I was captivated by the Temple of the Foliated Cross in a way that reminded me of the Pantheon in Rome—another building famous for its use of the golden mean and sacred geometry.

When modern Maya build their traditional houses, they still use ropes to trace arcs from a fixed point and intersect them to mark distance—as one might have done with a protractor in grade school. It makes perfect sense to me that this combination of cartesian and polar coordinates would yield all sorts of beautiful mathematical shortcuts—which Mother Nature is happy to incorporate. I could even be convinced that the nature inside my brain resonates on some level when viewing a physical object constructed with these ratios. I know *something* deeply aesthetic is going on.

I wandered to the end of the cleared section of the compound, then climbed some ancient steps to another raised platform. A small fence at the top marked the end of the public portion of the site. Beyond the fence, I could see more buildings poking through the ground foliage.

I joined a small group soaking in the golden hour on a high platform. The view was so mesmerizing I couldn't process it all in one sitting. I can see why so many feel this is a magical place. I could have easily spent a few more hours contemplating the view from my perch, but a park steward announced it was closing time and began herding us stragglers toward the exit.

MÉRIDA

Next, I headed to the city of Mérida, where I hoped to get my foot examined at Star Médica, reputedly one of the best hospitals in Mexico. Along the way, I got my first glimpse of the Gulf of Mexico, which looked as brown and lackluster as it does in Galveston, Texas. Nevertheless, I'll always have a soft spot for the dingy Gulf—my first encounter with the ocean.

I wanted to stay near Star Médica in case I needed to return over multiple days. I found a City Express **Jr.** (whatever that means) on booking.com. In a few minutes, I pulled up to the belly of the beast. The building had the same branding as a regular City Express but with a slightly different color scheme and "**Jr.**" tacked on to the exterior signage.

Allow me to briefly channel the late great Bill Hicks: If your crowning career achievement is adding "Jr." to "City Express," or if you find yourself in a corporate boardroom pitching hard for Double-Fisted Bacon Cheeseburger Ruffles (which is a real thing I did not make up) or Cookies and Cream Oreos, you might want to re-examine your life's trajectory. Oreos *are* cookies and cream, Brad. You're stuffing them with crushed-up versions of themselves. It's wrong.

So, I said not today, Satan. At the risk of losing bland comfort, I'm going to find a hotel with some character. Maybe I'll even get lucky and stumble onto a traveler hot spot.

I found a hotel called La Quinta Real, one of the only other reasonable options in the area. When Google Maps directed me into a gated residential neighborhood, I started to suspect something was amiss. It turned out "La Quinta Real" was a bedroom in someone's house. I suspect they gamed booking.com to make the listing look like a hotel.

My room had character to spare. The bed was of the old-school super-squeaky-frame variety. The curvy lacquered-wood dresser and matching nightstands would have felt very comfortable in my grandmother's house. Lace doilies on all flat surfaces added a nice touch. I got a feeling that *La Quinta Real* may have been home to somebody's Nana until she passed away—hopefully not too recently.

The owners were a very nice middle-aged couple who spoke zero English, allowing me to practice my Spanish. I made pleasantries and inquired about Mérida and Star Médica. They also taught me how to say I have pain in my heel: "Tengo dolor en mi talón."

Mérida sits on the Northeastern tip of the Yucatán peninsula—a perfect location during colonial times for trade with Mexico to the West, the US to the north, and the Caribbean and Europe to the East. Mérida's key historical export was *sisal*: rope or twine made from yucca fibers. Sisal twine can be boiled to make soft but surprisingly strong fabric products like hammocks that feel like yarn.

With all this mercantile opportunity, it is said that turn-of-the-century Mérida was home to more millionaires than any city in the world. The older part of Merida felt like a combination of New Orleans and Beverly Hills, with second-story balconies lining the immaculate streets and pristine stonework on all the buildings.

The next morning, I showed up at Star Médica, prepared to spend the day if necessary. I was directed to a combination urgent care and emergency room, which was busy but still nowhere near the chaos of a Los Angeles emergency room. Within a half hour, I saw a doctor who listened to my story and agreed that an X-ray would be a good idea.

The X-ray showed a bone spur that looked like a small hook protruding from the inside of my heel toward the front of my foot. The spur made *mi talón* actually look like a talon.

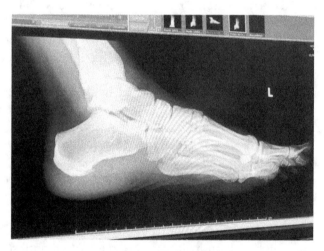

Don't mess with mi talón!

The doctor gave me a prescription for muscle relaxers and strong ibuprofen. He told me to put Icy Hot on my heel and gave me some calf-stretching exercises. He **did not** recommend I tape my heel, as I had been doing. I was in and out in under two hours, and the whole thing cost 2,000 pesos ($100). I left very impressed with the system.

Later, I went online and discovered that bone spurs and plantar fasciitis are common companions. The treatment for plantar fasciitis matched what he told me: try stretching, then maybe a cortisol shot down the road, then surgery as a last resort.

Plantar fasciitis is inflammation caused when the muscle that runs under the foot is stretched beyond its normal capacity. It's unclear if a bone spur is a symptom or a cause, but they seem to go together. One problem could be that my left leg was generally curled up underneath me while driving, which may have caused the calf muscle to contract. This was the one time I regretted not having a manual transmission, which would have kept my left leg busy in Mexican traffic.

At least I was no longer operating from my self-misdiagnosis of "policeman's heel." Unfortunately, this meant I was officially out of the Patagonia expedition, although I'd been suspecting that for some time.

I had set aside all day for the hospital but found myself free by 11 a.m., so I went for my first oil change of the trip, got my car washed, and then wandered around a mall basking in the sweet, sweet air conditioning.

CANCÚN

The following day, I said goodbye to the nice family at "La Quinta Real" and headed to Cancún, where I was to pick up my friend in two days. For my one full day in Cancún, I took a ferry to Isla Mujeres (Women Island). I was disappointed to find that, while the island had many women as advertised, it also had plenty of dudebros. I feel that should be in the brochure.

I wandered much of the island, including some sleepy neighborhoods running along a malecón on the far side. The beach was just as breezy but maybe five degrees cooler than Playa San Augustín, which was perfect for me. At sunset, I found myself at a little beach bar that made one, two, three of the best piña coladas I've ever had.

As one does, I took a lovely photo of my piña colada against the sunset backdrop, framed by the thatched roof of the beach bar. Of all the sweeping vistas, dramatic ruins, and other stuff I personally found fascinating on the trip—that picture garnered the most interaction on social media. Many of my friends from the Midwest had either been to Isla Mujeres, or they had heard of it and were hoping to go, or they just loved the tropical scene.

Sunset from Isla Mujeres

Which I get. If you live somewhere like Kansas City or Pittsburgh and get a week off in January, the last thing you and the family need is a big, crazy driving adventure. You just want to park your toes in warm sand and decompress for a few days. Then, once you're nice and relaxed, maybe look for an activity or a day trip with the kids.

So, while it's easy for overlanders and backpackers to disparage a place like Cancún, I understand that it makes perfect sense for many people. I just don't know how to do beach vacations—as we've clearly seen.

Eventually, I wobbled out of the beach bar and took the ferry back to Cancún, where the next day would bring a whole new phase of my trip: traveling with other humans.

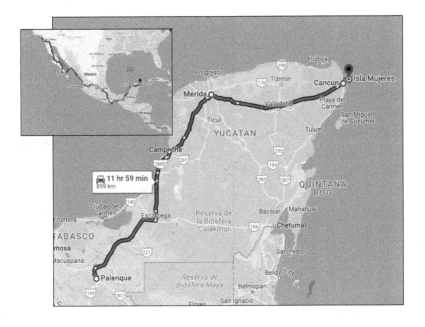

CHAPTER 21

POOR TULUM

FOR SUCH A TINY AIRPORT, Cancún makes knowing where to wait for someone impressively confusing, compounded by my friend Diana's lack of cell phone coverage.

Diana and I had worked together for years on multiple high-stress projects. She could be a bit high-strung as a project manager, and I'm no picnic to manage by anyone's account, but we'd always pushed through and worked it out. I assumed this trip would be no different. Plus, she'd lived in Baja for a few years as a teenager and picked up fluent Spanish, which could always come in handy.

Eventually, I saw a tall blonde in the distance towing a large suitcase and correctly guessed it must be her. We hugged and said our hellos and headed south to Tulum.

The Yucatán doesn't offer much to see from the road other than endless, flat Florida-esque greenery dotted with signs for resorts, amusement parks, and natural freshwater pools called cenotes (pronounced like sih-NO-tay).

The billboards for a place called Xel-Há, in which exuberant children careened down a spiral water slide set against the backdrop of a Maya pyramid, confused me. Was this a ruin or a water park? It turns out there are so many Maya ruins in the Yucatán that some of the lesser sites have given way to amusement parks. You can still visit the crumbling "Prehispanic Wall" at Xel-Há when you want a break from zip lines and water slides. According to their website: "Although the majesty of the old structure has been reclaimed by nature, its echoes still sound off in Xel-Há for the amazement of future generations." I have to say, that's quality blurb.

The next day, we left Tulum to pick up Diana's friend Baron in Playa del Carmen, which sits between Cancún and Tulum. I put on some chill EDM (electronic dance music, a.k.a. "techno" if you're Gen X, a.k.a. "Do they ever start singing?" if you're a Boomer) that I was into at the time.

There is a backstory to this music: Diana was on this trip by virtue of taking the same layoff as me. On our way to get a celebratory drink after our last night of work, she expressed pleasant surprise at the music playing in my car. So, I figured we were set for a primary listening option, and we could always dabble in other stuff if the chill music got old.

Turns out she wasn't into it.

"Do you have anything else?" she asked.

"I thought you liked this kind of music. You seemed impressed I had it on back in LA."

"I was. That doesn't mean I want to listen to it."

"Okay. Hmmm. Well, you know we can't just plug in Spotify out here. I have about 5,000 random songs on my iPod, mostly from the mid-2000s —many of which suck, so we'll be doing a lot of skipping. Also, there are some CDs under your seat."

She pulled out the carrying case and flipped through the CDs—all from the '70s through around 1994—when I and the rest of the world stopped buying CDs. Admittedly not the most scintillating selection in 2018. She got to the last CD, closed the case, and sighed.

I played my last card: thirty of my favorite anthems, the best of the best, compiled into a playlist on my iPod appropriately titled "Songs that rock your dick in the dirt." This wouldn't put a dent in the trip, but it would kill a few hours at least.

She didn't like any of them.

Not the most auspicious start to a three-week road trip.

I hadn't met Baron before, but he seemed like an affable enough guy on the ride back to Tulum. Diana wanted to check out the fancy restaurants along the beach. I would have been thrilled with one of the cheaper, easier-to-access places in town, but I'm boring like that. The road narrowed and became crowded along the beach, with a lot of tight, makeshift parking. We peeked into several restaurants, finally settling on an upscale Italian place. There were no downscale or midscale options.

Our host led us to a beach dining area where rustic, distressed wood furniture littered the sand. Strands of lights drooped between gazebo-like structures and an empty door frame that brought to mind the odd piece of a house left standing after a tornado. Every surface had the same beach-worn finish and aesthetically optimal ratio of peeling paint to exposed gray wood. I remarked that it looked like a Restoration Hardware catalog had thrown up all over the beach. Diana called it "very boho," which I gathered must mean something like "trust fund hippie."

The food was fine, but nothing memorable. The highlight of my meal was watching the diners closest to the ocean gradually sink into the wet sand throughout their meal. The bill with a couple of bottles of wine came to $80 per person. Obviously, this is several multiples of my usual meal budget—especially when most of that price was clearly going to the decor. But it was our first night together, so I sucked it up. They're on a short vacation while I'm on a long road trip. Of course, our budgets are going to diverge.

I think I was just cranky from the long day of driving and still worried about getting my car out of that crazy beach scene. Tulum, unfortunately, had no Uber. Towns with and without Uber would become a stark dividing line throughout the trip. With Uber, I could relax, eat, and drink to my heart's content, then still be whisked home in whatever distressed state I'd gotten myself into. Without Uber, unless we were close to our lodging or near a taxi stand, I had to worry about driving home after dinner.

In the morning, we found a lovely coffee/breakfast spot everyone could agree on, then headed down to the beach. When we reached the sand, I took off my shirt. My companions did **not** go snow-blind, and not a single well-meaning local tried to drag me back to the sea to rejoin my pod of beluga whales. Mission accomplished. Everyone doubted my sunburn plan, but I knew what I was doing.

Later, we stopped at a beachside Thai place for ludicrously priced drinks and appetizers. From our vantage point, we could see scattered piles of seaweed up and down the beach. The whole east coast of the Yucatán has a problem with these increasingly prodigious seaweed blooms, known as sargassum. Sargassum blooms first arrived in Tulum in 2015 and have increased yearly. Crews clean it off the beach every night, then dump it in parts of town where locals live. I'm told it stinks for a few days, then disintegrates into dust and blows away. I can't imagine breathing in all that seaweed dust is healthy.

Diana, Baron, and I rented bicycles for the rest of the week, which gave us much-needed mobility and independence. They were free to hit up chichi beach spots for a two-hour cocktail lunch, while I was free to wolf down a few street tacos with a beer. When we did decide to do something together, I still got outvoted by two to one **a lot**. "Ah well," I told myself, "it's only one week. I can suck it up."

We spent one day at a popular local cenote, which offered multiple swimming, snorkeling, and diving locations. The grand finale of the snorkeling tour involved swimming through a short tunnel into a large underground chasm. Most of the light came from the tunnel we'd just swam through—bathing the chasm walls in dreamy flickering blue-green light. The ceiling was covered with bats. Cool, right? Underground tunnel to the bat cave! Then I looked around at the bat guano floating on the surface and picked up the ammonia smell of bat urine. I wasn't disappointed when our guide said it was time to go back through the tunnel.

That night, we hit up the beach area for drinks. Diana led us to a popular hangout she'd read about. The outdoor bar area featured swinging wicker chairs with big velvet pillows, various New-Agey adornments, and, of course, absurdly priced food and drinks. A pool table sat right on the sand, which I thought was cool until I realized it was the most out-of-balance pool table I'd ever played on.

I started wondering, "Who's buying all this faux hippie crap? None of the hippies I'd seen in Mazunte or San Pedrito would come near this place, even if they could afford it, which they can't. How can Tulum support this weird attempt at eclectic New-Age luxury, with prices that make Cancún and Playa del Carmen seem budget by comparison?"

Before the trip, I'd heard about Tulum as an artsy hippie rendezvous place, so I pictured something like Mazunte. However, once I was on the trip, I'd heard from other travelers that maybe those days were gone, that Tulum had become a victim of its own success.

Then I read that Tulum has been "discovered" by the young Hollywood party crowd and their ever-present hangers-on: the failsons and faildaughters of the global rich. Everything instantly clicked into place. Only the megayacht and private jet crowd—who **never** get called out for their bad taste—could buy into all this overpriced Disneyfied-hippie-boho shlock.

From everything I've read, you do **not** want these people invading your town. Justin Bieber isn't allowed back to the Tulum ruins after he reportedly "pulled down his underpants and tried to climb one of its off-limits structures"—which more or less sums up the sad state of affairs in poor Tulum.

It's not just the annoyance of the international fuckwit set with their $2,000-a-night hotel rooms and "Vibrational Concert for World Peace" multi-day beach ragers. The money they're bringing in is destroying the environment. Between Tulum's main drag and the beach lies a protected mangrove watershed—an ecologically important drainage for the whole region.

The Mexican government seems to be trying to do the right thing, passing laws to keep development out of this sensitive area. But the outrageous amount of money pouring in from private jet setters is bringing condo flippers and intense pressure to build. New developments are springing up on the edges of the protected area—breaking the law but greasing the right skids to get away with it. The article I read on this subject showed a picture of one of the quasi-rogue condo buildings, which I'm 95% sure is where we stayed. Great. I'm part of the problem.

Poor Tulum. You don't deserve this. Hopefully, the Rich Kids of Instagram get bored with you someday so you can return to your former life as a funky alternative to Cancún.

Who knows, maybe the seaweed inundation will turn out to be a blessing in disguise.

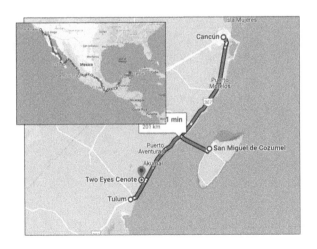

CHAPTER 22

TWO TO ONE

DIANA, Baron, and I had planned to visit the ruins of Chichén Itzá—an anticipated highlight of the trip—the day after our cenote excursion. However, each of us woke up with some malady. I had a sinus thing that would ultimately bug me for two months. Baron had a sore throat. Diana spent most of the day face down on the couch as the human embodiment of nausea. I suspected it was the bat cave, but Diana and Baron had sushi for dinner, which muddled the variables.

Diana tried to rally throughout the day, but each time, she'd throw up and then collapse in a heap back on the couch. She was really bummed about losing an entire day of her trip. I felt for her.

She felt much better the next day—lending credence to the food poisoning theory. Although I'm still pretty sure I had bat guano metastasizing in my sinuses for two months.

We arrived at Chichén Itzá to find the site thronged as expected. On entering the grounds, there it is—El Castillo, a.k.a. The Temple of Kukulkan—the Jude Law circa *Talented Mr. Ripley* of ancient pyramids. Simply mesmerizing.

El Castillo is a four-sided step pyramid with nine terraces and a staircase running up each side, topped with a square temple. When you add up all the steps, you get 364. If you count the temple on top as one shared step, you get 365—the number of days in the year. The Maya loved playing with numbers and celestial events like this. Every year, on the Spring Equinox, tourists gather at El Castillo to see the shadows on one stairway form an undulating, serpentine body that connects to a carved snake head at the base of the pyramid. Scholars disagree on whether this effect was intentional on the part of the Maya. There's no debate that it's a huge crowd-pleaser.

El Castillo at Chichén Itzá

Our energetic guide, Sergio, led us to a building known as the Nunnery —a name the Spanish tended to give any large rectangular structure.

The Hall of the Thousand (ahem, 200) Columns

Near the Nunnery sits a round building that served as the only dedicated celestial observatory in the Maya world. The Observatory has various doorways and stairs lining up with the equinoxes and solstices, including one for the farthest north passage of Venus.

Next, Sergio led us through the Hall of a Thousand Columns, built in a later phase in which the Itzá Maya seemed to share power with the Toltecs. Naturally, I spent the entire time tuning out our guide while I counted the columns. It turns out there are only 200. I knew it!

Radical! I'm gonna bring this on the bus tomorrow!

This corner of Chichén Itzá is overrun by jaguars—or at least the thunderous, lifelike jaguar roars emanating from ingeniously designed water pipes sold by a row of vendors. I imagined some poor prey animal nearby in a state of constant terror. Either that, or it learns to ignore the roars and stumbles onto an actual jaguar.

At one vendor stall, I was drawn to a solid wood carving of a half-human/half-skull emerging from a jaguar's mouth—which fifteen-year-old me would have thought was just about the coolest thing he'd ever seen. Later, I returned and pulled the trigger on the $30 purchase. Apparently, forty-eight-year-old me still had some fifteen-year-old in him, and I felt good about supporting the local craftspeople.

Sergio was kind enough to share his theories that the Maya were of Asian descent or at least Asian influence. He showed us a picture marking the similarities between a Chinese Terracotta Warrior and a figurine of a Maya warrior clad in cotton armor.

This is the fun part of getting a local guide: you get the basic story, plus whatever crazy theories they personally hold. If you want scholarly accuracy, you might book a top-tier guide through a tour agency. (I hear Fact-checker Ed does this sort of thing.) Otherwise, get a guide at the gate who seems fun, and enjoy the ride.

Hmmmm

Lastly, Sergio took us to Chichén Itzá's massive ball court. At 225 by 545 feet, the playing surface is nearly twice as large as the next largest Mesoamerican ball court ever found.

Sergio explained that the game was played until one team scored more points, or a team could get the ball through one of the hoops mounted at the top of the wall—*thirty feet above the ground*. Per the rules, a player couldn't throw or kick the ball; he had to hit it with his head, shin, or hip. I was astounded anyone could **ever** knock a ball that high.

As it turns out, most scholars agree it would have been impossible to play an actual ballgame on this court. They believe it was an oversized replica of a working court created for religious and royal ceremonies. The competitive ballgame—known as "Pitz" in classical Maya and "Ullamaliztli" in Nahuatl, among many other names—was generally played in residential neighborhoods.

The ball court at Chichén Itzá, with the impossible rings highlighted

For the Maya, the ballgame is integral to their origin story: the Popol Vuh. In the story, human twins enter a cave to play the ballgame against the Gods of the Underworld. Though hopelessly outmatched against the gods' might, the twins still pull out a victory through cunning and guile. Because of its underworld origins, the playing surface of a ceremonial ball court should appear sunken from its surroundings.

A Mesoamerican ballgame with three forward players and one "goalie" on each side

Remnants of over 1,200 ancient ball courts have been found from Northern Mexico to Nicaragua, the oldest dating to 1400 BCE. Most ball courts were I-shaped, often using a stucco surface to add bounciness. Teams lined up on each side of a centerline, past which only the ball could cross—somewhat like volleyball without a net. A team scored points by getting the ball past their opponent's end line at the back of the court. In a common variation, a team was awarded an instant victory if they could hit the ball through one of the vertical rings placed along the centerline. While the most common team size seems to be four to six players, the game could be played one-on-one or with dozens on each side. Other variations allowed players to hit the ball with their hands, while others involved smaller balls hit with bats.

The game itself could be brutal. The rubber ball, generally stuffed with lighter material but still quite dense, could weigh as much as a bowling ball. Players sometimes wore thick cotton pads to protect themselves. A Spanish priest described seeing players die from direct hits to the face and stomach. More commonly, players were maimed, which they wore as a badge of honor. The players were generally poor—as the game didn't pay. Their reward was fame.

Cities had teams and fierce rivalries. Nobles and commoners alike gambled on the games. Commoners sometimes lost their entire harvest or even had to sell themselves into slavery to settle ballgame debts. When a game concluded, nobles were expected to throw gifts to the winning team. If the nobles tried to sneak out early, ball players were allowed to tackle them and steal something.

The Spanish observed live ballgames at contact—which would have been the first time they ever saw a rubber ball or a team sport. I'm told there's a fairly popular team sport played in Spain today with a bouncy ball that players can't touch with their hands and a goal at each end. It's plausible that modern soccer owes its roots to the Mesoamerican ballgame, and by extension, so does rugby, American football, basketball, hockey, dodgeball, and any other team sport with a rectangular playing surface and goals at each end.

A basketball hoop has obvious similarities to the ring used in the Mesoamerican ballgame. There is no evidence that Dr. James Naismith, the inventor of basketball, was aware of the Mesoamerican ballgame. Yet, we can still wonder if the idea somehow filtered up from America's southern neighbor.

Today, Nahuatl speakers in the Mexican state of Sinaloa still play a version of the ballgame known as Ulama. Several other regions in the Maya world have revived the ballgame as a vital piece of their cultural heritage.

A modern Ulama player

Sergio told us that the winning team's captain was sacrificed after a match at Chichén Itzá. As evidence, he led us to a mural in which one of the team captains has snakes spurting out of his neck where his head should be. Based on his attire, scholars think Captain Snakes was likely Toltec, while the other captain was Maya. The ballgame may have been a source of heated rivalry between the Maya and the Toltecs.

My first thought was, "If I were the team captain, would I *really* be trying that hard to get the ball through that little ring?" Oh darn. Missed again. It seems like sacrificing the *losing* team's captain would produce a more exciting game.

Come to find out, there's no evidence *anyone* was sacrificed after the game, although it's certainly possible. One of Chichén Itzá's earliest guides admitted to making the whole idea up to titillate his guests.

Toward the end of the tour, I asked Sergio, "So, what really happened to the Maya? Why did they abandon this place?"

Without hesitation, he answered, "It was a peasant revolt. The commoners were fed up with being exploited by the elites. They went back to farming, and there was no one left who knew how to build pyramids."

I thought—maybe this explains why so many Americans are under the impression the Maya just *disappeared*. Our secondary school curriculum may have wanted to avoid planting ideas about peasant revolts in our impressionable young minds. Especially since most of the history textbooks I grew up with seemed to have been written in the tumultuous 1960s—as evidenced by the single page on the Vietnam War tacked onto the end of the book.

But as it often turns out, peeling back the onion layers of history reveals a more nuanced and messier picture. There are aspects of peasant revolt in the potential reasons the Maya abandoned their great cities. There are also political factions, natural disasters, famine, Old and New World diseases, esoteric reasons such as nobody remembering the long-dead ancestors the giant buildings were dedicated to, and even simply because it was the end of a b'ak'tun—the 394-year-cycle seen as a time for change and renewal in the Maya belief system. Chichén Itzá's abandonment coincides with the end of the 11th b'ak'tun. It's possible everyone just *walked away* from the great city.

After the tour, we were left to our own devices. I circled El Castillo and took pictures from up close, from far away, framed by trees, with foregrounds, etc. I would have been happy to sit there and soak up El Castillo all day.

Eventually, Diana and Baron dragged me away. Everyone was hungry, so we grabbed a bite at the on-site restaurant. I don't expect much from restaurants at major tourist attractions, but this one offered traditional Maya delicacies. I got salbutes de cochinita pibil—Maya-style crispy, puffy tortillas with shredded pork, tomatoes, pickled onions, and avocado. They were fantastic and perfectly hit the spot.

As we ate, I was pumped to talk about El Castillo and everything else we'd just seen, and how it contrasted with some of the buildings at Palenque. A few words into my story, Baron and Diana looked straight at me, then in perfect unison, looked down at their phones—completely tuning me out.

Flabbergasted, my first thought was, "I know I'm eight years older than you guys, but I don't think I'm quite into 'old man rambling story that doesn't go anywhere' territory yet."

To give them the benefit of the doubt, they each may have thought the other was listening to me.

Nevertheless, it was going to take some extra lung power to suck this one up. If this was a video game like Mortal Kombat—except instead of a life meter at the top of the screen, you could see my goodwill meter—I just took a Liu Kang bicycle kick to the face. I was still in the green but down significantly from 100%.

To really be fair, I should have addressed this slight when it happened. I could even have made the same joke about old man story hour. But, of course, I didn't do that. I abhor confrontation and rarely think that quickly on my feet. I prefer to let things fester and stew. I told myself to shake it off. Clearly, that failed, given I'm writing about it three years later.

On the drive back, I discovered Baron was a huge Pixies fan. So I put in a bootleg of a 1992 Pixies concert that I've listened to so many times the studio versions don't sound right anymore. We **cranked** that CD the whole way back to Tulum. For those unfamiliar, the Pixies are VERY LOUD; some might even say SCREECHY. I could tell Diana hated it and would have instantly vetoed the selection if it had been just her and me.

But hey, it's two to one—what can you do? ¯_(ツ)_/¯

That was an *extremely* satisfying car ride.

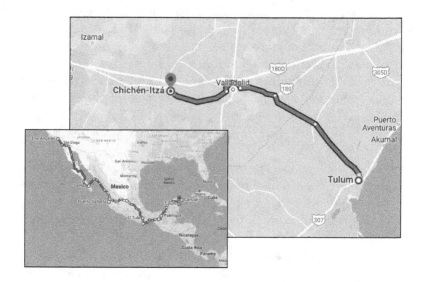

CHAPTER 23

GO SLOW

BARON left early in the morning to catch his flight. Loading up the car, Diana and I had our first little spat. I don't remember what started it. I just remember her saying, "What?"—as in, "**What** is your problem?" Apparently, I was being a pill.

I let her know that I didn't appreciate being constantly outvoted. I also brought up the cell phone incident at Chichén Itzá and how I dislike driving in silence. We didn't have any real breakthroughs, nor did I expect any. But it felt good to speak my mind and clear the air. We had worked together for years, dealing with the inevitable conflicts that crop up during intense projects. So, it wasn't like we barely knew each other. I thought it was a good talk and felt optimistic about the rest of the trip.

Our plan for the day was to check out the Tulum ruins, then head to Chetumal just north of the Belize border, where we would spend the night before crossing the border in the morning.

At the entrance to the ruins, we ducked through a low gate in the wall that opened up to an ancient causeway with buildings spread along each side. Some of the most impressive structures—including the dominant three-story temple, naturally known as "El Castillo"—sit on the edge of a sixty-foot bluff overlooking the sea. Several temples have outward-sloping walls that give off a vaguely drunken appearance. It's possible this angle protected them from collapse during hurricanes.

It took some willpower, but I resisted the urge to pull down my pants and climb on the buildings.

Tulum's Ceremonial Center

By around 800 CE, Tulum had grown from a small fishing village to a key trading port between the Yucatán and the Petén and, by extension, farther points south along the Caribbean coast. Obsidian, jade, feathers, cotton, cacao beans, and exotic treasures like turquoise and copper from as far as present-day Arizona all came through Tulum.

A reef just offshore provided abundant fishing and shelter for trading canoes but was tricky to maneuver, even in daylight. To test a theory that two small windows in the main temple could be used to navigate the reef at night, an archaeologist placed candles in each window, then set out in a canoe. Once he could see both candles, he was lined up to sail through a narrow gap in the reef—Maya ingenuity in action.

Five hundred years, almost to the day, before Diana and I toured the site, conquistador Juan de Grijalva first spotted Tulum. A priest described Tulum's buildings—gleaming in bright green, powder blue, and vermillion red—as "a village so large that Seville would not have appeared larger or better."

This encounter was the first time a European laid eyes on a New World city and the first time the populace of a Maya city saw a Spanish ship. The conquistadors had undoubtedly heard stories of the great cities on the mainland. But back then, European explorers entertained tales of cities made of gold, islands populated with Amazon women, and the lost city of Atlantis. This was the moment the Spanish **confirmed** that the New World was home to thriving cities with walls, towers, and temples.

Tulum continued as a working city and trading port after contact with the Spanish but was abandoned by 1600. Local Maya continued to visit the site to burn incense and pray for hundreds of years.

Tulum meets the sea

Back on the road, I started fiddling with the radio, hoping to find something Diana and I could both tolerate. Most stations were playing the traditional accordion-heavy stuff that makes me feel like I'm in a mid-priced Mexican restaurant back in the States. I stopped on one station in the low 90s and listened for a few seconds. We realized the DJ wasn't speaking Spanish, which meant she must be speaking Maya. Then, we found another station speaking Maya. As silly as it may sound, this was another *Eureka!* moment for me. The "disappeared" Maya still have multiple radio stations! I had to admit there was some upside to Diana's finicky musical tastes in that it forced us to explore our environment a bit more.

We took a side trip to Mahahual, a dowdy beach town just north of the border that seemed to cater to a more domestic crowd than Tulum or Cancún. There, we saw first-hand what happens to a beach that doesn't have the resources of Tulum to clear off the sargassum. Only a few hardy tourists waded through the carpet of seaweed to get to open water.

Mahahual—a beach with fluffy carpet for your toes

We arrived at Chetumal at sunset and pulled into what would be my last City Express of the trip. The next day would bring our first border crossing, which meant the Mexico sticker on my tailgate would finally have some company.

We slept in the next day. Getting into the car, Diana offered, "I see what you mean about that City Express checkout time."

Hah! See? It's not just me!

BELIZE

We planned to rendezvous with our friend Charlie in Belize City, then take the next ferry to the town of San Pedro on Ambergris Caye (pronounced like *Key*), the larger of two main tourist islands off the Belize coast. Ambergris Caye is actually the end of a long, marshy peninsula that originates in Mexico. No roads connect to the Belize side of the peninsula, so it's effectively an island.

I was a little nervous for my first real border crossing of the trip, but the border couldn't have been sleepier. Belize is the only country in Central America whose official language is English, which smoothed the process.

You immediately know you're in another country the first few hundred yards into northern Belize. The standard home changes from Mexican pueblo style to colonial style in Caribbean pastel colors, usually on stilts. We shared the drive through lush lowland farms with convoys of trucks piled high with sugar cane.

I found a local station playing fun modern reggae or dancehall or raggamuffin or whatever it's called. The language is a creole that supposedly contains a decent amount of English, but they could be aggressively reading the ingredients of Kraft Macaroni and Cheese for all I could make out. I looked up the lyrics to one song, only to find out the rapper was very agitated about breadfruit for some reason. Thankfully, Diana was into the music, too, which meant we were set for road music in Belize. Yay! No more driving in silence. Score another point for not just riding around in a self-curated music bubble.

The dominant ethnicity in Belize is "West Indian"—a loose mix of African, native Caribbean Islander, European, and South Asian descent (mostly the first two). West Indians form a metaculture encompassing the Caribbean and the east coast of Central America. They generally speak a creole of English, Spanish, French, or Dutch mixed with some native West African languages. English-speaking West Indians, from my limited experience, seem to have their own vibe versus Spanish-speaking West Indians. Think Reggae versus Reggaeton. The English-speaking subculture stretches from Central America to Jamaica, the Bahamas, Barbados, and the Virgin Islands—1,500 miles from Belize.

The rest of the population of Belize draws from a hodgepodge of indigenous Maya, Hispanic, Chinese, Koreans, and Russian Mennonites who speak Plautdietsch, an archaic Germanic language influenced by Dutch. The tiny nation's most unique subculture, the Garifuna, are descended from the survivors of a slave vessel that shipwrecked in 1675 off the coast of St. Vincent island—who then intermarried with local Carib Indians. Their offspring escaped colonial persecution and slavery to found coastal fishing villages from Belize to Nicaragua while maintaining their unique mix of African and Carib cultures.

One of the reasons I don't fantasize about chucking it all to go live on a tropical beach, other than sunburns and my dislike of heat, is that I got my "Jimmy Buffett Syndrome" out of the way early in life. Immediately after college, my best friend Ande and I moved to St. Thomas in the US Virgin Islands—my first immersion into another culture. We planned to teach school, which only requires a bachelor's degree in the USVI. However, upon hearing our roommate's epic struggles to corral his unruly students, including one student pouring formaldehyde in his coffee, we decided to just wait tables and party instead.

The people, sights, accents, and music of Belize instantly made me pine with nostalgia for that crazy fun in my life. There's no way I could have made a life in the USVI, though. I'd end up like one of those old sea captains who looks like a dehydrated pomegranate.

One commonality the USVI shares with Latin America is norms with regard to polite conversation. In St. Thomas, if you didn't say "good afternoon" before asking for something in a store, you risked the attendant making a sucking sound between her teeth and tongue (a.k.a. "sucking her teeth at you")—a grave personal insult. I wondered if Latin Americans had been doing some similar subtle tic every time I rudely forgot to make pleasantries. In either case, I've concluded that offering a smile and greetings before casual commerce is an objectively superior way to live.

We pulled into Belize City to meet up with our mutual friend and ex-coworker, Charlie. I arranged to leave my car in the Marriott parking lot for a few days while we were on the Cayes. Then, we made our way inside the hotel, where Charlie greeted us with big hugs.

We walked to the ferry terminal and shared another important ceremonial moment—first beer in a new country. Belize's national beer is called Belikin, which means "Route to the East" in Maya. The beers seemed to go down awfully fast, even for me. I kept picking up the weirdly heavy empty bottle, thinking it still contained beer. Finally, I looked at the label—9 ounces! What the hell? To make it the same size as a 12-ounce bottle, they simply add more glass. That's not right. I had half a mind to scribble out a nasty note to the Belize Ministry of Standards and Practices, assuming such a thing exists. But then our ferry to Ambergris Caye arrived.

AMBERGRIS CAYE

We settled into our condo, which offered a jaw-dropping view of the turquoise Caribbean, relaxed a bit, then headed out to find some dinner. On the way, we came across a circular crowd of people in a state of frenzy. We had to climb onto a pile of seaweed to see the source of their excitement, which turned out to be a bingo-type game with a live chicken serving as the random element. For good luck, players were directed to blow on the chicken's butt before releasing it onto the bingo board—which is just common sense, really. Purportedly, all chickens used in the game were sent to a rescue farm to live out their natural lives in peace and harmony.

Chicken Butt Bingo on Ambergris Caye

As enthralling as this was, our hunger got the better of us, so we pressed on, eventually landing at a casual beachside establishment. Our waiter led with his standard line, "Here in Belize, we have one rule: no shirt, no shoes, no problem!" I realized how different the tourist experience is when I can banter with locals in my native tongue. In Spanish, I could establish where you were from, how many kids you had, and *maybe* what kind of work you did. I was a long way from making casual jokes with the waitstaff. While my Spanish would improve dramatically throughout the trip, Belize drove home that I'd need to live in a Spanish-speaking country for a few years to get over that conversational hump.

As we wandered the island the following day, I fell in love with the charming old wooden houses rising right out of the sand. In the afternoon, we went on a snorkeling trip that ended amidst a nurse shark feeding frenzy. Nurse sharks' mouths are recessed, so they can't bite. Still, it was pretty wild to be engulfed by a writhing, twisting mass of sandpaper-skinned seven-foot-long sharks. I learned later that the practice of feeding nurse sharks for tourists is discouraged. I can't seem to help being part of the ecological problem wherever I go.

That night, for dinner, we tried a place in the heart of town called Caramba, which we had noticed earlier putting out fresh seafood in display tubs. I'm not generally the biggest crab fan, as I'm a lazy eater and don't like to work for my food. But I saw people at another table eating stone crab claws that looked so good I decided to give them a try.

Yay me. The claw meat was succulent, sweet, creamy, buttery, custardy, and sublime. With each bite, I did a marble-mouthed impression of Meg Ryan in the iconic diner scene from *When Harry Met Sally*. The buzz from the excellent mojitos certainly contributed to my taste bud mass-orgasm.

I still dream about those stone crab claws—my favorite meal of the entire trip. Every night thereafter, I tried to nudge my compatriots back to Caramba, but they understandably wanted to try other places. When I'm traveling and stumble onto a place like Caramba, my culinary curiosity evaporates. I'm done trying new places. I don't expect my traveling companions to share the same quirk, but it's nice when they do.

The next few days were similar—beachy days, buzzed afternoons, and blurry nights. I enjoyed interacting with the local islanders. I could speak their language, more or less, and their accents and music made me feel like I was back in the USVI.

On our last full day together, we rented a golf cart to explore some of the farther reaches of Ambergris Caye. We headed to Sunset Beach on the island's west side, which involved a long, bumpy cart ride over a gravel causeway.

Sunset Beach turned out to be nothing like we anticipated. A few families seemed to be finishing their picnics, and the lone beach bar was about to close. We had hoped to eat dinner on Sunset Beach, which is a bit of a challenge when there is no restaurant.

I'm not sure why you name a place *Sunset Beach* and then close everything before the sun goes down. I washed down some banana bread with a beer while Charlie grumped and Diana took selfies against the admittedly gorgeous sunset. Then we piled back into the golf cart for the forty-five-minute ride back to civilization in hungry, bumpy silence.

Again, I pleaded my case for Caramba, but Diana and Charlie wanted to try a food truck pavilion. Of course, neither was happy with their meal. We did make it to Caramba later, but the kitchen had just closed.

Ay, Caramba! You will live in my dreams forever. Maybe it was better this way. I'd be sad if a second helping of stone crab claws didn't live up to my original mojito-fueled memory. A great meal is such a subjective experience. It takes phenomenal food **and** the right moment. The moment was far from ideal that night.

An abandoned boat on Caye Caulker (not our ferry)

The following morning, we all got on the same ferry. Charlie had to return to the real world while Diana and I stopped off to explore Caye

Caulker. Unlike Ambergris Caye, Caye Caulker is so small that no vehicle larger than a golf cart is allowed. The island's official motto is "Go Slow."

Diana and I wandered the island, soaking in the relaxed vibe and colorful, rustic beach scenes. We found a sleepy bar to while away the afternoon and even found a place with stone crab claws for dinner. They were fine but not quite orgasmic.

Slow Going on Caye Caulker

Charlie was bummed when we told him about Caye Caulker. Apparently, sleepy, laid-back *Go Slow* was exactly how he'd envisioned his vacation. Instead, he got chicken butt bingo.

Having seen both islands—next time, I'd do it the other way around—spend three nights on Caye Caulker and one night on Ambergris Caye, mainly for the stone crab claws. After Caye Caulker, I started seeking out car-free islands.

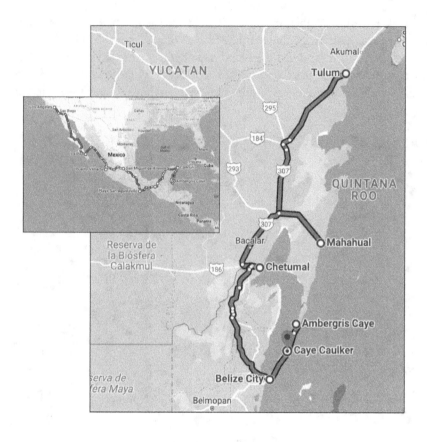

CHAPTER 24

LATE-STAGE EMPIRE

DIANA and I woke up early and caught the ferry from Caye Caulker to Belize City. We had ample time to get to our accommodations in the southern end of the country, so I checked out the nearby Belize Museum while she shopped in town. My walk to the Belize Museum passed a few dozen old colonial mansions—some crumbling, some still in good repair. I'm not sure how I'm supposed to feel about these houses, as they represent a legacy of slavery and oppression. They are quite photogenic, if poignant.

The Belize Museum, housed in an old jail, is easily the smallest national museum I've ever visited. In a room dedicated to the slave trade, a life-size recreation of the quarters on an African slave ship caught my attention. The exhibit described the unimaginably deplorable conditions, which generally killed a third to half of the captives in transit. It occurred to me that I couldn't recall ever seeing an exhibit quite like this in the United States. Being in the presence of a life-size replication of a slab of wood, with ropes and chains that were used to bind a human being in place for months, was a visceral experience.

Belize, known as British Honduras until 1973, didn't gain full independence until 1981. For a time in the early 1800s, Belize was a British slave territory, while Spanish-controlled Guatemala to the west had abolished slavery. Museum exhibits illustrated how people escaping slavery in Belize slogged through nightmarish terrain to reach the relative safe harbor of Guatemala's Petén jungle.

After the museum, I rendezvoused with Diana back at the Marriott, where I managed to leave behind my hat and sunglasses—both of which are impossible to find for my giant head in Latin America. From then on, whenever someone came to join me on the trip, I proactively bought a new hat online and had it shipped to them ahead of time.

Belize City south of the river had been described as a high-crime, "no go zone" by almost everyone I asked. I'm sure it would have been fine to drive through. But you never know when Google Maps is going to send you down a dead-end hot block that requires a 17-point U-turn to extricate yourself from. So, we gave the area a wide berth on our way to the town of San Ignacio.

SAN IGNACIO

Before this trip, most of my knowledge of Belize came from John McAfee, of McAfee Virus Protection crapware fame. Mr. McAfee cashed out his chips and moved to Belize to do bath salts with prostitutes, kill his neighbor's dogs, and participate in other activities that I'd rather not mention in this book. (If you're still curious, there's a Netflix documentary. You've been warned.) McAfee owned property near our Airbnb. So, we expected a relatively upscale enclave and were not disappointed.

Our two-bedroom bungalow shared a campus with three other cabins of various sizes. The grounds overflowed with colorful foliage and various flowering plants. A small river, the Mopan, ran through the back of the property. Steps led down to a bathing platform and rope swing over the river. The setting couldn't have been more idyllic if it was a painting.

An avuncular West Indian gentleman with curly gray hair emerged from one of the cabins. He introduced himself as Ernesto, the caretaker, and explained he was there for anything we needed. Ernesto was one of those people you want to hug even though you've only known him for five minutes. He gave us a tour of the immaculate bungalow while he explained how everything worked.

I immediately surmised we'd want to extend an extra night, which we could steal from our Guatemala stay, and I told Ernesto as much. Diana looked at me, surprised. I wasn't trying to decide for her. I just knew what her answer would be. I asked her, "Do you **not** want to spend an extra night here?" She looked around, thought about it for a second, then concurred. Ernesto also said he could arrange a driver to take us to the Lamanai ruins in the center of the country on the second full day of our stay. A low-key, relaxing first day in paradise sounded lovely.

The best Airbnb ever—in Bullet Tree Falls (look for Ernesto in the listing)

We got settled in, then headed into town looking for something to eat. San Ignacio is a charming, gritty little city—with crowded streets and healthy hustle and bustle. We stumbled onto a popular restaurant called Ko-Ox Han-Nah, which may or may not mean "Let's Go Eat" in Yucatec Maya—depending on whether you believe the restaurant or people who translate Maya for a living.

While waiting for our food, a young woman who had seen me parking on the street approached our table and asked, "Are you an overlander?"

Finally! This was the moment I'd been waiting for the whole trip—a normal mortal tourist—awestruck that I had **literally driven my own car** to [insert exotic location here].

"Why, yes. Yes, I **am** an overlander. What is your question, my child?"

It turned out she and her boyfriend were considering a similar drive and wanted any advice I could give them. I told her it's safer than you probably think, illustrating my point with the anecdote that I had shared the road with families, including kids, on bicycles. I also told them to bring camping equipment because they wouldn't want to miss out on magical places like San Pedrito in Baja.

I imagined that the farther I got from the US, the more attention simply being in my own car would garner. Sadly, this would be the only time on the trip I got to bask in overlander limelight.

Diana was underwhelmed by my newfound celebrity. I promised her I wouldn't forget the little people who knew me in the before times.

Belizean food is a hodgepodge of various African, Mexican, and indigenous influences. The country also has sizable East Indian and Chinese communities. The menu at Ko-Ox Han-Nah seemed to pull from a wide range of cuisines—from smoked pork tacos to shikar vindaloo. I ordered a "Belizean favorite"—coconut rice and stewed pork, which came out succulent with a perfect balance of sweet, salty, and sour flavors. Diana couldn't stop raving about her smoked pork tacos.

Having bought ourselves an extra day in San Ignacio, we slept in the next morning and, in the afternoon, checked out a nearby Maya ruin called Xunantunich. Accessing the ruins required transporting my FJ across the Mopan River on a ferry barely larger than my car. I had to take a leap of faith and assume that if they were in the business of dumping people's vehicles in the river, they'd probably get bad reviews on TripAdvisor or something.

Xunantunich was smallish but still had impressive pyramids, including another "El Castillo," which at 130 feet is the second tallest building in Belize—the tallest being another Maya temple. Xunantunich, in its day, was a large Maya city—rivaling its famous neighbors Caracol and Tikal.

El Castillo at Xunantunich—home of the Maiden of the Rock

Xunantunich means something like "Sculpture of Lady" or "Maiden of the Rock" in Yucatec Maya. The name was given to the site in the late 1800s, owing to a legend that a female apparition with glowing red eyes haunted the site. It was said she could be seen, dressed in all white, ascending El Castillo and then disappearing into the stone wall.

Archaeologists unearthed one of the largest royal tombs ever found in Belize at Xunantunich in 2016. At the bottom of a hidden stairway, they found a noble who died in his twenties adorned with jade jewelry, animal bones and teeth, ceramics, and obsidian weapons. If a tomb this rich can still be found after a thousand years of grave robbing and more than a century of continuous excavation at the site, imagine how much is still out there to find.

A couple shares a contemplative moment on the plaza at Xunantunich

Diana deserves credit for prodding me to see Xunantunich. I hadn't heard of the site and probably would have spent the day catching up on the internet in a coffee shop. After thronged Tulum and Chichén Itzá, Diana and I found Xunantunich relaxed and contemplative.

At least until the howler monkeys started up. Howler monkeys produce an ominous, piercingly loud, guttural roar that sounds like a death-metal singer getting sucked into a wood chipper. At an ear-splitting 128 decibels, howler monkeys are the loudest animals on land—not pound for pound—period. These furry little twenty-pound monkeys blast out more noise than a bull elephant or any big predator.

The loudest animal of all is the mantis shrimp, whose spring-loaded club-like "dactyls" generate over 200 decibels while blasting its prey to bits. The mantis shrimp's dactyls also clock the fastest movement in the animal kingdom (as fast as a .22 caliber bullet) and the most powerful force applied per square inch. On top of all that, mantis shrimp can see dozens of colors we can't even imagine. The Amish call this type of show-off behavior "grossfeelich." It is rightly frowned upon.

The single-record-holding howler monkeys have a specialized horse-shoe-shaped bone in their neck that amplifies sound coming from their throat. They tend to sound off together at dawn and dusk to mark their territory and avoid confrontations with rival groups.

Howler monkeys—built for sound

It is difficult to stay in contemplative mode when howler monkeys get going full swing. Your frontal lobe is saying, "Isn't this lovely? I'm immersed in the sounds of nature." But your amygdala is saying, "I'm in danger. Something in those trees is really pissed off." I can see how early New World explorers might have entertained King Kong myths, unable to wrap their heads around small monkeys putting out that much noise.

That night, Diana and I perused our TV options at the Best Airbnb Ever. One of the on-demand channels offered *Apocalypto*, the Mel Gibson-directed ancient Maya epic. Since we had just seen Xunantunich and planned to see Lamanai the next day, we figured it might be nice to learn a bit about the Maya world.

The movie's first fifteen minutes fit the bill—a slice of life in a Maya village, with playful hijinks and poignant moments. *Apocalypto* then turned into the bloodiest movie I've ever seen—with kidnappings, murders, and, above all, endless, lingering, painstakingly graphic scenes of hearts-ripped-out-of-chests, priests-bathed-in-blood human sacrifice. We came close to turning it off but felt invested for some reason.

Mel Gibson's bonk-you-over-the-head thesis is that the Maya by this point were in "late-stage empire." Commoners were fed up with being exploited by the ever-expanding elite leisure class. In the movie, our heroes from the village are kidnapped and brought to the big city to fill the insatiable need for new sacrifice victims. Along the way, they see famine and pestilence in the city's outer reaches. When they reach the city center, they see opulence and lounging courtesans who seem to have no function whatsoever. The outfits, makeup, and hairstyles are so overdone that it would be impossible for their wearers to even *participate* in actual work. Clearly, no parallels can be drawn with contemporary Renaissance-era royal courts across the Atlantic.

The leisure class in Apocalypto

Unsurprisingly, *Apocalypto* landed with a giant thud in the Mesoamerican academic community and the Maya world at large. Scholars groaned at the lurid violence, historical inaccuracies, and portrayals of Maya villagers as naked simpletons who somehow remained unaware of the giant stone cities they had shared the jungle with for a thousand years. And the idea that a common celestial event would send the city-dwelling Maya elites running around in a panic is laughable. Astronomy was their whole bag!

The Maya around the time of contact with the Spanish did practice human sacrifice but, by all appearances, on a much smaller scale than the Aztecs and other Mesoamerican civilizations. Making human sacrifice the central tenet of the movie seems gratuitous. Guatemala's Department of Race and Equality banned *Apocalypto* as racist and inflammatory. Nobel Peace Prize winner Rigoberta Menchú, Guatemala's internationally prominent indigenous rights advocate, refused to watch the movie, saying, "For my mental health, I don't watch violent movies because we've already suffered enough violence in Guatemala."

In a nod to the encounter at Tulum, *Apocalypto* ends with our villagers spotting Spanish ships just offshore as they're on the run for a new life, which means things just went from bad to worse. Given their ancestors are still around today, I guess the movie's only positive message is perseverance?

Diana and I agreed we would never look at those peaceful, contemplative pyramids quite the same—not with images of headless, blood-spurting bodies flopping down the steps. In summary, I don't recommend viewing *Apocalypto* the night before visiting a Maya ruin—or any pyramid-shaped structure, really.

LAMANAI

The Lamanai tour, described as "can't miss" by multiple sources, included a boat ride/riverine nature tour. On the water, our guide pointed out crocodiles, turtles, and various colorful birds. Along the way, we saw a few homesteads built by Dutch Mennonites, who began migrating to the area in 1790. I spotted several plainly dressed Mennonites toiling away in their field.

People lived at Lamanai for some 3,000 years, until the early 1800s—making it one of the longest continually occupied sites in the Maya world. Because Lamanai survived into the nineteenth century, we know the site's real name, except it's still been butchered. Lamanai means "drowned insect" in Yucatec Maya, which doesn't sound like the name of a glorious city. It turns out the actual name is Lam'an'ain, which means "submerged crocodile"—borne out by a preponderance of crocodile iconography around the site. A thirteen-foot carved limestone face adorned with a crocodile headdress serves as Lamanai's star attraction.

The Mask Temple at Lamanai

Unlike most Maya sites, which arrange their buildings around a ceremonial center with a sacred courtyard, Lamanai's monuments are laid out along the banks of the New River Lagoon. At thirty meters, Lamanai's High Temple, completed in 100 BCE, would have been the tallest building in Mesoamerica at the time. Lamanai was an important trading port for the region. Obsidian and jade came from present-day Guatemala. Cinnabar was mined in the mountains to the south. Salt, honey, and cacao made their way in from the coast.

On request, our tour guide was kind enough to howl at the howler monkeys until they howled back, which in turn set off every troop of howlers in central Belize. Naturally, I learned later that intentionally riling up the monkeys is frowned upon. My trail of ecological destruction continues.

That night, we headed back to Ko-Ox Han-Nah. I mixed it up this time and got the smoked pork tacos—which were mind-blowingly good. Ko-Ox would turn out to be my favorite restaurant of the entire trip.

I did not expect my best meal (stone crab claws at Caramba) **and** favorite restaurant of the trip to both be in Belize—which isn't exactly known as a world-class culinary hub—especially when I spent a month in Central Freaking Mexico and ate like a Roman Emperor. But that's the unpredictable magic of travel. For the record, Mexico probably holds spots two through ten on both lists.

Smoked Pork Tacos at Ko-Ox Han-Nah

The following day, we said goodbye to the Best Airbnb Ever and our beloved host, Ernesto. We both seriously pondered if we could squeeze in another day—or week. Despite our best brain-wracking, the math didn't work if we wanted to get Diana to Guatemala City for her flight in a week.

As we headed to the border, I had a request for Diana: "Look, this is our first real border crossing. It might get stressful. I may have to deal with random people aggressively hawking things. Guatemala has real crime, and I've heard this border town is sketchy. I don't need the extra stress of arguing with you while I'm also dealing with chaotic border stuff. Can we agree to be a team and support each other?"

She assured me that we would be a team.

I thought it was a good talk and felt optimistic about the day.

I parked at the border and realized I'd done a dumb thing. I'd been so good about spending all my Belize dollars that I had nothing left. Further-more, I had no loose change in USD, just a few $100 bills. These borders often have silly little things you have to spend $1 or $2 on—like spraying under your car for invasive species. Also, I wanted to buy a SIM card as soon as possible so I wasn't flying blind. Waving a $100 bill around asking for change in a dodgy border town didn't seem like the best idea. Luckily, a portly gentleman holding a fat wad of bills stood a few feet from our car—ready to change my money.

Diana, however, was concerned that I'd get a shitty rate of exchange. She wanted me to find an ATM where the rates are better. However, at the ATM, you get hit with fees, which mitigate the better rate to some degree, and I'd been to enough border crossings to know ATM machines are scarce.

I pulled the trigger and exchanged $100 for Guatemalan Quetzales. I'd heard crisp $100 bills might command a better rate, so I tried unsuccessfully to haggle with the guy. My anti-negotiation superpowers strike again. I found out later that these guys never budge off their standard daily rate on penalty of getting their ass kicked by the other money changers.

For some inexplicable reason, my money changing upset Diana. She wasn't just telling me I screwed up; she seemed legitimately mad about the transaction. We still had all the border stuff to deal with, and I didn't need to be having a wildly disproportionate argument over throwing away maybe $3 to $4 in exchange rate.

In a sense, I get that she was looking out for me. She was my project manager at work, so she saw us as in this together, and she was helping to project manage me. I appreciate it. I need to be project-managed sometimes. But in that moment? I think the road stress was getting to both of us and manifesting in weird ways like this nonsensical argument.

As we walked to the building, a well-groomed kid of maybe fifteen approached, offering his services as a helper. The big question from the overlander forums is whether or not to get one of these border helpers—a local who wants something like $10 to guide you through all the various windows, forms, stamps, signatures, and other bureaucratic foofery. Some overlanders oppose paying helpers on principle, but I figured I could support the local youth.

My helper effectively turned me into two people: one waiting in line for car customs and one waiting in line for people customs. At one point, the Aduana (car customs agent) handed my car title to the helper, who scurried off with it. This was a bit unsettling. Traveler forums say **never** hand over your original documents to helpers. They could hold the documents hostage until you cough up $50 or more to get them back. Again, I had to go with the flow and assume the Aduana wouldn't give the kid my title if he had any reason not to trust him. Imagine a DMV worker in the US handing your car title to some random person off the street who then runs off with it.

The kid reappeared a few minutes later with my title and a stamped form. The rest of the border went about as smoothly as entering Belize. I seemed to be running well compared to some border-crossing horror stories I'd read. We did have to pay $1 to spray the car, which amounted to a bored attendant waving a barely dripping wand vaguely in the vicinity of my undercarriage. I paid my helper $10 in quetzales, for which I was glad to have exact change and not have to whip out a $100 bill.

As I headed to my car with all my papers in order, a nicely dressed man in his 40s approached. He stuck out his hand and said, "Welcome to Guatemala. I hope you have a wonderful time in my country."

I shook his hand and thanked him, waiting for him to invite me to his hotel or offer to take me opal shopping or something. But the other shoe never dropped. He had nothing to pitch. He just wanted to welcome a traveler and make a good first impression for his country.

It worked. I drove into Guatemala with a smile on my face, my border anxiety melting away.

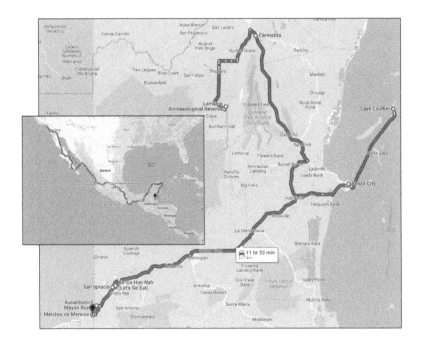

CHAPTER 25

LOST IN THE PETÉN

DIANA and I consternated over our next accommodations, knowing no place could live up to the Best Airbnb Ever. We found a rental on the shores of Lago (Lake) Petén Itzá with a charming little dock in a great location to explore the Tikal ruins—another anticipated highlight of the trip. Multiple reviewers had complained about the bumpy ride to the Airbnb, but my FJ scoffs at your bumpy road. One reviewer emphasized the word 'rustic' to describe the compound, which gave me pause. Nevertheless, we pulled the trigger, hoping to catch lightning in a bottle twice.

"Bumpy" turned out to be a drastic understatement for the road along the lake's north end. "Road" was an overstatement. We spent forty minutes bouncing along five miles of undulating, pothole-ridden dirt track—so brutal it made me nostalgic for Baja.

We arrived well before our check-in time, so we planned to just scope the place out, then head to the town of Flores on the south side of the lake. Eyeing a set of steep steps that led down into the compound, I suggested, "Maybe we should each take a suitcase now to avoid multiple trips."

Diana replied, "No, let's just check the place out first."

I started to protest that this was inefficient. But then I decided to just let her have this one.

As we descended the steps, I was confused as to which of the small buildings were ours or if the whole place was ours. The view of the lake with the little dock was picturesque, as advertised. Score one for that. Farther in, we came across a mother and daughter in the process of cleaning. Diana explained that we were only stopping by to check the place out. But the pair still seemed befuddled at our presence. Neither smiled nor had much to say, which is so odd in Latin America that it stood out. Maybe the 5'10" blonde speaking accent-free Spanish threw them for a loop.

Farther into the compound, we came across the family patriarch, who also seemed distracted and confused as to why we were there. He showed us our rooms, which each resided in their own bungalow and were separated by a hundred feet of open space. Diana appeared bothered by this arrangement. I noticed that neither room was sufficiently sealed, which is typical in this part of the world. It's how most people live. But it does mean you need to tolerate bugs in your room, even in your bed, from time to time. I assumed that's what Diana was fretting about.

After the gentleman had shown us our rooms, we walked down to the dock. There, Diana revealed her concerns that if a nefarious person, or a jaguar, or the Maiden of the Rock came sniffing around her room at night, she'd have to sprint across the compound to safety in my room. We had no cell coverage, so calling me to come save her wasn't an option. I thought this was a bit silly and told her so.

The dock of our dreams

But after brief consideration, I had to admit she had a point. We were more or less in the first fifteen minutes of a teen slasher movie: isolated compound in the woods, lake for skinny dipping, foreboding unsettling vibe from the local caretaker. Her concerns about personal safety also happened to dovetail with my concerns about bugs in my bed. We took a few pictures on the dock, let the family know we'd be back later, then left without depositing any bags.

ISLA DE FLORES

The road around Lago Petén Itzá connects to Isla (Island) de Flores by a causeway that leads from the lake's southern shore. The island is less than a kilometer in diameter, all taken up by the touristy colonial town of Flores, which we figured should have plenty of dinner options. I drove the slightly longer route along the lake's western edge, hoping it wouldn't be as bumpy as the eastern route, which turned out to be the case. We took the causeway to the island, found parking, and grabbed a drink at a restaurant along the lakefront.

Diana was apoplectic at the prospect of staying at the place we had booked. There was no getting a refund this late, which meant we'd have to eat $400 between the two of us. Neither of us wanted to blow that much money. I told her I didn't see any way out.

Flores was gorgeous, with interesting colonial architecture, tons of restaurants, and, most importantly, hotels we could stumble to after eating and drinking to our hearts' content. After a couple of beers, with the sun getting low, I was very much not looking forward to the one-hour drive in the dark on the road to hell, and I had thoroughly warmed to the idea of trying to wriggle out of the rental.

But I wasn't going to let Diana off that easy.

I told her, "Look, I can tell this is really upsetting you. I'm fine with that place, but I'm willing to do this **for you**. Let's come up with a plan."

I'm a giver like that.

I continued, "But if there's any talking, you have to do it. You know I hate awkward situations."

Our problem was that the owner would know we'd already been there, which killed most of our potential excuses—such as saying we were stuck in Belize or our flight was delayed. We also didn't want to tell her the real reason. If she took offense, she might be less likely to give us a refund. Plus, it's just not nice. We decided to tell her I had blown out one of my shocks—

utterly believable with that road—and we were stuck in Flores until I could get my car fixed.

I cannot give a big enough shoutout to Diana for not listening to me and instead insisting that we leave our bags in the car. Dropping our bags at that place would have blown the whole plan to smithereens.

Diana typed out a lengthy message on her phone and hit send. The owner got back to us within a few minutes. She graciously offered to refund the balance if we'd just pay the $20 cleaning fee, which we were more than happy to fork over to the weirded-out family.

Hallelujah! Diana and I high-fived. For one shining moment, we were a team—a euphoric, supportive team.

Returning to the car, we discovered that several hundred of the thousands of riotous red-lored parrots that call Isla de Flores home had been kind enough to turn my hood into a Jackson Pollock painting—possibly as payback for lying to one of their neighbors. I was happy to take my karmic medicine if it meant no hell road. We found a hotel as far away from the parrots as possible. I've never heard a flock of birds that loud. Maybe they feel the need to compete with the howler monkeys.

Neither of us liked the menu at the place on the water, so we cleaned up and went back out to look for a proper dinner. As usual, we checked one menu, then another. I knew the drill by now—the third place would usually be fine for some reason. But the second menu looked perfect this time. It had burgers! Two couples emerged from the restaurant. I asked them how it was. They couldn't stop raving about their meals.

Usually, I'm a human garbage disposal. Unless the restaurant serves nothing but liver and asparagus, I can find something to shove down my gullet. But just this once, I decided to break protocol and play the *I want to eat here* card.

I applied my best Jedi mind trick: "I really like this menu. Those people all gave it great reviews. I want to eat here."

Diana seemed deeply unsure. The best place ever could be just around the corner, and how will we know if we don't peruse at least **three** menus? Eventually, she acquiesced.

We sat down and looked over our menus. A club next door bumped bass through the walls at a modest volume. Occasionally, a door to the club would open, whereupon it would get loud, but not ear-splitting, until the door closed again. As the minutes went by, Diana became more and more visibly uncomfortable until it looked like she was wearing a hair shirt.

"What's wrong?" I asked.

"It's just so loud," she replied.

I protested, even though I knew it was hopeless, "Are you sure? It's really only when the door's open."

She just looked at me with a plaintive expression.

Sigh.

What was I going to do, make her sit there in her hair shirt all meal? I should have known better than to break protocol. We found a forgettable place nearby which did **not** have burgers.

TIKAL

On the drive to Tikal the next morning, we enjoyed the semi-tongue-in-cheek crossing signs for jaguars, turkeys, snakes, and other animals. The Maya Biosphere Reserve, which encompasses Tikal, is the most extensive stretch of rainforest north of the Amazon and one of the most biologically diverse ecosystems in the Western Hemisphere. It has some 450 species of birds, 60 species of reptiles, and 800 species of trees. In addition to the ubiquitous jaguars, tapirs, coatis, and monkeys of Central America,

Animal crossing signs on the way to Tikal

the reserve is also home to a freshwater crocodile, a flamboyantly colored turkey that looks like a peacock, the Mexican tree porcupine, and a fox that climbs trees—the only member of the dog family to do so.

We paid the entrance fee and parked, expecting to be approached by legions of guides like Chichén Itzá. None appeared. The whole vibe felt very laid-back. Tikal is so remote that there's no resort area nearby to supply busloads of day-trippers. One generally has to make a special trip to see Tikal and stay at least a night.

After a short jungle walk, we came up behind the imposing Temple of the Great Jaguar (a.k.a. Templo I), then circled around to the ten-acre Great Plaza, flanked by Templo II and the North Acropolis—a terraced complex of smaller royal funerary temples. Nearby sits the Central Acropolis, a raised platform with multiple structures that once housed the royal families of Tikal. Dozens of stelae monuments depicting past rulers have been restored and mounted in the center of the courtyard, where they were initially discovered in the late 1800s. Using these stelae and other sources, scholars can trace a dynastic line of at least thirty-three Tikal rulers dating back to July 6, 292 CE.

The Great Plaza and Temple of the Jaguar (Templo I)

Tikal has six giant temples, conveniently named Templo I through VI, and one colossal pyramid called the Mundo Perdido. If a tall structure has a temple perched on top, it's referred to as a temple; otherwise, it's a pyramid. Atop Templo I sits a wedge-shaped "roof comb," a feature common to most of Tikal's tall structures.

Another positive outcome of the low flow of tourists at Tikal is that, unlike Chichén Itzá, visitors can climb most of the pyramids (although climbing pantsless is still frowned upon). The downside, as I would discover, is that when you travel with Diana, you have to climb **all** the pyramids.

We climbed to the top of Templo II for the spectacular view of Templo I and the surrounding plaza. Then, we headed to the North Acropolis to clamber around the various structures. We met a guide who told us he roamed the grounds as a kid and even saw burials within the tunnels. What a childhood playground.

With no natural rivers or springs, Tikal seems an unlikely place to support a giant city. To capture seasonal rainfall, Maya engineers lined their limestone quarries with water-sealing stucco to create reservoirs. They also tilted the plazas an imperceptible one degree, so that rainfall would flow into catchment basins.

I bowed out of following Diana up a few medium-sized temples, choosing instead to spend quality time with the howler monkeys in the nearby Ceiba trees. My position on the raised platform put me at the same height as the monkeys and maybe fifty feet away. Standing under a troop of howler monkeys is not advised, as they seem to enjoy relieving themselves on their fellow primates. The ancient Maya associated howler monkeys with scribes, but for some reason only carved spider monkeys into stone, never howlers. Maybe it was the golden rain.

The map they give you for Tikal is one of those cartoony brochures with oversized buildings, which doesn't convey the enormity of the grounds. Tikal is the size of a large zoo or amusement park, easily dwarfing other ruins I've visited. The site contains over 4,000 structures, the vast majority of them still unexcavated. Recent LIDAR (lasers that can see through gaps in trees) surveys have pegged the area within city fortifications at forty-seven square miles, suggesting Tikal may have been home to as many as 400,000 people at its height.

Carved monuments and one piece of pottery depict the arrival of an interesting visitor to Tikal in 378 CE. According to the texts, a man named Fire Born arrived as an emissary of Spearthrower Owl, the king of Teotihuacán, then at the height of its power 630 miles away in Central Mexico. On the same day Fire Born arrived, Tikal's king, Jaguar Paw, died of unspecified causes. A year later, Fire Born crowned Spearthrower Owl's *son* as the next king of Tikal. The timing seems suspicious, as does Fire Born's rapid ascendance from visitor to kingmaker.

A Maya noble meets Teotihuacán warriors—seen with
spears and their distinctive atlatls

What archaeologists *haven't* found is evidence of warfare or large-scale violence in this transfer of dynastic power. The pictograph shows Teotihuacán warriors carrying spears and their distinctive spear-launching atlatls.

The spears are pointed down, and the atlatls are empty—which may signify the spears are being traded for quetzal feathers or are tribute as part of a transfer of power ceremony.

Whatever the mechanics of the coup, the signs are unmistakable. Tikal erected a temple in the talud-tablero style of Teotihuacán. Iconography of Teotihuacán's patron gods, including the goggle-eyed rain god Tlaloc, soon appears at Tikal. Access to Teotihuacán's trade network and technological know-how helped Tikal dominate the region, expand their influence, and seems to have fueled the rise of a warrior-king cult. While allied with Teotihuacán, Tikal founded or conquered many nearby city-states, including the great city of Copán in present-day Honduras. Palenque also rose to power as a strong trading ally between Teotihuacán and Tikal.

Tikal's ascendancy did not sit well with their non-Teotihuacán-aligned Maya neighbors. Nearby Calakmul, almost as big as Tikal, emerged as a blood rival—with constant warring between the two great cities. In the mid-sixth century, Tikal's longtime ally, Caracol, aligned with Calakmul to conquer Tikal. For over a century, Tikal was allowed to keep its dynastic line, but its kings were forbidden from erecting any new monuments or stelae. Tikal was forced to abandon all ties to Teotihuacán and only allowed to honor its Maya heritage.

This period is officially known as the "Tikal Hiatus." Although personally, I think scholars missed a golden opportunity to go with "Tikal Timeout"—which not only rolls off the tongue but also conveys the enforced punitive nature of the pause. Tikal had 130 years to think about what it did.

Eventually, Tikal had enough of sitting in the corner. Dos Pilas, a smaller neighboring city that Tikal had founded, started using Tikal's name in their glyphs—essentially calling themselves "New Tikal." When Dos Pilas attempted to contact Tikal's ancestors to curry favor with the gods, that was the last straw. Access to ancestors was everything to the ancient Maya. Contacting *someone else's* ancestors was the gravest offense.

Tikal attacked Dos Pilas and declared itself a first-class kingdom again, then went on to conquer Calakmul and regain its former glory. A carving in the Central Acropolis shows Tikal king *Stormy Sky* carried triumphantly through the city on a litter, leading a tethered captive who may be the defeated lord of Calakmul.

Tikal's kings built most of the giant structures standing today during this regeneration phase. In 830 CE, once again, at the end of a b'ak'tun, the city began to fade—along with most other classic-period Maya cities, including Palenque. In Tikal's case, signs of decline point to drought and overworked land as their influence shrunk and their populace had to farm closer to the city center. Tikal's leaders moved most of their sacred stelae to the Great Plaza in a last-ditch effort to please the gods. The last stela was commissioned in 869 CE. Soon after, without a trace of violence, the city was abandoned to the jungle.

Diana and I navigated Tikal's jungled grounds to the still-unexcavated Templo III, which gives an idea of how the overgrown buildings at Tikal may have appeared to explorers in the late nineteenth century. Then we climbed Templo V—which has one long, intimidating staircase.

As we wandered, I occasionally saw a tall structure poking the trees at the far end of the compound. From the cartoon map, I figured it must be Templo IV. I convinced myself that if this building were really as big as it looked, it would have a colorful nickname like the other

Templo I as found in 1882

major temples. This turned out to be a flawed assumption. At 230 feet, boringly named Templo IV is the tallest pre-Columbian structure in the Americas.

Well, maybe. Naturally, a debate rages over which ancient structure holds the height record. It's possible that Teotihuacán's Pyramid of the Sun and a pyramid called La Danta at a nearby older, mostly unexcavated site known as El Mirador, may have been a little taller before losing their temples. Either way, Templo IV, the Pyramid of the Sun, and La Danta were the tallest buildings in the New World until skyscrapers went up in New York and Chicago in the late 1800s. *(The Washington Monument was completed in 1848, but it's technically an obelisk, not a building. I don't make the rules.)*

Most of Templo IV is not restored, but you can still climb to the top via a LONG wooden staircase. On the way up, drenched in tropical sweat, I decided this was my last temple climb of the day. Once the stairs finally wrapped around to a platform in front of the temple, the view was well worth the effort. From Templo IV's vantage point, we could see the tops of the other giant temples rising from an endless sea of green treetops.

The view from Templo IV seemed vaguely familiar. Later, I learned the setting was used in the original Star Wars as the planet Yavin, where the Rebels amassed for the climactic attack on the Death Star. The scene shows a rebel sentry tracking the Millennium Falcon as it lands amidst Temples I, II, and III. Yavin must have an interesting backstory.

The Millennium Falcon stopping to pick up something at the Tikal gift shop as seen from the top of Templo IV

Climbing down off Templo IV, it was getting dark, and we still had to find our way back to the park entrance. I was convinced we should go right, through a wooded trail that I thought was a shortcut, whereas Diana was sure we should go left.

Diana had been deriding my sense of direction the entire trip. It is true that I often get East and West mixed up, and North and South. Also, I usually say right when I mean left, and vice versa. And I'm a blank slate when it comes to remembering how I got into a place in order to get back out. But I think the information is actually buried in my subconscious somewhere—because I seem to pick the *wrong* direction 90 percent of the time.

However, I was quite sure of myself this time and itching to prove her wrong. I took my stand: "The exit is that way. I know it."

"Fine. I'm going this way," she retorted as she headed to the left.

In retrospect, splitting up in the dark might not have been the smartest or safest idea. I planned to make my way to the next group of buildings and then wait for her to show up. But I hit a dead end. I had to jog back to our split-up point and then follow her route to catch up to her. Huffing and puffing, with my tail between my legs, I admitted she was right.

Ever the good sport, Diana only reminded me of this incident two, maybe three dozen times.

We got back to town, both famished. This time, we only had to peruse two menus. Bonus! The menu was outside on street level, and the restaurant was upstairs. As we ascended the stairs, the music volume steadily increased. When we got to the top, the din was louder than the place she couldn't tolerate the night before. I turned to her, assuming she'd want to head down and find something quieter.

"No," she said, "this is fine."

Oh.

So that's how it is. And the place **still** didn't have burgers.

The following day, we spent some time exploring the island. Diana shopped while I took shots of colorful colonial architecture. It's a tragic irony of Latin America that next to beaches, the biggest economy-driving tourist draws are quaint, charming colonial towns. Towns that were often built literally from the dismantled temples of conquered indigenous cultures—representing centuries of exploitation, oppression, and genocide. Even among the sad fraternity of Latin American colonial cities, Isla de Flores stands out as one of the most lamentable chapters in New World history.

Nojpetén

Before it was Isla de Flores, the city on an island was known as Nojpetén—the capital of Petén Itzá, a vast kingdom of Itzá Maya centered around the lake, Lago Petén Itzá. These were the same Itzá Maya who migrated from the Petén to found Chichén Itzá in the Yucatán in 830 CE, then migrated back around 1200 CE. Nojpetén residents whitewashed all their houses, palaces, and twenty-one temples, giving the city "a white glow that could be seen from leagues away," according to one Spanish account.

By the mid-1500s, conquistadors had taken the Yucatán to the north and Guatemala to the south. The Itzá had no gold to plunder, and the dense jungle wasn't suited for crops. So, the Petén remained a no man's land—providing a neutral buffer of empty country surrounding the Itzá kingdom. The rulers of Petén Itzá fought hard to preserve this buffer zone, as it protected them from colonial encroachment and provided a haven for escaped Maya slaves to join their ranks.

Cortés came through Nojpetén in 1530 and had a peaceful encounter with the locals. As a gift, he left them a lame horse. At the next contact, almost a century later, Itzá leaders showed a Spanish priest a sacred statue honoring Cortés' horse, which they had lovingly cared for throughout its days. This idol worship angered the priest, who tried to smash the statue with a rock. Relations with the Spanish went downhill from there.

An hotel in Isla De Flores

The Itzá were amenable to becoming part of the Spanish crown, but they refused to convert to Christianity. Hostilities arose, and in 1622, all priests were expelled from the city. Other than a brief visit from a priest in 1650 that didn't end well, no further significant contact with the Itzá occurred for over 70 years. This ended in 1695, when the governor of the Yucatán, Martín de Ursúa y Arizmendi, deliberately commissioned a road through the heart of Itzá territory.

Over the next three years, the Itzá, who by this time had almost two centuries to observe Spanish treachery and subterfuge, played Lucy with the football to Ursúa's Charlie Brown. The Itzá continually tricked him with offers of surrender, then attacked and sacrificed his men: "No, really. This time, we mean it. We're surrendering. No seriously. This won't be like the last three times." And then boom, more priests and soldiers wind up with their hearts cut out and their heads on stakes. The Itzá donned Spanish military uniforms to lure Ursúa's men into traps and even dressed as women to sneak into the soldiers' camps.

As usual, the Itzá had local indigenous enemies who were happy to team up with the Spanish to weaken the kingdom—eventually forcing them to their last redoubt on Nojpetén island. In 1698, Spanish soldiers built a galleon on the lake, armed with six cannons. After one last fake surrender by the Itzá, Ursúa's men launched the galleon and circled the city —pummeling the great whitewashed temples and houses with cannon fire. The ship circled a few times, and then the Spanish stormed the city, slaughtering indiscriminately. Nojpetén fell in one hour, and with it, the last indigenous kingdom in the Americas.

Ursúa wanted credit for the defeat of the Itzá but had no interest in governing the conquered subjects, so he gave the land and its inhabitants to the governor of Guatemala. If you've ever wondered why that square Texaspanhandle-looking chunk at the top of Guatemala isn't part of Mexico, this is why. Find a straight border anywhere in the world, and you'll probably find a tragic colonial tale behind it.

Today, there are fewer than ten fluent Itzá Maya speakers left—all very old and living in a village on the north side of the lake. It will soon be a dead language.

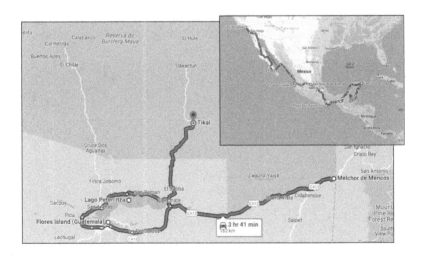

CHAPTER 26

ROAD RAGE

DIANA and I headed into the mountains with plans to spend the night in the town of Cobán and then continue on to Antigua, a massive colonial city that served as the capital of Central America for two centuries. For hours, we wound through Guatemala's central highlands, enchanted by rolling hills in dozens of shades of green.

We arrived in Cobán after sunset to find a hilly grid of one-way streets jammed with chaotic rush-hour traffic. Diana found a hotel on booking.com that looked promising. After one miss, which required a stressful, time-consuming circle of the block, I located the small entrance, checked the height of the overhang, and drove in. The hotel seemed perfectly pleasant, with two stories of old-Spanish-style rooms and a decent restaurant. I couldn't have been more relieved to park the car after a long day of driving.

I piped up, "All right, we made it! Let's go get our rooms."

Diana came back with, "Well, let's just check this place out first. I'm not sure."

Oh no no no no. This is no good. I was with her on the rustic teen slasher place. But not on this. I **cannot** get back in that car. This town doesn't have a Holiday Inn or City Express. We could drive around for hours in that traffic looking for something better. I needed to start selling.

In the most soothing, confident voice I could muster: "What? This place is fiiiine."

"Are you sure it's safe?"

"Of course—look at that gate. It's like a fortress in here."

"Maybe we could find a place that's not in the middle of town."

"Trust me. I have a lot of experience with hotels like this. I can already tell the rooms will be very nice, and it's super safe. We hit the jackpot."

We headed to the office to talk to the proprietor. The low $27 room rate seemed to make her even more insecure—not a good sign. Then we checked out our rooms, to which Diana showed no visible distress—a much better sign. Back in the office, I sat there like a car salesman, waiting for the customer to say those magic words, internally PRAYING she'd accept this place. I may even have been hunched over in my chair with my hands clasped and my lips touching my knuckles.

Finally, she blurted out, "Okay, we'll take it."

Hallelujah! Beer time!

Back at the car, I loaded my backpack with the usual overnight items: laptop, dopp kit, clean underwear, and shirt. Diana tugged at her giant hard-shelled suitcase, which seemed to contain a third of her possessions in life, and I'd come to dub "Old Ironsides" after two weeks of dragging it around.

"It's just one night. Do you have a smaller bag you could throw stuff into?" I asked.

"No. Everything is all mixed up together."

(Of course. What was I thinking?)

"I'll carry it up the stairs," she shot back in response to my audible sigh and recalcitrant body language.

"No, I got it." I grabbed the bag and dragged it up the stairs, huffing and puffing, groaning more loudly with each step—until, by the end, you'd have thought I was passing a kidney stone. For I am a gentleman above all.

While I was busy patting myself on the back for my amazing salesmanship in convincing Diana to accept our accommodations, she spotted a mosquito on the ceiling. I robotically spun into action. Must kill mosquito. Cannot let Diana change her mind. I grabbed a towel out of the bathroom and, for once in my life, nailed the bug on the first try.

I stood there, beaming with pride at fulfilling my role as household protector. But instead of sharing the joy in one man's triumph over nature, Diana looked perturbed.

I was afraid to ask, "What?"

"You got it on my towel."

[SCREAMING INTERNALLY]

I twirled around and left the room without saying a word, just hoping she didn't find a pea under her mattress.

While waiting for Diana the next morning, I walked around downtown Cobán. Apparently, school was out that day. Except instead of letting the kids run and play, they were marching and singing in the streets, wearing matching t-shirts. I didn't catch the entire gist of the occasion, but I gathered it was something local, possibly an organized protest. The kids seemed to be having fun, at least.

Cobán was a key military base used to launch campaigns against guerrillas in the surrounding highlands during Guatemala's thirty-six-year civil war. Although "civil war" may be a misnomer for what was essentially an endless guerrilla hunt and terror campaign against Maya villagers.

On the way to Cobán, Diana and I had driven through a small town called Chisec. In 1995, on a farm near Chisec, a patrol of soldiers, chagrined at being told to leave the local celebration, fired on the crowd, killing eleven people, including two children. The soldiers were easily identified, but civilian authorities initially declined to punish them, as had been the norm throughout the war.

Guatemala's Civil War could trace its roots back to 1954, when the US Central Intelligence Agency engineered a clandestine coup known as "Operation Success." The democratically elected president at the time, Jacobo Árbenz, had flirted with communism, and his agrarian reforms—which included distributing uncultivated land owned by foreign interests to indigenous communities—rubbed some the wrong way, specifically the United Fruit Company, at the time the largest private landowner in Guatemala. United Fruit used its influence within the US government to convince President Eisenhower that the CIA, fresh off its rousing success in Iran, should facilitate a similar coup in Guatemala.

Six years after the coup, two ex-soldiers of indigenous background led a small uprising against Guatemala's repressive US-backed military regime. The unrest was quickly put down but inspired more guerrilla revolutionaries. Though never numbering more than a few hundred fighters, some of these groups had loose ties to communism. This naturally drew in the US to provide support and training to the Guatemalan military and, most catastrophically, to its intelligence units.

For the next thirty-six years, a series of despotic generals, when they weren't coup-ing each other, waged something akin to the US war in Vietnam—fighting an overmatched but resilient insurrection force on their own dense, inaccessible home terrain. Over the ensuing decades, with varying degrees of US support, the Guatemalan military grew into a monster—consolidating power and spawning its own wealthy socio-political class that drew from a pool of hardened killers to protect its interests.

As in Vietnam, civilians suffered the most. The military raped, tortured, and murdered civilians, including children, to gain information or punish them for perceived collaboration. In the early 1980s, the notorious general Efraín Ríos Montt carried out a genocidal purge that was actively supported by US foreign policy. A United Nations Truth Commission found the Guatemalan military responsible for 93 percent of the 200,000 known civilian deaths during the war, documenting over 400 massacres of *entire villages*—with countless more undocumented.

Our high school history curriculum didn't just skip over the great ancient civilizations in this part of the world. It also brushed aside the genocidal terror campaigns still being waged against those same indigenous communities while *Friends* was in its third season.

In December 1996, under pressure from the US and the international community, Guatemala's military agreed to a truce—on the condition that they be held accountable for nothing. Their power and intelligence structures remained intact, their enforcers still capable of staggeringly cruel political violence. By 1998, only one member of the military had ever been convicted of an extra-judicial killing.

In 1998, Guatemala's leading human rights activist, Bishop Juan Gerardi, was murdered just before the release of a damning human rights report sponsored by his diocese. Chaos, threats of violence, and disinformation campaigns reigned as Guatemala's trial of the century and its appeals dragged on for nearly a decade. Witnesses, judges, journalists, and lawyers risked their lives for a chance to lift their country out of its corrupt, military-dominated morass.

In the end, to the surprise of many, a half dozen high-ranking military personnel were sentenced to substantial jail time. An independent judiciary with the power to stand up to the military—a pipe dream for most of Guatemala's history—had established a tenuous foothold.

Prosecutors tried the soldiers from the Chisec massacre along a parallel timeline, resulting in fourteen convictions. Efraín Ríos Montt was convicted in 2016 and later acquitted on appeal. He died in 2018 while awaiting another trial. As prosecutors continue to launch new trials, the other surviving ringleaders of decades of terror hope to run out the clock in similar fashion.

I thought about the people hustling about their day in Cobán who were old enough to be alive for all this. How many had seen, or done, terrible things? How does life go back to normal after thirty-six years of terror?

TACTIC

Diana and I hit the road for another long day of driving. Along the way, she wanted to check out a bustling Maya market in a town called Tactic. As we got closer to town, we saw crowds of people a few blocks ahead. Google Maps led me down a one-way street that kept getting narrower, with parked cars on both sides. By the time I was a block away from the market, people filled the street, surrounding my car. As I inched closer, I saw no way to turn right or left, meaning I would have to back out through several blocks of tight roadway full of people.

Something didn't seem right. Why would there be a funnel like this with no way out? Before starting the delicate multi-block reverse, I rolled down my window and motioned to a gentleman passing by. I pointed forward and backward, adding the universal facial expression and shoulder shrug of: "I have no idea what I'm doing. Please help." The man indicated that I should keep going "derecho" straight through the crowd. Diana and I looked at each other, "Well, this should be fun."

We crawled forward, and sure enough, when my car got within a few feet, the sea of humanity began to part. We drove through a gap between stalls, maybe a foot wider than my car on each side, with just enough room for people to squeeze out of the way. Diana could have grabbed an orange from the stall outside her window.

We parked and wandered the market for an hour. The ladies tending the produce stalls loved Diana and her excellent Spanish. One lady started bantering with Diana like old friends busting each other's chops. I guess it says something about human resilience that the unfailingly friendly Maya women we met were all old enough to have lived through the worst of the government's terror campaign.

Diana's Collage of the market in Tactic

An hour later, back on the road, we came to a crossroads. Diana was dozing off. I could have easily just gone the way I wanted, but I wanted her buy-in, which is another way of saying I wanted to deny her the pleasure of blaming me if things went wrong. I told her we could take the safe bet—the long way around the mountains, through Guatemala City, and on to Antigua. Or we could take a semi-shortcut that bypassed Guatemala City, winding down out of the hills on a very crooked road, which are always scenic and usually fun.

The last stretch of the shortcut was a small white line, which means it's usually going to be an adventurous road, if not a full-blown "Oh Google Maps—you so crazy!" experience. To me, taking this route is like a micro-cosm of the whole trip. Will it work out and be a cool experience? Yeah, 95 percent of the time, it probably will. Will something go wrong, causing it to be a pain in the ass, like having to backtrack? Yeah, maybe, but that's the adventure. Of course, there's the .01 percent chance something bad happens—like getting robbed, and perhaps a .0001 percent chance something unspeakably terrible happens. But I couldn't say the other way didn't carry the same risk.

I made my case to bypass Guatemala City: "Look, this isn't northern Guatemala anymore. Guatemala City has gangs and real crime. My concern is Google gets us off track, as we know it loves to do, and we wind up in a dangerous neighborhood. I haven't really done any research on Guatemala City's no-go zones. Even though Google says this route through the mountains takes a little longer, I'm willing to bet that with late afternoon traffic, it will actually be faster. I think we should do it. What do you think?"

"Well, where is the road? I can't find it on my phone." Diana had been fiddling with Google Maps on her phone throughout my entire spiel.

"Trust me, it's a route. Here, look at my phone."

"I don't know; I don't think there's a road there"—still fumbling with her phone.

"There's a road. Look at the blue line on my phone. It goes through. Why do you need to see it on your phone?"

"I don't want to go that way. I don't know if it's safe."

I got frustrated. "You know, just once, could you trust my judgment? Just once, can we do the thing I want to do?"

"What are you talking about?"

"Well, for starters..."

And then it all came out: The mosquito on the towel. Her curiously fluctuating ambient noise tolerance in restaurants. Stressing me out about changing money at the border. Stuff from Belize. Stuff from Tulum. Stuff I can't even remember now.

Was that all warranted by me? No. Looking back, free from the frustration of the moment, she had every right to veto the shortcut. I couldn't guarantee that route was as safe as the main road. It's her life, too. There is one stretch in Guatemala—the south side of Lake Atitlán—that you're never supposed to drive without a police escort, or you will get robbed. So, there's some precedent for dangerous roads in rural areas.

But in that moment, I was cranky and unaccommodating.

"Fine. You win. You always win," I blurted, reveling in my petulance. I put the car in gear and proceeded down the main highway, passing the shortcut turnoff.

After a few minutes, she offered an olive branch, "Put on your chill music."

I put on DJ Thorin's Progressive Sounds, the best of the best. But I wasn't going to crank it in that tense environment, and unfortunately, you need decent volume to hear the nuance in the music. At low volume, it just sounds like a monotonous drone. And yes, I know some would say it

sounds like a monotonous drone at **any** volume. Har har good joke. Didn't
see that one coming.

[...two minutes and seventeen seconds of monotonous droning later...]

"But I was right. There is no road."

"That's it." I yanked the car off to the shoulder so I could safely SHOW
HER that there is a road. "**See**, you have to actually **click** the **button** to
complete the directions. **Then**, the road appears. You can't just keep
zooming in. It doesn't work that way."

"I don't have to listen to this—" and she got out of the car.

I got out, too, where the argument continued. As it happened, I had
pulled over to a panoramic view of the blazing green valley below. So, there
we were: big red-headed gringo and tall blonde gringette, yelling at each
other in front of a jaw-dropping backdrop of lush scenery—like some scene
out of *Romancing the Stone*. I can't imagine what the woman tending the
nearby fruit stand thought of us.

Eventually, we calmed down and got back on the road. I saw some guys
standing around at a gas station and pulled over. I approached them, "Pre-
gunta por favor. Es el paso a la ciudad de Guatemala—muy peligroso?" I
was trying to ask, "Is the way through Guatemala City very dangerous?" By
their responses, it was clear they thought I was asking if the *road itself* was
dangerous, as in driving off a cliff or something.

So I made pistols with my fingers, firing them like Yosemite Sam as I
asked, "Banditos?"

They looked at me like I was an idiot, which was **exactly** the response I
was hoping for. Chuckling, they assured me I could drive through
Guatemala City without fear of banditos pointing their fingers at me and
making pew pew sounds.

I returned to the car and told Diana I felt much better about the drive
through Guatemala City. I felt cautiously optimistic that we had finally
gotten all the angst and road stress out of our systems, and things would be
copacetic going forward.

Then we hit road construction. For several hours, we were either at a
crawl or a dead stop. It became apparent we'd be arriving in Guatemala City
just in time for evening rush hour. Which meant I'd *yet again* be breaking
the first rule of overlanding in a stressful, dangerous, unfamiliar city.

Did I call Diana out for nixing the shortcut and putting us in this mess?
No. I knew it. She knew it. I didn't want to give her the satisfaction of
airing it out. I preferred to let her bathe in the pregnant, unspoken silence
of her wrongness. Just lather that stuff all over.

Eventually, she made an overture to the effect of "Maybe we should have taken the other route," to which I grunted some guttural, non-verbal reply.

After a few minutes, I softened a little: "Well, who knows, the other way might have been worse." Which was very true.

ANTIGUA

The traffic through Guatemala City was horrible, as expected. But we still rolled into the outskirts of Antigua with the last of the fading light. Our last Airbnb of the trip turned out to be part of an old stone mansion with modern luxurious features inside. Diana had chosen well. Hooray for a home base and **no more driving** for a while!

Starving, we asked our host for restaurant recommendations. He pointed us to a place called La Fonda de la Calle Real for traditional Guatemalan food, which sounded wonderful.

The Uber ride to the restaurant took us past endless colonial blocks on bumpy cobblestone streets. The restaurant had old-world Spanish decor with antique furniture, and our waitress wore a traditional patterned dress with a foofy white top. I got the stuffed chiles, which were delicious. Diana fell in love with her cilantro chicken and onion soup. If Guatemala has a signature dish—I believe it's that soup.

After dinner, we wandered the cobblestone streets, checking out the colonial architecture and a few still-ruined churches. I quickly fell in love with Antigua, which, at 5,000 feet, is my kind of climate.

On the way back to our lodging, I told Diana, "I've had a long, very stressful two days of driving. I'm exhausted. I really need to sleep in tomorrow and relax. Okay?" She agreed to let me sleep in.

I'm a light sleeper, so I heard Diana rummaging around from 8 a.m. onward as I drifted in and out of sleep. At 10:30, I emerged from the bedroom to find Diana sitting on the couch, looking eager to get moving.

"Ready?" she asked.

"What?" I replied in exaggerated groggy confusion. "No... I need to have some coffee and wake up a little. I said I want to relax, not hit the ground running." As I sipped my coffee, I could feel her restlessness permeating me from across the room. This lasted a few minutes before I gave in and headed up to shower.

I finished my shower, got dressed, and went to her room, where she was doing something in the mirror.

"I'm ready whenever you are," I told her.

"Okay, give me five minutes."

I lay on my bed and got out my laptop.

After ten minutes or so, she called out from her bedroom, "Are you ready?"

"Yep!"

Five more minutes passed.

"Are you ready?" she called out again.

"Yes!" I was perfectly content to surf the internet as long as it took her to get ready.

A few more minutes passed, then she appeared in my doorway.

"Why didn't you come and tell me you were ready?"

I thought I had gotten all the frustration and angst out of my system the day before.

I was wrong.

I shot up out of the bed, "What are you talking about? I said I was ready **twice**."

"Well, I didn't know. Why didn't you come to my room?"

"That makes no sense. I **told** you I was ready."

"I don't want to argue with you, Matt. You're so passive-aggressive."

[PAUSE FOR CEREBRAL ANEURYSM]

"I just...What?... I mean...WHAT? *I'm* passive-aggressive?!?!!"

"Stop arguing with me. You always do this. I don't want to argue with you."

And so it went—back and forth like that. I've had some inane arguments in my life, but none as profoundly stupid as that one. It was the Peter Griffin of arguments. It was the nut low, as we say in poker, of arguments. Napoleon had a better argument for invading Russia. The guy who sold his stake in Apple for $800 had a better argument.

History's dumbest argument spilled down the stairs and into the courtyard on the way to the car. Of course, I was now the bad guy because I had raised my voice and potentially embarrassed her in front of our host and the other guests. And in all seriousness, she was right. Although she did start the whole thing by being ridiculous.

We cooled down and drove into town, where we met up for coffee with a woman from El Salvador whom Diana had gotten to know on a hiking retreat in Ecuador. It turns out Diana's friend was on the board of the National Maya Council of El Salvador. She told us how the El Salvador government had massacred tens of thousands of Maya in the 1930s. And how after that, unlike in Guatemala, El Salvador's Maya abandoned their traditional dress. She explained that she moved to Guatemala because the situation in El Salvador is still less than ideal.

After a half hour, I said my goodbyes so Diana and her friend could catch up. Diana said she could find her own way back—meaning we were mercifully untethered for the first time since Ambergris Caye.

I returned to our place, took the last of the muscle relaxers I'd been given for my foot, and fell into a catatonic, stress-purging eighteen-hour sleep. When I finally woke up, all traces of piss and vinegar had drained out of me like pulling the plug in a bathtub. I knew I was really done this time.

I apologized to Diana for losing my temper and my patience. I didn't care who was right anymore. I just wanted to get through our last three days together in something resembling peace and tranquility.

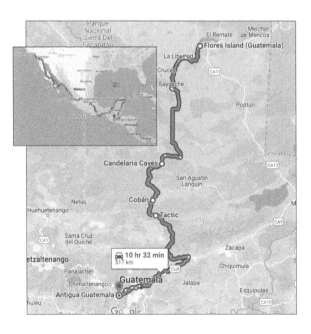

CHAPTER 27

SETTLING IN

BY NOON on my first day of exploring, Antigua had bumped El Tule out of the top spot of my "places to settle someday" list. What's not to love about cobblestone streets lined with centuries-old Baroque haciendas and the occasional old church left in ruins for dramatic effect—all set against a backdrop of active volcanoes?

Antigua's haciendas aren't much to look at from the street: just a wall, a door, and a few small windows—often in a state of rough restore. But a peek inside can reveal a shimmering garden courtyard flanked by tiled walkways and immaculate interior quarters. Antiguans have converted their haciendas into restaurants, hotels, shops, art galleries—and the world's most beautiful McDonald's. The Burger King isn't bad, either.

A typical restored Antigua hacienda

Did I mention the weather? After months in heat and humidity, I cannot overstate the extra spring that mild weather puts in my step. In hot tropical climates, I'm an old dog—shuffling along, moving my body the bare minimum required for the task at hand, lest sweat burst forth from every pore. In my natural, cooler climate, I'm as frisky as a middle-aged dog before the arthritis sets in.

Diana and I spent the day wandering, punctuated by an encounter with a towheaded crying toddler lost in a bustling square. Diana sprang into action, comforting the distraught child while I searched for a police officer and/or a parent in a wide-eyed panic. I found a police officer, but ten minutes later, still no parent. Finally, a woman of indeterminate European origin showed up with a stroller and two other kids in tow. She seemed incredibly blasé about losing her child for fifteen minutes in a crowded square in Guatemala. I think the kid would have rather stayed with Diana, who was wonderful with him. The whole incident caused me to see Diana in a new light. I began to suspect that I was probably the asshole in most of our kerfuffles.

Restaurant with quite a view of Volcán de Fuego (if only that parked car would have moved)

To cap off the day of exploring, Diana and I enjoyed a lovely dinner with a view of Volcán de Fuego periodically spewing puffs of smoke and fiery lava.

Volcano eruptions and earthquakes repeatedly rocked Antigua during its 222-year reign as the colonial capital of Central America. In 1773, a massive earthquake destroyed much of the city. Instead of rebuilding, the colonial authority relocated to the nearby Valley of the Shrine, on the site that would become Guatemala City. Antigua sat largely abandoned for the next century and a half—until the textile industry moved in and saved the city from total ruin. By the mid-twentieth century, Antigua's unique architecture began attracting locals and expats to restore the haciendas. In 1979, Antigua was declared a UNESCO World Heritage Site. I'm told that a mansion worth a million dollars today could be had for a hundred dollars in the 1940s.

LAKE ATITLÁN

Diana and I spent our last day together exploring Lake Atitlán, the deepest lake in Central America and Guatemala's most popular destination with backpackers. We parked in the city of Panajachel, then hired a tiny boat to take us around to several towns on the opposite side of the lake.

Our boat captain, a charming older Maya gentleman named Thomas, first pulled up to the town of San Pedro. There, we disembarked and walked past a few bars filled with raucous midday partiers. We continued uphill until we found a quiet coffee shop with a nice balcony. Our expansive view of the lake was dulled somewhat by smoke from burning crops.

We watched as both bars suddenly emptied into the street below. A man wearing a golden crown and purple robe waved his costume scepter like a shepherd's staff to herd the gyrating mob onto a double-decker party boat. Eventually, the boat sailed off; its **OONTZ OONTZ OONTZ** beat slowly fading into the distance—much to the relief of our waiter and the other denizens of the cafe, who seemed to be on the raggedy end of an all-nighter.

Next, we stopped at the sleepy town of San Juan, where we hired a tuk-tuk to shuttle us to various Maya craft demonstrations. We stopped at a farm and tried some honey harvested from small, stingless bees, which was delicious. I tried a honey beer, which was not.

Our driver took us to a textile store, where we observed traditional Maya weaving. I am always blown away trying to understand the mechanics and spatial gyrations involved in wrapping each piece of yarn around the others. I feel like a dog trying to understand a mirror. I try to think of the weaving apparatus as a mechanical computer and each pattern as an individual program, but I still can't wrap my head around what's happening on a string-by-string basis.

The woman who explained and demonstrated the weaving had the sweetest, most pure demeanor. As she wove for us, I daydreamed a whole fantasy that living a simple village life— never losing one's innocence, free from gizmos and other soul-sucking distractions—is perhaps the real key to human happiness. Maybe knowing you'll be cared for by a tight-knit community

Traditional Maya weaving

from cradle to grave somehow makes up for hardships like a lack of quality medical care. Then again, the Zapatistas specifically listed "dying from curable diseases" as one of their complaints. And the Maya here have had to endure centuries of persecution, first by the Spanish and then by the

Guatemalan government. So, it seems doubtful that my idyllic fantasy is anything close to their reality.

Still, there has to be a reason city people fantasize about chucking it all for the simpler ways of a small town. Hallmark Christmas movies wouldn't exist if the "disaffected Big City Businesswoman who's missing something in her life" trope didn't resonate. Although, I prefer the Lifetime movies. They're less dark, without real villains, just confused people who mean well. Unless a young person is back in town from Los Angeles, then they're a nefarious plot device. New York = good. LA = evil.

And no, I'm not just bitter because Hallmark rejected *Quantum Entanglement,* my script about particle physicists finding love in the most uncertain of places: "She was charmed. He was strange. When he spun into her world, they clashed like matter and antimatter. But the result was pure energy." Come on, Hallmark! It practically writes itself. Call me!

Where was I going with this? Oh yeah, the lesson is if you're a hard-charging Big City Businessman with an equally career-minded fiancée, DO NOT—under any circumstances—let her go back to her hometown for Christmas or even fly *near* her hometown where she could be diverted in a freak snowstorm. Lurking in wait is her chisel-cheeked high school sweetheart, Luke, who's finally ready to date again after his wife's tragic thresher accident and just wants to raise his adorably precocious child as best he can. Once your fiancée offers her big city businesswoman skills to organize the floundering Christmas Parade/Ball/Gala/Pageant/Formal/Cotillion (every small town has one), it's over. She's never coming back.

Last, we stopped at the town of San Marcos, which presented an interesting dichotomy of extremely dreadlocked gap-year hippies hanging out in various states of undress—amidst Maya women in traditional conservative dress going about their business. I noticed that Maya women in Lake Atitlán wore a thicker version of their traditional patterned floral blouse and black, floral-striped skirt than in the hotter lowlands around Lago Petén Itzá and Tactic. If Maya men have a traditional outfit, they don't wear it very often.

The cooler climate didn't seem to faze the hippies, however, who, let's just say, were *not* of the inordinately attractive variety like in Mazunte. One girl wore a burlap sack, almost entirely split down each side with nothing underneath. It seemed wrong to me. My first thought was, "You can be hippies anywhere. Why do it in this peaceful Maya village?" How utterly alien they must seem to the local Maya. Then I thought maybe they contribute enough to the economy that it's a net positive. Still, Diana and I both found them extremely annoying, which I realize could be an "us" problem.

I was so stressed about driving back in the dark that I didn't really enjoy the lake. Which I know is a "me" problem. I need to be more in the moment when I travel. To my great relief, we made it through the rough mountain roads and back onto the main highway before dark.

Just outside of Antigua, we passed a hubbub of activity on both sides of the road. Closer inspection revealed women in scanty outfits strutting around in some kind of brothel district. Prostitution is legal in Guatemala, but "procuring" it is not—whatever that means. In a scene out of the Wild West, a boustiered woman stood in a backlit doorway holding two saloon doors open.

"Wow! Did you see that?" I exclaimed, flush with excitement. Diana was nonplussed.

The next morning, the time for Diana and I to part ways had arrived. On the drive into town, Diana suggested maybe we do this again in Argentina/Chile. My initial thought was, "Yeah, right. You're nuts, lady."

But then I thought, "Well... if we make sure we have music we both like, I guess that's half the battle? And then maybe we could talk about the restaurant stuff. That covers most of our issues, right?"

She did drag me to places like Tactic and Xunantunich that I never would have seen on my own, her impeccable Spanish came in very handy, and she was amazing with kids and locals. So I guess stay tuned for *The Adventures of Matt and Diana II—What Was I Thinking?*

Diana gave me a friendship bracelet, which further melted my icy heart. We hugged it out, and I loaded her suitcase into the trunk one last time. Goodbye, Old Ironsides. I'll miss you most of all.

And that was it. For the first time in three weeks, I was the boss of me again. I could sleep in when I wanted, get going early when I wanted, eat burgers three times a day if I wanted. Naturally, I wandered the city in an aimless stupor, unsure what to do with myself. I came upon a travel agent offering various tours and signed up for a group volcano hike the following day.

My buddy Ande was coming in a week, and after that, the End of All Roads motorcycle guys, who had resumed their ride, were set to arrive—which meant I would be staying put in Antigua for almost a month. I was eager to study more Spanish and kick the tires on expat life. I located a Spanish school I had heard about named Tecún Umán and signed up for Spanish classes.

Then I discovered Reilly's, a sports bar just down the street from the school. Not really one for coffee tours or volcano hikes, I knew Ande would be thrilled if I found a place to park our butts and watch the NCAA Basketball Tournament. This was turning into a productive day after all. Time to celebrate with a burger and beer!

Hiking up Volcán Pacaya the next day, several local guides followed us with a trio of horses whose services were available should one of us become fatigued. The guides all eyed me, red-faced and drenched in sweat, as a potential customer. I didn't know how to explain to them that I only *look* like I'm going to die, but I rarely actually die.

Sorry you didn't get to carry me buddy. Here's a cookie.

To my great surprise, a store selling jewelry made out of lava stood just before the summit. The expat proprietors explained that all the proceeds go to displaced victims of a 2015 major eruption by Pacaya (the mountain on which we stood). Around Antigua, poor people tend to live on the most dangerous slopes.

Our guides brought a bag of marshmallows for hikers to roast over a still-smoldering vent. Once I saw how long the process was taking, I just ate my marshmallow raw, proving you're never too old to fail the marshmallow test.

I started Spanish school at Tecún Umán the following day, where I was paired off with a teacher named Jorge for one-on-one instruction. Our day started with conversation, which tended to produce awkward silence once I ran out of words. Over time, the awkwardness forced me to venture into more complex topics—marking possibly the first time my extreme aversion to awkward situations has been put to good use. During the instruction period, Jorge noticed I liked learning new verb conjugations, which I find similar to computer syntax: more conceptual, with less memorization. So, while someone at my level has zero practical use for the pluperfect subjunctive, Jorge taught me anyway.

The school's name, Tecún Umán, comes from the last leader of the K'iche' Maya, who lived in what is now known as El Quiche—not coincidentally the region that suffered the worst in Guatemala's Civil War. Tecún Umán distinguished himself in battle for years until finally succumbing to the conquistador Pedro de Alvarado. In 1960, he was declared a national hero.

Tecún Umán—telling the Spanish to "Come At Me Bro"

After the tour, I checked in at a homestay the school had arranged. My room was part of a compound of four other rooms and the host family's house. The homestay comes with three meals a day, at which you speak nothing but Spanish.

Naturally, the subject of where I had already been in Guatemala came up with my homestay hosts, as it did with my Spanish teachers and other locals. During those discussions, I didn't meet one Anitguan who had ever been to Tikal. It seemed like Tikal and northern Guatemala might as well be another country for them. I didn't get the impression that a road trip vacation would be cost-prohibitive for the people I talked to. But I suppose the prospect of driving through a war zone put a damper on any budding Clark Griswold/Family Truckster road trip culture. Hopefully, that's changing for Guatemalans. They have such a beautiful country with so much to offer.

As I fumbled through stilted pre-dinner conversation with the host family, a flying unicorn that farts rainbows entered the room and sat down next to me. And by that, of course, I mean a solo female traveler within fifteen years of my age on either side.

The unicorn had a name: Sophie. What's more, she seemed fascinated with my trip. Sophie was studying at a different Spanish school that used the same homestay. After dinner, we wandered the city for a few hours and got to know each other. I found out Sophie works as an engineer on race cars and has various daredevil hobbies like hang gliding and dirt bike racing.

As it turned out, our homestay sat next to a primary artery for chicken buses—a ubiquitous term the world over, as far as I can tell, for cheap local buses. Guatemalan chicken buses are retired Bluebird school buses from the States. They're also, literally, the most colorful thing in Guatemala. Their owner/operators put in hundreds of hours customizing them, adding chrome trim, neon lights, intricate color schemes and patterns, musical horns, and any other accouterment they think will enhance the *wow effect*. The sales pitch seems to be that the better the bus looks on the outside, the safer it will be for people on the inside. Or maybe the owners just do it for the love of the game.

Starting before dawn, chicken bus ayudantes (helpers) ride in the open doorway or run ahead of the bus yelling names like "GUATE! GUATE! GUATE!" for Guatemala City, or "XELA! XELA! XELA!" for Xelajú— the original Maya name that everyone still uses for the city officially named Quetzaltenango. I wake easily, but I can also fall back asleep once my brain habituates to the noise. Sophie, on the other hand, was eternally vexed by the ayudantes and the rumble of buses down our cobblestone street.

After a few days of Spanish school, I settled into something of a routine for the first time since leaving the US. Along the same block as my school, I had Reilly's pub, a gym, laundry, a favorite taco place, and my favorite coffee shop—Guate Java—where I hung out after class while coffee nerds came in to ask about the "personality" of the coffee.

Spanish classes felt a little like a job—but the good kind of job where you only work for four hours, then have the afternoon to explore a beautiful city. Our Spanish lessons were held at the Italian restaurant next door to the school, which had a gorgeous, if distracting, view from their rooftop patio. If I faced one way, I'd be mesmerized by Volcán de Fuego puffing smoke and fire every few minutes. If I turned the other way, toward the restaurant's decorative fountains, I could watch a male great-tailed grackle perform an elaborate courtship display worthy of *Planet Earth*.

One day, some of the students were building an "Alfombra" as a craft project. This was described as a brightly colored "carpet" that Antiguans spend countless hours creating in the streets for the fast-approaching Semana Santa (Holy Week before Easter). Having not seen an Alfombra before, I took the "carpet" part literally. I thought the end product would be some kind of rug. I absorbed zero Spanish from poor Jorge that session as I watched the students pour different colors of milled corn, using screens and molds to give the layers texture and add fine edges. I kept trying to guess what ingenious method they were going to use to somehow turn their creation into an actual rug. Finally, it dawned on me that "carpet" wasn't meant literally, and this pile of stuff wasn't going anywhere until somebody swept it up.

Our classroom Alfombra—definitely not a carpet

On Thursday, I drove to Guatemala City to pick up my old friend Ande at the airport. For four days, we ate great food, watched endless college basketball, and drank too much Cabro beer. Good times, boring story. Funny how that works. We spent our last night in Guatemala City, where Ande treated me to a sizzling ribeye for my 49th birthday.

Float practice

The traffic and excitement for Semana Santa seemed to build every day, with giant floats under construction and float-bearers practicing in the streets. The float-bearers, called Costaleros, train for months to make sure they're synchronized and strong enough to hold up the heavy floats. Each float is built and maintained by a Catholic charitable organization known as a Cofradías. Every Costalero pays something like $80 (not a paltry sum in Guatemala) to the Cofradías for the *privilege* of carrying the float for a few blocks. It is a very big deal to be part of a float in Antigua, home to the largest Semana Santa celebration in the world.

Back at Spanish school, somehow my teachers found out it was my birthday. Much to my embarrassment, all the teachers and students sang Feliz Cumpleaños to me, which is sung to the tune of *Happy Birthday*—except, given the general chattiness of Latin Americans, has two extra verses. It's also apparently a school custom for everyone who sings to shake the birthday person's hand. I was touched.

Inside a structure still in ruin, a parade float is prepared

Finally, the actual week of Semana Santa arrived. Classes ended on Wednesday, as Thursday and Friday are national holidays. With uncanny timing, Dan and the rest of the End of All Roads crew arrived in town, randomly driving down my block a few minutes after I got out of Wednesday's class. I met the other guys, Bob and Justin, for the first time. All three of them have the same BMW 850 adventure bikes—loaded with duffle bags and multiple hard-sided "paneer boxes" that store even more stuff. My first impression was how tall and bulky the bikes are. I've ridden a motorcycle a few times, but I'd be intimidated as hell to ride one of those. Not for beginners.

Their Airbnb conveniently had an enclosed patio to park their bikes and reorganize their stuff. As the guys extricated themselves from all their gear, I realized how much work this kind of travel entails. They have cameras on their helmets, an integrated communication system, and GPSs mounted on the front of their bikes. Their outfits consist of specialized pieces of fabric woven with Kevlar—basically to save them from scraping themselves raw if they have to lay the bike down at speed. Just getting out of it all was a process, like taking off a space suit. I never could get a straight answer on whether or not they have a pee reservoir in there somewhere.

I broke out the fancy mescal and shot glasses I had bought in Oaxaca. The guys made a few emotional toasts to Brian. They were all pretty tired from a long day of driving and dealing with the scorching Mexico/Guatemala border, so we had some dinner and called it an early night.

A giant Alfombra

The next night, we wandered the streets, checking out the parades with

Sophie and some friends from her Spanish school. Floats supported by twenty to thirty Costaleros depicted scenes of the Virgin Mary, angels, and Jesus carrying the cross. Some of the floats appeared incredibly heavy. Directors in silken robes helped steer, standing at the ready to make sure the whole thing didn't topple over to one side. Brass bands followed the floats around playing somber funerary music.

A Semana Santa float lit up at night

On Friday night, the sidewalks were so crowded that just *walking* to the guys' Airbnb was a challenge. If the street wasn't filled by a giant float, it was taken up by a massive Alfombra waiting for the parade to come trample it. Several times, I popped out of a crowd and almost stumbled onto a bus-sized Alfombra that teams of people had worked on all night. I have nightmares of falling into one of those things.

I met up with the guys for dinner, where we were joined by an expat biker they had met earlier in the day. The expat made us all very nervous about our plan to cross into El Salvador on the Saturday of Semana Santa. He was convinced the border would be insane, and we should wait until at least Wednesday. He also told us El Salvador was so dangerous that we'd probably get killed within a few days. We asked him if he'd ever been to El Salvador. The answer was no.

At 11 p.m., the town was still riddled with parades. We called it a night so we could get up at the crack of dawn, prepared for an all-day wait at the border. When I left the guys' place, the contents of their pannier boxes were still scattered all over the floor—like three intermingled 3D jigsaw puzzles.

On the walk back to my place, I said goodbye to Tecún Umán, Reilly's Pub, Guate Java, Cactus Taco Bar, Antigua's Gym, and my nice laundry lady. Okay, the laundry lady had long gone home, but I said goodbye to her in spirit. I got a little verklempt over my last night in Antigua, but I promised myself I'd return someday.

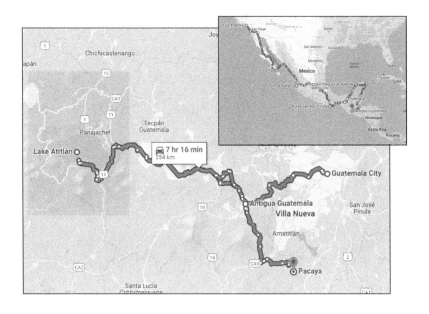

CHAPTER 28

DON'T SKIP EL SALVADOR

I MET up with the End of All Roads guys Saturday morning for what would be our first time riding together. I asked Dan how long it took to reassemble all their stuff the night before. "We didn't get much sleep," is all he grunted. I commiserated with him, chronicling my own five-minute struggle to corral all my stuff into my backpack in time to meet them at 7 a.m.

We started with me riding in front, which I liked, as I was terrified I might run into one of them. Given what had already happened, this prospect was unthinkable beyond all comprehension. But it soon became apparent that having me in front wouldn't work. I'd straddle a big pothole only to see Dan forced to take abrupt evasive action in my rearview mirror. At one point, a car in front of me slammed on its brakes to avoid a pothole, causing me to slam on my brakes, whereupon Dan appeared at my driver's side window.

Oh, hi Dan.

He wasn't sure if he could stop in time, so he swerved around me. The three of them passed me for good after that.

Whenever we stopped for a break, I'd get out of my air-conditioned car and saunter over in flip-flops to where the guys were busy creating a small lake of sweat. I never got tired of asking them stuff like, "Is it hot under all that gear?" and "Why don't they make air conditioners for those suits? You have everything else." I'm sure they appreciated the humor, too.

El Salvador and Belize are the only two Central American countries that don't span from the Caribbean to the Pacific, which means you can drive around them to get up or down Central America. Many overlanders skip El Salvador due to safety concerns or to make one less border crossing. However, I'd read glowing reviews about El Salvador from the Pan-Am travelers' group and other overlander sources. There's even a hashtag imploring overlanders and backpackers: #**DONTSKIPELSALVADOR**.

As we headed to the border, my new place anxiety was kicking in big time. Sure, Guatemala had crime, but this was El Salvador, the big leagues, land of MS-13. The expat biker's prediction of our imminent deaths wasn't helping matters.

We rode through through the steamy lowlands of southern Guatemala for a few hours, then rolled up to a completely deserted border. Saturday of Semana Santa couldn't have been a better time to cross if it was the zombie apocalypse. We hoped this meant the expat also had no idea what he was talking about with regard to El Salvador's safety.

While I pondered a large map of El Salvador, two scraggly gringos who had just walked across the border approached. I had a feeling that as soon as I struck up a conversation with these guys, they'd ask me for a ride. They seemed okay, if slightly odiferous. I told them our destination was the nearby surf town of El Tunco, then asked where they were going. "Well, we don't really know. Do you think we could get a ride with you to El Tunco?" Yeah, sure.

It turned out one was from Israel, the other from Bulgaria. They were doing the cheapest *dirtbag traveler* (it's a common affectionate term, really) experience possible. Their tales of trying to live on $0 a day fascinated me. They jumped into trucks with locals for free rides whenever possible. Traveling this way, they were certainly seeing more of how real Central Americans live than I was. The downside was a two-hour hell ride crammed into a small pickup with twenty other people and a piss-drunk driver screaming at everyone. But they lived and got a good story out of it.

EL TUNCO

Dan and the guys rolled into El Tunco ahead of me, snagging the last three rooms at La Guitarra, an iconic surfer compound in the center of town. I got stuck at a hostel across the street full of aloof surfers who refused to acknowledge my existence. Later, the hitchhikers I picked up messaged me that they had found a half-built house on the beach to crash in with other dirtbaggers. I envied them a little, but not enough to sleep on a concrete floor exposed to the entire pantheon of biting night bugs this part of the world has to offer.

I bought a SIM card in town and asked the local kid about safety in El Salvador. He told me, "You'll be fine. The gangs don't go after tourists. Just don't—"

I cut him off, "—try to hit on a gangbanger's girlfriend?"

Yeah, way ahead of you on that.

We regrouped and found a casual beer and burger place on the water. For the first time, I had a chance to relax and shoot the breeze with Dan and the guys. Antigua was hectic with Semana Santa and the guys constantly organizing their stuff and arranging travel schedules. I got to know Bob and Justin better in the relaxed environment of El Tunco.

I could tell they were still out of sorts from Brian's death. I was surprised they started up their trip again so soon. It would have been understandable for them to wait a while, but they all figured they wanted to get back at it before they fell into a funk. And it's the oldest cliché, but also true—they knew Brian would have wanted them to continue the ride.

El Tunco in a sleepy early morning mood

That night, the town filled with young people coming in from the surrounding area to party. From our vantage point on a second-story terrace, I could feel the heat coming off the revelers packing the street, adding to the already steamy ambient temperature.

On my way back to the snooty surfer hostel, I found myself drawn in by the hypnotic pull of a woman working an open griddle in front of a packed restaurant called Mamaguaya. She slapped a ball of dough back and forth between her hands fifteen times in lightning succession (I had to slow down my video to count) until it took on the shape of a three to four-inch disc. Then she molded the disc into a clamshell, stuffed it with cheese, and sealed it with raw egg. Finally, she lightning-slapped the sealed clamshell another fifteen times until it flattened into an oval a half-inch thick and six inches wide. I realized these must be the legendary stuffed "pupusas" I'd been hearing about the closer I got to El Salvador.

I ordered one pupusa with garlic and cheese and one with beans and cheese. Upon receiving my food, I found the cheese in my pupusa had fused with the surrounding porous corn cake. I couldn't tell where the filling ended and the shell began. Think of the most dense, rich, moist corn-bread you've ever eaten, then double that and make it cheesy. The first bite was one of those wide-eyed "Holy crap!" mouthgasm moments that are the absolute joy of travel, especially when you stumble onto them.

Pupusas!

I returned to Mamaguaya the next day and sat at a breezy second-story table overlooking the canal that runs through town. Since I wasn't wolfing down my pupusas on the street, I tried them with the standard condiments: curtido (sour carrot-slaw) and a mild runny salsa that soaks into the pupusa. Peppers are provided to add heat. As with most great dishes, I found pupusas delicious with or without accouterments. Later, I brought Dan and the guys, who all had their own "Holy crap!" moments. Pupusas easily win best street food in Central America.

After a few days of fun in El Tunco, Dan and the guys headed south to attempt the unheard-of two border crossings in one day—Honduras, then Nicaragua. They only had a few days to get to Costa Rica, where they planned to park their bikes for a month.

I also got the vibe that they didn't want to stick around in this turbulent part of Central America very long, given their god-awful experience with the police and medical institutions in Mexico. I was happy they had seen some of the good side of this part of the world when they met Roy, the guardian angel taxi driver who drove them around Zacatecas and translated for them. When the ordeal was over, the guys collected donations for Roy and his family. A few months later, Roy named his new baby *Brian Felipe* in honor of Brian.

*New El Salvador and End of All Roads sticker with Dan,
Justin and Bob, from left to right*

On my own again, I pondered my next destination. One El Salvador tourist spot that came up repeatedly was the Ruta de las Flores (Route of the Flowers)—a procession of five colonial towns surrounded by a few national parks in El Salvador's cloud forest. Cloud forest, you say? **Not** ninety degrees and humid, you say? Sold.

You had me at "cloud."

Heading up to the Ruta de las Flores on El Salvador's busy four-lane southern highway, I spotted a man off to my right, walking swiftly up a driveway toward the road, brandishing an Uzi-type submachine gun that hung from a strap over his shoulder. He seemed agitated, desperately scanning passing cars, looking for someone that I'm glad wasn't me. He was uncomfortably close by the time I passed him, so I could see he was fortyish with slicked-back hair, wearing an untucked dress shirt, slacks, and nice shoes. He had no tattoos and seemed too old to be a gangbanger. I'd seen plenty of M-16/AR-15-style assault rifles on cops and security guards on the trip. But this was my first Uzi sighting, well, ever.

If I had to guess, maybe he was a local business owner defending himself against gang extortion or robbery. The driveway led to what looked like an auto repair shop and a few other similar businesses. Or, more troublingly, maybe I drove through some organized crime turf war. I did see a souped-up Toyota Hilux with blacked-out windows abruptly pull over a quarter mile up the road. I did *not* stick around to see how it turned out.

Street gangs have been a problem in Guatemala, El Salvador, and Honduras since the 1980s, *before* the mass deportation of Central American criminals from US jails in the '90s and '00s. So, it's a misnomer to say the US caused the gang problems these countries face today. But it is accurate to say the US significantly amplified the problem. MS-13 and other notorious Central American gangs originated in the US, became hardened in US jails, then took street violence to surreal new heights back in their home countries. From 2007 to 2013, over 900 Guatemala City chicken bus drivers were killed as part of extortion schemes. That is not a typo.

The problem can trace its roots to Central American refugees arriving in the US in the '70s and '80s, fleeing the various US-sponsored dirty wars raging back in their home countries. Because the US government supported the regimes they were fleeing, most refugees were only granted "economic migrant" status—which doesn't include a path to citizenship. Relegated to the lowest rung of society, the children of these refugees grew into restless young men without prospects who naturally got into trouble. They formed street gangs to protect themselves from the already established Chicano (born in the US) and Mexican (born in Mexico) gangs in their neighborhoods.

Mara Salvatrucha (MS-13), Barrio 18, and some lesser-known but equally violent Central American gangs came to collectively be known as "Maras." Mara is short for "marabunta," which literally means "a massive migration of voracious army ants who devour anything that can't get out of their way," i.e., a migratory mob. Their gang culture, specializing in drug dealing and extortion, demands unconditional loyalty, starting with brutal rites of initiation. They distinguish themselves with head-to-toe tattoos, making it difficult to transition to a regular job. The penalty for leaving the gang is death.

In the US, mara gangs earned a reputation for ruthlessness and extreme violence that shocked even the local Latino gangs, who sometimes hired maras to carry out their dirtiest jobs. When these young men went to jail, they continued their gang activities and learned even more organized criminality. After they had served their sentence, they were deported back to their home country—with predictable results. Spanglish-speaking Mara gangsters, strangers in their own country, stuck together and quickly dominated the local gangs. Marabuntas, spawned by refugees fleeing government terror, would go on to spawn their own wave of refugees fleeing gang violence.

Other than the guy with the Uzi, the drive was extremely pleasant. El Salvador does a great job of promoting and clearly labeling tourist routes and directions to national parks—much more in the US style than Mexico or Guatemala. Roads also tended to be nicely paved, with guardrails even. There's a saying in El Salvador: "The people can eat pavement,"—meaning the populace may not always have food, but the roads will always be well-maintained.

Along the rim of one scenic valley, I pulled over to a viewpoint where a high-pitched whistling emanated from seemingly everywhere. I queried a passerby and found out the sound was produced by cicadas. I get nostalgic for the rhythmic pulsing song of the midwestern cicadas I grew up with. El Salvador's cicadas sound like one of those sonic death rays that force Captain Kirk to cup his ears and writhe in scenery-chewing agony. I'm not sure I could ever get nostalgic for that.

I made my first stop along the Ruta de las Flores at the town of Juayúa. Ringed by palm trees, bougainvillea, and other brightly colored landscaping, the town's square featured a pristine white fountain as a centerpiece.

As I wandered around amidst the colorful haciendas and shimmering flowers, it occurred to me that all these people going about their day in this fairy tale setting must have never gotten the message that they live in a "shithole country." Then I walked around angry for a while just thinking about that. Yes, El Salvador has real problems. But as Americans, given our own country has had such a big hand in creating and exacerbating those problems, the least we can do is have some empathy.

I spent the night in Concepción de Ataco—a grid of cobblestone streets and colorful haciendas centered around a central square lined with restaurants and craft shops. While dining on pupusas, a vehicle in the form of a giant purple stiletto pump took laps around the square. Standard.

Stilettos—never the best idea on cobblestone streets

The following day, I decided to take a fun-looking back road to the town of Tacuba. I had enjoyed traveling with fellow humans, but I was happy to get back to crooked roads and spontaneous adventure. I'm guessing the road I took doesn't get much non-local traffic. When I'd wave at kids along the road, they'd stare slack-jawed at the red-bearded gringo in the silver marshmallow car before sometimes waving back.

TACUBA

Off the dirt road and onto Tacuba's paved streets, I turned a corner and came up against the frenetic phalanx of miniature humanity that only forms when legions of schoolchildren are released en masse. There was no time for evasive maneuvers. I could only stop, brace myself, and hope for the best as wave after wave of giggling uniformed kids engulfed my vehicle, then moved on. Shaken but unharmed, I pressed on to the only accommodation in town: Mama y Papa's Hostel.

"Papa" arranged a trek the next day into Parque Nacional El Imposible —so named for a long-gone, extremely hard-to-negotiate cable bridge. I set out to explore Tacuba with the only other guest at the hostel, a young Aussie guy. The town proved to be quite sleepy when it wasn't swarmed with school kids. Buildings similar to Ataco, if a bit dowdier and not as brightly colored, lined the gently hilled streets. The town had only a few basic restaurants, but everything I tried was quite tasty. Tacuba's singular tourist attraction is a ruined old church. If you'd like a closer look, you need to find the caretaker who will open the gate and let you poke around the overgrown grounds. We were content to peek through the fence.

Sleepy Tacuba

William, my guide for Parque Nacional El Imposible, showed up the next morning. From the start, I surmised this guy was a little off-kilter. He had a mischievous twinkle in his eye, which isn't typically the first quality I look for in choosing someone to lead me into the Central American jungle.

We hiked through various stages of cloud forest, passing the occasional homestead amidst farming terraces tenuously carved into the steep terrain. William pointed out trees and herbs that had medicinal value. The bark of one tree was supposed to be good for prostate troubles. I asked him if the forest had anything for a sore heel. It did not.

We saw a torogoz, or turquoise-browed motmot, the national bird of El Salvador and, according to William, not a common sight in those parts. The bird's iridescent coat seemed to change from blue to green to orange with slight variations in viewing angle. It also had two "wires" at the end of its tail that led to tail fins, reminding me of a toy glider. Known as a "racketed tail," the torogoz swings this feature back and forth, like a wagging finger, as a signal to predators that they've been spotted and should try their luck elsewhere.

When we reached a steep ravine, William offered, "I'm going to do something special for you. I've never done this before." With that, he took off the coil of rope he'd been carrying and tied it to a tree. He had harnesses for both of us, which we attached to the rope and lowered ourselves down a steep bank. When we reached a straight drop-off down to a pool below, William said he'd lower me into the pool, then haul me back up.

Torogoz—the national bird of El Salvador

Hmmm. Let's see. You've never done this before, I outweigh you by eighty pounds, and I haven't climbed a rope since sixth grade. But you're going to somehow pull me up out of that?

I passed on his gracious offer. So he had me lower him down instead.

He splashed around in the pool a bit, then told me to wrap the rope around my back and help pull him up. I leveraged my body weight to pull him up, leaning backward and using a tree as a pulley. Eventually, I couldn't descend the bank any farther, so I yelled down that he'd have to pull himself up the rest of the way. He yelled up, "Okay, just hold the rope tight!"

At this point, my right arm came to rest on an anthill swarming with tiny black ants. Naturally, this being Central America, even tiny black ants stung like hell. But I couldn't move my arm, or William would fall. Thankfully, they weren't bullet ants, purported to have the most painful sting in the animal kingdom, or William would already be back in the pool.

I gradually repositioned myself to get my arm off the anthill. But ants were still all over the rope and crawling up my arm, stinging happily as they went. As soon as William reached the top, I did a little dance, scraping them off my body and out of my shirt. Still, I doubt William lowering me into the pool would have ended any better.

After the hike, I had a Baja-esque moment listening to cicadas in the crow's nest hammock at Mama y Papa's. What is it about hammocks? Maybe it's because I'm always on vacation when I'm in a hammock.

To start up the whistling chorus, a few individual cicadas would start making slow clicks. Then, more cicadas would join in, increasing the pace and intensity until they reached some harmonic threshold that merged the clicks into a high-pitched whistle. I pondered the physics of this as I listened to cicadas, chickens, car horns, bike horns, barking dogs, construction, songbirds, and a car stereo blasting reggaeton—all melding together to form a blissful cacophonous medley. It sounds weird, but the combination just worked.

Then, a baby started crying, which tore through the whole symphony like a rusty machete. Damn behavioral evolution.

Later, I went out for dinner, now the only gringo in town as far as I knew. I found it refreshing to walk the cobbled streets of Tacuba as the lone tourist in a place with zero tourist amenities. After dinner, I sat outside the local church, listening to a choral event with the concession vendors.

On the way back to the hostel, I passed a dozen teenagers milling around in an alley. They looked like the Sharks or the Jets—just hanging out, waiting for trouble. I wondered if I'd finally seen some gang trouble in sleepy Tacuba. Then I realized the kids were playing games on their phones. Apparently, that block was the only place in town they could get a decent cell signal.

I still had a week before I planned to meet up with some friends in Honduras. I was trying to figure out what to do with myself when my new friend Sophie texted that she had missed her flight to Costa Rica and was instead headed to El Tunco. Well then, I guess I'm headed back to El Tunco for a few days. Fortunately, nothing is more than a few hours away in El Salvador.

Along the way, something possessed me to take a shot of a welcome sign to a nondescript town called Sonsonate and then post it on social media. I always post pictures of lovely places and maybe of dodgy places, but I never post shots of a typical, gritty, non-touristy city in a place like El Salvador. I figured that might interest me as a voyeur following along with a traveler.

To my surprise, a friend I knew from an exercise boot camp replied that Sonsonate was her hometown. This was one of the unexpected pleasures of the trip—finding out which of my friends and acquaintances had roots in Mexico or Central America as I rolled through their home region. She finished with, "I hope you enjoy my little Pulgracito!" Salvadorans lovingly refer to their tiny country as "El Pulgracito de America"—*The Pinky of the Americas*.

The next day, Sophie and I set out to visit a local hiking attraction—Volcán Santa Ana. Much to Sophie's chagrin, we arrived a few minutes too late to snag one of the required guides for the hike to the top. We did find a guide to take us on a flat loop hike, which was pleasant but didn't satisfy Sophie's need for adventure. On the way back to my car, two families approached me. They'd seen my California plates and wanted to welcome me to their country. Both families had relatives in Los Angeles. This scene would repeat throughout El Salvador.

In the parking lot, I decided to try a popular local delicacy called yuca frita—made from fried sweet yucca (a rooty, squash-like plant), sour slaw, red sauce, and fried baby sardines. The dish looked so revolting, I figured it had to be good.

This turned out to be a flawed assumption.

It tasted like one would assume, with the unexpected delight of little fish skulls popping between my teeth like Rice Krispies.

Sophie and I separated again the following day. She was headed to Nicaragua. I said my goodbyes to her

Yuca Frita—tastes almost as good as it looks

and El Tunco and headed east across the country, where I planned to visit El Mozote, the site of a horrendous 1981 massacre. Steamy El Tunco had grown on me much more than I thought a hot beach town ever could, melting my heart like the proverbial dog that Dad didn't want.

I worked my way to the Morazán region in the northeast end of the country, near the border with Honduras. Around 5 p.m., I was very close to the town of Perquín, my destination for the night—when I crested a hill and saw a police cruiser at a crossing a few hundred yards away. The cruiser pulled out onto the highway ahead of me. My spidey sense tingled that these cops might be interested in me. But they were going so slow I had no choice but to pull up behind them, lest I look suspicious driving 10 miles an hour. After a minute of this, they pulled over to the side of the road, then got in behind me and fired up their flashers.

I pulled over. Three men appeared at my window, all smiles. The lead guy in the middle looked like a cop. The other two wore green fatigues like the Army or National Guard. The whole scene was very convivial, except for the assault rifles strapped across their chests—which I noticed were different models between the cop and the two Army guys.

I gave them my ID. They seemed very curious about where I was going and expressed concern that I didn't want to be driving at night in this part of El Salvador—a sentiment I wholeheartedly shared. I mentioned the name of the hotel I was headed to in Perquín. (I didn't mention El Mozote.) That seemed to put them at ease.

But then we had this weird exchange:

"Tu arma?" the lead cop asked me.

"Como?" I asked ("Come again?"—more or less).

"Tu arma?"

"Lo siento, no comprendo."

"Are you armed?" (Apparently, he was sandbagging me on his English.)

"No, no. That's you guys, not me." I held up my hands to show I wasn't carrying any weapons, gingerly pointing a finger at their conspicuous hardware.

This finally satisfied them, and they sent me on my way. I think they just wondered what I was doing in that area so close to dusk. Nonetheless, those long guns combined with their catlike curiosity was a bit unnerving.

That night, having nothing better to do, I posted my little vignette of getting pulled over by heavily armed cops on Facebook, starting with: "I got lit up today for the first time on the trip..."

I made sure to come off as calm and collected under fire as possible. I have a few women following me who I wouldn't mind if they saw a bit of my dangerous side—as I'm painfully aware I land squarely on the "Harmless Teddy Bear" end of the Bad Boy Spectrum.

Of course, the chances that this particular story would move the needle are basically nil. But a guy can still try.

Within minutes, my mom replied:

Way to be cool, "Dude" 😎 🖤 😀

Yeah, that should pretty much cement the bad-boy image I was going for. Thanks, Mom.

Imagine if turn-of-the-century explorers like Earnest Shackleton had to deal with social media:

Have fun on your little adventure to the South Pole, son, and BE SAFE!!! 😄 😄 😄

His men would mutiny.

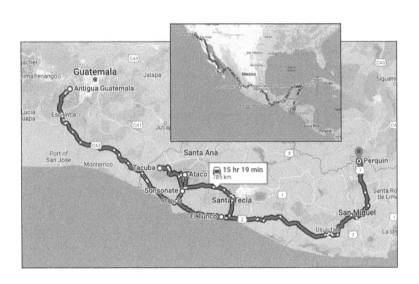

CHAPTER 29

THIS IS WAR

CONTENT WARNING: If, like me, horrific crimes deeply upset you and the mental images stay with you, sometimes forever, you might want to skip this entire chapter. I'm not going to recount every monstrous detail I came across, most of which come from Mark Danner's heart-wrenching book, *The Massacre at El Mozote*. However, some specifics are necessary to tell the story. In a perverse way, our aversion to discussing *unspeakable* horrors in polite company seems to benefit those who commit the worst atrocities. Survivors risked their lives to tell the truth of what happened at El Mozote to anyone who would listen. It seems the least I can do to tell their story here.

PERQUÍN

AT 3,600 FEET, crisp mountain air fills the town of Perquín with the sweet smell of oocarpa pines, reminiscent of a southern US pine forest. The three-room Museo de la Revolución, not officially promoted by the government of El Salvador, is surrounded by large armaments from El Salvador's thirteen-year civil war. Just off one corner of the building, next to a display of an unexploded bomb with US markings, a proudly preserved bomb crater gapes twenty-five feet across. Nearby, the twisted wreck of a downed aircraft sits prominently displayed under a dedicated shelter.

Inside the museum, long guns are displayed in conical "teepee" formation, along with stolen radios, which were invaluable in helping the rebels track the Army's movements. Propaganda posters and photos of the foot soldiers and leaders of the Farabundo Martí National Liberation Front (FMLN) line the walls. The images, generally candid shots taken during a lull in the fighting, give the appearance that life as a guerrilla for the FMLN was something akin to a fun summer camp with semi-automatic rifles.

Two young FMLN rebels enjoy a jocular moment

One room is dedicated to Radio Venceremos, the FMLN's highly effective underground radio station. Its suitcase-sized portable transmitter reached the entire country from the station's hiding place in the steep, dense terrain of El Morazán, the Department in northeast El Salvador that encompasses Perquín and El Mozote. Radio Venceremos, broadcasting "from somewhere in the Morazán," drove the Salvadoran government up the wall. The station put on a wildly popular satirical serial that mocked high-ranking government and military leaders. Even the targets of their satire tuned in to "hate listen."

Unlike Guatemala, the revolución in El Salvador actually stood a chance. The Salvadoran Army outnumbered the FMLN by roughly 13,000 to 4,000, but the rebels had terrain and asymmetrical warfare advantages. The Army could put the guerrillas on the run but didn't have the numbers to occupy their territory. The United States, desperate to avoid El Salvador following the same path as Nicaragua's Sandinista revolution, poured millions of dollars into El Salvador's military and trained its elite squadrons.

Just as in Guatemala's Civil War, mutilated corpses of suspected leftists showed up every morning in El Salvador's streets. Women had conspicuously been tortured and raped. Men had their genitals mutilated. In 1980 alone, death squads carried out an estimated 10,000 political murders. The government eventually ran out of hit lists in the cities, then began killing anyone even *suspected* of being a leftist. Wearing blue jeans and tennis shoes could be enough to get one killed as a possible rebel sympathizer. The American Embassy knew El Salvador's right-wing military regime was behind the killings. Nevertheless, US intelligence publicly upheld the facade of uncertainty as they couldn't risk Congress turning off the aid spigot.

One of the most feared death squads took its name from General Maximiliano Hernández Martínez, architect of El Salvador's La Matanza (The Massacre) in 1931—during which an estimated 10,000 to 40,000 peasants, mostly Pipil Maya, were executed in broad daylight. This was the event that Diana's friend told us about, which cowed El Salvador's indigenous Maya into abandoning their traditional dress. The idea behind La Matanza was that if the rebels are the fish, then the civilians living in their zones are the sea. If you can't remove the fish, you drain the sea. You kill enough innocent civilians that everyone else flees the zone. La Matanza was incredibly effective, paving the way

An unlabeled picture in the Museo de la Revolución

for fifty years of barely challenged military rule. Invoking the name of Martínez in El Salvador to terrorize indigenous peasants was akin to invoking Hitler to terrorize Jews. Not surprisingly, Martínez himself was a big fan of Hitler.

By 1981, most of the FMLN's urban supporters had either been murdered or had taken to the hills to join the rebels. But in January 1981, the rebels took the fight to the cities anyway, hoping to inspire a national uprising as Nicaragua's Sandinistas had done in 1978. The offensive failed to gain traction, putting the rebels back on the run in their rural strongholds.

In early December 1981, El Salvador's army initiated the Orwellian-named "Operation Rescue," a massive "Eunice y martillo" (hammer and anvil) maneuver. Their official objective was the command post of the

Revolutionary Army of the Poor (ERP), one of five regional groups that comprised the FMLN.

The idea was to deploy the regular army in a massive offensive sweep through the countryside—*the hammer*—often using a natural barrier like a river or mountain range to funnel the rebels toward an elite fighting force —*the anvil*. While the nimble guerrillas generally escaped the "anvil" in these operations, villagers and peasant farmers caught in the dragnet had nothing but bad options. Families could remain in their homes and pray the soldiers passed them by, perhaps with nothing more than a combative interrogation. Or they could flee to the surrounding hills and ravines, knowing the price of being caught was most likely execution as a suspected FMLN sympathizer. On top of that, soldiers would often burn down empty houses on the assumption they had been abandoned by guerillas.

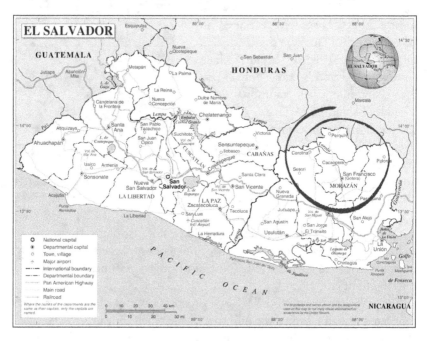

Departamento de Morazán, El Salvador

The "anvil" role in Operation Rescue was to be played by the elite US-trained Atlácatl Battalion, ironically named for a legendary indigenous warrior who fought against the conquistadors. The leader of the Atlácatl, Lieutenant Colonel José Domingo Monterrosa Barrios, was one of America's star pupils. A Salvadoran General described him as "that rare thing: a pure, one-hundred-percent soldier, a natural leader, a born military man with the rare quality of being able to instill loyalty in his men."

Lt. Colonel Monterrosa trained at the US Army's School of the Americas in Panama before taking on his role as founding commander of the Atlácatl. The US hoped he would become a model for reform and tighten up the Salvadoran military. Before the start of Operation Rescue, Monterrosa reiterated the goal to capture the rebels' command post **and** Radio Venceremos, adding, "So long as we don't finish off Radio Venceremos, we'll always have a scorpion up our ass."

EL MOZOTE

After the museum, I took a winding, rust-colored dirt road to the town of El Mozote. As the road dropped in elevation, the air became thicker and warmer, and pines gave way to tangled tropical brush. Prominent flags with FMLN in white letters on a red background flew high above some homesteads.

A mural at the entrance to town depicts a church set amidst a pastoral farmland scene, with a waterfall flowing down into a river and the caption "Bienvenidos a El Mozote" (Welcome to El Mozote). The mural's most prominent feature is a family of four holding hands—silhouetted, as if erased from the scene.

Welcome to El Mozote mural

Few pictures of El Mozote from before 1981 survive. I did stumble upon this loving depiction of the town from writer and journalist Renan

Alcides Orellana, who taught literacy in El Mozote in 1951. Filtered through the oblique flourishes of Google Translate, it reads:

> *[El Mozote was] a faithful replica of a butterfly garden. A long street, flanked by lush forests of 'fart apple,' was the vital nerve of the village. The cornfields grew; the cane fields threw honey stabs into the sky; the maguey trees sharpened their points of light; the water ran limpid, humming along the red mud gutters; the fruits were honey slices everywhere. Many 'little mountain plants' filled the mountains with strange colors. The cattle grazed calmly, as if chewing patience, while countless clouds of little birds saturated the landscape with wings.*

Notes:

1. Crabapples are sometimes known as "fart apples," owing to their effect on dogs who eat too many of them.
2. Maguey is a giant form of agave with long spiked leaves that can grow up to twenty feet tall.

The 300 residents of El Mozote and the immediate surrounding countryside knew Operation Rescue was coming. The local paper reported that only residents would be allowed to enter the zone. Marco Diaz, the owner of a small store and the town's wealthiest and most respected resident, returned from a supply run with further news: A local officer and friend had pulled Marco aside to tell him he should hunker down in town for the duration of Operation Rescue. Only in El Mozote could the officer guarantee Diaz and the other townspeople's safety. The officer further implored Marco to tell everyone in the nearby hamlets and surrounding countryside to seek refuge in El Mozote. It is likely this officer had no idea what was coming.

El Mozote's residents had experienced similar military pushes in the past and come out largely unscathed. As an enclave of evangelical Protestants who were by nature deeply suspicious of anything that resembled communism, particularly the leftist Catholic priests who worked closely with the FMLN, El Mozote had always had good relations with the Army. The guerrillas might occasionally buy food and supplies from merchants in town, but that was the extent of their interaction. El Salvador's government knew the residents of El Mozote weren't collaborators, and the local ERP knew El Mozote was useless as a recruiting ground.

Operation Rescue went into full swing on December 8. Soldiers from the Army's Third Brigade swept the countryside north from the Torola River. At the same time, the men of the Atlácatl Battalion started moving south from Perquín using conscripted local men as guides. According to a guide, the Atlácatl had lists of people in villages along the way. At each stop, they would interrogate and then execute anyone on their list. This continued to the town of Arambala—a mile north of El Mozote.

Along the way, word got back to company commander Captain Walter Oswaldo Salazar that another officer had said residents should be treated with respect until they were proven to be guerrillas. Salazar angrily replied, "No, these are all guerrillas!" and further added that the soldiers could go ahead and kill any of them or all of them. After Arambala, the Atlácatl commanders had no more lists. Still, they pressed on to El Mozote.

By the time the Atlácatl walked into El Mozote late in the day on December 10th, Marco Diaz's house, like the other houses in town, was full of people who had flooded in from the surrounding area. Forty-one-year-old Rufina Amaya and her husband, Domingo Claros, considered hiding in the mountains but ultimately elected to stay in El Mozote, largely on the weight of Diaz's advice. Inside the packed house, Rufina did her best to calm her nine-year-old son Christino and his younger sisters, Maria Dolores, five, and Maria Lilian, three, while occasionally nursing her eight-month-old daughter, Maria Isabel.

The Atlácatl forced everyone out of the houses, commanded them to lie face down, then walked around kicking people and interrogating them with questions like, "Where are the guns?" Marco Diaz protested that there were no guns and no guerrilla supporters in El Mozote. A soldier screamed at him, "No motherfucker, now you have to pay!" and stomped his head into the dirt. Soldiers demanded people hand over any rings and jewelry they had on their bodies. After several hours of this, everyone was ordered back inside their houses. Outside, the men of the Atlácatl sang and fired guns in the air throughout the night. Inside, Rufina and the other mothers did their best to calm their children, which was difficult since they couldn't take little kids who were soiling themselves outside to be cleaned.

Just before dawn, soldiers again rousted everyone into the plaza, ordering men and older boys to one side and women and children to the other. Everyone was again threatened, punched, and interrogated.

According to a later legal report, even the soldiers didn't know what they would be ordered to do next.

At 7 a.m., a helicopter hovered over the town. Soldiers herded the men into the church, then crammed over a hundred women and children into a three-room house in the center of town. The helicopter touched down, disgorging a half dozen officers who were received by the commanding officer on the ground. Some officers headed to the church, while others went to the house with the women and children. The officers struck the women with the butts of their guns and jabbed at them with bayonets, accused them of being collaborators, and again demanded to know where the guns were. After less than an hour, the officers piled back into the helicopter and lifted off. The "interrogation" seemed to have been a cursory formality. A junior Salvadoran intelligence officer stationed nearby expected to spend several days helping to interrogate 600 people. But he was never summoned to the scene.

Not long after the helicopter faded into the distance, men in the church started screaming. Rufina and her son stood on a bench to see out of a small back window. They saw her husband Domingo and another man bolt from the soldiers toward the bush. Both men were gunned down before they could get very far. Rufina and her son looked on in horror as the soldiers walked up to the two men lying motionless and beheaded them with machetes. According to several reports, the soldiers started out beheading every man. But their arms grew tired, so they shot the remaining men instead.

By afternoon, the gunshots and screams of the men had died down. Rufina's son begged her to take him out of the house so they wouldn't be killed. Soldiers again came to the packed house, where they announced that women would be taken out in groups, after which they would be free to go back to their homes or anywhere they wanted. But they only picked out young women and girls, some as young as ten, knocking the younger girls loose from their mother's grasp with the butts of their guns. Screams soon poured down from the hills above town as soldiers started raping the girls and young women.

While this was happening, one or two helicopters returned (stories vary). One of the conscripted guides recognized several officers, including the commander of the Third Brigade and Lt. Colonel Monterrosa. Amidst the screams from the women and girls echoing from the hills, the officers were ushered into an empty house, where they conferred for a short time, then got back in the helicopter(s) and left.

After this, the soldiers returned for the rest of the women. Rufina describes, "When they came back, they began separating the women from their kids. They pulled the mothers away, leaving the children there crying. They took one group of women and then in a while they came back and took another. That was the saddest thing—little by little, the mothers disappeared, and the house became filled mostly with crying children."

When the soldiers came for Rufina, it took two of them to pry baby Maria Isabel from her arms. They marched the twenty or so women in Rufina's group single file toward another house. When the woman in front reached the open doorway, she started screaming. She saw the blood and dead bodies and knew they were being led to slaughter.

Rufina, at the back of the line, dropped to her knees and began to pray, "I was crying and begging God to forgive my sins. Though I was almost at the feet of the soldiers, I wasn't begging them—I was begging God. Where I was kneeling, I was between a crabapple and a pine tree. Maybe that was what saved me. In all the yelling and commotion, they didn't see me there. The soldier behind me had gone up front to help with the first women. They didn't see me when I crawled between the trees."

As the soldiers in front grabbed the struggling woman to shove her into the killing house, one of them told her, "Don't cry, woman, here comes the devil to take you." Rufina watched as all the women in her group were forced into the house, followed by screams and gunshots. When the screams finally stopped, the soldiers rounded up the last group of women— to the same sequence of screaming, hugging, resisting, and shooting. When those women stopped screaming, Rufina could again hear the screams of the girls and women in the hills. Once all the mothers had been executed, the soldiers razed the killing house.

Rufina worried the fire would ignite the tree that was giving her cover, forcing her to flee and reveal herself. Soldiers sat only a few feet from her at one point—close enough to touch. She had to remain perfectly still, frozen in terror, as soldiers discussed what to do about the kids. Some soldiers wanted to keep the kids they had been raping "for a while." Another soldier told them that was absolutely out of the question—that this was a scorched earth operation on the Colonel's orders. Everyone must be killed.

Screams started up again as the Atlácatl began killing the children in the house. The soldiers used their bayonets and rifle butts to kill some of the smaller children. Another group was led crying and screaming to the Sacristy, where they were gunned down.

Rufina heard her son Cristino screaming for her: "Then I heard one of my children crying. My son, Cristino, was crying, 'Mama Rufina, help me! They're killing me! They killed my sister! They're killing me! Help me!' I didn't know what to do. They were killing my children. I knew that if I went back there to help my children I would be cut to pieces. But I couldn't stand to hear it, I couldn't bear it. I was afraid that I would cry out, that I would scream, that I would go crazy. I couldn't stand it, and I prayed to God to help me. I promised God that if He helped me I would tell the world what happened here."

Hiding herself within a passing group of cows, Rufina snuck away from the scene, then crawled several hundred yards down a dirt road past a sleeping soldier. Under a bright full moon, soldiers spotted her moving from a distance several times, prompting them to search for her and fire bullets in her direction. Yet, they never found her hiding place in a little ravine filled with maguey. She covered herself with corn husks and spiny maguey leaves, even as they tore her clothes and stabbed her flesh. Then she dug a small hole and buried her face in it, so she could cry without being heard.

Once the children's screams finally died down, the soldiers set fire to everything. This forced people who were still hiding or playing dead to reveal themselves, resulting in sporadic gunfire throughout the night. In the morning, the bulk of the Atlácatl moved out to continue the massacre in the nearby hamlet of Los Toriles.

After the Atlácatl had wiped out El Mozote, Los Toriles, and a few other hamlets, they finally moved on to their official objective—the rebel base at nearby La Guacamaya. The guerrillas, of course, had long fled. While punching through enemy lines, an ERP soldier burdened with heavy radio equipment was mortally wounded, losing the transmitter down a ravine. Radio Venceremos was knocked off the air. Monterrosa had removed the scorpion from his ass, at least for a while.

The Atlácatl spent a few more days winding down operations, then packed up and left the area. Guerrillas flowed back in and were gobsmacked at the utter devastation. Bodies in gruesome poses littered the streets and hillsides. The streets were so thick with vultures that they were described as a moving black carpet. The Atlácatl had also killed every animal, burned the crops, and razed every house to the ground, many of them with dead bodies inside. Peasants hiding in the hills saw the smoke and said the smell of burning flesh lasted for days. FMLN commanders, stationed elsewhere in El Salvador, initially refused to believe the scale of the carnage the rebels on the ground were describing. Over the course of two day's work, the Atlácatl had slain almost a thousand human beings, half of them under twelve years old.

More villagers began to straggle in from the hills, filling in bits and pieces of the story for the guerillas. Many survivors fled the Morazán to refugee camps in Honduras, "depriving the fish of its water" as intended.

A few days later, the rebels found a hysterical, half-naked Rufina being tended to by peasant farmers. To escape, she had walked for days through maguey, which left her bloody and scarred. The ERP got Radio Venceremos back on the air, then let Rufina tell the world what happened. Rufina lived up to her promise to God, risking her life to tell her story as the sole surviving eyewitness from El Mozote.

The aftermath of El Mozote (Susan Meiselas/Magnum)

Sensing the time was right to apply international pressure, the ERP accepted long-standing interview offers with US media. The ERP also offered safe passage to anyone from the US Embassy who wanted to investigate the scene, which no one took them up on.

The New York Times correspondent Raymond Bonner trekked over the border from Honduras with photographer Susan Meiselas to see the carnage. They were followed by *The Washington Post* correspondent Alma Guillermoprieto, who had this to say: "The most traumatizing thing was looking at these little houses where whole families had been blown away—these recognizable human beings, in their little dresses, just lying there mummifying in the sun. We kept walking, got to El Mozote. We walked down these charming and beautiful roads, then to the center of town, where there was this kind of rubbly place [the sacristy] and, in it, a stupefying number of bones."

Six weeks after the massacre, *The New York Times* and *The Washington Post* ran front-page stories on El Mozote. Todd Greentree, a junior reporting officer from the US Embassy, and Defense Attaché John McKay traveled to Morazán to investigate. Under the watchful eye of army leadership, the pair interviewed soldiers, local villagers, and refugees who had gathered in nearby camps. Unsurprisingly, the refugees and local residents weren't very effusive in the presence of the Salvadoran Army. McKay said the general mood felt like Vietnam, and it was clear to him something had happened. When the two men tried to visit El Mozote, the soldiers refused to escort them, saying guerrillas made the area too dangerous.

Rufina Amaya shortly after the massacre (Susan Meiselas/Magnum)

Greentree and McKay ultimately filed an ambiguous report that didn't find proof of a massacre and contained curious pieces of misinformation, such as noting that only 300 people lived in the immediate vicinity of El Mozote. Just reading the first few paragraphs of either *The Washington Post* or *The New York Times* article made it clear that the massacre spread to many other nearby hamlets and that people had taken refuge in El Mozote from the surrounding countryside. *The Wall Street Journal* ran an editorial titled *"The Media's War"* attacking Bonner and Guillermoprieto, parroting the same nonsense talking point about El Mozote's population, and snidely jabbing, "There is such a thing as being overly credulous."

The New York Times recalled Bonner back to the US, claiming the move had nothing to do with El Mozote. But according to author Mark Danner: "Bonner and his 'credulity' had become a minor cause célèbre in the press and on the television talk shows. *The Times* editors appeared to have 'caved' to government pressure, and the Administration seemed to have succeeded in its campaign to have a troublesome reporter—the most dogged and influential in El Salvador—pulled off the beat." Bonner would go on to write a book titled *Weakness and Deceit: America in El Salvador's Dirty War.* He's still on the case today, reporting for *The Atlantic.*

US Ambassador to El Salvador Deane Hinton embraces Lt. Colonel Monterrosa

Congress received the Reagan Administration's certification that El Salvador was "making a concerted and significant effort to comply with internationally recognized human rights" and increased aid to El Salvador. By 1987, US aid totaled $608 million per year, more than El Salvador's entire governmental budget. A number of the key perpetrators of the El Mozote massacre received promotions. Captain Walter Oswaldo Salazar retired as General Salazar. Lt. Colonel Monterrosa would go on to command the eastern sector of the war.

El Mozote was the biggest massacre—but not the last. The Army seemed to decide small massacres of fifty or fewer could be just as effective without bringing as much international attention. In 1986, a unit of the Atlácatl murdered six Jesuit priests and two female helpers at the Central American University. The widely denounced crime finally began to turn the tide against further aid from the US.

By the 1990s, the Cold War was over, and US support had dissolved. In

1992, the right-wing government declared a truce with the FMLN, officially ending El Salvador's civil war after thirteen years and some 75,000 deaths. The treaty disbanded the Atlácatl battalion and formed a coalition government. The FMLN received a few seats alongside the right-wing Arena party, which was made up of the same military leaders who had ordered massacres and led death squads.

Soon after the 1992 truce, a team of Argentinian forensic experts under the auspices of a UN Truth Commission excavated several sites in and around El Mozote. Almost immediately, the forensic team unearthed twenty-five children's skulls at the Sacristy, confirming the stories were true.

One child was found still clutching a bright orange plastic toy. Under normal forensic circumstances, a find like this could be highly valuable, since it could help parents identify the body. But in this case, there was no point, as the child's parents were also undoubtedly dead.

In the Sacristy, investigators confirmed 143 victims whose average age was six years old. After their initial find, the forensic team stopped by Rufina's house to tell her the news. She shot back, "Didn't I tell you? If only you could have heard that enormous screaming."

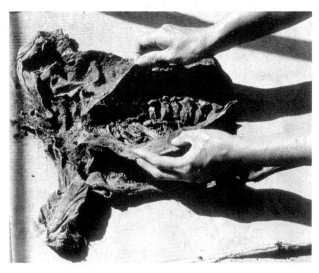

A tiny body exhumed at El Mozote in 1992 (Stephen Ferry)

The forensic team analyzed 245 shell casings. All but one came from an M16, the standard issue rifle in the El Salvador Army. Most of the cartridges could be traced to a US government manufacturing plant in Missouri.

The Chief of the Armed Forces Joint Staff and the Salvadoran Minister of Defense told the Truth Commission that they had no way to identify the units and officers involved in El Mozote and had retained no records for the entire period. In 1993, El Salvador passed an amnesty law for anyone implicated in UN investigations, which effectively exempted the Army from prosecution and benefited the military holdovers much more than FMLN rebels.

The Wall Street Journal, for its part, doubled down. An editorial entitled *"The War's Over, but El Salvador Still Fights Propaganda Battle"* conceded that while "it appears that a massacre of some kind took place, questions remain," including, "Who were the true perpetrators of this awful crime?" Talk about credulity and utter lack of accountability.

So why did the military do it? According to Mark Danner, "El Mozote was, above all, a statement. By doing what it did in El Mozote, the Army had proclaimed loudly and unmistakably to the people of Morazán, and to the peasants in surrounding areas as well, a simple message: In the end, the guerrillas can't protect you, and we, the officers and the soldiers, are willing to do absolutely anything to avoid losing this war—we are willing to do whatever it takes."

Lucia Annunziata, a correspondent who traveled frequently with Colonel Monterrosa, agreed with Danner's assessment: "The point was to create a turning point, a watershed, to turn the tide, and to do it by scaring the hell out of the enemy. It was a deliberate demonstration of cruelty to show them that the guerrillas couldn't protect them. And he understood that you do this as cruelly, as brutally as possible; you rape, impale, whatever, to show them the cost."

Most of those in the area around El Mozote fled after the massacre and only began to trickle back when the war was winding down. Militarily, the operation was a success.

When Operation Rescue had moved on to Los Toriles, word filtered up to the Atlácatl leaders that some of the men were feeling uneasy about the children they'd murdered back in El Mozote. According to the guide from Perquín, Captain Salazar angrily addressed his men: "Señores! What we did yesterday, and the day before, this is called war. This is what war is. War is hell. And, goddammit, if I order you to kill your mother, that is just what you're going to do. Now, I don't want to hear that, afterward, while you're out drinking and bullshitting among yourselves, you're whining and complaining about this, about how terrible it was. I don't want to hear that. Because what we did yesterday, what we've been doing on this operation—this is war, gentlemen. This is what war is."

On a personal note, these quotes sent me down a very dark, very depressing rabbit hole thinking about the proven methods by which otherwise ordinary men can be whipped into a murderous fraternal frenzy; when it is and isn't okay to kill civilians in war; and whether it matters much to the dead if their life was extinguished by a bayonet, a bullet, or a bomb.

The official memorial to the victims of El Mozote is a grid of black tiles, each displaying the names and ages of ten victims, formed into a large semicircle around a central memorial dedicated to Rufina Amaya. The number of single-digit ages is staggering. Some children are only listed as "son" or "daughter" because no one who knew their names survived.

A small open-air shop selling tourist items and knickknacks sits adjacent to the memorial. I stopped in to talk to the woman tending the store. She spoke no English, and my Spanish was particularly dumbfounded that day. I didn't have it in me to ask her for a tour of the famous sites—the crabapple tree that concealed Rufina from the soldiers and the remnants of the sacristy. I bought a few small items and donated to the memorial.

The El Mozote Memorial *(Amelia Rayno for The Star Tribune)*

After some time in a Honduran refugee camp, Rufina moved back to El Mozote. When she wasn't traveling to other countries to tell the story of the massacre, Rufina could be found tending the same outdoor shop I visited, offering tours of the site where she had endured the most unimaginable trauma and anguish a human being can experience. (To hear Rufina in her own words and see her tour of the massacre site, look for YouTube account: **S.I.T. Media Library**. A full link is provided in the bibliography.)

Rufina continued speaking out about the massacre and giving tours until she passed away in 2007. Her daughter Marta, born after the massacre, continued Rufina's tradition until 2017, when she had to flee to the US with her daughter after being threatened. Marta explained her decision to carry on her mother's tradition of spreading the word, "At first, I didn't know why she cried, and as I grew older and I understood, I would cry with her, dry her tears. I always shared with her the weight she carried because of it. I helped her to carry it."

Marta Amaya (center) with her nephew Henry and niece
Ana Yanci (photo credit: Marta Maritza Amaya)

Marta had left the country before my visit. It's heartening to know women are still at the memorial, carrying on Rufina and Marta's tradition.

In 2016, bowing to international pressure, the Salvadoran Supreme Court overturned the 1993 amnesty agreement. Prosecutors filed charges against the ringleaders of the massacre in El Salvador's high court. Seven years later, nineteen elderly men continue to drag out the pre-trial process. The military and government have stonewalled at every step. Expert observers are not optimistic the men will ever be brought to justice.

Notably absent among the defendants is Lt. Colonel Monterrosa.

By 1984, Monterrosa had changed his modus operandi to a "winning hearts and minds" strategy called "beans and bullets." His approach was to helicopter into a village, hand out food, and then deliver a speech. But the rumors about El Mozote still dogged him. In a candid moment, Monterrosa confessed to James LeMoyne, Bonner's replacement at *The New York Times*: "Yeah, we did it, it was a limpieza (cleaning). We killed everyone. I thought that's what I had to do to win the war. And I was wrong."

The Architects of El Mozote await trial

Despite his newfound gentle side, Monterrosa remained the FMLN's enemy number one. On October 22, 1984, he arrived by helicopter in the tiny Morazán town of Joateca, where he gave a speech to the locals. "We are your true brothers," he began. "We're not the caretakers of the rich. Do you see any rich among us? We give our blood to the soil, but it's up to you to make it fertile."

While Monterrosa was in town, the guerrillas sent a column of fighters into an obvious ambush. In their retreat, they left behind a transmitter covered in rooster blood to simulate it being dropped in a firefight. Listening to their stolen radios, the FMLN heard soldiers excitedly announce the discovery of the transmitter to their superiors. As the rebels had hoped, the radio was brought to Monterrosa, whose vanity blinded him to a situation that should have aroused suspicion.

Radio Venceremos skipped its nightly broadcast, and the rebels waited.

Monterrosa announced plans to display his prize for the national and foreign press in the nearby city of San Miguel. He had the transmitter loaded into his helicopter and lifted off, joined by his successor in command of the Atlácatl and five other battalion commanders.

As the helicopter passed over an FMLN position on its way to San Miguel, a rebel watching from the ground remotely detonated eight sticks of dynamite hidden inside the transmitter. The helicopter erupted in a ball of flame and plummeted to the ground, crashing very close to El Mozote.

The twisted hulk of metal I saw in Perquín was Monterrosa's last ride. According to Mark Danner, it is the most cherished monument in all of Morazán.

The remains of Colonel Monterrosa's helicopter in Perquín

CHAPTER 30

NAKED AND AFRAID

HEADING west along El Salvador's verdant, mountainous Northern Highway, my traveler anxiety ramped up once again. I was headed to Honduras, the scariest country yet, one of the murder capitals of the world.

Yes, El Salvador had MS-13 and real crime, but that was largely confined to the capital city, San Salvador. Honduras had two (2!) world-class crime cities: San Pedro Sula in the north and the capital, Tegucigalpa, in the south. El Salvador was tiny and welcoming once you got to know it. Honduras was much bigger—far too big to care about coddling tourists, or so I imagined.

One Honduras expat had posted in the Pan-Am Traveler group: "Forget about not driving at night. In Honduras, you better be off the roads by 3 p.m." That stayed with me.

At the border, I turned in my paperwork to leave El Salvador. On the way back to my car, a man ran up to me with a $5 bill that had fallen out of my pocket. This might have surprised me earlier in the trip, but not once I'd experienced Mexico and a chunk of Central America. In fact, it would have surprised me if someone *didn't* come running after me with the money. Now juxtapose that with the average American's image of El Salvador, or mine before the trip. This, in a nutshell, is why I travel—to have my misconceptions blown out of the water.

But Honduras? Still scary.

I cleared the Honduras border and set a course for a hostel called D&D Brewery on the shores of Lago Yojoa. Like Overlander Oasis in Oaxaca,

D&D Brewery kept coming up as a must-stop on the Pan-Am Highway circuit. Leaving the border, I climbed through rolling hills carpeted with oocarpa pines and almost no signs of civilization. I'm not sure why so few people live in this relatively temperate, stunningly gorgeous part of Honduras. Maybe it's one of the world's last undiscovered gems.

A half-hour into Honduras, I saw a man walking beside the road at the top of the next rise. I thought, "That guy looks naked." Then, I immediately dismissed such a stupid idea, convincing myself that he must be wearing tan shorts.

As I got closer, I could see that, no, I was right the first time. He was just flopping along, completely naked except for his sandals.

Mr. Natural looked to be in his twenties and very tall for Central America, with no tattoos. To my untrained eye, he seemed like a student or recent college grad, certainly not a gangbanger. He carried a large plastic drinking glass—so at least I knew he was hydrated.

As I passed him, we made eye contact. He gave me the sheepish "office welp face"—the one you exchange with your coworker when you meet in the hallway for the fourth time that morning. Basically: "Welp, this is awkward. But here we are."

I cannot overstate my relief that the guy didn't plead with me to help him. I've played it out dozens of times and still don't know what I would have done. We were surrounded by nothing but pine trees and empty farmland. I would have been terrified it was some kind of gang set up. Although you'd think they'd use a naked woman. But maybe people are on to the naked woman trap, or you work with what you have, or something. When nothing makes sense, everything makes sense.

I guess the most plausible explanation is that he got robbed and then was sent on his way without any clothes. I vaguely recall hearing that bandits do this to delay the victim from calling the cops or getting help. But he didn't seem distressed when I passed, just mildly embarrassed. And how did he get the plastic cup? Did the gangbangers take all his clothes except sandals and give him a cup of water? It was all just weird.

On top of new country anxiety, Honduras-specific fears, and the naked guy, I was flying blind without a working SIM card, which is always unsettling. As soon as I came out of the mountains into civilization, I went looking for a new card. This turned out to be a lot more complicated than in Guatemala or El Salvador. I had to supply my passport and fill out a government form, which then became input to the SIM activation process —I assume to crack down on drug dealers using burner phones. We spent the better part of an hour trying to activate my SIM, without success. So they sent me to another place down the street, which eventually got it sorted. But I was now looking at arriving at D&D Brewery by dusk at best. So much for being off the Honduran roads by 3 p.m.

As I bounced along the washboarded road to Lago Yojoa, dodging potholes with the setting sun in my eyes, my brain started talking to me like Rain Man: "It's definitely past 3 p.m. Pan-Am Forum says no driving in Honduras after 3 p.m. Definitely shouldn't be on the roads past 3 p.m." My new turf anxiety, compounded by Honduras and redoubled by the naked guy, rose to a brain-fogging crescendo. I got a vision of me walking naked down the road, robbed of everything I own.

Then, a moment of clarity washed over me. I looked around and thought, "Look at where you are. You're surrounded by farms. Mothers are walking their kids along the road. MS-13 is not going to jump you here. Relax, dumbass."

I know I shouldn't be so hard on myself. But sometimes, I just get on my last nerve.

LAGO YOJOA—D&D BREWERY

I pulled into D&D Brewery with the last of the fading light, still fully clothed with all vital organs intact. A sign directed "Overlanders" to park off to the left in a grassy field. I parked and headed across the road to check in. The campus had paths through the jungle leading to single rooms, dormitory hostel accommodations, and an outdoor restaurant beside a campfire surrounded by Adirondack chairs.

The reception desk doubled as the restaurant bar—a good sign in my experience. The clerk/bartender spoke very good English. While he was checking me in, I told him about the naked guy, then queried:

"Is walking naked a thing that people do in Honduras? For fun or something?"

After a pregnant pause, he replied, "No. This is not something that people do in Honduras."

But I wasn't going to let it go that easily, "Well then, why do *you* think that guy was walking naked along the road? Any ideas?"

Another long pause, "He was probably crazy."

I persisted, "I don't think so. The guy seemed perfectly sane. He looked like a college student."

With that, the clerk/bartender paused his paperwork and studied me with a look that could only mean, "Oh, great. Now I have a crazy person staying at my hostel."

I settled in and came out to the common area, where I discovered the beer was pretty good. They even had cheeseburgers, which also weren't half bad. The fact that I didn't have to wander all over town for them elevated both to *exquisite*. The chairs around the fire soon filled with people and lively conversation. I talked to three twenty-something guys from Belgium who, for some weird reason, seemed genuinely interested in my old man stories. My new turf anxiety drained away with every beer-induced trip to the bathroom.

The D&D common area—what more could you ask for?

Another thing D&D did well was post available activities, with detailed descriptions and pictures, on a wall at the restaurant. A very personable local guide, Ramón, gauged interest and set group outings for the next day. I signed up for a hike the next morning.

Along the hike, I talked to Ramón about the area. Once I felt like we had established that I was a sane, normal person, I told him the naked guy story, including my take that the dude did not look crazy. Then I asked if **he** had any idea what was going on.

Ramón gave me a side-eyed look that said, "Oh great. I'm leading a lunatic into the bush. I wonder if he'll kill me or go for the women first?"

What was I supposed to do, snap an action shot of the poor guy on the worst day of his life?

I stopped asking about the naked guy after that. Some mysteries just aren't meant to be solved.

Our hike led us through lowland scrub and fields of banana plants. Honduras has been synonymous with bananas since American author O. Henry famously coined the term "Banana Republic" in his 1904 novel *Of Cabbages and Kings*. O. Henry based the book on his time living in Honduras, where, at the time, bananas comprised two-thirds of the country's entire export output, and three fruit companies owned nearly all the prime lowlands. Fruit companies only built infrastructure needed to get their produce to the nearest harbor, which left swaths of Honduras undeveloped. Central Honduras remained such a backwater that the road between San Pedro Sula and Tegucigalpa wasn't paved until the 1950s.

Always a bit behind the curve, Honduras didn't have its military coup until 2009, ousting socialist-adjacent president Manuel Zelaya. The first coup in Central America since the end of the Cold War had dissident killings, disappearances, and even a pirate radio station called Radio Progreso. Since 2009, under the ostensibly pro-business, military-backed government—crime and unemployment have skyrocketed, and the minuscule social safety net poor Hondurans once relied on has evaporated.

As we hiked, banana plants gave way to trees and a cooling breeze. The summit of our little hill offered a spectacular view of Lago Yojoa and the surrounding valley. This area marks the ancient border between the Maya and the Lenca, a cultural and ethnic group that could be described as "Mesoamerica-adjacent." The Lenca seem to have taken the things they liked from the Maya: the ballgame, stelae, pottery, food, religion—while eschewing the need for god-kings, human sacrifice, and giant pyramids.

After the hike, we headed back to D&D and had more lively conversation around the fire. The Belgian guys were heading out with Ramón to some club in a nearby town. I declined their invitation to come along. I know a night of deep regret brewing when I see one.

D&D seemed to have that rare quality where people of all ages—backpackers, retiree overlanders, and me in that awkward in-between age—could effortlessly shoot the shit together. I like Halloween parties for the same reason. In costume, your age and social class aren't immediately the first business card you present about yourself. Weekend nights on San Francisco's Ocean Beach seemed to attract a similar milieu, at least when I lived there. I've stood around the same bonfire with Dotcom wizzes and homeless kids from Haight Street. I miss that.

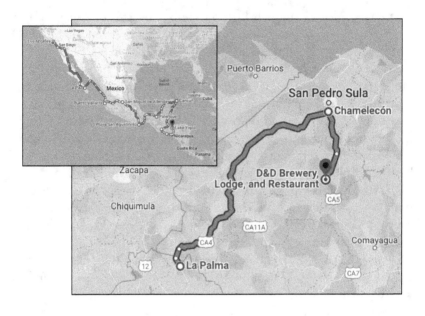

CHAPTER 31

ECHOES OF A LOST DYNASTY

I MET my friend Tommi and her friend Steph at the San Pedro Sula airport. Tommi and I have been friends for over twenty years and traveled together in the past. You learn all you need to know about someone after the long drive back from Burning Man, when everyone just wants to sleep for the next thirty-six hours, but the playa-dust-caked rental RV still needs to be cleaned. If someone pitches in without complaint and doesn't even feel out the possibility of begging off? That's an energy giver. So, if Tommi and I had any strife, I'd have to seriously consider that I might just be a lousy travel companion.

We headed south to the town of Copán Ruinas, which, as one may have guessed, sits adjacent to the Copán ruins. Along the way, Tommi and Steph wanted to stop at Jaguar Hot Springs.

I've always been kind of tepid on hot springs (get it?). The experience never feels worth the work of changing into bathing clothes, getting wet, getting out (brrrrr), drying off, and changing back into dry clothes. I don't like phase changes. If I'm dry, I want to stay dry. If I'm wet, I want to stay wet. I'm weird, I know. But Tommi and Steph were really into it, so we went.

We took the backroads since I knew the highway was clogged with construction. Near the hot springs, I was skirting around a group of cows a little too fast when we heard and felt a gigantic **BOOM!** I looked in my rearview mirror and didn't see any cows rolling around, so I kept moving, lest some angry farmer come chasing after me with a shotgun.

Once clear of the scene, I stopped to inspect the damage. My passenger side door had a massive dent and a greenish-brown poo streak running from the door to the rear fender. Apparently, I had spooked one of the cows into backing its butt straight into my car. When we got moving again, Tommi discovered her window wouldn't roll up. Oh great. A permanently rolled-down window just in time for the rainy season.

By the time we got to the hot springs, however, her window magically worked again. Tommi's attempts to roll up the window seemed to have popped out the main dent. Score one for self-healing cars and not having to search for the Munentec of Copán Ruinas.

The hot springs had many levels, different temperatures, therapeutic mud, etc. I enjoyed myself more than I expected, which is usually how it goes for me at hot springs. I just need someone to drag me there.

COPÁN

We arrived at Copán Ruinas, settled into our hotel, had a nice dinner, and headed to the ruins in the morning. In 1839, explorers John Lloyd Stephens and Frederic Catherwood would have taken a similar route, as their local guide led them out of the colonial town of Copán, across a cornfield, and into the dense underbrush.

By the early 1800s, many ancient Maya sites were still "lost" to the jungle, known only to locals, and possibly a centuries-old account from a Spanish priest or conquistador. Of the known ruins, popular theories of the day speculated that ancient Egyptians, the Phoenicians, or the lost tribes of Israel could have built them. No one believed the forefathers of the local indigenous Maya—who had been exploited and relegated to the bottom rungs of colonial society for centuries—could have built such wonders.

Stephens and Catherwood followed their guide to a river, where they saw a one-hundred-foot-high stone wall running along the far bank. The trio crossed the river and climbed a crumbling stairway riddled with gnarled tree roots. When they reached a flat terrace at the top, their guide began hacking a path through the maze of underbrush, strangler figs, and giant ceiba trees with their distinctive buttressed roots. As more features came into view, the explorers realized that one wall of foliage was actually the side of a pyramid.

Hacking through more jungle vines, they came upon a still-standing twelve-foot-high stela cut in full relief, which Stephens compared to the finest statues of ancient Egypt. He then went on to describe their epiphany in that moment:

> *The front was the figure of a man, curiously and richly dressed, and the face, evidently a portrait, solemn, stern, and well-fitted to excite terror. The back was of a different design unlike anything we had ever seen before and the sides were covered with hieroglyphs. The site of this unexpected monument put to rest once and forever, in our minds, all uncertainty in regards to the character of American antiquities, and gave us the assurance that the objects we were in search of were interesting, not only as the remains of an unknown people, but as works of art...*

Catherwood visited the site every day for weeks, creating photorealistic paintings with the help of his camera lucida—an optical device that projects the scene onto paper. The explorers went on to visit Palenque, Chichén Itzá, and forty-seven other Maya sites. In 1842, Stephens published *Incidents of Travel in Central America, Chiapas, and Yucatan,* which paired his evocative prose with Catherwood's lifelike recreations. The book became an international sensation and is generally credited with introducing the ancient Maya to the modern world.

Stela with altar (Frederick Catherwood)

By the 1960s, the Copán River had cut into the site's platform, known as the Acropolis, revealing strata of clay and stone that had been used to build up the structure over centuries. Using this cutaway as a guide, archaeologists began tunneling horizontally into the Acropolis. In 1989, a tunnel dug by archaeologist Ricardo Agurcia Fasquelle unearthed the most well-preserved large building ever found in Mesoamerica.

Rosalila Temple, as it came to be known because of its rose color, was buried under the tallest pyramid on the Acropolis. Generally, when a Maya king builds over a previous king's work, he reduces the older structure to fill rubble. But Rosalila was first encased in plaster, likely as a way of ritually embalming the building, then packed with thick clay, an excellent preservative. This careful burial kept Rosalila's original paint and elaborate stucco artwork in a near pristine state for over a thousand years.

Professor Barnhart, our esteemed fact-checker, was working at Copán as a student at the time. He describes being on hand for one of the greatest finds in archaeological history as a pivotal moment in his budding career. Yes, I would imagine so.

Rosalila appears to have been a working temple for over a hundred years, an uncommonly long lifespan in the Maya world. Offerings were found inside the temple, including jade jewelry, conch shells, jaguar claws, exquisitely-carved obsidian eccentric flints, remnants of flowers (which are still used in modern Maya religious ceremonies), and even the body of a five-foot shark—which had to be dragged eighty kilometers from the nearest ocean. Agurcia immediately recognized these as part of a termination ritual, a common Mesoamerican practice when retiring an important structure.

Steph enters a life-size recreation of Rosalila Temple

Tommi, Steph, and I stopped first to see a full-sized reproduction of Rosalila, which sits in an open-air courtyard surrounded by the Copán Sculpture Museum. I didn't think another building could muscle in on my love affair with Chichén Itzá's El Castillo. But Rosalila is jaw-dropping. Painted blood red and the size of a three-story house—flamboyant molded stucco decorations in blazing yellow, green, and white festoon Rosalila's top two stories.

Inside, we followed the path to the inner chamber, which spirals through three outer rooms, symbolizing the passage a king would take to enter the sacred cave of the underworld. In the inner chamber, Agurcia's team found stingray spines, jade flowers, and ceramic incense burners with charcoal still inside.

As part of a ritual to communicate with his ancestors, a periodic act foundational to his right to rule, a Maya king would pierce his ears, his tongue, and even his penis with a stingray spine. His sacred royal blood was then captured on paper or cloth and placed in an incense burner. An ancestor would appear through the incense smoke to share wisdom and knowledge. Modern Maya still burn incense in religious ceremonies. Piercing genitals with stingray spines, not so much.

After the museum, we made our way to the Acropolis, the pool-table flat platform rising above the Copán River. Still interspersed with a few giant ceiba trees, the platform supports several massive pyramids and the second-largest Mesoamerican ball court outside of Chichén Itzá (which is in a class by itself). In its heyday, the buildings of the Acropolis would have been painted blazing red with white trim, which was easier to visualize with Rosalila still fresh in my mind.

Blessed with abundant, easy-to-carve volcanic tuff rock, Copán's kings commissioned elaborate three-dimensional stelae, giant heads, and intricately carved altars—all of which have provided scholars with a bonanza of information. The most noteworthy of these public monuments is Altar Q, located in front of Pyramid 16, under which Rosalila Temple was found.

Altar Q depicts sixteen kings in a dynastic line, starting in 426 CE when a foreigner named Yax K'uk Mo' took the throne by means never fully expounded on. From texts around the Maya world, it's apparent Tikal provided direct military support to install Yax K'uk Mo' at Copán. Teotihuacán may have played an indirect role—motivated to set up Copán as a friendly trading outpost with access to the rich jade mines of the nearby Motagua Valley.

The inscription on top of Altar Q states that Yax K'uk Mo' traveled for 153 days to reach Copán, carrying with him the emblems of office from a place associated with Central Mexico—likely meant to be Teotihuacán—before finally "resting his legs" at Copán. The baton that Yax K'uk Mo' is shown passing to the next king on the side of Altar Q is one of those sacred emblems passed down from king to king for centuries, like crown jewels. Imagine finding that baton buried somewhere. I wonder if it ended its life as a family heirloom, relegated to a curiosity whose significance no one could remember: "Sure, grandpa, the scepter of eternal life... Yeah, yeah, we'll pass it down to our kids... Uh-huh... Got it."

Passing of the baton on Altar Q (Arian Zwegers)

Rosalila Temple wasn't the only structure buried under Pyramid 16. It had been built on top of an older temple known as Azul, which was itself built over an even older temple, and so on. In 1992, archaeologists started a new tunnel, aiming for 1,600 years into the past. When their tunnel reached the vertical line of Pyramid 16, they found a stunningly well-preserved facade of a collapsed building. The platform was nicknamed Margarita Temple, keeping with the flower theme they started with Rosalila. Margarita's decorations functioned as a blazing billboard for Copán's dynastic founder, Yax K'uk' Mo.

In a nod to Raiders of the Lost Ark, archaeologists discovered a vessel of liquid mercury emitting poisonous fumes from inside the temple. This delayed excavation for months while, presumably, the team checked for trapdoors, poison darts, and giant rolling stones. After five years of careful digging, Sharer and team reached a tomb under the temple, where they found a skeleton coated in red cinnabar, adorned with 30,000 pieces of jade. It was one of the most richly decorated tombs ever discovered in the Maya world.

Scholars assumed that this spectacular burial must be Yax K'uk Mo'. But the skeleton turned out to be female, likely Yax K'uk Mo's queen, making it the most lavish woman's tomb ever found in Mesoamerica. Sharer and team probed below the Margarita, where they found a skeleton posed with Teotihuacáno atlatl weapons and a distinctive goggle-eyed headdress. The deceased man wore a single jade bar, ear-flare jewelry, and a ceremonial chest ornament known as a pectoral—which all matched Yax K'uk Mo's likeness on the side of Altar Q and elsewhere.

Incense burner depicting Yax K'uk Mo'

Enticing clues suggest Yax K'uk Mo' could be Fire Born, the mysterious visitor who installed a new dynasty at Tikal in 378 CE—forty-eight years *before* Copán's dynasty began. Yax K'uk Mo' only reigned for eleven years, and the bones in his tomb were those of an older man. So, the timelines add up. Also, a monument dedicated to Yax K'uk Mo' has a glyph of an upturned frog that looks similar to Fire Born's name glyph. It's plausible that in his AARP years, Fire Born was given the kingship of Copán as a reward for his service. If true, Yax K'uk Mo'/Fire Born can lay claim to founding two of the Maya world's longest-lasting, most powerful dynasties.

After some wandering, Tommi, Steph, and I came to the other big architectural highlight of Copán—sixty-three rows of steps made from 2,200 carved hieroglyphs, each roughly comparable to a word. The Hieroglyphic Stairway is one of the longest ancient stone passages ever found. Over the centuries, all but the bottom fifteen rows slid down and became jumbled, which created an impossible puzzle before epigraphers had deciphered Maya script—and then just incredibly difficult after that.

With temples like Rosalila and Margarita, epic monuments like the Hieroglyphic Stairway, and the evolution of stelae to full relief statues—

something rarely seen in the Maya world—Copán is perhaps the most artistically rich Maya city ever built. The dynasty also introduced new forms of glyphic writing and advanced Maya knowledge of astronomy and calendrics, leading to Copán's reputation as the Athens of the New World.

John Lloyd Stephens summed up his visit to Copan with a conjecture: "One thing I believe, that its history is graven on its monuments. Who shall read them?"

He was right. But he couldn't have imagined it would take another 130 years to decipher Copán's engravings or the cast of eccentric characters to rival any of the *Cannonball Run* movies that would ultimately piece it together.

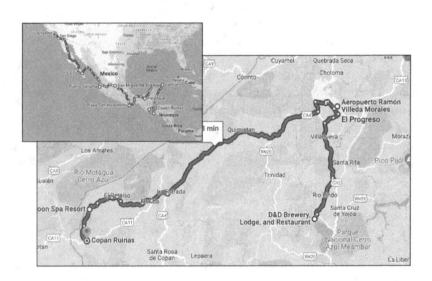

CHAPTER 32

CRACKING THE CODE

IMAGINE if human civilization disappeared and our only surviving expressions were the words and images carved into our monuments and plaques. That's roughly where the first "Mayanists" in the early nineteenth century found themselves. At early sites like Palenque and Copán, explorers pondered the curious script of square "glyphs" made up of recognizable and unrecognizable symbols combined in endlessly varied layouts.

Was it phonetic—where each glyph represents a pronounced sound? Was it ideographic—where glyphs represent nouns, verbs, or ideas? Or was it just gibberish—at the whim of the artist creating it? Did the inscriptions represent history, as John Lloyd Stephens predicted? Or were they a religious proclamation or prophecy? If the ancestors of the local indigenous Maya had created the monuments, could the script be read in a local Maya language or at least an archaic antecedent? It was a tantalizing possibility.

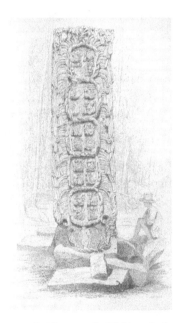

A stela covered with hieroglyphs
(Frederick Catherwood)

The contemporary Maya living on the fringes of post-colonial society certainly didn't know.

Remarkably, the first seeds of the resurrection of Maya writing were planted by a man responsible for much of its original destruction. In 1562, a Franciscan priest named Diego de Landa, acting as the church-appointed leader of the Yucatán, discovered the local Maya were still making sacrifices to their gods. In response, he ordered an auto-da-fé—which literally means 'act of the faith' but, in Inquisition-era parlance, meant the burning of a heretic. He had Maya men tortured and burned at the stake, destroyed thousands of their precious statues, and burned every Maya book he could find.

De Landa was reportedly surprised at how much this last act upset his subjects:

> *These people also used special characters or letters with which they recorded in their books their histories and knowledge, as well as figures, and particular signs in those figures explained it all, and lent it meaning and understanding. We found a great number of books containing such letters, and as they did not contain an iota in which there was not superstition and falsehoods of the devil, we burned them all, which dismayed and distressed them greatly.*

Maya scribes wrote on sheets of whitewashed tree bark, which they then folded up like a fan and bound together with wooden covers, sometimes wrapped in jaguar hide or animal skin. A typical page featured glyphs in sections made up of two or more columns, but a page could also feature a full-color painting surrounded by dozens of glyphs. Glyphs consisted of a primary symbol, to which other symbols could be added as "affixes" onto any side. Glyphs could be combined, overlapped, or even placed inside one another.

The same two syllable word—chumtun—written four different ways

This variety of layouts gave Maya scribes enormous artistic latitude to convey their words on paper, pottery, or stone in endless permutations. Maya scribes sometimes depicted themselves as rabbits or playful monkey men holding brushes and conch-shell inkwells. A Maya scribe must also be a good artist. So, it follows that monkeys are the patron animals of artists *and* scribes throughout Mesoamerica.

Scribes held a very high position in Maya society, passing down the skills of writing, carving, and engraving from generation to generation. Even after they had long lost the ability to read or write Maya hieroglyphs, scribes carried the essential tradition of recording their sacred texts and calendrics into modern times. For centuries, with no formal education, one generation of scribes taught the next how to write spoken Maya in the same archaic form of Latin script that Spanish priests forced on them in the 1500s. The Popol Vuh, the epic Maya creation myth, was discovered written in Latin script, presumably transcribed from a long-lost hieroglyphic original. Passing down their sacred knowledge, prophecies, and prayers has always been paramount for the Maya, even if they had to do it in someone else's writing system.

Today, only four pre-Columbian Maya books are known to survive. The rest were burned by the Spanish or transformed into wads of organic goo by the oppressive humidity in most of the Maya homeland. Collectively known as the Maya codices, three of these surviving books are housed in Europe, where conquistadors originally sent them as tribute and curiosities. One resides in Mexico City after being discovered in 1960 in a dry cave in Chiapas.

By the early 1800s, the Madrid Codex was split into two pieces housed in private collections, while the Paris Codex sat unnoticed in a basket of old papers in a chimney at Le Bibliothèque Impériale. Only the Dresden codex was known to academia, and only five pages had been mass-reproduced. No one had yet figured out that the Dresden codex contained the same writing seen on Maya monuments.

Diego de Landa was cruel, but for a Spanish priest, he was also abnormally curious to learn about the culture of his indigenous converts. He kept journals recording Maya social organization, economy, politics, calendars, and religion. In an attempt to document Maya writing, de Landa instructed a Maya noble named Gaspar Antonio Chi, who was literate in both Maya and Latin script, to write down the glyphs for common words like days, months, and the four directions. Then de Landa pronounced each letter of the alphabet as it's pronounced in Spanish while the scribe wrote down the symbol for each sound: "ah" for the letter A, "bay" for the letter B, "say" for the letter C, etc. De Landa understood that this list made up only a small subset of Maya phonetic glyphs, but he considered it too cumbersome to try to record them all. For a longer example of Maya writing, de Landa asked Gaspar Antonio to produce a sentence—to which the scribe dutifully wrote "I don't want to" in Maya hieroglyphs.

Maya writing on a recreation of a stela from Piedras Negras

Ultimately, de Landa proved too tyrannical for even the conquistadors, who sent him back to Spain in chains for ordering an inquisition without the proper authority. While languishing in a Spanish prison, de Landa compiled his notes on Maya beliefs and society into a book called *Relación de las cosas de Yucatán* (Relation of Things in the Yucatán). Most importantly, he included the "alphabet" that Gaspar Antonio had produced for him. But as with most of the codices, de Landa's manuscript disappeared for 300 years, only resurfacing in the mid-nineteenth century.

The first break in deciphering Maya script came in 1832 when an American-born self-described polymath (basically a Renaissance Man before the term existed) named Constantine Samuel Rafinesque-Schmaltz became interested in Maya writing. As archaeologist Michael Coe puts it in *Breaking the Maya Code*: "During the first half of the nineteenth century, Americanist research was replete with eccentrics: the dead hand of the academy had yet to stifle the unbridled enthusiasms of a small band of amateurs in Europe and America."

Rafinesque had only the five reproduced pages of the Dresden Codex and some laughably inaccurate pre-Catherwood drawings of a few Maya ruins. For example, a drawing made in 1832 by a French artist/explorer named Jean-Frederic Waldeck depicts a Maya glyph in the form of an elephant's head. As it turns out, Waldeck was predisposed to the idea that Babylonians, Phoenicians, or Hindus built Maya pyramids. The actual glyph doesn't look much like an elephant.

*Waldeck's drawing versus the actual glyph—yeah that's a bit of
a stretch*

Working under these hamstrung conditions, Rafinesque still somehow managed to:

1. Determine that the writing at Palenque and in the Dresden Codex was the same script and was unique from Aztec writing.
2. Hypothesize that if Maya script was based on a language still spoken in the region, then it could be deciphered, much like Coptic was used to crack the code of Egyptian writing.
3. Deduce the base-20 system of Maya numbers—where each dot represents a count of one, and each bar represents five dots.
4. Recognize that the Maya had a symbol for zero—as a number itself and as a useful placeholder to indicate large numbers—a concept the Romans never figured out, and an idea that didn't appear in Europe until the twelfth century, whereupon the church promptly banned it as the work of the devil.

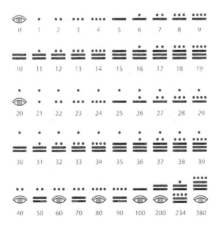

*Using a shell symbol for zero, the Maya could represent large
numbers much less awkwardly than Roman numerals*

In addition to his Maya script breakthroughs, Rafinesque made legitimate contributions in the fields of botany and zoology. He also, however, told a slew of tall tales in his vanity publications, such as claiming to have translated the Delaware Indians' origin and migration story from writing on tree bark. Rafinesque's publications on the Maya glyphs were ignored by the academic community along with the rest of his non-naturalist work.

Less than a decade later, Stephens and Catherwood's explorations proved Rafinesque's assertion that the Dresden Codex and the writings at Palenque and Copán were the same script.

No more real progress was made on cracking the code until 1862 when a French abbé and amateur epigrapher (one who studies inscriptions) named Charles Étienne Brasseur de Bourbourg came across an abridged copy of de Landa's *Relación de las cosas de Yucatán* in Madrid's Royal Academy of History. Brasseur had lived with the K'iche' Maya and helped translate an early copy of the Popol Vuh from Spanish to French and K'iche'. He also had access to one of the few complete copies of the Dresden Codex available at the time. He immediately understood that de Landa's *alphabet* could be a Rosetta Stone for Maya writing.

Diego de Landa's "alphabet" as discovered by Brasseur

Armed with the symbols for months and days from de Landa's work, Brasseur used the Dresden Codex to work out the Maya base 20 number system—thirty years after the forgotten Rafinesque. Understanding Maya numbers and calendar signs, Brasseur was able to determine any Maya date within the fifty-two-year "Calendar Round" cycle.

But Brasseur wasn't done. When one of the two pieces of the Madrid Codex surfaced in 1866, Brasseur added his own "translation" as a companion piece to the reproduction. Brasseur assumed he was dealing with a literal phonetic alphabet, not an incomplete syllabary, which sent him off in predictably disastrous directions. He wasn't even reading the glyphs in the proper order. Compounding these epigraphic misadventures, Brasseur's translations tended to veer into the fantastical to support his pet theory that Mesoamerican civilization had been seeded by refugees from the Lost City of Atlantis. He gradually lost all standing in the budding Mayanist community and spent his last decades publishing increasingly unhinged theories into the ether.

Brasseur didn't just ruin his own reputation. His translation failure cast a shadow of doubt over the accuracy of de Landa's alphabet. Scholars openly speculated that the entire set of glyphs could have been deliberate disinformation fed to de Landa by Gaspar Antonio Chi.

In 1882, a Tennessee frontiersman named Cyrus Thomas, working for the US Bureau of Ethnology, made a name for himself by establishing the correct reading order of Maya glyphs: two columns at a time—left to right, then down to the next row—in a repeating Z pattern. Thomas also began to suspect that Maya script was largely phonetic, and he correctly postulated that Maya writing could be logosyllabic, where some signs stand for whole words, while other signs, whose symbolic meaning may be long forgotten, stand in for single phonetic syllables. Unfortunately, Thomas ran into the buzzsaw of fallout from Brasseur de Bourbourg's failed translations. The "dead hand of the academy" convinced him to reverse some of his groundbreaking claims, which would only be appreciated much later.

And that's where the decipherment of non-calendric Maya writing stood for the next sixty years. By the early twentieth century, academia's position on the nature of the untranslated glyphs had hardened into doctrine that assumed all unknown glyphs must be superfluous and unimportant. The most influential Mayanist of this time was a passionate American archaeologist named Sylvanus Morley, who discovered several Maya sites and considered himself an epigrapher above all. Morley took his assumptions to what he felt was their logical conclusion: Maya societies were run by peaceful astronomer-priests who were primarily concerned with tracking celestial bodies and timing eclipses.

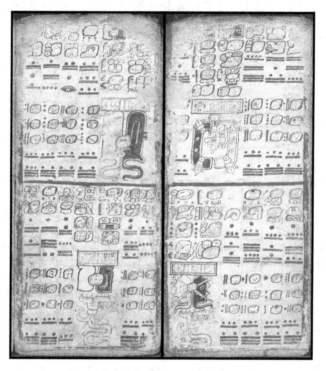

Eclipse Tables in the Dresden Codex

In 1924, Morley hired an ambitious young English anthropologist named Eric Thompson to work with him on excavations—based mainly on the qualification that Thompson had studied Morley's publications and could compute Maya dates on sight. From this humble start, Thompson went on to make enormous contributions to Maya studies over a storied fifty-year career, receiving a knighthood from Queen Elizabeth shortly before his death in 1975.

Sir Eric Thompson applied his extensive knowledge of pre-contact Central Mexican societies to pinpoint commonalities across all of Mesoamerica—like various gods and the long count calendar, which Thompson anchored to a definitive first day of all creation: August 11, 3114 BCE (or 0.0.0.0.0 in Maya Long Count calendar nomenclature). Thompson created an extensive catalog system for glyphs that is still in use today and contributed untold advances to the understanding of Maya calendrics—all of which he published in massive ponderous tomes, densely packed with broad literary allusions of questionable relevance.

Thompson took Morley's assumptions about Maya writing and, by extension, the nature of ancient Maya society and cemented them into dogma. Thompson had lived with several different groups of Maya, where he became enamored with their culture and made deep, lifelong friendships. He seems to have projected some of his affections for his contemporary Maya friends, and possibly some of his own deep religiosity, onto his extrapolations of the nature of pre-contact Maya society. Like Morley, Thompson believed that Classic Period Maya cities were run by astronomer-priests who were chiefly preoccupied with acquiring celestial and spiritual knowledge, having little ambition for warfare or conquest.

By the 1950s, Thompson, without ever occupying a position of real academic power, had, through sheer force of personality, browbeat most of his colleagues into accepting that there was no more significant Maya script left to decipher. Thompson asserted that the 90 percent of hieroglyphs that were as yet undeciphered would probably *never* be translated and likely consisted of something he called "esoteric time worship"—an activity which, apropos of nothing, I once embarked on following the ingestion of eight ounces of Robitussin.

Thompson's obstruction of Mayanist thought was so thorough that during his lifetime, it may have been impossible to break the dam from within the interconnected American and European halls of academia. So, it follows that Russian epigrapher/linguist Yuri Valentini Knorozov, toiling away behind the Iron Curtain in a cramped office in St. Petersburg, would make the breakthrough of the twentieth century.

In 1945, at age twenty, Knorozov found himself stationed in Berlin with the Red Army. Yuri's official story for decades purported that he raced into the burning Prussian State Library *during* the Battle of Berlin—with allied bombs carpeting the city—and rescued a book containing rare copies of the Dresden, Paris, and Madrid codices (which were extremely difficult to reproduce in pre-Xerox days).

However, in an interview much later in life, Knorozov claimed he had been misunderstood. The library was **not** on fire, and the book was found in a group of boxes that were to be shipped to hiding places around Germany. Yes, I often confuse "found in a box" with "rescued from a fire." Probably just a language barrier thing.

Oh, Yuri! Why let facts get in the way of such a great story? I had the screenplay half-written in my head.

Back in St. Petersburg after the war, Knorozov went to work with his new find. Like Cyrus Thomas, Knorozov started with the assumption that the glyphs in de Landa's alphabet represented the pronunciation of the *names* of Spanish letters and comprised an incomplete syllabary. A truly syllabic writing system, like Japanese, should have roughly 200 to 300 signs. But there were over 800 known Maya glyphs—too many to be a syllabary and too few to be a logographic system like Chinese, which can represent disparate spoken languages like Cantonese and Mandarin using thousands of non-phonetic, idea-based characters.

Yuri overcame this stumbling block through his broad knowledge of ancient writing systems such as Sumerian, Hittite, and ancient Egyptian. He knew that no writing system contained one kind of sign. It was possible that 200 to 300 of the known glyphs were phonetic syllables, while the rest were non-phonetic idea-based logograms. Knorozov also understood that polyvalence—a system where a sound can be represented by more than one glyph, and a glyph can represent more than one sound—was a common feature in early writing systems.

Eric Thompson, for his part, had no use for comparative studies when it came to Maya writing. He was convinced that, like his concept of Classic Maya society, Maya writing was unique in the history of civilization.

Knorozov's greatest leap forward was to speculate that glyphs represented many words that could still be found in modern Maya languages— the same way that Jean-François Champollion used Coptic, a modern descendant of the language of the Pharaohs, to decipher Egyptian hieroglyphs.

Following the same path as Thomas, Knorozov looked at one of de Landa's signs, the glyph for ku, found above a picture of a turkey in the Madrid Codex. The Maya word for turkey is 'kutz.' Knorozov speculated that the second glyph must be the sound for tzu.

Yuri knew that in syllabic writing systems, it's common to drop the vowel sound of the last symbol but also use a symbol with a vowel that matches the syllable before it. For example, if English were written as a syllabary, the signs "coo" and "loo" would combine to make "cool," while the signs for "baw" and "taw" would become "bawt" (spelled "bought" in English, because screw you that's why).

Knorozov found his proposed tzu sign, combined with the known sign for lu, in a glyph that appears above a picture of a man and a dog in the

Dresden Codex. Yuri then found 'tzul' in one of his Maya to English dictionaries as a lesser-known word for dog. And with that, the first crack in Thompson's dam had appeared.

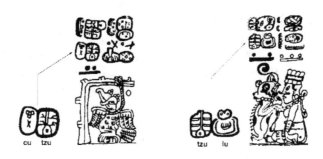

The symbols for kutz with a picture of a turkey in the Madrid Codex and tzul with a dog in the Dresden Codex

Knorozov went on to unravel more phonetic connections to modern Maya languages, too many for any expert to reasonably refute. As part of his doctoral dissertation in 1952, Yuri published his work in a landmark paper that landed in the West with a fizzle. It didn't help that any scientific work coming out of the Soviet Union at the time had to begin with pages and pages of boilerplate to the tune of "Only the great Marxist/Leninist system could come up with such groundbreaking work, which the Imperialists had completely failed at for a hundred years... yadda yadda..." You get the idea.

Thompson, a virulent anti-communist, forbade his students from even *reading* Knorozov's work. As per the pattern of his predecessors, Thompson found flaws in some of Knorozov's translations but ignored any arguments that weren't as easily rebutted.

A few years later, Michael Coe was on honeymoon with his new bride Sophie, browsing through a second-hand bookstore in Merida, when he stumbled upon a copy of Knorozov's paper that had been translated into Spanish by the Mexican Communist Party. Michael read it and quickly concluded that Knorozov's paper was the first sensible treatment he had read of the non-calendric portion of Maya script. His wife Sophie, the daughter of an exiled Russian scientist, translated the paper into English, while Michael began corresponding with Knorozov. Coe and his wife published her English translation of Knorozov's work, which circulated amongst an underground following of Mayanists, many from outside established academic silos. Thompson still dominated the landscape, but the seeds of resistance had been planted.

In the late '50s, Tatiana Proskouriakoff, a Russian-born artist who created stunning depictions of Maya cities as they would have looked in their full glory, noticed that dedication dates on the stelae within a group were always spaced five years apart. The first stela in the sequence always showed a human figure in a niche. Thompson assumed this was some sort of god. When Tatiana looked at the dates on the stelae, she realized the dates on most groups of stelae fell within a range of forty to sixty years. She also noticed multiple stelae in a group would reference a date twelve to thirty years *before* the first stela's dedication date. She realized that these date ranges perfectly matched a typical human lifespan and the reign of a king. The earlier date, which was never referenced until after he became king, fit perfectly as his birthday. The seated figure wasn't a god but a king ascending to the throne. The stelae were honorifics erected every five years in front of the current king's eventual tomb.

Without translating a single glyph, Tatiana showed that the inscriptions were history, not *esoteric time worship*. It was a stroke of genius that, in retrospect, had been staring Mayanists in the face for nearly a century since the first date translations. She showed her paper to Eric Thompson, whose initial reaction was that she couldn't possibly be right. To Thompson's credit, he studied her work overnight and came back the next morning with, "Of course you're right."

When she showed her work to Michael Coe, he was floored:

> *I was truly thunderstruck. In one brilliant stroke, this extraordinary woman had cut the Gordian Knot of Maya epigraphy, and opened up a world of dynastic rivalry, royal marriages, taking of captives, and all the other elite doings which have held the attention of kingdoms around the world since the remotest antiquity. The Maya had become real human beings.*

Mayanists now had people, places, dates, and a little glue to bind them together, courtesy of Yuri Knorozov. But in the twenty-odd years since Knorozov's breakthrough, scholars had only matched about thirty glyphs to the eighty possible syllables in spoken Maya. They could piece together some dynasties and other histories but were still mainly in the dark as to the non-calendric content of the inscriptions. As Eric Thompson persuasively argued, if Knorozov's approach was correct, why hadn't there been a flood of new phonetic glyphs and decipherments in the succeeding decades?

That dam finally cracked open for good in 1973, when Linda Schele, a young art teacher (and Fact-checker Ed's eventual mentor), organized the Mesa Redonda de Palenque (Round Table of Palenque)—the first collaborative interdisciplinary Mayanist gathering of its kind. Thirty epigraphers, art historians, astronomers, archaeologists, and enthusiasts showed up at Palenque, many meeting for the first time. The group gathered daily for trips into the field, made forays to an offsite library of Maya inscriptions, and gave presentations to each other under the thatched roof of the home of Palenque's first tour guide—Moises Morales.

Schele collaborated with several scholars one afternoon, looking for Palenque's emblem glyph. The glyph usually appeared with various "event glyphs" that the team suspected must be verbs, for example, "[event glyph] Lord Shield of Palenque on 9.12.11.5.18." This was the first time anyone had rigorously approached Maya writing using the same verb-object-subject sentence structure as modern spoken Maya, which is rare among languages. Working from the premise that the event glyphs would most likely be ceremonial records like "born," "died," "married," or "ascended to the throne," they were able to piece together a previously unconnected line of six kings spanning 200 years.

That night, they presented their findings to the group. The thirteenth ruler in the dynasty, whom they had nicknamed "King Shield" because his emblem glyph looked like a shield, became king at age twelve and served for sixty-eight years—one of the longest reigns ever recorded in any civilization. At this point, an agitated Moises Morales asked, "Why are these ascribed royal nicknames always in English or Spanish and not Maya?" The group decided Moises had a good point. So they looked up the word for shield in Yucatec Maya: *pakal*. "King Shield" would now be known as King Pakal (whom you may remember from my visit to Palenque as the alien astronaut king).

After the conference, Michael Coe and another attendee both remembered seeing a purely phonetic version of the same king's name with the symbols for Pa, Ka, and La—which, after dropping the last vowel sound, combines to from Pakal. In that *aha!* moment, scholars knew that for once, their *nickname* for Pakal was also his *actual* name—as pronounced over 1,300 years ago. It was a beautiful confirmation that even proper names like people and places could be phonetically deciphered. The wide aesthetic latitude Maya scribes gave themselves to convey spoken words, combined with their aversion to repeating themselves, created a significant hindrance to decipherment but also provided a powerful tool to corroborate decodings.

PAKAL   PAKAL-la   pa-ka-la

Some of the different ways Pakal could be expressed

Soon, a wunderkind scholar named David Stuart, who had tagged along with his father on Maya excavations since he was a toddler, made multiple breakthroughs that blew the dam wide open. New decipherments and translations started pouring in. With the advent of the Xerox machine, everyone had access to a vast corpus of Maya writing. Tenured professors made copies, then got down on the floor like kids, cutting things out and moving them into different combinations.

Rich history slowly came to light. The great city of Calakmul, with some 6,000 structures, the largest Maya city ever built, had been forever mute, its soft sandstone weathered beyond readability. However, once Mayanists worked out Calakmul's snake-head emblem glyph from other sites, they began to piece together a Maya world of warfare and political intrigue dominated by two feuding superpowers: Tikal and Calakmul.

Mayanists were surprised to find that many of the smaller cities served as vassal states to the great powers (at least until they rose up like Dos Pilas did against Tikal). Tatiana Proskouriakoff made the first link between Tikal and Teotihuacán, then showed that Yax K'uk Mo's installation in Copán was connected to Tikal. David Stuart found the phonetic spelling of Yax K'uk Mo' hidden in plain sight, creatively incorporated into the king's headdress on Altar Q.

Michael Coe began to look at Maya pottery with the help of a rotating pedestal setup that produced high-quality "rollout" images of hundreds of vases recovered from royal tombs. This novel source of less formal writing opened up new vistas, replacing some of what was lost in the destruction of Maya books. According to Coe, old-school "dirt archaeologists" were dismayed to find out that much of the elegant writing on the vases basically amounted to: "This is a vase. It was made on 13.0.3.1.13. It is owned by King Whatshisname."

My favorite part of this story is what happened when the nearby

Lacandon Maya, who still live a very traditional existence, wanted to know more about what the epigraphers were doing at Palenque. The team began briefing the local Maya on their breakthroughs. In the ensuing years, indigenous Maya everywhere came forward, desperate to learn a history they had never been taught in school. Linda Schele and others started workshops for the local Maya in Antigua. Those workshops spawned similar efforts around the Maya homeland, which continue today. Maya who participated in the early workshops as students now teach what they learned to a new generation.

As Linda Schele concludes in the 2008 documentary *Breaking the Maya Code*:

> *One of the most precious gifts that any group of humans on earth has is history. It's a gift that places people in time. It's a gift that gives people resilience. It gives them identity. The process of actually deciphering it, that's only the first tiny step to understanding world view, to understanding history, to being able to create this enriched pattern of what this great civilization contributed to the heritage of humanity.*

Today, Maya parents in Chiapas, Yucatán, Petén, and the Guatemala highlands are christening their children with newly unearthed names of Maya gods and kings. Maya school kids learn their heritage and history and are even being taught to read and write Maya glyphs. As far as anyone knows, this is the first time in history a culture has lost its written language, then gotten it back.

CHAPTER 33

SERENDIPITOUS TREASURES

TOMMI, Steph, and I spent one more night at Copán Ruinas, then headed back to D&D Brewery via another scenic drive through pine-strewn rolling hills, but no naked guy this time. I slept in the next day while Tommi and Steph picked one of the activities on the D&D big board: kayaking on an idyllic lake clogged with water lilies.

Later that afternoon, we toured a nearby orchard where Tommi and Steph obsessed over sneaking out some of the ubiquitous airplane plants that grow on all the tree limbs. When we got back from our stroll through the orchard, I was ready for a cheeseburger, a beer, and parking my butt in one of the Adirondack chairs by the fire. But Tommi and Steph weren't digging the cheeseburger vibe.

Tommi: *We want to try something in that little town. Are you up for it?*

Me: *You realize they have cheeseburgers and beer here, right?*

Tommi: *We want to try something different.*

Me: *Okay. I hear what you're saying. But I feel like maybe there's been a breakdown in communication. The cheeseburgers and beer I mentioned? They require **zero** walking. The nice people at D&D bring them to you! Right over there, in those comfy chairs around the warm fire.*

I gestured provocatively in the direction of the fire, feeling confident that the internal logic of the cheeseburger-beer-butts dialectic would win the day. But apparently, they hadn't traveled all the way from LA to eat the same inoffensively average food every night—butts or no butts.

So we trudged to the nearby town and started poking around. A fried chicken place looked okay to me, but not much else. Down the street, they spotted a hole-in-the-wall restaurant draped with a big vinyl sign depicting tacos, enchiladas, burritos, and all manner of standard Mexican food. Steph went in and asked for some of the things on the sign. "Oh, we don't make any of that," came the basic reply. All the while, I was grumbling internally, "Of course, they don't make that. It's just a sign to grab your attention. This is not a foodie area. Why are we here? I should be eating a cheeseburger right now."

I'll just say it—I was being a pissy traveling companion. Tommi and Steph wanted to try something different on the only trip they may ever take to Honduras. But my foot hurt, and I wasn't having any of it.

"Well, what **do** you make?" Steph asked. Something we couldn't understand came the reply in Spanish. There were no pictures. We did manage to understand that they were going to close soon, so whatever we ordered would be to go.

"Okay, we'll take three," Steph replied, holding up three fingers. The proprietor disappeared into the kitchen before I could explain that I planned to have a cheeseburger when we returned to D&D. Tommi had the proprietor come back out and told her, "No tres, only dos." The woman sternly replied, "No, tres," then returned to the kitchen. Okay then. I guess we're getting three of whatever this is.

Sounds of furious chopping drifted from the kitchen. I figured whatever we were getting, at least it should be fresh. The chopping continued for at least ten minutes, followed by more indeterminate food preparation sounds. To keep me entertained, a kid and a grownup were playing an intense game of Xbox FIFA soccer, complete with spectators and endless trash-talking by both sides. Eventually, the chef-proprietor emerged with three dinner-sized Styrofoam containers in a plastic bag.

"Well, whatever you just ordered, it's as heavy as a bowling ball," I told Tommi and Steph—making it clear I wanted no part of whatever mystery meat chef-d'oeuvre they had just ordered. I was a seasoned Central American traveler down here living this life, whereas Tommi and Steph were just tourists. I could tell when food options were going to be subpar just by the look of an area. They were going to be sick the next day, and I was going to laugh at them.

When we got back to D&D, Tommi opened her mystery box to reveal a giant pork chop slathered with a chunky red sauce, resting on a bed of slaw, tomatoes, and fried banana chips. I tried one bite of the seasoned pork with tangy red sauce and immediately regretted ordering a cheeseburger.

Just then, a young backpacker sitting next to Tommi excitedly blurted, "Is that chuleta con tajadas?!?" Uhh, maybe?

I got out my phone and eventually landed on a spelling close enough to find the dish in Google Images (a godsend for food lookup). We had stumbled onto a genuine travel treasure—a beloved local delicacy that flies under the tourist radar for whatever reason. And a seemingly very well-prepared version at that. Mom's home cooking—the Holy Grail of food travel.

Well, Tommi and Steph stumbled on it, dragging me along as I grumbled to myself about their silly quest. I was about to dig in to the chuleta, on top of the cheeseburger, which would lead to the inevitable groaning and rolling around on my bed all night like an engorged tick. But the backpacker looked hungry, so I offered her the third box. Her face lit up like a kid receiving a surprise puppy. On a primal level, I was happy to see all that food go to someone more deserving than me.

UTILA ISLAND

Next, we drove to the port of La Ceiba, where I parked my car so we could ferry to Utila island. Utila is all about diving, with at least a dozen dive resorts. The island sits at the southern end of the Mesoamerican Barrier Reef, the second-largest reef system in the world. Utilans know the reef is their lifeblood, and they protect it accordingly. The preponderance of dive shops and remote location make Utila one of the cheapest places to get a divemaster certification. Many young people take advantage of this, coming to Utila for a three-month vagabond experience while they attain divemaster.

We arrived at Utila to a chaotic scene, as dive shops waited to pick up guests—some with golf carts, some with just a wheelbarrow to haul luggage. Tommi and Steph didn't make reservations in advance, which added to the chaos as multiple dive shops tried to recruit us. I've experienced Tommi's laid-back "wait until you get there to pick a place to stay" style of travel before. Somehow, it's only guaranteed to work when Tommi is part of the equation.

We wandered the island for a bit and finally settled on Alton's Dive Center, which seemed to run a tight ship, had good reviews, and was reasonably far away from the loud part of town. Alton's had no AC rooms available, and none of us were too keen on the non-AC dorms— which are usually free if you dive with the resort. So, we found a couple of adjoining rooms at Trudy's Dive Hotel next door and ended up diving with both resorts. As it turns out, Trudy is Alton's sister. It's a small island.

We arranged for some dives the next day and headed out to explore. The island is eleven miles long by two miles wide, with most of the action along a strip on the Bay of Honduras side. Newer houses sit back from the road on stilts, while historic homes and buildings rise out of the sand at the road's edge. Just as on Caye Caulker, the lack of any cars larger than a dune buggy created a tranquil vibe. A pleasant afternoon breeze added to the paradise feel. I daydreamed about what it must be like to grow up with the Caribbean as your backyard, endless beaches to play on, and a whole island to roam. I wondered what local kids think the first time they see the mainland and realize not everyone lives their Mayberry meets Gilligan's Island lifestyle.

I asked a shopkeeper if anyone born on Utila ever leaves.

He thought for a second, "Yeah, but they always come back."

I was glad we put care into choosing where to stay and dive. We strongly considered Captain Morgan's, which seemed very popular and was close to the ferry dock and most of the bars and restaurants. But we realized after passing by a few times that it was also **the** party dive shop—with mostly people under thirty going **hard** and **loud** until the wee hours. Trudy's was fun. Captain Morgan's looked a little *too* fun. Some of the other dive resorts looked stuffy and boring.

Captain Morgan's isn't just a catchy name. The famous pirate Henry Morgan settled on Utila. Naturally, his treasure is rumored to be sunken somewhere offshore. Utilans, many of whom still have the last name Morgan, are descended from a mishmash of English, French, and Dutch pirates, British naval officers, Afro-Caribbean Garifuna, Spanish settlers, Indigenous islanders, and migrants from the Cayman Islands. That's a heck of a *23 and Me* test. Utilans speak English and are very proud of it. Shopkeepers will answer you in English even if you address them in Spanish. I had plenty of practice with this, as I became addicted to the local banana bread, progressing to a three-a-day habit by the end of my stay.

After a few days of diving, I realized I was already a third of the way to earning an Advanced Open Water certification, so I decided to go for it. The next dive was a night dive, which made me a little nervous. But I had a blast with no panic whatsoever. I think I bonded with diving for good that night.

What I like most about diving is that I'm one hundred percent present while I'm underwater. I'm not stressing about my weight, my car, the next border crossing, some stupid internet argument, or the myriad other hobby horses that circle my mind in a never-ending merry-go-round of shit. I'm in the moment and focused on what I'm doing. Diving is like meditation that actually works for me, right down to the focus on breathing.

One day, the Belgian guys from my first stint at D&D showed up at Trudy's. This happens a lot where you wind up on the same circuit as other travelers—especially in Central America, where everyone can only move up or down the narrow spine. We had another drunken pow-wow, and once again, they seemed inexplicably interested in what someone twenty years older than them had to say about life and whatnot.

Bill, a retirement-age gentleman, occupied the room next to mine at Trudy's. Bill would dive during the day, then sit out in front of his room, whiling the night away with a giant bottle of Bombay Sapphire and tonic mixer. Bill liked to talk **a lot**. His stories didn't always go somewhere, but they were always interesting. He'd been sailing the Caribbean and stopping at Trudy's to dive for twenty years. Bill and I spent a few enjoyable nights swapping rambling stories as we watched the sun go down. I realized I might be the Belgian guys' Bill, and I decided I was okay with that. Life's too short to spend on people with impeccable social graces and nothing to say.

Sunset from Trudy's deck

On another night, we wandered down to Treetanic, one of those oddball expat labor-of-love projects you stumble onto in nether corners of the world. Artists Neil and Julia Kellera, with the help of a ton of local input and labor, have created a profoundly weird restaurant/club/hotel that I can only describe as if *Pee-wee's Playhouse* was set in *The Flintstones'* universe. No right angle or regular curve exists in the whole place. Gazebos, arches, elevated walkways, fountains, tunnels, and various standing plat- forms wind their way among lush mango trees. Every surface is festooned with kaleidoscopic mosaics of salvaged glass, marbles, bottles, plates, dolls, coins, seashells, and any other shiny detritus they could find—in composi- tions of turquoise, pink, purple, orange, chartreuse, and other blazing psychedelic colors.

(Black and white pictures here wouldn't do Treetanic justice, but you can always see color pictures on my blog: ushuaiaorbust.com.)

We walked back to our hotel around 10 p.m.—passing a large group of dive shop employees heading *out* for the night. This would be a recurring evening theme of the trip—old farts headed in, kids headed out.

We did hang with the kids at Trudy's one night, starting with the world's largest, most disorganized game of flippy cup. This led to a blurry night at one of the island's ironically named clubs—*Rehab, Relapse, Delirium Tremens, You're a Drunk Loser and I Want a Divorce*—or some- thing like that.

One cool thing about diving is that it tends to break down age barriers. At Trudy's, it didn't matter if you were twenty or seventy—if you wanted to party after the dive, you were welcome. You were also welcome to spend the following day in bed for insulting Mother Nature by trying to keep up with the kids.

On our last day, I walked down to the beach and had a little moment saying goodbye to the island. I never would have gone to Utila, which turned out to be one of my favorite places on the whole trip, if Tommi hadn't pushed for it. But unless you work in the dive industry, I don't think Utila makes sense as a place to settle. The island isn't big enough to accom- modate hordes of expat retirees or digital nomads driving up rents—all while contributing little to the local economy other than sending the banana bread baker's kids to college.

While waiting for the ferry, we saw a newly minted divemaster returning to the real world, tearfully hugging her friends and saying good- bye. It reminded me of the sad "summer's over" scene in *Grease*. Her friends continued to wave from the dock as we steamed away.

On the boat ride back to La Ceiba, I stressed inordinately about my FJ. What if someone had broken into it? The port didn't seem very secure. What if one of the propane bottles exploded in the baking heat, and we returned to nothing but a hunk of charred metal? Tommi admonished me that I need to think positive in order to manifest good outcomes. I explained to her that this isn't how it works with me. I need to **worry** about worst-case scenarios so that they **don't** happen.

"See?" she said when we returned to a perfectly intact car.

"Yeah," I replied, "Nothing happened—because the universe wanted me to look stupid for worrying about it. That's the power of **negative thinking**."

She shook her head and made a sour face, demonstrably displeased with my *Reverse Secret* philosophy.

PICO BONITO

Tommi and Steph wanted to spend our last two nights together at Pico Bonito, a jungled national park near La Ceiba, whose headliner is white-water rafting. The rafting was fun, if a bit shorter than I expected. We mostly just ran a few rapids and jumped off rocks.

The day also produced one of the goofiest photos I've ever been in. Our guide had Tommi, Steph, and me sit in the back seat of the raft to keep us from burrowing into the water as we went over a small falls. The picture taken by one of the other guides shows three blue helmets all in a row, doing nothing as our guide furiously paddles, looking like the Three Chipmunks on a rafting adventure.

Shot from my rejected Most Interesting Man in the World demo tape

Tommi and Steph had an early flight the next day, so we found a hotel on the outskirts of San Pedro Sula. Later, we went out to dinner and then stopped for ice cream. The strip mall also had a pizzeria with outdoor seating and a big tent serving food from an open grill. The parking lot seemed to be something of a local hangout.

I was a little trepidatious about sitting outside, being so exposed at night, adjacent to one of the murder capitals of the world. What if we got caught in a drive-by shooting? But as I took in the genuine laughter and smiles of the people around me, I realized no one seemed nervous, so I relaxed, too.

I don't think I fully bonded with Honduras, at least the mainland, until that moment on my last night in the country. As I watched the crowd enjoying their night out, I didn't get the impression many of them would trade their lives in Honduras for a new life in the United States. The Hondurans I'd met were universally proud of their beautiful country, lighting up at any chance to talk about all the things to see and do. Of course, I didn't spend time in the gang-run barrios or impoverished rural villages, where things are a different story.

So, for our next chapter, let's just grab the third rail with both hands and have an imaginary Q&A session with America over my take on ***The Crisis at Our Southern Border™***.

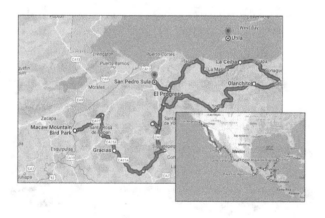

CHAPTER 34

Q&A WITH AMERICA

HELLO AMERICA! Welcome to our Q&A session on immigration and the crisis at our southern border. Let's focus on Honduras as a case study and dive right in.

Some political issues seem to have no good answers, just an assortment of messy, complicated, least-bad partial solutions. Homelessness and drug addiction come to mind. But from where I sit, Central American immigration is **not** one of those issues. The situation at our southern border is only a massive problem because we make it one.

Here's my answer: Just let 'em in.

Honor legitimate asylum claims. Offer work visas to the rest. Educate their children and give them a path to citizenship if they stay out of trouble. Don't force undocumented teenagers into a marginal existence that becomes an ultra-ripe recruiting ground for gangs. Streamline the process. Find a way to make it work. Just let 'em in.

Okay, America, time's yours. Fire away...

BUT WON'T WE BE OVERWHELMED AT THE BORDER?

Not if we set up Ellis Island-like processing facilities around airports and seaports. Migrants sell their houses and farmland to pay a human smuggler, known as a coyote, $2,000 to $5,000 when their chances of success are less than 50 percent. That's easily enough to pay for a plane ticket to Houston with money left over to get set up in the US. Under the current system, all that money goes to organized crime. Along the way, migrants have to dodge robbery, rape, and murder on the notorious "black train." Or, if they're really unlucky, they could die an agonizing death in a locked shipping container abandoned in the desert. We're helping to create a humanitarian crisis by making migrants run this hellish gauntlet.

If we give them work visas, won't they just stay?

Well, we have no idea because we hardly issue *any* work visas to Hondurans. Migrants left to their own devices until their asylum hearings generally have a good track record of showing up. According to *The Broken Village: Coffee, Migration, and Globalization in Honduras* by Daniel R. Reichman, even Hondurans who sneak into the US illegally usually go back home after saving money and sending remittance back to their family for a few years. Migrant remittances now comprise the largest chunk of Honduras's economy—eclipsing agriculture and manufacturing. People don't send that much money back home if they plan to leave their families.

Honduran citizens make up the largest share of undocumented immigrants in the United States because, unlike Salvadorans and Guatemalans who fled extreme violence in the middle and late twentieth century, most Hondurans don't have generational footholds in the US. Migration from Honduras was almost non-existent before the late 1990s and only really picked up in earnest after the 2009 coup. The new military-backed regime destroyed the social safety net and the rule of law, which—along with the United States' mass release of incarcerated Central American criminals—has paved the way for unprecedented levels of gang violence.

The US foreign policy brain trust seems to finally agree that extending temporary work visas to Central America, as they've done with Mexico for decades, might be a better answer to the border crisis. Almost no one apprehended at the border these days is from Mexico. You have to wonder if issuing a quarter-million work visas has something to do with that.

In 2009, Mexico was issued 37,000 H2A farm and H2B unskilled labor visas, while Honduras was issued a grand total of fifteen. In 2020, the Trump administration, despite blasting the "MS-13 is coming to eat your babies!" alarm for years, quietly allocated 10,000 new slots for H2A and H2B visas to Honduras. But Hondurans have been slow to realize the availability of these new work visas, and many have gone unfilled. Even now, with Biden continuing Trump's policy, in 2021, the US issued 244,000 work visas to Mexico versus 1,100 to Honduras. In Honduras, visas are seen as something only available to rich people, and the application is a cumbersome eighteen-step process. We will improve that as part of my "just let 'em in" policy.

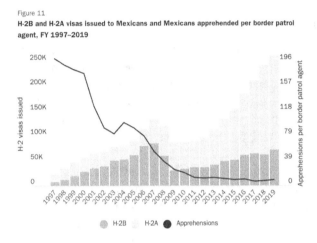

Figure 11

H-2B and H-2A visas issued to Mexicans and Mexicans apprehended per border patrol agent, FY 1997–2019

As more work visas are issued, border apprehensions plummet

BUT WHAT ABOUT MS-13?

I'm not saying we should literally open the gate and let anyone in without processing or due diligence. If some steel-eyed teenager shows up covered in face tattoos, yeah, we might want to send him back. The overwhelming majority of the people who show up at our southern border just want to work—very hard. It's their *children* who eventually get sucked into local US gangs because we relegate them to a marginal life in major cities. We can fix that with education, intelligent planning, and a path to citizenship. Hondurans made up 80 percent of the first much-ballyhooed immigrant **CARAVAN!**, which blew up just in time for the 2018 midterm elections and intensified the abhorrent child-separation policy.

I recently saw a clip where a reporter for some American-flag-branded news network breathlessly caught up with the latest **CARAVAN!** The migrants he found stoking fear in the hearts of cable television viewers nationwide? A group of bedraggled women and children huddled together under a tree. The horror. I only hope that brave reporter made it out in one piece. A crying Honduran woman who had just been tormented by a group calling themselves "Concerned Patriots for Law and Order" or some such asked, "I just want to come here and work hard. Why do they hate me so much?" Good question.

BUT THE US IS ALREADY TOO CROWDED!

First of all, that's not a question. Second of all—bollocks! Hong Kong is too crowded. The US has one of the lowest population densities of any major country. America's birth rate has been dropping for years. We have room. Houston has remade itself from an oil town to a thriving city full of diverse immigrant communities working in a healthy assortment of industries. Houston, and other cities like it, would seem to have plenty of capacity.

And let's get real for a second. "Too crowded already" is almost always a euphemism for "I don't want my city to turn brown." The irony being that the people most vehemently opposed to immigration tend to live the farthest from the immigrant communities they fear. Maybe I live in a bubble, but no one I've ever met in Los Angeles frets about the size of the Latino population. On the contrary, LA without Latino culture would be dreary and unthinkable.

WON'T THEY TAKE JOBS FROM AMERICAN WORKERS?

You don't hear this one as much these days. Everyone now seems to realize that Central American immigrants sign up for the jobs zero Americans want. As I write this book, the current made-up cable news nonsense crisis du jour is that we're in a dire labor shortage due to unmotivated American workers. Apparently, we gave the working poor too much Covid stimulus, and now they only want to lay on the couch pulling bong hits and watching *The Price is Right*.

Listening to this level of extreme derp unleashes my inner angry comic, Sam Kinneson-style:

> *"Hey. Hey there, mister talking head. You know where there's a huge source of people willing to work these jobs you keep blathering that Americans are too lazy and entitled to do? I bet you do. Think hard. See this little country right here on the map of North America? It's called—**HONNDOOORAAASSS! AUUGHH! IT'S RIGHT**

IN OUR BACKYARD! AUGH! AUGH! AAAUUUGHH-
HHHHHHHH!!!"

Of course, we all know the reply: "No, no, no. Not like that. We just
want to make *Americans* more desperate."

WILL LATINO IMMIGRANTS ASSIMILATE?

Now you're just being absurd. If the Latino families I see in Los Angeles
aren't the living embodiment of the American Dream, I don't know what
is. The first generation works their tail off doing jobs no one else wants, so
the second can get a foothold and an education, often becoming the first in
their family to go to college.

If you'll indulge me in some positive stereotyping for a moment, the
Latino immigrants I know in LA are more American than I am. They love
baseball and Chevy trucks, work blue-collar jobs, and set off a battleship's
worth of fireworks on the Fourth of July. The Latino extended families I see
at the parks and beach near my house remind me of my mom's big Irish-
Catholic family. I envy them. I wish I had the kind of family support and
level of community their neighborhoods seem to have.

I walk twenty to thirty miles a week throughout the Los Angeles area. I
see many upscale enclaves that are house-rich and community-poor—with
no children playing in the street, yards hidden behind massive privacy
bushes, and no signs of life beyond a few people walking their dogs. If
assimilation means dead streets, you can have it.

I have one question for the "concerned about assimilation" crowd, to
which I've never heard a remotely satisfactory answer: What is fundamen-
tally different about Latin American immigrants now versus my Italian,
Irish, Scottish, and German ancestors arriving at Ellis Island around the
turn of the century? Germans and Italians also speak a different language
(and Scots when you get a few pints in them). New arrivals form tight-knit
immigrant communities, stoking fears they won't assimilate? Yes, my ancestors faced that. See: Queens. Fear of gangs and violent criminals? My Italian
great-grandfather, Beniamino, definitely had to deal with that.

As late as the '60s, my dad was denied a plum government job and told
flatly, "I will never hire an Italian." (Hiring managers could proudly admit
stuff like that back in the good ol' days before pesky discrimination laws.)

Assimilation fears were baseless then, and they're baseless now.

THE UNRESTRICTED DUMPING-GROUND.

Anti-Italian propaganda from 1903—very stabby

SHOULDN'T WE TRY TO MAKE THINGS BETTER BACK IN THEIR HOME COUNTRIES SO PEOPLE DON'T *WANT* TO MIGRATE?

Yes! Finally, something we can all agree on. In no way am I claiming migration is a panacea for all that ails Hondurans. On the contrary, *The Broken Village* describes first-hand how disruptive the migrant economy has been to life in one rural mountain town.

The coffee harvest runs from November to February, leaving residents with no income for the better part of a year. One of the town's largest landholders travels to Atlanta to wash dishes. Three of the town's best students, all with law degrees, emigrated to work unskilled jobs in the US. American movies and TV shows inundate Hondurans with visions of a glamorous lifestyle they can't afford. Some villagers are seen as migrating to the US out of necessity, some out of ambition. The latter is frowned upon—at least until the first remittance wires start rolling in. Migrants who send back the most money set the bar for the village. A migrant whose remittance doesn't measure up is seen, sometimes even by his own mother, as a lazy *haragán*— a loafer. A favorite joke among village locals depicts migrants ensconced in the United States as so fat and lazy they won't bother to pick up a $10 bill lying on the street.

The book tells the story of the first waves of migrants returning to the village, which had no electricity or running water at the time. They built houses like they'd seen or even helped build in the US—with amenities like swing sets, barbecue grills, and hot tubs. Rural Hondurans generally don't even like bathing in hot water and have zero use for a hot tub. It's just an expensive status symbol to inform the village that a big shot who returned from the States lives here.

One migrant worked seventy hours a week at a deli on Long Island for six years, making $12 an hour—enough to send generous remittances to his family and still roll back into town like a returning king. He built a fancy house, stocked it with the latest appliances and electronics from the US, and married the prettiest girl in town in a grand ceremony that had campesinos from all over the countryside peeking into the church windows. Six months later, bored and worried about running out of money, he paid a coyote to sneak him back into the US. His young bride grew lonely in the dream home and moved back in with her mother.

I have no idea what the moral of that story is. But the point is that everyone involved agrees that it would be better if Hondurans didn't *feel the need* to migrate to the US in mass numbers. Aid is being poured into Honduras right now for this express purpose. But these programs must be targeted strategically and take time to work. You can't just fix global coffee prices or eliminate the mara gangs overnight. So, in the meantime, I say let's try the Mexico program and issue a ton of work visas.

BUT IT'S THE LAW!

Again, not a question. So, while you're in timeout, let me reply with some questions of my own. What would you do if you could only afford to live in the poorest parts of some of the most dangerous cities on the planet, where your thirteen-year-old son was under pressure to join MS-13 or die? What would you do if you were a coffee farmer barely getting by in the good years, now financially shattered by a global price collapse? Imagine having a family to feed, and the apparel factory you worked at just shut down—all due to a race-to-the-bottom system where capital is free to fly around the globe in search of ever-cheaper products, but the human beings who produce those goods are confined to the place they were born.

At least acknowledge that you'd probably try to migrate as well, given similar circumstances, law or no law. Harriet Tubman broke the law. Toddlers carried across the border by their parents technically broke the law. The Chinese Exclusion Act was law. The law turned away 937 Jewish refugees fleeing the Holocaust aboard the SS St. Louis. The law is not the final moral authority. Especially when the United States has historically promulgated a nudge-nudge-wink-wink mixed message that could best be summed up as: "It's illegal to come here, but if you manage to sneak through our defenses, there will be plenty of work waiting."

Won't they just go on welfare?

This is the myth that won't go away. Undocumented immigrants receive schooling and emergency medical care but **not** welfare, food stamps, Medicaid, or most other public benefits. They still pay sales tax, and they often pay income tax and social security tax via a fake social security number, ensuring they will never get credit for paying into the system. One study concluded that immigrants, documented and undocumented, pay on average $80,000 more in taxes over their lifetime than they consume in government services. But we can have dueling studies all day. The idea that Hondurans and other Central American migrants undertake that hellish trek just to go on public assistance in the US is laughable on its face, as anyone who's spent a few days in Los Angeles can attest. First-generation Latino immigrants are the backbone of California's economy, which is larger than all but a handful of countries. The whole state would shut down without them.

Will immigrants bring diseases?

Okay, no more AM Radio for you.

Well, America, it looks like we have time for one more question...

Are you calling me racist?

Alrighty, that's a wrap, America. Time to get back to our regularly scheduled road trip. But first, let's give a big round of applause to the first-generation immigrants who set up the conference room, put out the coffee and bagels, and stand off to the side waiting to clean up after us when we leave.

PART FOUR

NICARAGUA

The Somoza clan marches into exile while Augusto Cesar Sandino wanders freely throughout Nicaragua, showered by flowers, half a century after he was executed by firing squad. This country has gone mad: lead floats, cork sinks, the dead are fleeing the cemetery and women the kitchen.

— Eduardo Galeano, *Memoria del Fuego*

What Are You, Nicaragua?

By Giaconda Belli

What are you—
a little triangle of earth
lost in the middle of the world?

What are you—
a flight of birds
guardabarrancos
cenzontles
hummingbirds?

What are you—
a roar of rivers
bearing polished, shiny stones
leaving footprints of water in the mountains?

What are you—
A women's breasts made of earth
Smooth, pointed and threatening?

What are you—
Singing of leaves in gigantic trees
Green, tangled and filled with doves?

What are you—
Pain and dust and screams in the afternoon
—screams like those of women giving birth—?

What are you—
Clenched fist and loaded gun?

What are you, Nicaragua
To cause me such pain?

CHAPTER 35

EVERY CHILD A POET

ON APRIL 18, 2018—as Tommi, Steph, and I were en route to Utila Island—protests broke out in Managua, León, Granada, and other Nicaraguan cities. Crowds of mostly students and senior citizens made their feelings known about a decree by President Daniel Ortega that reduced the social security benefit, while raising taxes on those paying into the system.

For reasons known only to himself, Ortega cracked down on these peaceful rallies, HARD. If he intended to squelch future protests, it failed miserably. Footage of police and Ortega's Sandinista Youth shock troops battering young and elderly demonstrators exploded onto social media. Massive violent protests erupted in cities all over Nicaragua. After five days of riots that left thirty people dead and countless more injured, Ortega rescinded the reforms, and the country fell into a shaky simmering détente.

I monitored the situation from Honduras, thinking there was no chance in hell I'd be heading to Nicaragua any time soon. Then, the riots stopped, and the message from anyone I contacted in the Nicaraguan tourism industry was, unsurprisingly, "You can come now. It's okay."

I had an inkling by this point that I wasn't going to make it to South America. But the thought of turning around and missing Nicaragua, Costa Rica, and Panama really bummed me out. So, I pressed on, figuring I could always bug out of Nicaragua and head to Costa Rica at the first sign of trouble.

I didn't want to race through Nicaragua, though. Sabrina, my Spanish tutor in LA, had inspired me to add the colonial cities of León and Granada to my "places to settle some someday" list. According to her sales pitch, Nicaragua offers bountiful natural wonders like Costa Rica **and** boasts Central America's richest literary and intellectual tradition. Nicaragua's national literary hero, turn-of-the-century poet Rubén Darío, is considered the father of Modernism in the Spanish language. According to Sabrina, every Nicaraguan is assumed to be a poet until they prove otherwise. Children are affectionately referred to as *poeta* or *poetisa*, not unlike the way my uncles called me *tiger*.

At least some of my fascination with Nicaragua had been primed much earlier in life. The Iran-Contra scandal broke in 1987 during my senior year of high school. Even though my pressing concern at the time was how to hide the latest dent in my Camaro from my mom, I still managed to absorb that 1) the Sandinistas were evil communist revolutionaries who should be feared, 2) Ronald Reagan was a naughty boy who got caught with his hand in the cookie jar—selling arms to Iran and using the proceeds to fund the counter-revolutionary Contras, and 3) when testifying before Congress, Oliver North, the scheme's mastermind, came down with the most inexplicable case of early-onset selective amnesia known to medical science.

THE BORDER

The forums teem with tales of woe from overlanders held up at the Nicaraguan border—sometimes for days—owing to some rejected document, accidentally pissing off a customs agent, or just because the big boss was having a bad day and wanted to throw his weight around.

One traveler told a story about dealing with a very picky Nicaraguan border agent: "She was taking forever to inspect every bill I gave her. She kept rejecting bills for the tiniest tear or imperfection and pushing them back to me. Finally, she accepted a twenty-dollar bill that met her standards. When she returned my change in córdobas, I mimicked her, squinting as I meticulously inspected each bill. Then I made a face and pushed one of the bills back to her, just like she had done to me."

I asked him how this legendary act of insubordination turned out.

"They kept me there for three more hours. But it was worth it."

I salute you, sir.

My streak of sleepy border crossings came to an end at Nicaragua. So, I got a helper on the Honduras side who was reasonably helpful but did not explain that he'd be taking my $10 and then handing me off to a *different* helper on the Nicaraguan side. It was not immediately clear if I was expected to also pay the second helper. Once clear of Honduran exit customs, we waited for my Nicaraguan helper to show up. After a few minutes, a wiry, weather-beaten, dour-faced man of about sixty pedaled up on a bicycle, and I was officially handed off.

My new helper grunted and pedaled off, waving for me to follow him. Once again, I had somehow snookered myself into having nothing smaller than a $100 bill. So, my first order of business was to ask my helper, who hadn't yet looked me in the eye and clearly had no time for my nonsense, where we could get some cambio (change). When he saw the $100 bill, his eyes lit up, and his whole demeanor changed. He comically exclaimed, "Amigo!" and put his arm around me. We had fun going back and forth with that. "Oh, **now**, I'm your amigo? Okay, I see how this works." It was my first taste of the snarky Nicaraguan sense of humor and the perfect response to put me at ease.

My helper earned his keep—steering me through a bureaucratic maze of stamps, signatures, and grumpy functionaries reminiscent of the movie *Brazil*. He would put me in line to wait for one form while he pedaled off across the compound with $2 to get another piece of paper stamped. Navigating the whole process on my own would have been a nightmare.

The air conditioning in the main building was on the fritz, so the border workers had all pushed their giant metal desks outside. At one of these desks sat a portly, sweaty Aduana agent with his uniform shirt unbuttoned down to his abdomen. He asked me for a "propina" (tip) before he would sign the form that my helper had just gotten stamped somewhere off in the hinterlands. I laughed, gave him a big smile, and indicated that I was already paying my helper, who was standing right there. How could I possibly pay **two** propinas? Crazy talk.

In response, the flustered agent crossed his arms and puffed out his lower lip in an exaggerated pout, like a cranky toddler. I have to say, when I walked through the various bribe coercion techniques I might be faced with on the trip, I did not consider extreme pouting. Once the corpulent official realized his comical pout wasn't going to melt my icy resolve, he signed the paper.

And that, friends, was the only time on the entire trip someone in authority asked me for a bribe—a situation I'd wasted countless hours fretting over during pre-trip research and planning. I was proud that I didn't give in. Paying a bribe makes life tougher for future overlanders and just makes the world a slightly crappier place in general. Then again, it's not like Pouty McPoutface put me in a crucible.

When it came time to pay my helper, I gave him $20. By the way his face lit up, I think I made his month. Overpaying border helpers is another thing overlanders complain about, as it jacks up expectations for everyone coming after you. But my helper earned it. I can't imagine how often the poor guy has been stiffed by overlanders who refuse to pay more than the $10 they'd agreed to on the Honduran side. Yes, it's a bit of a scam. But your vehicle is probably worth more than your Nicaraguan helper will make in his lifetime. Let's have some perspective.

By GDP per capita, Nicaragua is the poorest country in Central America. The drop from Honduras, the second poorest, was palpable. Taxis and tuk-tuks ferried people to and from the border on the Honduran side. The only vehicles I saw for hire on the Nicaraguan side were bicycle rickshaws whose poor drivers looked like they were about to keel over in the scorching heat. Even the foliage seemed to turn brown and dusty just past the border. Many rural Nicaraguans still cook with firewood, which, as one would expect, has led to deforestation.

It's always nice to have a concrete destination after the ordeal of crossing the border. Sophie had gone on to Nicaragua after we parted company in El Salvador. She recommended the aptly named, as I would come to find out, Volcano Hostel. I plugged the address into Google Maps and headed for the colonial city of León.

León

I drove a few laps around León's cobblestone streets, admiring the colorful architecture, until I spotted a sign for the Volcano Hostel. Inside, the hostel was laid out like a typical modest colonial hacienda, with rooms along one side, a garage area, kitchen and storage along the other side, and an open-air courtyard under a big tent that served as a rain and sun umbrella. As luck would have it, the garage area had just enough room to squeeze in my car.

I asked if they had any AC rooms. They did not. I asked if the rooms stayed hot at night. Remus, the congenial French vagabonder working the front desk, told me my room would cool down at night and had a good fan. I checked out the room, which was spacious and clean with old-world flair. I was a bit concerned that the room only had two small windows, both facing the courtyard. It did have a powerful working fan and high ceilings, which I presumed would help dissipate the hot air. The mid-afternoon

León heat was oppressive. But at least it was a dry heat, which tends to cool down at night. Or so I reasoned.

I decided it was time to stop being such a pampered AC-suckling wuss. I would tough it out and live like everyone else for once. I paid $11 for one night and $3 for parking with plans to stay longer.

In the open-air lobby, a few local residents and an American guy in road-bicycle gear were watching the Champions League semi-final soccer match. I decided to park my butt and enjoy a few beers.

"Victoria or Toña?" Remus asked, marking the first of countless times I would hear that question. Nicaragua has two national beers, and Nicas are as passionate about their beer allegiance as they are about baseball, poetry, and civil disobedience. Although I question if many could tell the difference between Toña and Victoria in a blind taste test. A few times, in congenial local company, I tried lightheartedly floating my opinion that the two beers taste pretty much the same. Each time, the reply came as stone-faced silence, convincing me to quickly drop the subject.

The gringo in bicycle gear had just gotten back from a four-hour ride in the mid-morning heat, which I couldn't even comprehend. Apparently, he was bouncing around Central America, doing this for fun. He asked about my car and my trip. I gave him the brief outline, to which he replied, "So, like a midlife crisis?"

I laughed. "Yeah, I guess so." I'd never really thought of my trip in those terms, but it seems to check most of the boxes. Still, it's not like I ran out and bought a Lamborghini. Maybe a "mid-life crisis" is just deciding that life's a journey, not a destination. You can learn a lot from Aerosmith.

After a couple of beers, I set out to explore León. I'd heard the city was trashed in the riots, and I was curious to see the damage. But I couldn't find any. The old city center seemed to be in great shape, with most of its colonial buildings freshly painted in vibrant colors.

I found a coffee shop, one of the few establishments in town with AC, and a perfect spot to cool down and wait for the sun to get low. I decided León was missing the boat if they weren't using "León: Hot as Balls" as their city slogan.

Leon's Iglesia La Recoleccion cathedral

On my way back to the Volcano Hostel, I passed several elderly residents sitting in little barred alcoves that jutted out from their haciendas. I guessed that these nooks, which looked like half a birdcage and could be square, round, or trapezoid-shaped, were good spots to cool down in the early evening. At a few feet above street level, the alcoves also sat at the perfect height for a seated senior citizen to interact with passersby on the sidewalk. Sunset seemed to be social hour all over León. The city buzzed with people conversing in the street, sidewalks, and shop entrances. The vibe reminded me of my Spanish tutor's bustling Hispanic neighborhood in LA.

When I arrived back at the hostel, the same group of people who had been drinking and watching the soccer match earlier, minus the bike-riding gringo, were still drinking and now creating their own entertainment. I checked my room. It was, unfortunately, still hot as balls. I turned on the fan and opened the heavy wooden door to let air in. I hoped the room would cool down as night set in. I had a few more beers in the courtyard while I waited.

Eventually, I bid goodnight to the raucous partiers and retired to my room, hoping the fan had worked its magic. It had not. If anything, the room seemed hotter than when I had checked it earlier. The air in the courtyard just outside the room was at least ten degrees cooler. I looked up at the vaulted ceiling, which came to a point directly above my bed. In Antigua, vaulted ceilings usually had an opening at the top to let the heat out. I always thought this was odd since it's rarely hot in Antigua, and the openings mostly just let mosquitoes *in*. Here in sweltering León, however, a hole in the ceiling would be a godsend.

I stripped down to my underwear and lay on top of the covers with the fan pointed at me on full blast. The ambient air was so hot and dry that the fan felt like a giant hair dryer.

I got my portable fan out of my car, thinking two fans might help move the air around and pull in cooler air from outside. They did not. The only noticeable difference was that I now had *two* hair dryers blowing on me.

The air was so dry that I didn't sweat. I'd spent a few brutal summers without air conditioning as a kid and a few more as a broke college student. At least in the midwestern humidity, I could generate my own puddle of cooling sweat to writhe around in. This was somehow worse. I felt like a pig on a spit, constantly turning, roasting in my own skin.

The only time the fans felt the tiniest bit cool was when I flipped from one side to the other. This would last for about thirty seconds until the thin layer of sweat on the part of me that had just been in contact with the bed dried up. Then it was back to dueling hair dryers.

I took a cold shower, which helped, for about fifteen minutes. By this time, the air outside my door had to be twenty degrees cooler.

Stupid Spanish! Why do you poke holes in the roofs in mild Antigua but not in hot-as-balls León? One freaking hole would create a sucking vortex of hot air that would pull in the cooler air from outside my room. I think vaulted ceilings without a vent hole might actually dissipate heat *worse* than low ceilings. The empty pyramid of space above my bed seemed to function as an upside-down heat sink, trapping the rising warmer air like a hot air balloon. I had a lot of time to ponder the thermodynamics of the situation as I lay on my bed of lava, staring up at the ceiling.

I should have known this was coming when Sophie recommended the place. Sophie would need a cardigan on the surface of the sun. If our ideal ambient temperatures were any farther apart, one of us would be a different species.

In desperation, I pulled my heavy queen-sized poster bed across the room and up against the open door, hoping to catch a little of the cool breeze from outside. I noticed a medieval-looking iron rod at the top of the arched doorway. I yanked and twisted the rod, which felt like it hadn't moved in years. This generated loud iron-on-iron screeches that would have awoken the partiers, now sleeping in nearby hammocks, if they hadn't passed out piss drunk.

Eventually, the rod came down. Then I yanked a similar rod *up* from the bottom of the doorway—to the same chorus of screeching. My efforts freed up a smaller, second door that I was able to open part-way, thus creating an extra six inches of open airway. #BLESSED

A seven-foot-tall wardrobe, which seemed to be carved from one solid block of wood, prevented the little extra door from opening to its full glory. After several failed attempts to shove the wardrobe out of the way, I realized it was bolted to the floor, presumably so some heat-deranged idiot didn't accidentally pull it down on himself. I considered getting my socket set out of the car. But ultimately, I decided that any attempt to dislodge the wardrobe would heat me up more than another six inches of open doorway would cool me down. Also, I might kill myself.

I finally fell asleep sometime in the wee hours. By dawn, my room in its current configuration was almost bearable. I decided to close my doors, lest the morning help arrive to the bewildering and disturbing scene of me spread-eagle in my underwear, my massive bed dragged across the room, strange doors akimbo that hadn't moved since the 1700s—and begin to wonder just what exactly we had gotten up to at the previous night's party.

Of course, with the doors closed, the room instantly heated up again.

I drifted in and out of heat sleep for a few hours. Finally, I gave in and got up, groggy and somewhat hungover, but with a mission: MUST FIND AIR CONDITIONING. When I left the hostel, the first thing I did was check the roof. I wondered if maybe there was a second story above my room, which would explain the lack of a heat vent. Nope. Such advanced technology as DRILLING A HOLE apparently never occurred to the colonial architects of León.

I wandered the streets for a few hours in my quest for cooler lodging. None of the hostels I found had AC rooms, nor did they know of any that did. It started to look like my only option was a stodgy $100-a-night hotel in a boring part of town. Then, I checked with a hostel I had been avoiding, as it sat right in the thick of the raucous bar district. They did have an AC room for $25 a night. Sold. I can easily live with a little noise over baking all night like a Christmas ham.

Sometimes, you just have to look yourself in the mirror and come to terms with who you are. I am an AC wuss. I will always be an AC wuss.

I am enough.

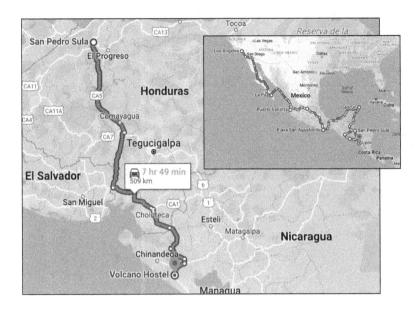

Chapter 36

Volcano Surfing

I QUITE LIKED LEÓN, other than the hot-as-balls part. My first question to anyone who seemed local was, "Is Granada any cooler than this?" After a few thoughtful replies of, "No, not really," I crossed Granada off my list of places to settle as well. Poor Nicaragua. Everywhere else in Mexico and Central America, the Spanish built their colonial cities in the mountains. But in Nicaragua, they picked the hot lowlands and then inexplicably refused to poke holes in the roofs.

I settled into a comfortable routine in León. The Volcano Hostel allowed me to store my car in their garage, so I went back often to hang out with Remus and crew. I also became a regular at the air-conditioned coffee shop. The French have a word for wandering a city wherever the moment takes you: *flaneuring*. Sadly, my hobbled foot and León's cobblestones put a real damper on my flaneuring.

As far back as Guatemala, I'd been hearing about volcano boarding as a "must-do" in León. Local guides have figured out that one of the nearby volcanoes has the proper slope, and the volcanic pumice rock has the right friction, to allow tourists to slide down the volcano on a wooden toboggan without bodily injury... for the most part. We did meet a woman at Pico Bonito in Honduras who tore ligaments in her knee while volcano boarding in León. So, that was on my mind. The volcanic dust may also be toxic, because they make you wear a face covering, goggles, and essentially a hazmat suit. The need for the hazmat suit was never fully explained.

A group of volcano boarders heading down to the launch
point in their hazmat suits

As for the board ride itself, the spooky part comes at the beginning. The slope gets steeper about halfway through, which gives the impression that you're about to sail off a cliff. The rest of the ride was anticlimactic, as my primary concern was staying under control and not tearing knee ligaments. You control the speed by using your feet as brakes and leaning back on the toboggan for full speed. Sophie had done volcano boarding when she came through, and she was proud that she had gone the fastest in her group. I gave a silent thanks that she wasn't around to ridicule my cheese-grater-like grind down the mountain.

If I had a chance to do it again, I'd have gone faster the second time. There are packages where you get to board twice. Just keep in mind that also means you have to hike up the volcano twice. Did I mention that it's hot?

On the ride back from the volcano, I talked to a young Dutch back-packer named Eva who worked at a hostel in León. She said that during the riots, people went about their business during the day, then all hell broke loose at night.

In these skirmishes, the cops used rubber bullets **and** real bullets, and Ortega's Sandinista Youth sometimes bombarded the protesters with Molotov cocktails. Protestors fought back using homemade rocket launchers they call *morteros*. Eva said the night the clashes came down her block was the scariest. As a precaution against stray bullets and mortars, hostel workers piled mattresses against the windows and then spent a long night huddled in the room farthest from the street.

According to the anti-Ortega protesters and some compelling video footage, Sandinista Youth foot soldiers would blend in with the protestors to launch a false flag attack on the police, giving the cops an excuse to retaliate with real bullets. A stray bullet killed a fourteen-year-old girl during one of the protests in León.

Figuring out who's who in these clashes and whom to believe when the shit hits the fan seems nigh impossible. The quote at the beginning of this section refers to a famous local aphorism, "Nicaragua is a land where lead floats and cork sinks," which, as near as I can tell, is a colorful way of saying, "Don't believe anything you hear, and don't try to make sense of anything you see."

I assumed that if things flared up again, the protests would stick to the cities and follow the same day/night pattern, giving me the option of heading to a more peaceful rural location or just bailing out of the country.

I never could find remnants of the riots. The only damage I found was a wall riddled with bullet holes that looked decades old. I wondered if the wall had been deliberately left in that state as a tribute to the 1979 Sandinista Revolution that ended the Somoza family dynasty.

Bullet-riddled wall in León

COLUMBUS TO SOMOZA

For 300 years of Spanish colonial rule, Nicaragua served as a trans-isthmus crossing between the Atlantic and the Pacific. Boats ferried passengers along the San Juan River from the Caribbean to the Eastern shore of Lake Nicaragua, the largest lake in Central America. After a leisurely sail across the lake, travelers had only a short eleven-mile overland passage by donkey or covered wagon to the Pacific Ocean.

Nicaragua's history begins to diverge from the typical Central American story with the discovery of gold in California in the 1840s. Suddenly, the Nicaraguan passage became vitally important to American interests. Cornelius Vanderbilt started a profitable steamship line across Lake Nicaragua, allowing trans-isthmus passengers to travel from sea to sea in twenty hours.

In 1855, the United States completed the Panama Railway. As a result, interest in Nicaragua waned for a bit but then rekindled when dreams of a trans-isthmus shipping canal materialized.

France took the first crack at building a canal across Panama. Besieged by engineering problems and endless waves of tropical diseases, the French finally surrendered to the jungle in 1889. With France out of the race, United States leadership set their sights on a canal across either Panama or Nicaragua. The French wanted to sell their exclusive rights to build a canal across Panama for $40 million, a price many in Congress thought too high. Nicaragua also had the advantage of a more stable political situation, less deadly wild jungle to plow through, and a shorter journey to and from the US by boat. In 1902, the US House of Representatives voted to build the canal across Nicaragua. The Senate seemed a lock to follow suit.

The 10 centavo stamp that may have cost Nicaragua the canal

As debate proceeded in the Senate, Mount Pelée erupted on the Caribbean island of Martinique, destroying the city of Saint-Pierre and killing 30,000 people. The French, desperate to unload their canal rights, seized on the disaster, promoting the idea that Nicaragua's many active volcanoes posed a catastrophic risk to the canal. As a clincher, a French lobbyist sent each undecided senator a Nicaraguan ten centavo stamp, which—in a quintessentially Nicaraguan ironic twist of fate—proudly featured the Momotombo volcano spewing smoke and lava. The Senate did an about-face, voting instead to build the canal across Panama. Nicaragua's future had been inexorably rerouted by an untimely eruption and a ten-cent stamp.

The US wanted to ensure that no one else would try to build a canal through Central America, so they browbeat Nicaragua into selling them exclusive rights in perpetuity. Nicaragua's popular president, José Santos Zelaya, had been a strong ally of the United States. But when Zelaya realized the US had no plans to build a canal across his country nor let anyone else build one, he ramped up rhetoric and actions against the US. When Zelaya started flirting with Germany and Japan to build a canal, President Taft sent in the US Marines, ostensibly to protect US interests. Zelaya fled to Spain.

The Marines stuck around for over twenty years, propping up one US-approved Nicaraguan president after another. In 1927, Augusto César Sandino, the son of a wealthy plantation-owning father and an indigenous servant mother, declared war on the United States, kicking off the first guerrilla war on the continent since colonial times. By 1933, the diminutive cowboy in his signature oversized Stetson hat and low-slung pistol holsters, commanding his army of between 300 and 3,000 men (depending on whose account you believe), had given the US enough headache to drive the despised Marines out of Nicaragua. Sandino became a national hero.

Augusto César Sandino in his trademark stetson hat and gun belt

As usual, the United States had the last word. On their way out the door, the Marines tapped an otherwise unremarkable thirty-five-year-old Army major named Anastasio Somoza García to head the feared and loathed National Guard—the real reins of power in the country. Somoza's primary qualifications seem to be that he was educated in the States and that the wife of the US ambassador found him "pleasant."

Once Sandino achieved the primary objective of driving out the Marines, he signed a peace treaty with Nicaraguan president Juan Sacasa, hoping to help steer Nicaragua on its post-occupation course. Acting without Sacasa's knowledge, Somoza had his guardsmen assassinate Sandino on his way home from a round of talks at the presidential palace.

Two years later, Somoza ousted Sacasa and installed himself as president, kicking off forty-two years of dynastic rule. Somoza remained a staunch US ally, reportedly causing President Franklin Delano Roosevelt to quip, "Somoza may be a son of a bitch, but he's ***our*** son of a bitch." Although some historians think Somoza made the quote up and promoted it himself—proud to be FDR's SOB.

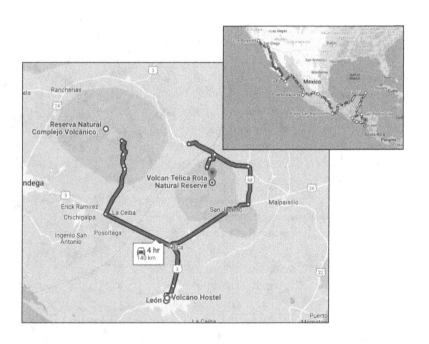

CHAPTER 37

PARADISO

I ASKED AROUND FOR A FUN, social, hopefully not hot-as-balls place to relax after León and received a recommendation for something called Paradiso Hostel. I've been to places with "Paradise" in the name that should be reported to standards and practices for false advertising. But Paradiso—perched on the edge of a clear crater lake called Laguna de Apoyo—lived up to its moniker. From the open-air dining area, colorful tropical foliage framed a picture view of the azure, perfectly round lake.

I sipped a few cold Toñas, soaking up the prevailing cool breeze, watching the mountainous crater rim transform from gold to burnt orange to ruddy brown as afternoon gave way to sunset.

Laguna de Apoyo from Paradiso Hostel

Paradiso didn't have AC rooms, which initially concerned me. The room turned out to be a tad stuffy, but nothing a fan couldn't alleviate. The silver lining from my traumatic night at the Volcano Hostel was that every other warm night for the rest of the trip seemed bearable by comparison.

On my second night, the Paradiso staff hosted a trivia competition to benefit a local charity. The proceeds helped pay for secondary school for local kids, which I thought was odd, since education was a hallmark cause of socialist Nicaragua.

For the competition, I was teamed with a group of twenty-somethings. Figuring my oldness would come in handy for once, I was feeling confident, bordering on cocky. I may even have let on to my teammates that I'd been known to play a mean Trivial Pursuit back in the day, and they should all get ready to hop on my back and ride me to Glorytown.

But I was dead weight. Some questions were clearly geared toward the youngs, like "What is the name of Beyoncé's kid?" But even on the questions a 49-year-old should have gotten, I whiffed. My sole contribution to our cause was recognizing the first few bars of *Push It* by Salt-N-Pepa.

Despite my anchor dragging bottom the whole way, our team still won. The prize was a bottle of rum, which we happily shared amongst the table and anyone else who wandered over. Eventually, the party whittled down to a half dozen of us huddled around the dwindling bottle of rum. Two young Nicaraguan guys sat nearby, the only other trivia participants who hadn't left or migrated to our table. They looked a bit dejected, so I invited them to join us. I peppered the two young men with questions about the protests and Nicaragua in general. In their answers, I detected a vibe that felt so out of place I didn't recognize it at first: deep cynicism.

Latin Americans, at least from all my experience, don't do *cynical*. These guys reminded me of myself and my friends in high school: nihilistic, pessimistic, sneering at anyone who earnestly thought they could make a difference. The key distinction being that my friends and I were just entitled, angsty little Gen X shitheads with zero actual problems. We weren't getting shot in the streets by government goons.

I asked the guys, "What's up with having to raise money so kids can go to secondary school? I've heard that even though Nicaragua is poor, at least the government provides decent education and healthcare."

"That is all a lie," came the depressing reply.

So, where did it all go wrong? Or did it ever go right?

SOMOZA TO ORTEGA

Once you remove the vilification lens I grew up with from the US media, what the Sandinistas accomplished seems downright monumental. In 1961, Carlos Fonseca, Tomas Borge, and a few other student revolutionaries founded what would eventually be known as the Sandinista National Liberation Front (FSLN), named in honor of national hero Augusto Sandino. A few of Sandino's original men were even still around to join the early FSLN. For nearly two decades leading up to the 1979 revolution, well-educated young bourgeoisie and landless peasants, known colloquially as "Muchachos and Campesinos," joined the FSLN, even though opposing Somoza often amounted to a death sentence.

FDR's "son of a bitch," Anastasio "Tacho" Somoza, enjoyed nearly twenty years of despotic rule before being assassinated by a famous poet. *(**Note:** in Nicaragua, assume all bomb-throwing revolutionaries are famous poets unless stipulated otherwise.)*

Anastasio's son, Luis, succeeded his father as president, kicking off the first family dynasty in Latin America. Luis died in 1967, followed by his brother Anastasio "Tachito" Somoza, who by all accounts was the most corrupt and barbarous of the three Somozas. Tachito was fond of dropping his political enemies out of helicopters into the Masaya volcano, at least when he wasn't feeding them to his pet panthers.

By the '60s, a new generation of affluent Nicaraguans, many educated abroad, grew disenchanted with their homeland and began agitating for change. In her memoir *The Country Under My Skin*, poet-revolutionary Giaconda Belli tells of a life-altering childhood encounter on her uncle's coffee plantation:

> *I was forbidden from going anywhere near the dormitories where the coffee pickers lived, a prohibition that only made me want to see them more. One afternoon I surreptitiously slid out from my nanny's watchful eye to have a look. It was like discovering one of the circles of hell. The rustic wooden barracks, dark and foul-smelling, only had a couple of crude openings just under the roofline and housed God only knows how many families. Each family occupied a kind of shelf set into a wall. There were many, stacked closely together. Crammed into that small space, the coffee pickers slept with their wives and children, lying on top of dirty rags. ... I would*

never forget that stench of humidity and filth, of being closed
in, airless. That spectacle left an indelible impression on my
memory and shattered any childish illusions I may have
harbored that the world I lived in was a happy one.

Nicaragua's opposition newspaper, *La Prensa*, voiced this generation's aspirations and concerns and remained a constant thorn in Tachito Somoza's side. In 1967, *La Prensa* published shocking accounts of the National Guard gunning down three hundred peaceful protesters at a rally to denounce the upcoming sham elections. That atrocity began a string of seminal moments that progressively eroded Tachito's support among the vast majority of Nicaraguans. As much as he may have wanted to shut down *La Prensa*, Tachito was in a bind. The paper was wildly popular, and the appearance of a free press and legitimate democracy were essential conditions for US support.

Just after midnight on December 23, 1972, a catastrophic earthquake measuring 7.5 on the Richter scale rocked Managua and neighboring cities. When the subsequent fires finally stopped, the quake had razed more than 600 city blocks, killed 10,000 people, and left another 300,000 homeless.

Within a day, planes stocked with emergency relief supplies began to arrive from around the world. But instead of distributing relief items to the earthquake victims as intended, government officials doled them out to connected cronies. Corrupt customs agents sold canned goods right off the planes, which showed up in markets the next day. Emergency tents intended for the newly homeless appeared in the backyards of National Guardsmen and other government employees who were still scared to sleep in their own houses. Only a few bags of rice and potatoes ever made it through this gauntlet of graft. *La Prensa*, again, was there to document the blatant corruption.

By the late 1970s, downtown Managua was *still* a blank pile of rubble. Public sentiment had decayed to the point that Tachito was essentially in command of a hostile territory—one which could only exist by virtue of unwavering support from the United States. To that end, Pedro Chamorro, the editor of *La Prensa*, exclaimed a sentiment echoed by countless Nicaraguan intellectuals over the years: "The US is the great overwhelming factor in our national life, and you don't even know we exist!"

Managua after the 1972 earthquake

Congress and the Carter administration, however, were finally growing weary of the endless atrocities and brutality. They scaled back unlimited aid and worked to engineer a peaceful transfer of power.

In January of 1978, Somoza had Pedro Chamorro assassinated. The dictator denied involvement, but no one was buying the floating lead and sinking cork stories on this particular event. The conservative Chamber of Commerce called for a general strike, and even non-radical students took to the streets. Everyone who didn't have their hand buried in the cookie jar had turned against the regime.

For their part, the Sandinistas pulled off a succession of brazen operations that progressively raised their mystique among the masses. In 1974, they raided a Christmas party hosted by a prominent Managua politician, taking a few dozen government bigwigs hostage. In the end, Tachito Somoza paid $1 million in ransom, agreed to publish an FSLN manifesto in local papers, freed fourteen political prisoners, and gave the kidnappers safe passage to Cuba. One of the released prisoners was a young Daniel Ortega, who had been incarcerated since 1967 for bank robbery.

In 1978, a would-be mistress lured Somoza's despised top counter-insurgency official into a deadly pants-down bedroom ambush that made for titillating national headlines. Later that same year, twenty-five Sandinista commandos took the Nicaraguan Congress hostage in a daring raid known internally as *Operation Pigsty*. A sympathetic Catholic Cardinal smuggled five rolls of film out of the besieged Congress, and the footage became international news. Again, Somoza paid ransom, published screeds, arranged a plane to Cuba, and freed political prisoners, including Thomas Borge, the only FSLN founder still alive.

Iconic "Molotov Man" photo—shot by Susan Meiselas, who was seemingly everywhere in Central America in the '70s and '80s (Susan Meiselas/Magnum)

The FSLN had more levers to pull than just guerrilla attacks and public spectacles. Throughout the '70s, thousands of day-to-day revolutionaries like Giaconda Belli worked regular jobs—in her case, writing ad copy—while secretly supporting the revolution. Although I can't for the life of me understand how being an award-winning poet helped her cover, given the reputation of Nicaraguan poets. Giaconda secretly organized meetings, transported arms, hid fugitives, and wrote Sandinista press releases and propaganda materials—all while raising a young family. This underground army did as much to undermine the Somoza regime as the guerrilla army staging raids from their mountain hideouts.

Giaconda Belli with another famous poet-revolutionary, Father Ernesto Cardenal (Giaconda Belli)

A few weeks after *Operation Pigsty*, the Sandinistas called for a long-planned national insurrection. Armed operatives rose up in a dozen cities, winning control of some neighborhoods. Somoza had to resort to tanks and bombing runs over his own cities to win the territory back. The Sandinistas regrouped in the mountains, gathered strength for six months, then launched several major offensives at once in May 1979. From this point on, things began to move fast.

A month into the FSLN's big push, with tensions on full blast, a National Guard soldier impulsively shoved ABC News reporter Bill Stewart to the ground and shot him. Astoundingly, Stewart's fixer convinced the dim-witted guardsmen that if they let the rest of the group live, the news crew would air a story claiming a Sandinista sniper had killed Stewart. Stewart's cameraman, who had surreptitiously recorded the murder from their van, smuggled the film out of Nicaragua that afternoon.

Somoza called a press conference, blaming the incident on a Sandinista sniper. Later that same night, the ABC Evening News aired footage of a uniformed National Guardsman shooting Bill Stewart in the back of the head as he lay face down on the ground. Any last shred of credibility the regime had within the United States was gone.

Tachito Somoza fled a few weeks later, raiding the national treasury and taking as much booty as he could fit onto a plane. He even dug up his brother's casket and flew it out of the country. The United States refused to let Somoza settle in Miami as planned, so he fled to Paraguay instead. Less than a year later, local rebels ambushed his motorcade and gunned him down. The Sandinistas never officially claimed responsibility, but many assume they were involved.

Nicaraguans celebrate the end of the Somoza dynasty

Even with Tachito Somoza out of the country, the FSLN assumed they would have to share power with the heavily armed and still powerful National Guard. But the moment Somoza left, the National Guard disintegrated. A large contingent of guardsmen fled to Honduras, committing atrocities against Indigenous villagers along the way, apparently out of nothing but spite. Many of those guardsmen would go on to become Contras.

The Sandinistas found themselves scrambling to rebuild and run a country in a disarray far beyond the bombed-out ruins of civil war. In 1979, 70 percent of Nicaragua's rural peasants were illiterate. Infant mortality and average lifespan were the worst in Central America by a significant margin. The Somozas had deliberately kept rural areas uneducated and poor to create ripe recruiting grounds for the National Guard. As a famous local saying went, "In the town of Somoto, they planted corn and harvested Guardias."

The FSLN's three major factions, known as tendencies, each contributed three members to form a nine-member National Directorate. For years, this secretive body made the country's important decisions in private. Daniel Ortega was on this council along with his brother Humberto. The brothers' alliance gave Daniel a natural advantage in consolidating power, leading him to serve as Nicaragua's first post-Somoza president in 1984.

When it came time to rebuild the country, the muchachos did not forget about their campesino compadres. In perhaps their finest hour, the Sandinistas initiated a national literacy campaign. Hundreds of idealistic teenage volunteers from the cities temporarily relocated to rural villages, where they lived for months, teaching illiterate peasant farmers to read. It was a manifestation of the volunteerism and collective spirit that the Sandinistas hoped would propel the country into a new awakening.

The campesinos, however, were generally not as thrilled with the muchachos' land reforms and price controls. Many farmers and ranchers refused to produce at the prices being offered. Instead, they found other sources of income, often migrating to cities to look for work. This lack of farm labor created the need for another brigade of volunteers from the cities, this time to bring in the coffee harvest. In a poignant full circle, Giaconda's Belli's teenage daughters went on some of those volunteer missions, where they happily lived in barracks like the ones young Giaconda had seen housing multiple families in squalid conditions.

Problems also came home to roost in Nicaragua's cities. Price controls on staple items resulted in waiting lists and a thriving black market. Government workers enjoyed priority status on the waiting lists, stirring resentment. Many of Nicaragua's conservative upper class, who vehemently hated Somoza, initially supported the Sandinistas. But when their kids came home from school proclaiming the bourgeoisie were the enemy of the people, that was too much to bear. Conservative *La Prensa*, which had been a thorn in Somoza's side, quickly became a thorn in the FSLN's side.

Ortega's Sandinista government eventually reversed some of its least popular land allotment policies and price controls. The eternal question is whether the FLSN could have overcome enough of these initial snafus to morph into a sustainable popular government. But that question is unanswerable. The FSLN had barely two years to figure it out before they were plunged back into war, sponsored by an incoming US president making good on his campaign promise to punish Nicaragua.

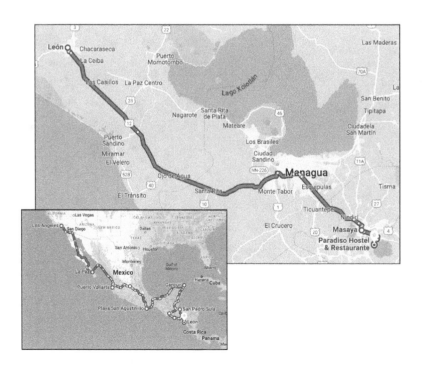

CHAPTER 38

EXPEDITION LIFESTYLE

PARADISO TRIVIA NIGHT got real blurry by the end, leading to an aggressively unproductive hangover in the morning. I spent the more lucid parts of my day planning my next move. I briefly considered driving to Puerto Cabezas on the Miskito Coast in the far northeast for a real off-the-beaten-path adventure. But Google Maps clocked the drive at fourteen hours, meaning it would take two days each way. I decided to drive to the town of Bluefields on the Caribbean coast, where I would spend one night, then fly out to Big Corn Island and finally take a ferry to Little Corn Island.

Heading out the following day, I passed through a large traffic circle on the outskirts of Managua, where I saw an orderly march of pro-Ortega counter-protestors carrying exactly equal parts Nicaraguan flags and red and black FSLN flags. From what I've read, these rallies are mandatory for government employees, who are forced to chant such soul-stirring battle cries as "The Commander stays because he stays!"

Most of the marchers looked to be in their 30s or 40s and a little on the pudgy side, supporting the government worker claim. Minders scurried around the group like sheepdogs, keeping everyone bunched in tight formation. The crowd seemed subdued for a rally but otherwise in good spirits. Maybe they were just happy to get the day off.

As an aside, this is why I hate being forced to lie to my boss, even if it's a nudge-nudge-wink-wink situation, like making up an excuse to work from home. Lying at work as a matter of unspoken policy feels like a baby step down the road to: "So, Bob, you didn't seem very enthusiastic at the rally yesterday. Are you feeling okay? We're just a little worried about you. Is there something you'd like to talk to HR about? No? Okay, well, we're **all** hoping you'll be back to your usual exuberant self at the next rally."

Subdued pro-Ortega rally near Managua

As I passed over the central spine of Nicaragua, dry season brown scrub gave way to lush rolling hills and lowlands. All along the drive, the smiling faces of Daniel Ortega and his wife, Rosario Murillo, beamed down at me from a steady procession of brightly colored billboards. Rosario serves as First Lady **and** Vice President—an understandable cause for concern in a country that has some history with family dynasties. The boisterously cheery vibe of Ortega's billboards seemed out of place with the level of tension in the air, to put it mildly.

Half an hour past the town of Nueva Guinea, I hit a long, hilly section of road construction. Over the next twenty miles, highway workers directed me through single-lane detours of dirt track covered with fill rocks. Past the construction, the road opened up to freshly paved tarmac the rest of the way to Bluefields.

BLUEFIELDS

I navigated the crowded, narrow streets of Bluefields to reach my home for the night, the Flamingo Hotel and Casino—a Bluefields institution that everyone still calls by its original name, the Oasis. I planned to stay one night at the Flamingo, where they graciously agreed to store my car while I was on the Corn Islands. I settled into my room and then headed out to explore.

I walked a block to the harbor, which seemed to be the town's main drag. Dowdy shops and restaurants that were clearly not geared to tourists lined the street on both sides. Outside one shop, two men played checkers while two others spectated. Bluefields lived up to its reputation for looking a bit gritty but also turned out to be quite friendly. Several local men went out of their way to say hello and welcome me to Bluefields.

A game of checkers with spectators

Like much of the east coast of Central America, a majority of the population of Bluefields are of Afro-Caribbean descent, referred to throughout Nicaragua as "Creoles." As with most places around the Caribbean once under British rule, Creoles in Bluefields speak English. They can also slip into their own Creole creole, if you will, which is unintelligible to anyone not from the area.

It was getting dark, so I headed back to the Flamingo. I checked out the casino, which consisted of a few dozen video poker and slot machines. I had a cheeseburger in the little bar, which wasn't terrible, but the flavor was just off in some weird way that I couldn't put my finger on. It was as if someone who had never actually eaten a cheeseburger tried to recreate one from nothing but a photo and a description of the taste.

On the plane ride to Big Corn the next morning, I met a married couple who take turns planning one trip a year. The planner keeps everything about the trip secret from their spouse, including the destination. This year was the wife's turn, so the husband had just learned they were going to the Corn Islands. This seems like an innovative and fun idea—as long as you both love to travel and are up for the adventure.

LITTLE CORN ISLAND

The ferry docked at Little Corn's harbor, where we were greeted by a few hotel employees bearing wheelbarrows for their guests' luggage. I'd heard wheelbarrows were the biggest vehicle on Little Corn, but I didn't fully believe it until I saw it—no cars, no golf carts, not even scooters. I did see one guy pulling a flatbed cart on two wheels. I joked with him that he was the semi-tractor-trailer of Little Corn.

I quickly settled into the sleepy rhythms of Little Corn Island life. Much like my banana bread habit on Utila, I got hooked on a small empanada-like pastry called a *pati*, which came stuffed with either meat, veggies, or a sweet version with pineapple. A lanky, older Creole gentleman showed up every morning bearing a Tupperware container full of pati and other tasty pastries. If he was late, you could find me frantically patrolling the waterfront asking if anyone had seen the pati guy yet.

One of the island's quirks is that the power goes off daily from 6 a.m. to noon. Light sleeper that I am, I'd hear the air conditioner shut off at 6 a.m. and know I had about fifteen minutes of snooze time before the room became unbearably stuffy. I actually grew to like the early wakeup call, since it got me out of my standard habit of sleeping in well past the time most productive tourists are out and about.

As I had to be up anyway, I scheduled as many early morning dives as possible. Diving seemed to run a little less by the numbers on Little Corn than Utila. After the first dive, I eagerly asked, "When do we fill out our dive logs?" This had been a staple post-dive group ritual at Alton's and Trudy's. Our dive instructor brushed me off with a response that basically amounted to, "Fill it out whenever you want, NERD." It felt like showing up on the first day of junior high and asking, "Hey guys, when's recess?"

I dove several times with a young doctor who said she planned to live an "expedition lifestyle," where she would work for a certain portion of the year, then travel for the rest. I thought, a) that's awesome, and b) damn, I wish I had thought of that in my twenties. If I had it to do all over again, I might pick a profession in the healthcare field—something highly portable that lends itself to taking large chunks of time off. Computer programming is project-based, which doesn't play nice with a six-month on/six-month off schedule. Then again, I like programming, and I'm not sure I'd enjoy working in healthcare, so who knows? Perhaps Aerosmith has some wisdom on this issue.

Otto Beach on the far side of Little Corn—the most idyllic beach of the trip

While I relaxed on Little Corn, word came through that big protests were planned for the day I was supposed to fly back to Bluefields. I assumed these would follow a similar pattern as the previous unrest—peaceful days and crazy nights. How that would affect the rest of my trip in Nicaragua, I wasn't sure. I knew that Bluefields hadn't seen anywhere near the level of chaos that León had, so I wasn't overly concerned.

I flew back to Bluefields in the morning and was on my way across Nicaragua by noon. I hoped to make it to Granada by nightfall, where the Belgian guys from D&D Brewery and Utila happened to be hanging out.

As I approached the intersection of NIC-71 and NIC-134, just before the town of Nueva Guinea, I saw a few parked buses and people sitting around. I crawled toward the intersection, searching in vain for any reason to be optimistic that the blockage was some temporary incident or construction. But I knew in my sinking heart it was a roadblock, or *tranque*, as they're known in Nicaragua.

I had no idea how long it would last. My best hope was they'd let everyone through after nightfall as the Oaxaca protesters had done. I could find a place to stay in Nueva Guinea and head to Granada the next day.

TRANQUE JUST BEFORE NUEVA GUINEA

I came to a stop behind a large box truck that blocked my view of the inter-section. A late model four-door pickup, which I'd passed earlier when it stopped to pick up a highway worker, pulled up behind me. The pickup's well-dressed driver got out and walked past my car toward the intersection. He reappeared a few minutes later, headed back to his truck. I could have gotten out of my car and asked him, in my mangled Spanish, what he had found out. But I didn't.

He started his pickup and pulled around me, disappearing around the big truck in front of me. "Dammit," I thought, "that was my chance. He's probably some big shot on the road construction crew who managed to talk his way through. Maybe I could have piggy-backed behind him, but instead I just sat in my car like a dumbass."

I did ask the next person coming from the roadblock if they knew how long it would last. I heard the word "dos," and my spirits lifted. Two hours wouldn't be that bad at all. A little later, I asked the trucker parked in front of me if he thought it would really be two hours. He looked visibly annoyed at my idiocy. "Dos horas? No. Dos días!"

Two days? That was much less optimal. Dejected, I got back into my car to wait it out, as I had no other options that late in the day.

My car was attracting a lot of attention from people walking past me on their way to the tranque. Invariably, one guy in each group would notice the big silver marshmallow car, then look at my California front plate, then look up at the big red-headed gringo sitting in the driver's seat. If the guy stared long enough, I'd wave. Sometimes, he'd wave back.

As dusk settled in, loud reggaeton music began to emanate from the intersection. Once it got dark, intermittent fireworks lit the sky with a thunderous **BOOM**. The party raging at the intersection dashed my hopes that this would be one of those "let 'em go after dark" roadblocks. I got out of the car to prepare one of my REI rations for dinner.

As I set up the jet boil stove, I caught a glimpse of someone watching me from the shadows a few feet away. Realizing he'd been seen, a squat, pot-bellied man of about thirty-five came forward and asked, "La cena?"

"Yes," I told him, "this is my dinner." I showed him how the stove worked and then poured the boiling water into the bag to let it cook for ten minutes. He seemed bemused by the whole process. I offered him some of my Santa Fe Beef Skillet, but he declined.

The man was the driver of the open-air bus parked directly behind me.

He was clearly buzzed and on his way to a healthy drunk. He continually called me "gringo." I don't remember his name, so for the purposes of this book, I'm going to call him Gringo Guy. I asked Gringo Guy when he thought the roadblock was going to end. He said four days.

Oy vey! Every time I asked, I got a worse answer.

Eventually, Gringo Guy's co-pilot, who was younger and less drunk, joined us. The co-pilot knew roughly as much English as I did Spanish. This created an interesting dynamic where we switched back and forth between English and Spanish, just as many Los Angelinos do, only very poorly in our case. He asked me if I was scared to walk up to the road-block. I thought, "Uh, should I be?" I hadn't worried about it until that question.

Gringo Guy, who was getting drunker by the minute, made me a little uneasy with his pushiness and instant familiarity. He made a lot of jokes at my expense, most of which I couldn't understand. I knew that ribbing stranded gringos is a national pastime in Latin America. Still, in that exposed context, it was a bit unsettling.

Later, two more men joined us who weren't as chatty. One of them had a dead-eyed stare that I didn't care for. The new guys kept scanning up and down the road. I got a little paranoid that they might be looking for a gap in the foot traffic, possibly to mess with me when no one else was nearby. As we talked, the four of them had a habit of leaning against my car and getting on all sides of me. I would reposition myself to the edge of the group, but soon, they'd surround me again.

I knew that Gringo Guy was almost certainly just drunk, and the other guys were probably fine. But just in case, I snuck a picture of the front license plate on Gringo Guy's bus. Then I posted it to Facebook with the caption, "Fun party bus parked behind me." I didn't want to unduly terrify my mom with the real reason for the post. I also texted the picture to some friends. My idea was that just in case things turned ugly, I could show my captors that they would ultimately be identified. I knew the chance of something happening was extremely low, but I figured it couldn't hurt to have an insurance policy. I gave thanks that, unlike the roadblocks in Oaxaca and Chiapas, this one had a cell signal.

Nothing ultimately happened, but the whole experience brought home that I was essentially in a lawless area where my car and I were attracting a ton of attention. I was at the mercy of the crowd to police themselves and not allow something to happen to me. Then again, in a country like Nicaragua, the police aren't much of an emergency reaction force anyway.

Even in the best of circumstances, they just show up well after the fact just to take notes and file a report.

After dinner, I put aside the unsettling question from Gringo Guy's buddy and walked up to the roadblock. Night gave me some welcome anonymity in that it wasn't obvious a gringo was coming from a hundred feet away. I noticed the truck of the supposed road construction boss. He hadn't gotten through after all. He'd just pulled closer for some reason. The barrier itself was just a few branches thrown over the road that anyone could have driven over. The real roadblock was everyone who milled in and around the intersection, enjoying the music and fireworks. I saw a few young protesters with scarves covering their faces. Otherwise, it was hard to tell a protester from a bystander.

I got a look at the fireworks they were setting off. A young bandana-clad protester had an apparatus made from a length of 2-inch diameter metal pipe, closed at one end, with two smaller pipes welded on as handles. I realized these were the morteros I had heard about in León. The rockets climbed fifty to a hundred feet into the air, then exploded with a report that sounded like the M80s from Mike's Sky Rancho. This weapon is obviously no match for cops with pistols and long guns, but still not something you'd want exploding in your face. A cop was reportedly killed by a mortero during the riots.

When they didn't let us go by midnight, I figured waking everyone up at 3 a.m. to let us through didn't seem likely. So, I settled in for the night.

My next hope was that the tranque supervisors would let us go at sunrise. When that came and went, I had a decision to make: Should I stick it out at the roadblock, potentially for days, or should I head back to Bluefields?

Waiting at the roadblock, where I stuck out like a sore thumb, seemed like a bad idea. I could, in theory, look for a place to sleep in Nueva Guinea, entrusting someone like Gringo Guy to look after my car. That, too, seemed suboptimal.

Gringo Guy, still drunk, told me the road to Bluefields was blocked, and I wouldn't be able to get through. I decided to take my chances anyway.

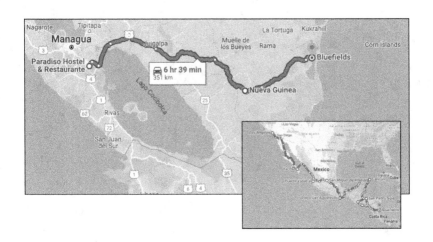

CHAPTER 39

BOTTLED UP IN BLUEFIELDS

I LEFT the roadblock amidst a heavy downpour. This gave me a whole new reason to be concerned. "When the rains come" is a trope in Nicaraguan literature. Some years, the rains come and don't let up for weeks, flooding cities and effectively shutting down many rural roads. What if I got stuck in Bluefields—not because of the roadblock but because of the rain? What if I was already trapped between the tranque and the construction zone, as Gringo Guy had suggested?

I arrived at the road construction, where the situation looked grim. Workers directing traffic were coated in gooey mud up to their waists. I joined a line of cars waiting to go down a long slope that had turned into a giant clay-mud slick. On one side, a bulldozer was climbing up the slope, towing a bus, which was towing a car. Nothing without tank treads was getting up that thing. I asked a motorist waiting with me if the rain shut down the road for days or weeks. "Yes, but only when it *really* rains," came his non-reassuring reply. Apparently, the deluge I'd just driven through didn't register as real rain.

While the bulldozer towed vehicles up one side of the slope, the crew laid rocks on the other side to make it passable. When the new rock-studded road was ready, the traffic director picked my car, presumably the most capable 4x4, to be the first down. I guess he figured if I went sliding off into the abyss, then the road definitely wasn't ready yet. On the way down, I hit some spots of bare mud that caused the car to glide effortlessly in the direction momentum and gravity wanted it to go—braking and steering mere suggestions to be ignored. Clay mud is nasty stuff. I reached the bottom, then prayed the "real rains" would hold off for a few more days.

A muddy mess at the road construction

I got back to Bluefields without running into any protests and checked back in at the Flamingo. I headed out to explore, looking for any signs that vehicles were escaping to the Pacific side of the country in some other way.

An older Creole gentleman, picking up on my distress, asked if I needed anything. I do not know the full range of goods and services he could have procured, but I imagine it's vast. I learned his name was William, and I told him my story. As we walked, I noticed a parked bus marked for Managua, also stuck in Bluefields. I figured if anyone would know when the road-block is letting vehicles through, it's a bus driver. I asked William if he could leave me word at the Flamingo if the bus moved or if he heard any other developments.

I grabbed some lunch while William checked around. I was thrilled to have a local source of information—and one who spoke English at that. William returned with the bad news that nothing was moving on the roads until at least Monday—three days away. We walked down to the harbor together to see if I could get my car onto a small barge known as a panga boat, which could take me upriver to the town of La Rama. William checked with the boat drivers, who all told the same story: The harbor was shut down until further notice.

During the first round of protests, a journalist had been shot and killed by a sniper in Bluefields while broadcasting on Facebook Live. So, the town was still a little on edge.

I stocked up on provisions and filled my extra gas cans. I planned to head back to the tranque the following day, hoping that the original two-day estimate somehow turned out to be correct. I was prepared to wait at the tranque for a few days, especially if I saw any evidence they were letting vehicles trickle through at night.

BACK TO THE TRANQUE

The next morning, I handed my key to the front desk girl at the Flamingo and told her I hoped she wouldn't see me again. She wished me luck. The Bluefields to Managua bus was still parked at the pier. William also told me a smaller roadblock had been set up outside Bluefields.

Either that local roadblock dissipated before 10 a.m., or it never existed. I don't think Bluefields' heart was ever really in the whole revolution thing. When the Sandinistas ousted Somoza, the diverse groups of Nicaragua's sparsely populated Caribbean slope were reportedly unfazed. To the Creoles, the Garifuna, and the Miskito, Rama, and Sanna Indians, who comprise the majority of eastern Nicaragua's population, the country's leadership had just swapped one group of "Spanish" for another.

At the road construction, I was happy to see the mud slick had been shored up. Whatever chaos was happening in the rest of the country, it never seemed to slow down the road builders.

A few miles after the road construction, I passed a tricked-out baby blue pickup coming the other way. A man was standing up in the bed holding a military-grade rifle—the only firearm I saw in Nicaragua not wielded by a cop or soldier. Unlike the truck full of armed Zapatista para-militaries I saw in Mexico, nobody in this pickup covered their faces. They all wore street clothes and didn't look like farmers or students. My guess is the men were pro-Ortega muscle, as I can't imagine rebels being that cavalier about showing guns in public.

I rounded a corner and saw the sign for Nueva Guinea, causing my heart to lift with a brief moment of hope. I was sure the intersection was just around the next bend, and I hadn't seen a vehicle yet. Then, I rounded the turn and saw a long line of cars, trucks, and buses.

I parked my car and proceeded to the intersection on foot. When I got closer, I recognized Gringo Guy's bus. I continued past a line of stranded cars and trucks. Everyone looked more settled in than when I left. Shirtless men played cards on makeshift tables. Truckers napped in hammocks under their trailers. Laundry had been hung to dry on the barbed-wire fences lining each side of the road.

When I got close to the intersection, I saw the presumed road construction boss who had pulled up behind me at the roadblock two days earlier, now stripped down to a sleeveless undershirt. I figured if this guy and his $40,000 truck couldn't get through, nobody was getting through. I was prepared to wait it out for a few days if necessary, especially if it seemed like they were letting cars trickle through. Clearly, that wasn't happening.

As I approached the intersection, I pondered a rutted track that disappeared into a cow pasture off to the right. The road to Nueva Guinea was a right turn from the intersection, not straight ahead. I wondered if I could drive through that field at 3 a.m. with my lights off and sneak around to the road on the other side. But I snapped out of that idea pretty quickly. If I got caught, which was likely, they'd probably destroy my car and beat me to a bloody pulp.

The general mood at the intersection was less upbeat than the first night. I could mostly tell who the protesters were this time since very few bystanders were milling around. As in the Sandinista Revolution forty years earlier, there were the Muchachos (bandana-clad students) and the Campesinos (farmers in straw hats and cowboy boots). Nicaragua had come full circle.

A protester carrying his mortero

Farmers appeared to outnumber students by at least ten to one. Only the student protesters carried morteros, the homemade rocket launchers made from either metal or PVC pipe that I'd seen and heard on the first night. I snuck a grainy picture of one of the weapons.

Someone behind me yelled, "Gringo!" It was Gringo Guy, now sober and cleaned up in fresh clothes. He had gotten a hotel room in Nueva Guinea. His new best estimate for when the roadblock would clear was four more days. He also admitted this was more of a wish than concrete information. None of this was good news. I asked Gringo Guy what he thought of my plan to sneak around the intersection via the cow pasture. He pantomimed holding a gun and made a rat-ta-ta-tat sound. They'd shoot me. Okay, so that's definitely not a good plan.

I did see one pickup allowed to proceed through the tranque toward Nueva Guinea. It was loaded with plantains from a nearby farm, presumably on some official mission to support other protesters or possibly to trade for pineapples, which seemed very popular based on the piles of detritus lying around.

The campesinos argued over how best to let the plantain-laden pickup through the main roadblock, now a low wall of cinder blocks and logs. The group sitting on the barrier wanted the driver to go around via a ditch, but that route looked very tight with the potential to get stuck. Finally, after much debate, it was decided to move the barrier—much to the chagrin of the guys sitting on it, who now had to get up and help take it apart.

It seemed obvious they weren't regularly letting vehicles through if the process was that much of an ordeal. Scores of motorcycles were parked on both sides of the intersection. If motorcycles weren't even allowed through, this tranque was serious business.

I had no idea how I would even begin to try to talk my way through, and I wasn't psyched to sit at the roadblock for four days. I had plenty of food and water, but I'd forgotten to bring any alcohol, which may have played a role in my decision to head back to Bluefields in defeat.

BACK TO BLUEFIELDS (AGAIN)

When I arrived back at the Flamingo, the front desk girl just handed me my key without saying a word. *Hotel California* started playing in my head: "You can check out anytime you like, but you can never leave."

I talked to my man on the street, William. He was under the impression that there would be big protests in Bluefields in two days. So maybe I could get out in three or four days. But also, nobody really knows. Most importantly, my real-world touchstone, the stranded Bluefields to Managua bus, was still parked by the harbor.

It finally started to dawn on me that I needed to abandon any hope of seeing Granada, Ometepe (a popular island in Lake Nicaragua), or the beach resort town of San Juan del Sur on this trip. I needed to focus on getting me and my car out of the country. A little-used border crossing with Costa Rica at Los Chiles, on the eastern side of Lake Nicaragua, seemed promising. I still had to get through the Nueva Guinea tranque, but at least the eastern route bypassed Managua, Masaya, and the other major problem areas.

The Flamingo's owner, Jerry, told me he could line up a place to store my car long-term if I needed it. The problem was if I overstayed my thirty-day Temporary Import Permit (TIP), there was no guarantee I'd ever get my car out. I doubted the excuse of being trapped by protests would hold any sway.

So, I bided my time in Bluefields in a state of low-grade anxiety, trying not to think about what could happen if the situation deteriorated. I dreaded the prospect of having to choose between my safety and my car.

I spent the time catching up on my blog and exploring Bluefields, whose gritty charms grew on me a little more every day. The town's architectural highlight, a white-plastered Moravian church, sits on a gorgeously manicured stretch of waterfront. Moravians arrived in the area from Germany in the mid-1800s and immediately set about converting the Afro-Caribbeans and indigenous tribes to their brand of evangelical Christianity. The second-most well-maintained property in Bluefields is probably the fire station, the product of a proudly proclaimed joint venture between Nicaragua and Russia.

I heard rumblings that if the tranques dragged things out long enough, the entire Caribbean side of Nicaragua could run out of supplies. The panga boats weren't running, the harbor was closed, and no road traffic was getting through. Yet, the stores and markets always seemed well stocked. I saw no panicked runs on staple items such as, say, toilet paper. If all else failed, residents always had the open-air fish markets, which were flooded with more product than usual since the processing plants had stopped taking new catch.

The most vital of supplies have been replenished!

I did, however, notice the crates of bottled beer in the Flamingo's outside storage area dwindling at an alarming rate. I could take days of whiling in Bluefields. But whiling without beer? Please pray for my soul.

I grew concerned enough to ask the owner, Jerry, about the situation. He assured me the Flamingo would not run out of beer. True to his word, just when the stacks were nearly depleted, dozens of new crates appeared. I don't know if a boat snuck it in at night, they flew it in like the Berlin airlift, or if Bluefields has some strategic beer reserve. All I know is that contingency plans were in place.

Bored with the weird Flamingo cheeseburger, I tried the restaurant at Casa Royale, the fancy hotel next door. The highlight of Casa Royale was

Clayberth—the best bartender in Nicaragua. Clayberth spoke English, which meant I had a captive audience with whom to commiserate over my situation. The hotel only had a few guests, and the restaurant was usually empty. After a few days, I started to feel like Jack Nicholson sitting at the bar in *The Shining*—just me and Clayberth—talking things out. Only replace the spooky gramophone music from the movie with an incessant rotation of Ed Sheeran, who had been chasing me all over Central America like the horror movie *It Follows*.

*The Bar at Casa Royale—you can all see Clayberth
standing there, RIGHT?*

On Sunday, I received an interesting tidbit from the Nicaraguan expat forum. A member claimed that protesters were now allowing ambulances and foreign-plated vehicles through. I had no idea who this person was or why I should believe them, but it was a glimmer of hope, nonetheless. Wednesday, it turned out, was to be the first day of talks between Ortega and the protesters. I asked myself when, in history, has the first day of talks **ever** gone well? With local protests scheduled for Monday and Tuesday, Wednesday seemed like the make-or-break day. I decided to go for it.

On Tuesday, I roamed around Bluefields, picking up potential bargaining chips. I bought two cases of beer and some ice for my cooler. I had seen the exposed, viciously hot roadblocks and knew an ice-cold beer would be like a kiss from an angel. I also picked up bottles of soda, water, vodka, and plenty of cash. Finally, I had my extra gasoline if anyone wanted that. The only thing I forgot was cigarettes, which would have made great currency. But smoking is bad for you. I don't want to encourage that.

At one point in my supply gathering, I stopped and had a moment with myself. Am I really doing this? Am I *really* going to load up my car with barter goods and extra gas, like I was Mad Max, then try to talk my way through multiple lawless gauntlets manned by bandana-clad revolutionaries with homemade rocket launchers?

I took a deep breath and decided, yes, I guess I'm actually doing this.

Once I was fully stocked with supplies, I posted my plan on the Pan-Am forum and the Nicaraguan expat groups, soliciting any advice that might increase my chance for success. Having time to kill, I tried out the Flamingo casino for the first time. I put a quarter into a slot machine and won $40 on my first spin.

While debating whether I should keep gambling, Ed Sheeran came blasting over the sound system: *"I found a girl..."* You always find a girl, Ed! You're soooooooo lucky to have her, and you can't believe your good fortune. Yadda yadda yadda. WE GET IT ALREADY!

I bet Ed Sheeran comes home to his wife, grabs a beer, turns on Battle-Bots, sticks a hand in his waistband, and says, "Honey, I'm sorry. I left it all out there on stage today. I got nothing left for you."

I took Ed finding yet another girl as my cue to cash out my auspicious winnings and save the rest of my luck for the big day ahead. I walked over to Casa Royale for dinner, where Clayberth and the rest of the staff wished me luck.

On the way back to my room, I found William to give him one last propina for being my man on the street. I had noticed that William would always refer to Ortega as "that guy" instead of just saying his name. I remembered the young Nicaraguan guys at Paradiso Hostel had done the exact same thing. Since no one else was around, I asked William, "You mean Ortega, right?"

He lowered his eyes a bit and quietly replied, "Yeah."

I'm no political historian, but it seems to me that reflexively referring to your country's leader as "that guy"—because you never know who might be listening—might be a sign you're under the thumb of a totalitarian dictator.

ORTEGA TO ORTEGA

Nicaragua under Ortega wasn't always so totalitarian. But the Contra War plunged the country into chaos, leading to unpopular draconian policies and debilitating the fledgling government. The Contras, many of them ex-

Guardsmen, had been organized and equipped by the CIA. They staged raids into the countryside from their bases around the Honduras border, causing havoc and committing atrocities in the mountainous regions, even killing volunteer Sandinista coffee pickers.

The war and US blockade created shortages in the cities and pushed the Sandinistas to institute an unpopular military draft for all men aged seventeen to twenty-one. American SR-71 spy planes made daily low passes over Managua to intimidate residents with window-rattling supersonic booms. Fearing a US invasion, the Sandinistas kept half their fighting forces in Managua, hampering the war effort in the mountains and exacerbating the need for more fighters.

The US House of Representatives initially voted 411 to 0 to fund the Contras on the condition that their mission could only be to stop Nicaragua from giving military aid to El Salvador, not regime change. When it became clear that this condition was preposterous, the Reagan administration played an ever-evolving game of cat and mouse to get more funding. Later, Congress allocated money only for "humanitarian aid," such as food, clothing, and medicine.

Mysteriously, the Contras never seemed to be without military supplies and fresh weaponry. This even though the Contras' other paramour—the military junta running Argentina—dropped out in disgust after miscalculating that the United States would back them in their ill-advised Falkland Islands War. (Argentina's humiliating defeat against the British led to the ouster of President Leopoldo Galtieri, ending over fifty years of military dictatorship in that country.)

Ronald Reagan shakes the hand of Contra leader Steadman Fagoth Muller

In 1986, the Sandinistas shot down a C-123 cargo plane in the act of dropping supplies to the Contras. Pilot Eugene Hasenfus, the only survivor of the four-person crew, parachuted to safety and calmly waited to be captured. Once in Sandinista detention, Hasenfus freely admitted to working for the CIA's Air America and began spilling the beans that uncovered the Iran-Contra scandal—the singular bit of history many Americans of a certain age remember about Nicaragua. Reagan's bagman, Colonel Oliver North, had arranged for the clandestine sale of arms to the United

States' enemies in Iran, with the proceeds going to fund the Contras. Naturally, no one ever faced a consequence for this subterfuge, including North for trolling Congress with his selective memory issues. To this day, you can still enjoy Oliver North's unique perspective on several cable news channels.

Sandinistas lead pilot Eugene Hasenfus out of the bush
(Reuters/Carlos Duran)

Despite the Sandinistas' fears, the US never had the stomach for an invasion, which meant the Contras were merely fighting a punitive war at the behest of the United States. The CIA never grasped that ordinary Nicaraguans would never support a counter-revolution led in part by notorious ex-Guardsmen from the Somoza regime. Eventually, Costa Rica helped organize a peace treaty, which granted some Contras a role in Nicaragua's government. With the Cold War over, the Contras and Sandinistas found they had much less to fight over.

The Contra War took the lives of 30,000 Nicaraguans and left the economy in shambles. Children suffered from malnutrition. Rampant crime plagued the cities. Doctors, engineers, and other professionals who could get out had long fled the country. In a hugely embarrassing incident during a multi-country ceremonial run, nearly the entire team of twenty-five Nicaraguan "torch of freedom" bearers—*who had been handpicked from the Sandinista Youth*—bolted across the border to Costa Rica, claiming their lives had become unbearable in Nicaragua.

Despite the catchy slogan "Everything Will Be Better," Ortega lost the 1990 presidential election, which was monitored by international election observers. No one expected Violeta Chamorro, Pedro Chamorro's widow and La Prensa's current editor, to actually win. To his credit, Ortega conceded defeat, marking the first non-coerced transfer of power in Nicaragua's tortured history. The Sandinistas took a cue from Somoza and stole everything they could on the way out, primarily by privatizing industries and selling the spoils to cronies.

A string of presidents, ranging from moderately to astoundingly corrupt, followed. Ortega vowed to "rule from below" when he left office, wielding power via street gangs. Ortega staged losing bids for president in 1996 and 2001, never receiving more than 40 percent of the vote. Before the 2006 election, he crafted a backroom deal to modify Nicaragua's electoral system so that thirty-five of the vote was sufficient to win the presidency, assuming no other candidates received more than 30 percent. Ortega won with 38 percent of the vote against a divided field.

Ortega booted out the independent election observers and, by all accounts, has rigged the elections ever since. He also ended term limits, gave himself power to rule by decree, inserted his wife as Vice President, and consolidated effective power over the military, police, and all branches of Nicaragua's government. Nearly all of the original Sandinistas have long since denounced Ortega as nothing more than an autocratic tyrant, including Giaconda Belli and even his own brother Humberto.

To be fair, Nicaragua is doing a few things right compared to its neighbors to the north. The country's homicide rate is the lowest in the region, less than one-tenth of El Salvador's. Strict gun control undoubtedly has something to do with that. This relative lack of violent crime could also be why, despite the crushing poverty, Nicaraguans haven't migrated to the US in droves like Guatemalans, Hondurans, and Salvadorans. During the unaccompanied minor border crisis of 2014, not a single child came from Nicaragua. However, as of 2021, Nicaraguans have begun to show up at the US border.

In 2013, a Chinese company purchased the rights to build a canal across Nicaragua, which would immeasurably improve the country's economic fortunes but would also wreak environmental havoc on Lake Nicaragua, destroy 1,500 square miles of pristine tropical habitat, and displace 35,000 campesinos and indigenous villagers. China lost interest following the 2018 riots, and the project is now effectively dead.

Until the riots, the general vibe among ordinary Nicaraguans toward Ortega could seemingly be characterized as one of disgruntled disgust with corruption and waste, yet falling short of the impetus to take to the streets. All that changed with the riots, and Nicaragua has been in a kind of low-grade civil war ever since. However, unlike Tachito Somoza in his last days, Ortega does have a solid base of support, mostly among government employees and those who do business with them. And this time, the government has all the guns.

As I write this, Ortega has jailed every significant opponent and shut down *La Prensa*. He even imprisoned some of the septuagenarian Sandinistas he fought alongside during the revolution. No one expects fair elections. The seventy-five-year-old president has lined up his wife to replace him and his son after that.

Blood of Brothers: Life and War in Nicaragua author Stephen Kinzer, writing for the *The New York Review of Books* in September 2021, quotes author Sergio Ramírez, one of Nicaragua's most influential intellectuals:

> *Nothing remains of the revolution, just a rhetorical pretext to justify repression and the consolidation of the Ortega family dictatorship," lamented Sergio Ramírez, the country's leading novelist, who was Ortega's vice-president in the 1980s and now lives abroad to avoid arrest. The hard-boiled Nicaraguan detective who is the central figure in his latest novel, Ramírez said, embodies "the disillusionment of an entire generation that has seen the revolution not only age, but decompose into a cadaver that smells in the sun.*

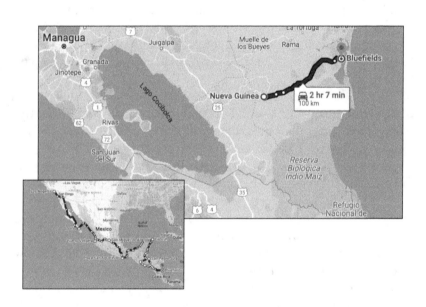

Chapter 40

Exodus

I woke up at 6 a.m. to a message from a backpacker named Lasse. He and his friend Stefan were stranded in Nueva Guinea. A friend of theirs had seen my post on the Pan-Am forum and alerted them that I could be their ticket out. I replied that I'd be happy to give them a ride—*if and when* I got through the tranque. They offered to help in any way they could.

I enjoyed what was hopefully my last breakfast on the Flamingo's rooftop patio, soaking in the view of the harbor and sparkling turquoise Caribbean. Gritty, dowdy, lovable little Bluefields had put on its best face to send me off. The owner, Jerry, joined me for breakfast. He wished me luck and told me that his friend, who owned a hotel in Nueva Guinea, was willing to go to the roadblock to help plead my case if need be. In my ideal world, Jerry's friend would meet me at the roadblock to do all the talking for me. But Jerry was clear that I should try on my own first, then call his friend if I couldn't get through.

I didn't relish the prospect of walking past all those other motorists, some of whom had been stranded for six days, to ask some armed tranque comandante to please let my privileged American ass through. I pictured the comandante gesturing out to the crowd, yelling in rapid-fire Spanish I couldn't understand, something to the effect of, "Why in the hell should I let you through when all these people have been sitting here for a week? You think because you're an American, that makes you **special?** Vete a la mierda, pendejo!"

I decided I would walk up to the tranque and play it by ear.

I wound my way through the road construction for the sixth and hopefully last time, on pace to hit the roadblock around 8 a.m. A mile before the
roadblock, I noticed an old farmer on the side of the road waving his arm
up and down, trying to hitch a ride. I thought, "Does this guy realize
there's a roadblock around the next bend?" Then, a lightbulb went on.
Maybe I could explain my situation to the farmer, and then *he* could advocate for me at the tranque. Surely, it couldn't hurt to have an old farmer tell
the tranque leaders about how this nice gringo with international plates
had given him a ride, even if it was a short one.

I pulled over and pushed open my passenger-side door. The old man
hopped into my front seat, cradling a giant burlap sack full of cotton that
barely fit in my car. He made some guttural noises as he gestured toward
the road, trying to warn me about the roadblock ahead. I told him I knew
all about the roadblock. Then he made the same guttural noises, but this
time pointed to his throat. I realized he was indicating that he couldn't
speak.

"Well, that's quite the ironic start to my day," I thought. "The guy I
hoped could be my spokesman at the tranque is a mute."

I pulled over behind a group of parked cars. The old farmer hopped out
and started dragging his giant sack of cotton toward the intersection. A
flatbed semi sat jackknifed across the road, blocking any new vehicles from
getting close to the intersection. Barbed wire had been strung from the semi
to a fence post to prevent cars from using the ditch to go around. I wasn't
sure how I'd get through this outer roadblock, but I figured I'd worry about
that when I got permission to go through the main roadblock.

I proceeded toward the intersection, my heart beating faster with each
step. I practiced my memorized lines: "Hay paso, por favor?" (May I please
pass?), "placa de internacional" (international license plate), and "solo
quiero dejar el país" (I just want to leave the country).

I saw Gringo Guy's bus parked off to the side, covered with a tarp.
Everyone still looked settled in for the long haul. The only differences I
noticed from the same walk four days earlier were more laundry hanging on
the fence and the vague whiff of poop, suggesting people weren't walking
far enough into the cow pasture to do their business. As I approached the
intersection, I saw the road construction boss's truck still parked in the
same spot.

The mood at the intersection this time was downright somber. The
party was long over, its revelers exhausted from six days of exposure to the
tropical sun. About thirty campesinos milled around inside the intersec-

tion. More were scattered about in all directions. I didn't see any bandana-clad muchachos.

I walked over to a group of campesinos. One guy with darker skin and a loose afro gave me a friendly look. I gave him a head nod. He reciprocated with a fist bump. I figured this guy seems as good as any, so I told him my story and asked if he knew who I should talk to.

In so many words, I had just said, "I am an American, and I would like to speak to the manager of this roadblock"—a concept I found utterly preposterous just a few days earlier. The man approached a group of campesinos huddled under a shade tree.

After a brief exchange with a seated campesino, my new friend motioned for me to come over. I repeated my spiel, "Hay paso, por favor? Placa de Unistados Unidos. Solo quiero dejar el país." In my nervousness, I replaced "International license plate" with "United States license plate," except instead of the correct "Estados Unidos," I actually said "Unistados Unidos," which in Spanish amounts to something like "United Uni-states." Fortunately, everyone understood what the stupid gringo was trying to say. I would continue saying "Unistados Unidos" for the rest of the day, like a nervous tick, long after I realized I was saying it wrong.

The still-seated council of campesinos held a brief discussion, after which the leader indicated that I would be allowed to pass. "Holy crap," I thought. "Is it really going to be this easy?" I thanked the men and bolted before anyone could change their mind. I had received official permission to pass, and I wasn't about to ask twice.

Just past the intersection, I heard someone call out to ask me if I was getting through. It was the road construction boss, still in his slacks and undershirt. I hadn't said one word to the guy on my previous trips to the tranque, but he might have remembered me, or maybe Gringo Guy told him about me. I hunched my shoulders and shouted, "Tal vez?" (maybe) and something about my "placa de Unistados Unidos" as I hustled by. I didn't want to rub it in that I was getting through, considering the poor guy had been living out of his truck for six days. He gave me a big thumbs-up anyway.

I speed-walked the rest of the way back to my car. My first order of business was getting around the outer roadblock. I pulled up to the flatbed truck, where some campesinos had set up a speaker and were having a little party. I explained to the guy standing nearest the blockage that I had received official permission to pass. He immediately set about disconnecting the barbed wire for me.

After I had pulled my car through, I got out to hand the man a beer in gratitude. His amigo was standing right there, so I offered the amigo a beer. In the time it took for me to reach into my cooler for the second beer, another amigo materialized. As I reached to get the third amigo a beer, two more amigos appeared. I realized I would run out of beer long before the supply of amigos exhausted itself. I gave the other two guys beers, then closed my cooler and said "no mas" to a half-dozen thirsty-looking men converging on my car.

It was a spooky moment. They could have easily just said, "Fuck you, gringo. We're taking the beer," and there wouldn't be a thing I could do about it. Thankfully, they respected my decision and walked away looking dejected. I learned a valuable lesson: Hand out all the beers at once. Doling out beers piecemeal is a recipe for disaster.

The start of my hopefully last drive up to the intersection

As I rolled up the final stretch to the intersection, my car began to cause a commotion. People realized I might be getting through and were excited for any break in the monotony. Naturally, my mind wandered to the climactic scene of *An Officer and a Gentleman,* in which Richard Gere strides into the factory in his service dress whites, scoops Deborah Winger off her feet, then carries her out past her cheering coworkers. I was more than happy to play Deborah Winger's role in this remake, if that's what it took to get me through.

I had "Love Lift Us Up Where We Belong" stuck in my head for days.

At least it wasn't Ed Sheeran.

When I arrived at the tranque, some campesinos removed the small pile of branches that blocked the entrance to the intersection. They were also clearing a roadblock on the *far* side of the intersection, indicating that I should drive straight ahead. I knew the road to Nueva Guinea was to the right, so this seemed odd. I had never explored the road across the intersection and had no idea where it led. I had to assume these guys knew what they were doing and must be sending me on some alternate route to Nueva Guinea.

When I got to the middle of the intersection, and it was clear they were going to let me through, I stopped my car and got out. I wanted to thank them for allowing me to pass without asking for anything in return. I handed out some bottles of cold soda and gave a twelve-pack of beer to the guy who had initially given me the fist bump. He strutted off as the big man on campus, doling out beers to his buddies.

As I shut my rear door, I heard a commotion off to my right. I snuck a peek and saw a few bandana-clad muchachos who did not seem happy with what was transpiring. I hopped in, started my car, and put it in gear. As soon as my car started to move, a cry of, "Hey hey hey! HEY HEY HEY HEY! **HEYYYYYYYY!!!**" rang out from the direction of the muchachos.

I pretended not to hear, plowing straight ahead as directed. I didn't want any part of whatever they were arguing about, which I knew had to involve me.

I started up the road on the far side of the intersection and climbed over a hill that put me out of sight from the roadblock. I continued driving until the road turned into a dirt track, then dissolved into a field. I kept going at twenty miles an hour, refusing to admit to myself that the road was no more, until my car started bouncing around like a pogo stick.

I came to a stop in the cow pasture, where I could see I was blocked by a ravine running between me and Nueva Guinea. I had no choice but to turn around and slink back to the intersection with all the enthusiasm of a dog that knows it's in BIG TROUBLE.

A campesino walked over the hill to wave me back to the roadblock. I considered trying my luck with a small road that disappeared off to the left in the direction of town. But that road almost certainly dead-ended at the ravine as well. I crested the last hill and came face to face with a diminutive bandana-clad muchacho who was aiming his mortero at me.

I figured a mortero round would probably just bounce off my car. But of course, if the situation deteriorated to the point that he fired his weapon, I'd be screwed no matter what.

I slowed to about two miles per hour, whereupon the pocket-sized warrior drew his weapon back to his chest.

As I inched forward and slowed to a stop a few feet from the mortero-wielding muchacho, a crowd converged on us. It seemed like every man in the vicinity had migrated to the intersection to be part of the unfolding drama. As the muchacho stood fast, the crowd began yelling in Spanish. Two campesinos stuck their heads in my passenger side window, making highly animated points I couldn't understand.

This was peak chaos.

Thankfully, most of the crowd seemed to be yelling at each other—not me. I heard the word "Internacional!" flying around a lot and noticed that some of the campesinos who seemed to be arguing the hardest **for me** had ice-cold Toñas in their hands. Score a big one for beer diplomacy.

Once Mini-Minuteman was satisfied that I wasn't going anywhere, he made his way around to my driver-side window. Still brandishing his weapon, he began rattling off rapid-fire paragraphs of Spanish that I couldn't begin to make out. A few rounds of me sheepishly offering, "Lo siento, no comprendo," got us nowhere. Clearly, this guy had never been taught *Dum Dum Hospitality Spanish for Gringos* at that fancy college of his. Running out of ideas, I offered, "Propina?"—trying to bribe him. He shook his head no. This was devolving into my worst-case scenario.

Campesinos continued yelling all around us throughout the exchange. Wee Guevara was becoming visibly frustrated with my idiocy, and I was growing increasingly uncomfortable with the tense impasse. Then, he uttered two words in isolation that I actually recognized: "Tu arma?"

I only knew this phrase because the heavily armed cops who pulled me over in El Salvador had asked the same thing: "Are you armed?"

I held up my hands in the universal gesture of **not** being armed and replied, "Yo no arma."

In response, the muchacho pumped his weapon from his chest and quickly pulled it back, as if to emphasize: "Damn right! **I'm** the one who's armed here."

My gears began to turn. A ray of clarity appeared through the fog of chaos. Maybe this guy is just trying to make a point to everyone else at the tranque. Maybe I should break my cardinal rule and ask twice. I didn't seem to have much else to lose.

I gingerly offered, "Hay paso, por favor?"

Nicaraguan Napoleon paused for a few seconds to give his verdict the solemn gravitas it deserved, then motioned with his mortero to indicate that I may proceed.

All along, he just wanted someone to respect his authority.

With that, a dozen campesinos started waving me in the direction I should have been going all along—down the road to Nueva Guinea. They'd engineered a detour system instead of having to dismantle the main road-block every time a car needed to pass. As the group guided me around the last outer roadblock, my original fist-bump buddy appeared at my window, asking if I could spare any change. I gave him about $6 worth of córdobas, which seemed to make him happy.

I was eager to find Lasse and Stefan and get out of Nueva Guinea before some even bigger muchacho honcho showed up to herd me back to the intersection. I knew this wasn't very likely, but I was still paranoid. I had already been told yes, and then no, once. Also we still had multiple roadblocks to run, and I had no idea if the Los Chiles border stayed open after dark.

I plugged the name of their hostel into Google Maps, which promptly led me down a dead-end, sparsely populated residential street with only a few small houses. Really Google Maps? Do we have to do this **NOW?** I had to fall back on the analog technology of asking people on the street.

I found the hostel and asked the woman at the front desk if she could please roust the two gringos for me. She told me they had gone for a walk. Gone for a walk?!?!! Before I could head out to look for them, she reappeared to tell me she was mistaken; they were in their room, after all.

A minute later, a shirtless young gringo appeared at my car, looking shocked. None of us expected me to get through the tranque that fast. I impressed upon him my desire to get the hell out of there as quickly as possible. The poor guy had about ten seconds to ascertain whether he was about to embark on a road trip through lawless territory with a psychopath. To my relief, Lasse and Stefan appeared back at my car, fully packed, in less than five minutes.

We made our introductions on the road. Lasse was from Denmark, Stefan from Switzerland. The two were taking a half-gap year between college and the real world. They had taken the bus to Bluefields just to see the town, which impressed me, as Bluefields is well off the backpacker beaten path. There, they stayed at a hostel that even my *Central America on a Shoestring* travel guide suggested was a bit dodgy. That earned them instant street cred with me. They'd taken a collectivo taxi to Nueva Guinea but could get no farther. Roadblocks had effectively shut down all traffic in the area. To get to the west side of the country, they would have had to walk over a hundred miles of countryside, exposed to the elements, not knowing where they were going to sleep at night.

Loading up the car for our midday run

Another tranque appeared only twenty kilometers outside of Nueva Guinea, giving me some concern that we might have to talk our way through dozens of them before the day was over. This tranque seemed to be manned by suburban dads, with no muchachos in sight. The amiable dads began taking apart their roadblock as soon as we started our story. I thanked them with some cold water and soda, and we were on our way.

We drove for an hour and a half through wooded countryside, almost entirely devoid of cars and human activity. We all agreed it felt like the zombie apocalypse. By and by, we saw a few people walking along the road, then more increased activity. As we approached a major intersection, a woman started frantically waving, trying to warn us of the tranque ahead. I tried to wave back that I knew about the tranque, but that's hard to get across in a wave.

Our sudden appearance around the corner surprised a scrum of people, who clearly were not expecting to see a car coming from that direction. Unlike the Nueva Guinea tranque, which had dwindled down to a few bandana-clad muchachos, this tranque had more of them than I could count. Some of the muchachos started waving aggressively at us, shouting, "NO NO NO NO NO!"—like we were supposed to just turn around and go back the way we came.

As we exited the car, the crowd of muchachos and campesinos closed in. Again, there was a lot of yelling back and forth. I scanned the crowd, trying to determine who was in charge. I made eye contact with one campesino who seemed sympathetic, so I gave him my spiel as others listened.

The muchachos were very suspicious at first. They wanted to see inside the car and search the rooftop cargo carrier. They weren't interested in my locking trunk, even when I offered to open it. They only seemed concerned with spaces big enough to hold a human being, presumably some enemy of theirs that I might be trying to smuggle out of the country. Although God help anyone in my black cargo carrier baking under the Nicaragua sun.

The idea behind nationwide tranques was to bring all commerce within the country to a standstill, which puts pressure on the government and could even create international pressure. This intersection was a key connector between east and west, and where we needed to veer off to follow the eastern side of Lake Nicaragua to the border at Los Chiles. I got out a map and showed the protesters the route we wanted to take. I kept repeating my phrases, "solo quiero dejar el país," and of course, "placa de Unistados Unidos."

One of the muchachos asked if I was a Contra. Uh... I knew the Contras hated Ortega... and the muchachos hated Ortega. But, of course, that didn't mean the muchachos loved the Contras. I just stared blankly, trying to look as aggressively stupid as possible, until my questioner lost interest.

After a few minutes, a tall bandana-clad muchacho who appeared to be of at least part African descent walked up to the group. I could tell by the crowd's body language that this guy was in charge. After some discussion with the other muchachos, he nodded that we could pass.

With that, I grabbed a twelve-pack of Toña from my cooler and handed it to one of the campesinos. He hoisted the beer above his head, then paraded it around to the front of my car for the whole roadblock to see— like a triumphant hunter returning to his village with a kill. A thunderous roar shot out from hundreds of people up and down the roadblock. Unistados Unidos: out here winning hearts and minds, one twelve-pack at a time.

The comandante muchacho led us down a long straightaway that formed a no man's land between the two ends of the highway connection. In the middle of the straightaway, we got a better look at the loudest source of cheering. A few dozen protesters had taken over a bombed-out gas station. In a scene straight out of *The Warriors* or any of the Mad Max movies, bedraggled muchachos sat on the roof, the gas pumps, some unfortunate cars, even the light poles. As we drove by, the scarf-clad squatters whooped and hollered and pumped their fists in the air. Stefan turned to me with his eyes as big as dinner plates.

I was happy he and Lasse had gotten a taste of the intensity I went through at the first tranque. After the suburban dad tranque, I feared they may have thought I was embellishing a bit.

When we got to the other end of the intersection, the comandante directed us down the road to the Los Chiles border, making sure we didn't try to veer off toward Managua.

We drove on for another hour through more zombie-apocalypse countryside until we came to an intersection staffed by a half-dozen nervous-looking cops in a small, raised outpost. The way they gawked at us, I might as well have pulled up in the Millennium Falcon. We smiled and waved as we drove past. They just stared, too stunned to wave back.

The police outpost had me hopeful that we were in government territory and that maybe the roadblocks were done. Then, we rounded a bend and again surprised a group of people who seemed the angriest of all the tranques so far. They were really confused as to how we got there. Fortunately, our story was the only thing that made sense. They also wanted to search the car and rooftop carrier. After they were satisfied with their search, the leaders huddled up to decide our fate.

As the leaders conferred, an older campesino gave me the universal palm-facing-down sign of "Just chill; everything will be okay." I decided right then that if society ever breaks down, I want to be in rural Nicaragua. These farmers have been living communally and looking out for each other for centuries with only the thinnest veneer of government to keep things in check. Americans, on the other hand, go into kill-or-be-killed mode when the toilet paper runs out.

When the tranque leader said we could pass, I pulled out some soda and beer, and this time, I finally got the nerve to ask for a picture. The campesinos had no problem having their picture taken. But to be safe, I blurred out their faces.

We were released from the tranque and sent down the right shoulder of the road, where we drove past a line of big rigs that seemed to go on for a mile. I figured this had to be the last roadblock, and it was.

Stefan along with a few campesinos bearing diplomatic gifts from Unistados Unidos

After all the supplies I had loaded up to barter for my freedom, no one asked for anything other than respect. Every campesino and muchacho I met at the tranques seemed far too proud of their purpose to ask for a bribe.

Throughout my trip and in researching for this book, I kept asking myself: Why is Nicaragua so different from its neighbors? Why did their revolution succeed where others failed? Why are their crime and emigration rates so much lower than their neighbors despite crushing poverty? Why are droves of protesters *still* risking imprisonment and death to push back against a brutal dictator?

The best answer I can come up with—is pride. Nicas are fiercely proud of their steamy little volcano/earthquake/flood-ridden land of poet-warriors—to a degree that most non-Nicaraguans can't fathom until they see it up close. Their national pride comes across in their writing and everything they do. Then and now, ordinary Nicaraguans from a spectrum of social classes have risked death to make life better for their compatriots. Not a lot of places can say that.

Note: None of the above applies to the diverse groups of Nicaragua's Caribbean slope, who mostly just want to do their own thing.

After clearing the tranque, we had smooth sailing through dense scrub forest. If the Nicaragua Canal is ever built, its eastern leg would connect to

Lake Nicaragua in this area. The entire region would transform overnight from a sleepy, pristine backwater to a global industrial hub.

We crested a hill to see the bridge over the Rio San Juan. Just before the bridge, a trio of police officers flagged us down. I asked the cop if the border was open. He replied that it was. From that point on, I've never been so thrilled to be questioned by grumpy cops in my life. We told them our stories and gave them them a bottle of soda. We kept the last of the beer for ourselves.

After a few minutes, they let us go. We crossed the bridge, crested a hill, and there it was—one of the prettiest sights I've ever seen: a giant Costa Rican flag waving in the breeze.

The GORGEOUS Costa Rican flag at the Los Chiles border crossing

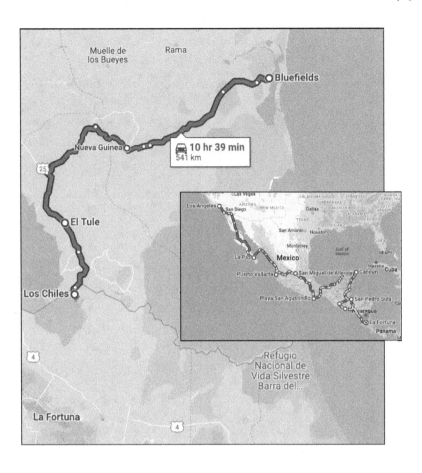

PART FIVE

CULTURE SHOCK

Daily life drives me crazy. I don't find enough salt in it.

— FRENCH ALPINIST JEAN-CHRISTOPHE "J.C."
LAFAILLE

CHAPTER 41

TYPE II FUN

BEFORE WE COULD SET foot on Costa Rican soil, we had to get out of Nicaragua, which I'd heard can be more arduous than getting in. The stamp and signature runs back and forth across the deserted compound were easy enough. But the border police still managed to fritter away two hours troubleshooting their shiny new multi-million-dollar, car-wash-sized X-ray scanner, then running my car through it multiple times. And to think Nicaraguans accuse their government of not spending their tax córdobas wisely.

From what I've heard, the border authorities are primarily looking for guns and flying drones. Nicaragua is fanatical about keeping drones out of the country, presumably so government activities can't be monitored from the air. Tick another box on the totalitarian dictator checklist.

We breezed through the Costa Rica border—a model of efficiency compared to Nicaragua. While I finished with the Costa Rican Aduana, I suggested to Stefan and Lasse that since it was getting late in the day, they should find us a place to stay close to the border. They found a hostel called Selina in the town of La Fortuna, a popular tourist destination an hour and a half away.

LA FORTUNA

We pulled into the Selina parking lot around dusk. As we waited in line to check in, I was jarred to be surrounded by loud American accents for the first time in months. The over-the-top retro-kitsch bursting out of Selina's every nook provided another affront to the senses. The only non-dormitory room they had available was a teepee for $60. Not exactly what I had in mind, but okay.

The front desk required a copy of my passport, another first in months. I went to retrieve it from the car, visualizing how drunk I was about to get and how I was going to live 100 percent in the moment for the rest of the trip. I'd had my big adventure. Nothing could phase me from here on out. No more indecisiveness, no more pissy traveler, no more new turf anxiety... Wait... Where's my passport?!?!

It wasn't in the clear zipper bag that held all my important documents and IDs. I tore apart the car, but I had an immediate sinking feeling that I must have left it at the border. It could only be at the last stop—the Costa Rican Aduana. I remembered handing it to him, but I had no clear memory of him giving it back. I was so focused on all the papers, I forgot about the passport.

The woman at the front desk accepted my driver's license. But of course, I had a much bigger problem than booking a teepee. The concierge at Selina tried to call the border for me with no luck. Nothing ever works over the telephone in Latin America. I considered driving back to the border in the dark, but I wasn't sure it would be open. So I decided to head back first thing in the morning, which meant I would have to temper my celebratory imbibing. I got settled in to my teepee, then met Stefan and Lasse at the bar.

Before the bartender would serve us a drink, he asked for a credit card so he could "open a tab." What? What's a *tab*? Are we back in the United States? I don't think I'd been asked for a credit card upfront during the entire trip until then. That's just not how things are done in Latin America. I also noticed a mini-fridge on the bar, filled with neon-colored cans of some disruptive alcoholic energy drink—another first since Los Angeles. Nevertheless, I was pumped to hopefully enjoy a non-weird cheeseburger for the first time in several countries.

The bartender interrupted our conversation to tell us he had a joke. I thought fine, whatever, just make it quick. But I misinterpreted his Australian accent. Turns out he had a *job* for us. He wanted each of us to fill out a TripAdvisor review in exchange for a free shot. "Oh, you can just piss right off with that!"... is what I restrained myself from blurting out.

What the hell is this corporate nonsense? Did we just teleport to a Dave and Busters? Stefan and Lasse were happy to comply for the free drink. I got out my phone and tapped on it a few times. As I expected, the shot was foofy and weak.

Me, Lasse, and Stefan toasting our great escape

While we waited for our food and relived our big day, a stream of over-stimulated, high-fiving, ballcap-wearing American bros filled the bar around us. Stefan, Lasse, and I didn't have to say a word. The looks we exchanged said it all. This was nothing like the sleepy backwater we had called home for the last few weeks. We were in legitimate culture shock. We all agreed we missed Bluefields.

I will give Selina one—and exactly one—kudo. That was the best damn cheeseburger I've ever eaten. The juicy, bacony, plump goodness that actually tasted like beef was everything I'd been craving for months.

I began talking to a couple at the bar who were also clearly not digging the coked-up frat bro vibe. Over time, our little corner of the bar became a refuge for other non-bros. Eventually, the refugees came up with a plan to check out some other bars in town. Stefan and Lasse decided to call it a night. It felt good for once to be the old guy heading out while the young-sters turned in early.

Our refuge excursion turned into a mini-pub crawl that featured dancing and blurry conversation. With my early morning run to the border always in the back of my mind, I took my leave of the group around midnight. In retrospect, losing my passport probably saved me from a brown-out drunk and the requisite debilitating hangover.

Later that night, when the rain came in sheets, I found the teepee to have one massive advantage over a regular room. Instead of having to sprint across the lawn to the communal bathroom, I could just unzip the flap of the teepee and pee out into the deluge.

There's your TripAdvisor review.

BACK TO THE BORDER

Despite holding back, I was still blisteringly hungover for the 6 a.m. drive. When I arrived at the border, I recognized the woman who had scanned my luggage the previous afternoon. The Aduana agent, who I was fairly certain hadn't given me back my passport, had not arrived yet.

The woman entered Aduana's office to search for my passport while I observed through the little window. My heart sank when the passport wasn't on the desk or in any drawers. Eventually, the woman and I agreed that my passport must not be in his office.

I walked around the compound, asking anyone I encountered if they'd heard of a passport being turned in. None had. Dejected, I got in my car to leave. I would have to return that afternoon when the Aduana agent was scheduled to show up. I imagined a scenario where the guy was already on his last demerit for various mistakes, like, for example, forgetting to return travelers' documents, and now his only hope to keep his job was to throw away my passport and deny everything.

I had to face the very real possibility that I was stuck in Costa Rica without a passport. I knew I could eventually get some kind of emergency travel document from the embassy. But could I even get into Panama with that—much less ship my car anywhere? I wasn't sure what the rest of my trip would look like without a real passport, but I knew it wouldn't be fun.

Mountaineers have what they call "type II fun," which by definition is god-awful while it's happening but sublime when it's over. My Nicaragua escape was type II fun—stressful and scary at the time, but glorious now that I'd had a big adventure and got a story out of it. Losing my passport, however, would be a type III ordeal—not fun when it's happening and not fun in retrospect. No one wants to hear a story about how I spent countless hours in one poorly air-conditioned government office after another, pleading with dead-eyed bureaucrats to just do their damn jobs.

On my way out of the parking lot, I stopped at the guard outpost to see if my passport had been turned in there. It had not. The guard, who turned out to be the big boss, wanted to check in some other places. So I parked and followed him back into the complex.

First, he wanted to recheck the Aduana's office. I almost told him to forget it, that the other woman had already scoured the room while I watched. But I figured, who am I to tell this guy how to do his job? The woman who had previously checked the room was understandably disgruntled that her boss didn't trust her searching capabilities. He looked in all the same places she had looked while I again watched through the little window. This time, however, I noticed a copy of my passport sitting in an otherwise empty tray on the Aduana's desk, proving my passport had been there.

Slowly, an idea began to permeate my bleary hangover-addled frontal cortex. There was a **copy** of my passport on the desk. ... Where have I lost documents, sometimes for months, until I eventually found them? ... (brain... thinky... hurty...)

Finally, I blurted out, "COPY MACHINE!" The boss didn't understand me. I pointed wildly toward the bulky device. He opened the cover, and there was my beautiful, sexy passport, still spread out on the glass like a centerfold.

I spontaneously screamed, "YES! YES! YES!" and pumped both fists in the air like I was Daniel Bryan. Several workers poked their heads out of their little windows to see what the heck was going on. I imagine they don't encounter jubilant screaming very often. Any other cause I can think of for such a border celebration must, by necessity, wait until one is well beyond earshot of the border authorities.

The glorious sight of my passport sitting on the copier platen

I drove back to La Fortuna in a happy, hungover, headachy fog, still reeling from the craziest twenty-four hours of my life.

BACK TO LA FORTUNA

When I returned to Selina, Stefan, Lasse, and I agreed we'd had our fill of the party bro scene. They wanted to check out Tortuguero, a national park on the Caribbean Coast, famous for its turtle nesting beaches. I had a week to kill before meeting up again with the End of All Roads guys, so the idea sounded great. I told Lasse and Stefan I wanted to record the previous day's events while they were still fresh in my mind. Equally important, I wanted another cheeseburger.

As I furiously typed away, I was vaguely aware of a thirty-ish American guy with a mullet gallivanting around the pool, blaring AC/DC out of a boombox, and just acting like a general jackass. Later in the car, Stefan told me that he had very nicely asked the mulleted man if he could turn the music down a bit, which sent the loudmouth into a rage, attacking Stefan with insults like "You're just traveling on your daddy's money!"

My first reaction was that if I'd heard what was going on, I'd have explained to Joe Dirt that while he's been spending his days coked-up around the pool at an upscale, over-decorated hostel that might as well be in Miami—Lasse and Stefan have been traveling on a shoestring, staying at sketchy hostels in decidedly non-touristy corners of the world, and handling themselves with aplomb in tense encounters with armed protestors. But, of course, we're never as witty or confrontational in real life as in our imagination.

The whole incident did nothing to improve my impression of Selina, which I would later learn is one of a chain of hostels that cater to "digital nomads"—a term I've come to reflexively despise, even though it more or less describes what I want to do with the rest of my life. I think my disdain for the term started with a BBC special on digital nomads in Bali, who were all running some useless middleman scam, like drop-shipping or online marketing, and only seemed interested in partying.

However, I have since come to accept, mainly through the writings and podcasts of my travel and writing guru, *Vagabonding* author Rolf Potts, that not all digital nomads are vapid soulless partiers who make no effort to understand or ingratiate themselves to the local culture. One undeniable positive to come out of digital nomadism is that ambitious locals, who often don't have the wherewithal to travel the world, are making valuable connections with nomads from wealthier countries and learning to become digital nomads themselves.

Nevertheless, if you ever find me calling myself a digital nomad, I've been kidnapped. Please call the police.

TORTUGUERO

We arrived at the dock just in time for the last ferry of the day to Tortuguero, which is only reachable by boat. Once underway, I handed out the last of my tranque Toñas to the other passengers and our captain, who hailed from Bluefields and still had family there. The captain was happy to hear my report that life in Bluefields seemed unfazed by the tranques. At a fork in the canal, the captain pointed out the channel to take if I wanted to sneak back into Nicaragua. I told him I was good with Costa Rica for the time being.

As dusk settled in, we motored up a large canal surrounded by thick bush on both sides, stopping at a few tiny docks to ferry local villagers to and from a water-based gas station/general store. We arrived at the Tortuguero town dock, where Stefan, Lasse, and I disembarked.

The three of us walked the length of the town, which sits on a thin strip of land between the channel and the Caribbean. We passed a series of restaurants and hostels and then houses on stilts painted in pastel colors, crisscrossed by narrow footpaths. We doubled back and found a cheap hostel built on a platform extending out over the channel.

Later, we found a lovely outdoor restaurant, where I ordered a dish called chifrijo that our waiter pitched as a local delicacy. Costa Rica is not known as a culinary powerhouse. But I found the chifrijo, which turned out to be something like nachos without the melted cheese, delicious.

After dinner, we retired to the hostel, where Stefan and Lasse fell into a vigorous debate about whether government should let its citizens make their own mistakes or try to coerce them into making better decisions. Stefan, from independent, free-market-minded Switzerland, felt that people should be allowed to fall on their faces. Lasse, the social-democratic Dane, felt that people often need to be nudged, if not prodded, in the right direction.

The revelatory part was that they were engaged in the same argument you might hear between two Americans, except with all the underlying positions shifted an octave to the left. Of course, you should have some form of universal healthcare and a social safety net. Of course, guns should be regulated in a sensible way. These things are taken for granted as common sense in Euro-land. They were arguing about *political philosophy* and *the fundamental purpose of government*. Where the actual policy lines were drawn on any given issue wasn't particularly important to the discussion.

I can imagine a similar schism between an American from a hundred years ago and an American from today: "What do you **mean** the government should provide healthcare, regulate public safety, and pay people in their retirement? Good sir, have you gone mad? That's not what government **does**. And what's this about no more child labor, a forty-hour work week, and Coca-Cola without real cocaine? The Communists must have won! Fetch me my top hat. I'm going back to the 1920s!"

In the morning, we grabbed breakfast and walked along the beach until we reached the entrance to Tortuguero National Park at the south end of town. Green sea turtles and leatherbacks, which can weigh up to a ton, lay their eggs on Torteguerro's black sand beaches. On the other side of the country, up to 150,000 olive ridley turtles crawl up on a few beaches to lay some ten million eggs in a single week. Known locally as an *arribada*, this mass laying is one of nature's greatest spectacles.

Apparently, the turtles got the message that the park was closed that day, as none were in sight. However, a week after we were there, a tourist snapped a gruesome picture of a jaguar devouring the soft parts of a giant leatherback on that same beach.

Tortuguero is part of a vast lowland forest that once spread unbroken from Colombia to the Yucatán. When North and South America connected about three million years ago, Central America became the meeting ground for plants and animals that had evolved in isolation for tens of millions of years. Many of these species found niches in the biologically hyper-productive lowland rainforests of the Caribbean slope. Others settled in Central America's highland cloud forests, grasslands, and seasonal dry forests.

As a result of its unique geography and hospitable ecology, Costa Rica supports five to six percent of the world's known plant and animal species within just .03 percent of the planet's habitable land. Costa Rica is home to 830 species of birds—more than the US and Canada combined, 350,000 species of insects, 1,000 species of butterflies, 6,000 kinds of flowering plants, including 1,000 species of orchids, and 240 species of mammals— about six percent of the world's total. Within Costa Rica, Tortuguero is one of the most biologically diverse hotspots—home to jaguars, pumas, ocelots, sloths, tapirs, monkeys, river otters, manatees, white-lipped peccaries, herons, parrots, great curassows, crocodiles, fer-de-lances, caimans, and poison dart frogs.

Before Tortuguero National Park was established in the early 1970s, poaching was a huge problem. Poachers would dig up turtle eggs and tie buoys to the nesting turtles so the animals could be easily picked up by boats offshore where turtle hunting is legal. Many other species were on the brink of disappearing entirely from the park. Caribbean lore maintains that manatees, a.k.a. sea cows, contain every kind of meat—chicken, pork, beef, fish, and even bacon. As one would expect, manatees tended to disappear from any region shortly after humans arrived. I know nothing about hunting sea cows, but I can't imagine it's significantly harder than hunting a land cow.

Through education programs, park managers convinced the local population to value and take pride in their natural heritage, allowing manatees to return to Tortuguero. Costa Rican park stewards also pioneered the initially controversial practice of hiring former ranchers, farmers, rogue miners, and even poachers—whose livelihoods had been impacted by the park's creation—to work as park guides and naturalists. Park managers reasoned that no one had better knowledge of the terrain and patterns of animal behavior and that giving these men a source of income could eliminate a potential threat.

Today, Costa Rica's parks are a huge source of national pride and international tourist income. Twenty-five percent of Costa Rica's land is protected as part of a national park or reserve. One in five Costa Ricans visits a national park annually—an impressive ratio for a developing country.

Given the national park was closed, and Stefan and Lasse had friends coming in, I decided to head back to the mainland. We said our goodbyes, and I wished them luck on the rest of their trip. Some travelers you meet, have fun with, then forget. But I know none of us will ever forget our crazy midday run out of Nicaragua.

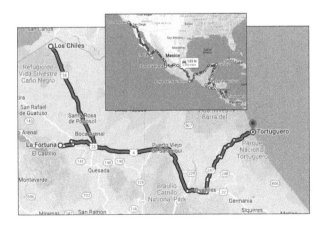

CHAPTER 42

THE ROAD ALMOST NEVER TAKEN

THE BOAT RIDE from Tortuguero back to the mainland took three times as long as the ride out—owing to a combination of full boat, low tides, sailing against the current, and the need to pull the outboard motor out of the water as we skimmed over an endless parade of invisible submerged logs. In short, the captain earned his paycheck that day.

I planned to spend one night in San José, Costa Rica's capital, before heading up into the cloud forest. I offered a young English backpacker named Ed a ride to San José. Ed had lined up accommodations in a neighborhood called Barrio Escalante, so I figured I'd drop him off and check the place out. Who needs to research neighborhoods or hostels when you can just pick up Euro backpackers and have them do the work for you?

SAN JOSÉ—BARRIO ESCALANTE

We pulled into the driveway of Finca Escalante, a villa-turned-hostel with white plaster walls, arched doorways, and a Spanish tile roof. The slightly overgrown grounds and bustling common areas exuded a relaxed, convivial vibe. As Ed checked into his dorm, the gentleman at the front desk told me they had a single room for $35 a night. Sold.

I dropped my bag in the room and headed out to explore the neighborhood. Block after block of restaurants, coffee shops, wine bars, gelaterias, and the like left me agog. This was the kind of culture shock I could sit with. Later, Ed and I met up at a brew pub, where I had my first beer stronger than 4.5% since Tijuana. At some point during IPA #2, I decided the cloud forest could wait. Decompressing and catching up on the blog suddenly seemed like high priorities. Did I mention that San José sits at 3,800 feet, and the weather is eternal spring? Poor Nicaragua.

The next morning, I got my first taste of real gallo pinto—literally "spotted rooster"—the marriage of fried rice and black beans that is perhaps the quintessential Costa Rican food item. There's even a saying: "I'm as Tico as gallo pinto." Breakfast does not happen without gallo pinto in Costa Rica. I'd had a few dried-out versions of the stuff in Nicaragua and didn't get what all the fuss was about. But the gallo pinto at Finca Escalante was moist and delicious, as were the pancakes.

That night, I hung out with Ed and a couple of his English buddies, who were well-versed in world politics and seemed to know more about the US than the average American twice their age. Ed had an interesting take that his generation, a.k.a. Gen Z, is the first generation to **know** they're fucked before they even get started in life. Millennials, according to Ed, had an optimistic childhood. Then came the realization they would probably never out-earn their parents, couldn't afford a home, and had inherited a looming environmental catastrophe. Ed felt it was preferable never to have had hope in the first place than to see one's life dreams dashed against the rocks like that. I felt like I was talking to myself at age nineteen.

I hung with the group for a few bars and a KFC run until they wanted to hit the clubs. Then, I reverted to the standard order of things and became the old guy bowing out early.

The next day, Mike and Geneva of *It's Not a Slow Car, it's a Fast House* overlander blog fame, whom I had been in touch with since before my trip, showed up at Finca Escalante. Over dinner, I told them about my foot problems. Geneva had undergone foot surgery in San José a few months prior and was in town for a checkup. She introduced me to her doctor, who did a few tests as I told him about my diagnosis in Merida and showed him the X-ray of my heel spur. He asked if I'd been stretching my calves daily as instructed. I fibbed a little and said I had.

That was all the doctor needed to hear. He said I needed gastrocnemius release surgery on both legs, explaining that he would slice part of the tendon that connects the calf muscle to the back of the knee joint. This lengthens the calf muscle, easing the tension on the Achilles and the plantar fascia that stretches across the bottom of the heel bone—the ultimate source of pain (in my case, compounded by a heel spur).

"Okay, Doc, let's just slow down a bit," I thought as I nodded along.

While the prospect of a quick fix to this frustrating malady held some appeal, I wasn't about to go under the knife when I hadn't given stretching an honest try. As much as I love buying things on impulse, cutting a slice out of both calf tendons felt like a decision I should sleep on.

Ultimately, this encounter reinforced my inclination to head back to the States. I needed to get back into a routine that allowed for stretching. If I had to get surgery, I wanted to know all my options regarding price and follow-up care between the US and Costa Rica.

One morning at breakfast, I started chatting with a lovely young British woman of around thirty named Lucy. We both had no plans for the day, so we decided to wander San José together. Lucy mentioned her boyfriend five times in the first few minutes—which was four times more than necessary for me to get the message that this was **not** a date. I was just honored she considered me close enough to her age to be a threat, and also relieved, since any kind of ambiguous possible flirtation situation sends me into a spiral of dread and anxiety.

We stopped at a cafe that had just opened, where we met the owner and learned that he and his partner had just moved to San José from Kansas City, my hometown. The chance meeting got my juices flowing about the idea of moving to San José, which was already rocketing up the charts of potential places to settle. The encounter made me realize how much San José felt like Kansas City—except in a cloud forest. Both cities have one and a half million people and give off a similar lively but not overly crowded or hustled vibe.

After the cafe, we headed toward what seemed like downtown. Along the way, we passed some of the most impressive street murals I've seen. We followed a set of overgrown railroad tracks flanked by a stone wall, behind which sat a row of old mansions in various states of repair. The whole scene could have been transported straight from the Plaza area of Kansas City, including the abandoned railroad tracks my Dad and I used to walk for miles when I was a kid.

A collage of San José's street murals

We checked out a fancy chocolate shop, where I decided to try 100% cacao for the first time. The girl at the counter warned me that it would not taste like chocolate or anything particularly edible, which I'd already seen enough food shows to know. She did **not,** however, inform me that the experience would be like blasting the contents of a Shop Vac into my mouth.

100% cacao—try it!

On our way back to Finca Escalante, we passed the Museo Nacional de Costa Rica, a striking mustard-colored faux-medieval castle that once served as the headquarters of Costa Rica's Army. In 1948, on the roof of this building, a ratification ceremony took place for an act that, to this day, has almost no precedent in world history. To cap off the event, visionary President José María Hipólito Figueres Ferrer—thankfully known by the much more succinct nickname "Don Pepe"—took a sledgehammer to one of the turrets, sending a chunk of the wall (which had been pre-loosened the day before) plummeting to the lawn below.

Costa Rica's National Museum

COSTA RICA'S VERY UN-CENTRAL-AMERICAN HISTORY

For most of the 20th century, brutal US-backed military dictatorships ruled Costa Rica's dysfunctional neighbors to the north. While all of these countries except Nicaragua are now more or less democracies, their military class still wields enormous power, and their former military leaders have never been held accountable for boundless crimes against humanity. Nicaragua's socialist revolution managed to purge Anastasio Somoza's military class (hooray!) only to replace it with a new military class of Ortega cronies (sad trombone).

So, which path did Costa Rica take? Well, it turns out there's a third option: Don Pepe disbanded Costa Rica's military.

As the standard guidebook story goes, Costa Rica's government put the money that would have gone to military hardware and salaries into infrastructure, education, nature conservation, and the arts—and the results speak for themselves. My first thought was that while I'm sure there's *some* truth to this idealized account, it can't really be that simple.

As it turns out, at least from everything I've read, no one materially disputes this interpretation of events. Costa Rica owes its status as the success story of Central America, in large part, to the money saved from not having a military and, perhaps more importantly, the lack of a military bourgeoisie to throw their weight around and look out for their own interests above all else.

To be fair, Costa Rica had favorable conditions in becoming the Switzerland of Central America, which might not have been as feasible for its friends to the north:

1. Compared to its neighbors, Costa Rica had never developed a pervasive military class. So, the resistance to Don Pepe's plan never reached coup levels.
2. The country had recently mustered a small army on short notice to repel a half-hearted invasion by Nicaragua's Somoza. Costa Rican leaders felt they could raise a fighting force again if needed.
3. Costa Rica took the prescient leap of faith that the US would never allow a hostile invasion by a foreign power from outside Central America to take place in its own backyard.
4. Ticos, as Costa Ricans call themselves, take great pride in their aversion to violence in favor of negotiation. Ticos have a reputation for dealing with conflict by talking, talking, and more talking. If a solution still isn't at hand, they table the discussions for a few days, weeks, or months—repeating this cycle until either a resolution is reached or the parties have forgotten what the dispute was about in the first place.

Costa Rica means "Rich Coast," owing to the gold lavished on the first Conquistadors to establish a foothold in the region. However, it turned out that the gold had been acquired via trade routes stretching from Mesoamerica to the Andes. Costa Rica lacked precious metals, and most of the countryside was too rugged for any of the cash crops of the day. This dearth of exploitable resources led Costa Rica to become the "Cinderella" of Spanish colonies—ignored, taxed, and neglected by the crown, administered in absentia from Nicaragua. Costa Ricans didn't even learn of their independence from Spain until a month after it happened.

The lack of an elite postcolonial landholding class seems to have given Costa Rica a more egalitarian outlook and a commensurate head start on the path to democracy. But by the 1940s, rising militarism and economic turmoil threatened to send Costa Rica down the dark path of its neighbors to the north.

After losing the 1948 elections, President Rafael Calderón claimed voter fraud and had his cronies in Congress annul the results. Don Pepe declared war on Calderón's government. As a popular coffee plantation owner, Pepe had the tactical advantage of support from peasants in the countryside. In one dramatic escape, he used his knowledge of local weather patterns to evacuate his army under the cover of low clouds.

After six weeks of fighting, Pepe's army forced Calderón and his inner circle to flee to Nicaragua. The 2,000 lives lost in Don Pepe's revolution mark the bloodiest conflict in Costa Rica's post-colonial history, which is saying something for Central America.

Pepe immediately set about reshaping Costa Rica's political future according to his vision. He limited presidential and congressional terms, gave more power to the legislative branch, nationalized the banking system, and ended nepotism in government hiring. The country's congress ratified a new constitution that gave full citizenry and voting rights to women and people of Afro-Caribbean descent—who not only couldn't vote at the time; they weren't even allowed to move to the western half of the country.

Pepe capitalized on a string of well-received reforms—such as subsidized healthcare, social security, and a school lunch program—to eventually push through his most audacious plan: abolishing the military. On December 1, 1948, from the roof of the Army Headquarters, Pepe unfurled an oversized scroll and delivered his historic pronouncement:

> *Today, the government of Costa Rica officially disbands all of its armed forces. From now on we will have no air force, no army, and no navy. Too often in Latin America, armies have been used by dictatorial regimes to crush opposition and to intimidate their own people. The governing Junta in Costa Rica has no reason to fear its citizens, and therefore feels that guns are not required in order to remain in power.*

Foreign VIPs in attendance, many of whom had ridden to power on the backs of their own military, reacted with little enthusiasm. US diplomats publicly supported their Central American ally but, behind the scenes, thought Pepe had lost his mind. Pepe, for his part, hoped to inspire other nations in the region and around the world to follow suit. It took forty-two years and the tumultuous reign of Manuel Noriega—a military kleptocrat who induced a major run-in with the US—but in 1990, neighboring Panama joined the tiny fraternity of countries to willingly disband their military.

Pepe also established the first political party in Costa Rica's history not tied to one person, a revolutionary concept for the region at the time. The remnants of Calderón's faction formed an opposition party, and the two parties took turns occupying the presidency for the next half-century. Don Pepe's second-greatest legacy is probably the supreme tribunal he established to ensure fair elections. Since 1948, no Costa Rican president has come to power by force, and its elections have been above board by all accounts.

Subsequent Costa Rican leaders have navigated the exceedingly treacherous Central American political waters with a deft touch—even openly defying the US at times, such as refusing to allow Air America to supply the Contras from Costa Rican airstrips. In 1987, Costa Rican President Óscar Arias earned the Nobel Peace Prize for negotiating an end to the Contra War.

Today, Costa Rica boasts a high standard of living, universal healthcare, the highest life expectancy in Latin America, and an education system on par with many developed nations. Costa Rica's low crime, robust infrastructure, and world-class national parks attract millions of tourists annually. The once-neglected Cinderella of Central America is now the belle of the ball—finally living up to the name Rich Coast, albeit from sources of wealth the conquistadors could never have imagined half a millennium ago.

President José María Hipólito Figueres Ferrer, a.k.a. "Don Pepe" with future first lady, American-born Henrietta Boggs (photo credit: Henrietta Boggs)

Following our walk, Lucy and I refreshed back at Finca Escalante, then met up at a nearby restaurant—just in time for a deluge the likes of which I'd seen maybe a handful of times in my life before the trip but had become accustomed to since. Costa Ricans have eight distinct words and dozens more colorful phrases for rain, ranging from *pelo de gato* (cat hair) drizzle to *cielo roto* (the sky is broken) downpour.

According to our server, this was the first real rain of the season, and it showed. Rainwater systematically probed the restaurant's defenses like velociraptors testing their enclosure in *Jurassic Park*. Lucy and I had to retreat to the restaurant's interior when an overloaded gutter created an impromptu water feature a few feet from our table. We continued to eye the roof warily between bites of nachos, our feet suspended above a rushing stream.

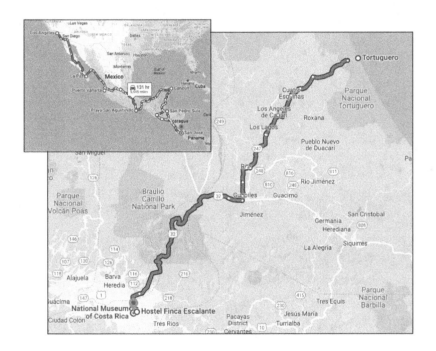

CHAPTER 43

PURA VIDA

FIVE DAYS into my stay at Finca Escalante, the End of All Roads crew showed up at the Intercontinental Hotel across town, ready to liberate their bikes from storage in the hotel's basement and get back on the road. For this leg, they also had passengers. Bob brought his girlfriend Nami, Justin brought his wife Lara, and Dan brought his college-age daughter Allaira.

I met them at the hotel, whereupon I was presented with an assortment of items they **could** have carried but **chose** not to, since I **had** offered my car. When the dust settled, I had six giant duffel bags stacked like cordwood across my back seats, two spare bike tires creatively strapped to the outside of my vehicle, and a large box of motorcycle parts in my front seat—destined for some guy in Panama named Paul.

No support detected

Note that in one of their earlier blogs, Dan had taken issue with someone who assumed they had a "support vehicle." He made it clear that the truck, driven by Dan's uncle Glen, was most certainly **not** providing any support but simply a guest driver tagging along—just like me—completely superfluous, as you can see.

BALDI HOT SPRINGS

Our first destination was, naturally, a hot springs resort—a thoughtful choice by the guys to help their riding companions decompress after their long flights. Baldi Hot Springs offers a dozen pools at various temperatures and a water amusement park featuring several multi-story water slides.

To my surprise, the water park was still open at night despite a lightning storm raging on the not-too-distant horizon. I was perfectly content to spend the rest of the evening lounging around the thermal pools, sipping Mai Tais. But the gang was super enthusiastic to hit the water slides, so I tagged along.

The wrap-around pool bar at Baldi Hot Springs

First, we approached a multi-story tube slide that seemed to empty into a colossal blue-and-green-striped toilet bowl. Water poured out of a human-sized hole in the bottom of the bowl, cascading down to a pool underneath. As we climbed the platform, I studied the whole apparatus, trying, and failing, to figure out how it worked. Where was the long skid pool that served to decelerate the rider in every other giant water slide I'd ever seen? Was the slide going to somehow shoot us through that hole in the bottom of the bowl? That seemed ludicrously dangerous on multiple levels.

Thankfully, Allaira volunteered to be the group's safety inspector, loading herself into the slide first. We all wished her good luck as she leaned back and disappeared down the tunnel. A few seconds later, she shot out of the end of the tube feet first, flying around the inside of the bowl like an Olympic luge racer rounding a sharp turn. She lost speed and height with each revolution until gravity won out over momentum—unceremoniously flushing her, if you will, through the hole at the bottom of the bowl.

Ah, so that's how it works. Yep, still terrifying.

Dan went next. The sheer velocity he managed to pick up during just a few seconds inside the tube was astonishing. The mind is not accustomed to seeing a completely unprotected human blob racing around in circles in a confined space at forty-five miles an hour. Dan flew around the inside of the bowl a dizzying five or six times—twice as many revolutions as Allaira—before coming to a stop, then rolling over into the catch pool like a walrus.

The great "toilet bowl" slide at Baldi Hot Springs (photo credit: Paradise Ventures Costa Rica)

I went after Dan. In the dark tube, I couldn't process how fast I was going. Then I shot out into the light and saw a blue and green-striped wall coming at me at highway speed. As my soul prepared to leave my body, my mind could barely take in the dizzying stripes whizzing by, followed by my own ungainly head-first dump into the pool below.

It took a few seconds to process that I was still alive. Flying around in circles, nearly naked, totally out of control, and utterly at the mercy of the designers of that crazy contraption was a surreal experience in ways a roller coaster could never match.

Next, we climbed up a five-story platform to a pair of behemoth tube slides that intertwined like two drunken snakes having sex. These slides emptied into the familiar catch basins, even though the pools looked like bathtubs from our vantage point. My first thought as I loaded myself into the tube was the same question I have boarding a giant roller coaster these days: "How bad will this hurt tomorrow?"

Small holes along the length of the tube created a frenetic, strobe light show that left no doubt as to how fast one was moving. While the toilet slide had been reasonably smooth, the snake slide was anything but. I slammed into the walls repeatedly, whacking my head several times. Finally, I came shooting out of the tube, feet first and upside down, ending in a violent tumble fifty feet through the skid pool.

A few seconds later, a 250-pound flesh-colored blur named Dan came rocketing out of the sister slide next to me in the same upside-down position, finishing with his own head-over-ass tumble that brought to mind some of the more epic hydroplane wipeouts on *ABC's Wide World of Sports*.

My big takeaway from these participatory physics experiments is that you can't have a water slide that's fun for a sixty-pound kid and not completely insane for a full-grown man of typical American girth. Waterslides, kids. Do your own safety assessments, at least in Central America, and Kansas—look it up. Er... actually, don't. Just trust me.

Most of the group went back for seconds on the snake slide. I decided one concussion was enough for the evening.

The End of All Roads crew attracted a lot of attention

TAMARINDO

Next, we headed to the beach town of Tamarindo, which took us on a scenic ride around the conical Volcán Arenal. The girls got a kick out of the attention the bikes received, taking GoPro video and waving at gawkers as we drove by.

Tamarindo was a pleasant beach town. A little warm for me, but they all are. We tried a restaurant called Nogui's, where I had a velvety slice of pineapple pie that still haunts my dreams. When I glance at a map of Costa Rica, I see a big piece of pineapple pie where Tamarindo sits. I may never remember which direction I need to go to get out of a place, but I have an eidetic memory for food. Show me a map, and I'll tell you what I ate there.

On our second day in Tamarindo, my traveling companions tracked me down to breathlessly inform me that I had a doppelgänger running around town. Is anyone ever actually excited to meet their supposed doppelgänger? No, I think not. Maybe Brad Pitt is okay with it. But that's the line.

Lara managed to track down the poor, ginger-bearded fellow, who seemed likewise unenthused about the whole doppelgänger business. Bracing for someone significantly more unattractive than the guy they produced, I was pleasantly surprised. Which means he probably lost the will to live for a while.

Sure, all ginger beards look alike

MONTEVERDE

After a few days of beach lounging, we headed up to the cloud forest town of Monteverde, which claims to be the birthplace of jungle zip-lining. The region has a reputation for being touristy and expensive, so I was a bit nervous that the $29-a-night place we booked, Jaguarundi, might be a bit too "rustic." But it turned out to be homey and wonderful. The grounds featured a mini-jungle catwalk and plenty of nature viewing. Throughout my stay, an endless parade of leafcutter ants denuded a tree just outside my door. I also saw an agouti, a long-legged rodent unique to Central and South America that looks like a tiny deer, foraging on the grounds.

The area around Monteverde wasn't settled until 1951, when a group of Quakers carved out a foothold in the rugged landscape. This late settlement may have spared the region the industrial-scale deforestation that befell many of Costa Rica's old-growth forests in the twentieth century. Scientists estimate it takes five to ten thousand years for a clear-cut forest to return to its virgin state.

In *The Quetzal and the Macaw: The Story of Costa Rica's National Parks*, author David Rains Wallace revels in a stroll through a virgin Costa Rican forest:

> *Yet one seldom gets a chance to walk for a morning through a forest of five-foot diameter trees whose trunks don't branch until they're forty or fifty feet from the ground. Every few minutes, the guardaparque (park guard) would nick a trunk with his machete and have a quizzical discussion with our Costa Rican guide about what species it might be. With leaves and fruit a hundred feet in the air, the color and taste of wood are among the more reliable ways of distinguishing among five hundred species.*

The marquee highlight around Monteverde is Selvatura Adventure Park, which offers zip lines, jungle canopy walkways, and various animal exhibits. The package for the whole day at Selvatura wasn't cheap. But when I saw the harness-clipping-in procedure, I was comforted knowing we were at the Cadillac of zip line parks and not the Geo Metro. On each platform, attendants would clip us onto a regular line and a safety line with a dizzying series of moves almost faster than the eye could take in, then send us on our way with a cry of "Pura Vida!"

You will hear Pura Vida (literally "Pure Life") a lot in Costa Rica, especially around Monteverde. Ticos in the service industry seem to use the term as an all-purpose salutation. In practice, Pura Vida means something like "to the simple life" or "to the good life." I scanned the Selvatura employees for hints that the whole *Pura Vida* ethos had lost its original oomph and was now just a hollow marketing gimmick. Other than a bit of understandable weariness from dealing with gringo tourists all day, they seemed upbeat and sincere.

The butterfly garden at Selvatura featured hundreds of species, including some true giants and a glass-winged butterfly whose wings look like empty frames. Scientists have determined that the wings use randomly sized and spaced "nanopillars" to prevent light waves from forming harmonic nodes, thus allowing the light to pass through the wings unimpeded, even at sharp angles where most see-through material would reflect. Nature's genius never ceases to amaze.

My favorite activity at the park was the relatively staid canopy walkway. I didn't see any animals, but the jungle plant life offered slow-motion violence in abundance. The whole game is to grab height however you can. When water is bountiful, the battle for sunlight becomes paramount. Life as a tree in the cloud forest seems exceedingly brutal. Hundreds of different organisms are either hanging off you, eating your leaves, or actively trying to strangle you.

Dan demonstrates the glasswing butterfly's see-through wings

It seemed like everywhere we went in Monteverde, a certain little street dog would find us and camp outside the nearest window or doorway. We could be a mile across town, eating on a second-story balcony, and look down to see this little dog. Much as the gang found my doppelgänger in Tamarindo, I decided the little dog was Justin's doppelgänger, drawn to his ethereal kin. I tried, but failed, to talk Justin and Lara into taking the little guy back to Seattle with them.

You be the judge

Another highlight of Monteverde is the night walk, where our guide Martín pointed out poisonous snakes, a toucan, and cloud forest bullet ants. While we scanned the trees with our flashlights for sleeping animals, Martín acquainted us with the local flora, which, unlike the animals, could reliably be expected to remain in one place. He showed us how the parasitic Ficus tree grows around its host tree until it smothers the tree to death, leaving only a giant Ficus with a hollow center that looks really cool when you put a flashlight inside it.

Martín continued to sprinkle us with fascinating information about Costa Rica's wildlife. Did you know that, unlike a bear, a jaguar will not crash into a tent? Not according to Martín anyway. Just don't unzip your tent fly, no matter how nicely the jaguar asks to be let in. Ogden Nash advised: "If called by a panther, don't anther." I humbly offer the following mnemonic addendum: "If visited by a jaguar, get inside some mylar."

The grand finale of the night walk was an encounter with a tarantula, which Martín lured out of her hole by tapping at the doorstep, mimicking the behavior of an amorous male. Any male tarantulas in the vicinity that evening should be grateful they weren't that stick. A very large, clearly not-in-the-mood female tarantula came charging out, ready to devour the hapless creature who disturbed her slumber.

BACK ON THE ROAD

After Monteverde, the girls flew back to their lives, and we headed south toward Panama. The drive's highlight was a stop at the famous bridge over the Tarcoles River, where Costa Rican wildlife officials bring problem crocodiles from all over the country, then feed them so they'll stay put. Directly below us, a dozen enormous crocodiles basked in the muddy shallows along the riverbank.

I immediately pictured stumbling over the bridge railing, which came up to mid-thigh, then landing in the soft mud amidst the crocodiles, alive but wounded, perhaps with a broken ankle. The crowd above could only watch helplessly as the crocs, surmising I must be some special holiday treat, fought over who got to devour the tastiest parts of me. I can't imagine many worse ways to go. This "negative fantasy," as my therapist calls them, still flashes through my mind occasionally, inducing a violent shudder.

I was hoping we'd have time to make a side trip to Finca 6, an archeological site that showcases Costa Rica's famous giant stone balls, which can also be found scattered throughout the country. Early European explorers were perplexed by these near-perfect spheres, ranging from baseball-sized to two meters in diameter. *Chariots of the Gods* postulated they were remnants of projectiles fired by starships. Because, of course, Occam's razor and all.

The creators of the stone spheres fell under the umbrella of cultures known as the Chiriquí, who thrived in what is now Costa Rica and Panama. The Chiriquí were part of the great trade route that brought jade from Mesoamerica and gold from the Incas and other cultures of the Andes. As many as ten thousand people lived in cities centered around conical great halls, resembling those still constructed by local indigenous villagers. Chiriquí cities featured public sculptures, reflecting pools, cobblestone causeways, and an aqueduct system still in use today.

The sun was getting low, so the balls would have to wait. We pressed on to the steamy town of Piedras Blancas, where we found a pleasant roadside hotel owned by a Cuban-Canadian expat and prepared to cross the busy border into Panama the next day.

Despite the terrible first impression at Selina, I liked Costa Rica more than I expected. I was prepared for something like Cancún or Cabo—an expensive American playground with slim chances for authentic interaction with local residents. To some degree, Costa Rica is those things. However, being more expensive also means its citizens generally enjoy a higher standard of living. I picked up a much stronger sense of optimism from the average Costa Rican than any other country in Central America.

Or maybe that attitude is just baked into Tico character. It would seem to follow that a society that avoids conflict at all costs would have a rosier outlook on life—even if it's not clear which aspect is the cause and which is the effect.

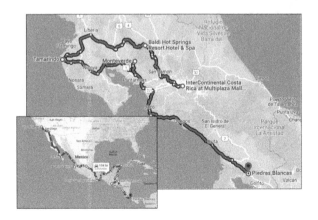

Chapter 44

Ride the Sea Slug

Across the border into Panama, the Pan-American Highway opens up into a four-lane thoroughfare lined with muffler shops, appliance stores, and car dealerships—which could easily pass for any busy stretch of commercial highway in the US.

One becomes accustomed to moving on a roughly south-by-southeast tack from one country to the next while driving through Central America. Panama, however, is disorienting. The country is shaped like an **S** lying on its side, or, more precisely, a sea slug as it contorts its body to perform one of nature's most awkward methods of locomotion.

Panama undulates so much that a ship entering the Panama Canal at Colón on the Caribbean side actually comes out farther **east** at Panama City on the Pacific side. Panama's tallest mountain, Volcán Baru, is the only place on earth where one can watch the sun rise over the Pacific and set over the Atlantic.

We reached the outskirts of Panama City just as the last light faded from the sky. Soon, we came around a bend to see a wall of skyscrapers lit up against the night sky as if we were driving into Miami. I was thankful to have experienced San José as a warmup to Panama City. The culture shock of coming straight from Bluefields to that skyline might have given me a stroke.

After a LONG day on the road, I had zero complaints about setting up camp at the swanky Marriott for a few days. As pilots, the guys get a sweet discount on rooms, and I was able to tag along on their deal. We had a ceremonial first beer in a new country, this one creatively named Panama Lager, and then called it an early night.

The following day, we drove to the Miraflores Locks of the Panama Canal. The visitor center provides an excellent history lesson on the canal, which employed some 75,000 workers from eighty-seven countries. One collage of canal workers who look to be from about twenty different cultures really helps explain the melting pot on steroids that is modern Panama.

Panama Canal workers from various regions of the world

How about one last pop quiz for old time's sake?

Q. Why does the Panama Canal have locks?

If you answered, "Why would they need to lock the Panama Canal?" you're in good company with a few friends who shall remain nameless.

If you answered something about sea level being different between the Pacific and Atlantic, you're not alone. That was my vague idea until I looked into it before this trip. Ditto for all three members of a certain motorcycle group, who shall also remain nameless.

The correct answer is that ships spend most of the Panama Canal transit on Gatun Lake, an artificial reservoir that sits at eighty-five feet above sea level. Each lock is essentially a giant bathtub that can raise a ship up to Gatun Lake or lower it back down to the sea.

There is a historical basis for the sea level disparity myth: For centuries, cartographers and engineers pondering a canal worried that the sea level in the Pacific was up to twenty feet higher than the Atlantic, which could mean a difference of forty feet at high tide. But by the mid-nineteenth century, scientists had determined that the Pacific sits only fifteen inches higher than the Atlantic due to its higher salinity and resulting lower density.

With this stumbling block out of the way, in 1881, Ferdinand de Lesseps, architect of the Suez Canal and hero of nineteenth-century France, led the first attempt at a canal across the isthmus. De Lesseps insisted on a sea-level canal, which meant an order of magnitude more digging than a lock-based canal. It would also require an untold number of dams and diversion canals to tame the volatile Chagres River and its tributaries.

The French made colossal mistakes that would be comical if they weren't so tragic. Like most leading minds around the turn of the century, French doctors believed tropical disease was primarily caused by swamp vapors and moral turpitude, and that building houses on stilts three feet above a swamp would protect against "miasma." In the hospital, nurses put the legs of each bed in small pans of water to keep ants off the patients, thus creating four ideal mosquito nurseries. Sick workers routinely ran off into the jungle to avoid the hospital, which they justifiably believed was a death sentence.

Jules Dingler, the chief engineer of the French project, was so confident in the virtuous living hypothesis that he brought his entire family to Panama. He believed that as long as they practiced good hygiene and stayed out of the seedier parts of town, his family would be spared the ailments that were claiming the lives of two hundred workers and a dozen company officers every month. In one year, Dingler lost his teenage daughter, then his grown son, then his wife to tropical disease. He somehow continued his work as an emotional zombie. The French project ultimately succumbed to insurmountable engineering challenges and mosquito-borne yellow fever and malaria, which claimed the lives of roughly 20,000 workers.

At the turn of the century, the United States appeared on the isthmus to take another crack, driven by what President Teddy Roosevelt called his "Great Enterprise." But there was a problem. Panama was still a province of Colombia at the time. US negotiators worked out a treaty with the president of Colombia for the right to build a canal and effective sovereignty over a zone five miles wide on either side. But in a surprise move, the Colombian Senate rejected the treaty, demanding more money and refusing to grant effective sovereignty—a dealbreaker for the US. Roosevelt began reviving plans to build the canal across Nicaragua instead.

But the day was not yet lost. Shenanigans were afoot.

An independence movement had been brewing in Panama, not encouraged by Roosevelt but notably not *discouraged* either. When five hundred Colombian soldiers disembarked at Colón with orders to proceed to Panama City to assert Colombia's authority, the prospective revolutionaries faced a now-or-never moment.

Rebel groups on each side of the isthmus, with the help of multiple actors representing US and French business interests, came up with a plan. The Panama Railroad superintendent escorted the landing party's leaders to a luxurious parlor car, explaining that the remainder of their troops would soon follow on another train. When the Colombian officers reached Panama City, they were treated to a luncheon and then presented with a military parade in their honor. Two lines of soldiers marched on either side of the seated officers, then, on cue, all turned and pointed their bayonets at the stunned guests of honor.

It turned out Colombia's top military officer in Panama City had been properly bribed and was now an enthusiastic supporter of the Panamanian independence movement. As the Colombian officers were being led to confinement, rebel leaders sent out a cable officially declaring Panama an independent republic.

A few days of tense standoff followed. The stranded troops were kept in the dark about the situation for as long as possible and ultimately convinced to leave Colón without bloodshed. Colombian warships were strongly encouraged to vacate the harbor by the presence of two American gunships—the Nashville and the Dixie—who were ostensibly only in Panama to protect the interests of the railroad. The ships' captains had orders to block any military force that might cause disruption, which meant any further invasionary landing—again, solely to protect the railroad, certainly not to impede Colombia from quelling a rebellion in her own province.

Eventually, the Colombians still loyal to their home country were convinced to leave through a combination of bribery and brinkmanship. One Colombian ship declared allegiance to Panama and stayed, as did several Colombian military officers. Only one person died in the revolution —an unlucky Chinese shopkeeper hit by a shell fired from one of the Colombian ships in a moment of panic.

Once Panama was independent, its fledgling government granted the

US the right to build a canal and control over the canal zone "as if it were sovereign" *in perpetuity*. What a fortuitous turn of events that whole sordid affair turned out to be for the United States! Sacré bleu!

When work on the canal finally began, US engineers solved the problems that had defeated the French by 1) building a lock canal well above sea level, 2) focusing on excavated dirt and rock (a.k.a. spoil) removal as a first-class problem, and 3) waging war on mosquitoes. Teddy Roosevelt visited the canal while it was under construction, causing a huge sensation as the first time a sitting president had ever traveled outside the US. On-site, Roosevelt made a habit of slipping free of his handlers and popping in on various operations unannounced to get a ground-level feel for how the work was progressing.

On August 15, 1914, an American cargo and passenger ship named the SS Ancon made the historic first passage through the Canal. The momentous event would have generated much more fanfare if not for the breakout of World War I two weeks earlier.

On the day we visited, no more ships were scheduled to pass through the canal, so we couldn't see the locks in action. However, I heard that recreational boats sometimes need volunteers to serve as line handlers during the canal passage. So, I planned to look into that after the guys returned to their jobs. I had visions of lounging on a luxury catamaran with 24/7 access to the open bar, perhaps even a masseuse.

We enjoyed a snack at the Miraflores Visitor Center while the gang discussed whether or not they wanted to check out the town of Yaviza—the last outpost before the notorious Darién Gap and the end of the Pan-Am Highway before it resumes again in Colombia. It seemed natural to contemplate—as we sat at the site of one of the greatest engineering feats in human history—why a simple road connecting North and South America has never even been *attempted*.

In the course of my research for this book, I somehow acquired a weathered 1954 hardcover entitled *The People of Panama*, which blithely assumes a road across the Darién is just around the corner:

> *Panama is the "Crossroads of the World." Thousands of ships use the Panama Canal each year to pass from one ocean to the other. Airplanes shuttling between the United States and South America pause in Panama and other planes take off for Europe. And when the last great obstacle to completion of the Inter-American Highway, the Darién Jungle in eastern*

Panama, is conquered, an overland route will add new luster to her title.

So, why is there no road? The obvious answer is that building one would be a herculean challenge. The Gap is an accordion of steep ravines, which would require dozens of mega-scale bridges, tunnels, and viaducts to tame. Yaviza is only sixty-five miles as the crow flies from the nearest road in Turbo, Colombia. But a large bay and the great Atrato Swamp, an impassable morass the size of Rhode Island, lie in the way. Any possible connection between the two continents would need to wind along river valleys, avoid or bridge the swamp, skirt the bay, and ultimately require much more than sixty-five miles of high-intensity roadbuilding.

Only a handful of expeditions have ever dragged a vehicle, kicking and screaming, across the Darién. In 1928, as part of a ten-year journey from Rio de Janeiro to the US to promote the Pan-American Highway, three Brazilians made the first vehicular crossing of the Gap in a Ford Model-T and support truck, using waterways whenever possible. A successful 1960 Land Rover expedition spent five months hacking through jungle and improvising bridges at an average pace of 200 meters per hour. Tires and one car still litter the jungle from a 1961 expedition made up of Chevy Corvairs, of all vehicles.

A Chevrolet Corvair resting in its forever home in the Darién Gap (Richard Emblin)

In 1972, a fleet of Land Rovers with a sixty-person support crew arrived in the Darién as part of an expedition to drive from Alaska to Tierra del Fuego. The rains came early that year, stranding the team for a month until special rafts could be flown in to float the vehicles across the Atrato Swamp. The bedraggled support team eventually staggered out of the jungle with trench foot and other maladies. The expedition's leader described the crossing as the most challenging ordeal of his career.

While the engineering challenges to building a road through the Darién are daunting, they could be tackled if the political will was there. In the early days of Panama's independence, the country's leaders welcomed the Gap as an impediment to invasion from Colombia. This fear was not unfounded. During Panama's nearly bloodless revolution, Colombia, blocked by the US from landing at either harbor, attempted to march 2,000 soldiers through the Gap. Ultimately, the expeditionary brigade succumbed to fatigue and disease and had to turn around.

In modern times, Panama's reasons for leaving the Gap in its pristine state stem from fear of Colombian drug traffic and the violence that comes with it. In 2016, Colombian authorities confiscated 8.8 *tons* of cocaine headed for the Darién and on to the US.

On top of the drug traffickers, FARC, and other Colombian revolutionary guerrilla groups have taken up residence in and around the Gap. From roughly 2000 to 2015, kidnapping by FARC and similar groups rose to epidemic proportions in the region. Journalists and orchid hunters were kidnapped. Several missionaries and adventure trekkers were killed. Even humble indigenous villagers were taken for months or years—shaken down for whatever meager ransom the guerrillas could squeeze out of their families.

In 2005, Colombian authorities floated the idea of building a road following an anticipated truce with FARC (which wouldn't actually come for another ten years). Panama's government shot the idea down, citing environmental concerns, disruption to semi-autonomous indigenous zones, and fear of cattle foot-and-mouth disease—which, to date, hasn't made the jump from South America. Some have also speculated that Panamanians still retain a vestigial fear, however unfounded, that a road through the Gap could tempt a future Colombian government to try to reclaim its former province.

Finally, in the last decade, the Gap has become a muddy death march for desperate people fleeing economic hardship and political repression in countries as far-flung as Congo, Nepal, and Cuba. Every year, hundreds of thousands of unprepared migrants make the arduous trek north from

Colombia, hoping to either sneak into the United States or claim asylum at the border. Some perish in the jungle. Many never make it to the US.

All this is to say—nobody is in any hurry to build a road through the Darién Gap at present. Check back in a decade or two.

The End of All Roads guys were aware of the dangers in and around the Gap, and we'd read a few traveler blogs about trips to Yaviza that made the town seem dodgy. Other travelers, however, had said that a day tour of Yaviza was no big deal and suggested the blogs were being a bit dramatic.

The gang seemed to be leaning against the trip until Justin pointed out that it would be a little weird for a motorcycle group named *End of All Roads* to not actually go **to the end of the road**. Bob and Dan briefly considered the internal logic of Justin's thesis, then nodded in thoughtful agreement.

And so it was settled, we were going to Yaviza.

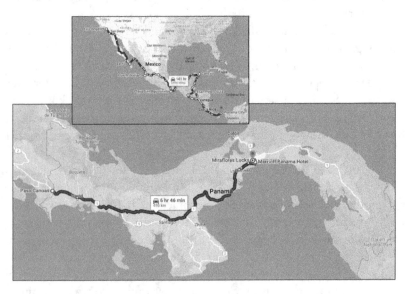

It's a sea slug! I know, right? Once you see it, you can't not see it.

CHAPTER 45

THE END OF THE ROAD

THE GUYS and I made good time to the outskirts of Panama City, where one moment we were still navigating a busy commercial zone, and the next, we passed through some kind of portal to *The Panama that Time Forgot*—a lonely two-lane highway lined with cow pastures and banana plantations.

It was immediately apparent that a road connection to South America would change **everything** about this region. Their sleepy cul-de-sac at the end of Central America would transform into a busy thoroughfare, jammed with cargo trucks and all the noise, pollution, and detritus that comes with them. Smuggled drugs and humans would flow in from South America. For better or worse, everyone's way of life in eastern Panama would turn upside down.

We wound through bucolic countryside for an hour, then Dan pulled over and came to an abrupt stop at a roadside bar/restaurant. As I pulled in behind him, my car started to skid on the gravel shoulder. I worried that I might bump into the back of Dan's bike, so I swerved to the right onto what I thought was a grassy embankment. Unfortunately, the grass turned out to be the end of an overgrown ditch.

My right tires sank into the ditch. I put the car in reverse and tried to back out. But my tires dug into the soft wall and dropped farther down. I tried to go forward, but I just descended farther into the ditch—my car now leaning to a concerning degree. This dance went on for a few more cycles until my right tires finally found the bottom of the ditch they had been yearning for all along.

At that point, less than a minute after the ordeal began, a small pickup pulled up beside me, its driver offering to help. Well, I was having none of that. I pretended not to see him.

In pure frustration and annoyance, knowing full well in real time that I was doing the dumbest thing imaginable, I slammed the FJ into reverse and gunned it. I wasn't climbing out of the ditch, but moving felt so so good. On some Paleolithic level, I was hoping to reach escape velocity and magically pop out of the back end. Then, I slammed into a concrete drainpipe with a jarring thud.

I hung my head in shame. I had dredged a foot out of the bottom of the ditch. My car felt like it was about to roll onto its side. I was defeated.

Can't park there, mate

I kicked open my door and hoisted myself out of the car. The pickup driver got into position to help tow me out. Another man appeared and asked if I had a tow strap. I did, but I had to remove a bunch of stuff in my rear compartment to get to it—not the most straightforward task when the car is half-tilted on its side. The man attached the tow strap while I climbed back into my vehicle. Justin appeared at my open window, offering a beer from the bar. Needing both hands for the wheel and unsure if the bottle would sit properly in my cup holder at such a steep angle, I politely declined.

Dan emerged from the bar, saw what was happening, and sprang into action. Some run from disaster; others rush toward it. As Mr. Rogers says:

"When calamity strikes, look for the helpers." Dan bristles at the word "hero." He'll tell you that plenty of ordinary people, in his shoes that day, would have done the same thing... Whip out their phone and start narrating my misadventure:

> *So, we have a support vehicle on this ride. But he's not really so much a support vehicle, as **we** are three support motorcyclists, for... [camera pans from Dan's face to reveal my car more or less lying on its side in the ditch]... **that guy**. [giggling]*
>
> *We're out here in the middle of nowhere, down near the Darién Gap. And the fact that these guys would even be cruising by. We've literally been here, ten minutes. I whipped over on the side of the road because I had an... **emergency**... that had to be tended to, if you know what I'm saying. And I suspect—we'll find out here in a minute—but I suspect that Matt swerved to miss me...*
>
> *So... I... uh... [we see the pickup move and the tow strap pull tight]... oh... oh... [my car starts to move forward] Come on baby! Come on, baby! [I crank the wheels, give it a little gas, and with a lot of help from the tow strap, my car rights itself and pops out of the ditch]... Heh heh heh **HEYYY!!!! YEAH-ESSS!!!***
>
> *[Bob can also be heard whooping and hollering in the background. None of us thought the little pickup would pull me out of the ditch that easily.]*
>
> *Nice. Alllll riiiight. And there he goes! And there's his pride... **right there**. [Dan pans to the torn-up ditch, then giggles at himself for a good while.]*

Dan goes on to give me shit about my muddy car and a piece of bumper that popped off in the ditch. Grass and mud coated the right side of my car, but I somehow had no new dents. I must have been at the perfect angle to lightly graze the side of the ditch.

I still wonder if I could have gotten out on my own—by plowing forward as I rocked the car from side to side. This attempt probably would have failed, may have damaged my car, and certainly would have left the bar's ditch in even worse shape. But it'll always bug me that I didn't get one more shot to escape on my own. They'd still be talking about my epic four-wheel-drive wizardry in that small corner of Panama—instead of the idiot gringo who drove straight into a ditch and had a temper tantrum.

The first order of business, of course, was to buy beers for my ditch angels. The pickup driver, who introduced himself as Saoul, owned a hospedaje (motel) just down the road. We checked it out and told him we'd love to stay the night on our way back from Yaviza.

Back on the road, we hit our first official checkpoint at the border of Darién Province, where a few humorless cops took our names and plate numbers. They stipulated that we were only allowed to visit Yaviza if we planned to return later that day. Spending the night in Darién Province would have required official permission.

Thirty minutes later, we hit another checkpoint, this one manned by relatively jovial young men in military uniforms. In 1989, following a string of unpleasant military dictators that came to a crescendo with Manuel Noriega, Panama followed Costa Rica's lead and disbanded its defense forces. The country does, however, have a National Guard and border police force, which can be hard to distinguish from the regular army. The soldiers fawned over the guys' bikes, peppering them with questions and taking selfies.

As we passed through a blip of a town fifteen miles from Yaviza, a man in acid-washed jeans and a black t-shirt came running out of a roadside hut, waving his arms. We pulled over, not quite sure what was happening, whereupon we all received a tongue-lashing for driving too fast. Apparently, the town's sheriff can't afford a uniform. Or maybe it was laundry day.

Welcome to Yaviza. Alaska—
12,580 kilometers thataway.

YAVIZA

The Pan-American Highway empties into the square grid of Yaviza, which makes pinpointing the precise end of the road an inexact science. Bloggers seem to have settled on a corner of the grid where a footbridge extends across the Chucunaque River to a tiny hamlet on the other side. I guess "from here you must dismount your vehicle and proceed on foot" makes as compelling a case as any for the southern end of the northern leg of the Pan-Am Highway.

On our way through town, we drove past an open-air bar packed with rough-looking men in various states of drunken excitement. It seemed like the kind of establishment where one could arrange for anyone or anything to be smuggled into or out of the Darién. We did not stop in for a beer. The Mos Eisley Cantina vibes were a bit strong.

The footbridge that marks the unofficial end of the Pan-Am Highway

We found the bridge and parked in front of a colonial-style house in seafoam green and black trim, which must have been quite a looker before it fell into disrepair. The guys completed their cumbersome dismounting process, and then we walked across the bridge.

The latte-colored, swift-flowing Chucunaque below us spanned about a hundred yards from shore to shore. Traditional dugout canoes lined the banks on both sides. A long, narrow, two-person riverboat loaded with green bananas worked its way downstream. Their dog had taken up the King of the World position on the boat's bow, looking ahead to a sweeping bend in the river.

Upriver, all transport takes place by boat or on foot. Outsiders call this impenetrable band of jungle the Darién Gap. Locals know it as *El Tapón*— "the stopper" or "the plug," depending on your translator.

A boat loaded with bananas navigates the Chucunaque

El Tapón's place in New World history can be summed up as a mostly forgotten backwater, punctuated by brief periods of intense interest from the outside world.

Conquistador Vasco de Balboa chose the Darién coast to establish the first European settlement on the New World mainland. (Newfoundland is an island, so the Vikings lose on a technicality.) There, a local chief told the conquistadors of a great sea beyond the hills and beyond that, "a king whose people eat from plates of gold." Balboa set off across the isthmus with 190 of his men, 1,000 indigenous conscripts, and a pack of attack dogs —conquering any non-compliant tribes he met along the way. In 1513, he and his men, among them Francisco Pizarro, became the first Europeans to lay eyes on the eastern shore of the Pacific Ocean.

Balboa set about building ships on the Pacific side of the isthmus, but he was executed by a jealous local governor before he could set sail for the fabled kingdom of gold. Pizarro finished building the ships and sailed for South America.

Local colonial authorities extracted tribute from Darién tribes for a few more years until their gold ran out. By that time, most of the Darién's indigenous population had been killed, shipped off into slavery, or succumbed to disease. New tribes came up from the Amazon basin to fill the void, a pattern that would repeat several times following European contact. For the rest of the colonial period, the Darién was largely ignored —except for a few Spanish-run gold mines that local tribes were happy to aid French and English pirates in ransacking.

The bulk of Panama's colonial activity took place around the site of modern Panama City, where gold from the Incas, shipped back from South America by Pizarro, was unloaded to be sent to Spain. Porters hauled tons of spoil from the conquered Andean empire across the isthmus on the cobblestone-paved "Royal Road," which ran roughly along the same route as the future Panama Railroad and Canal.

Having run out of indigenous conscripts, Spanish authorities imported enslaved Africans to build the Royal Road and the cities that sprang up on either end. As many as three out of ten enslaved people escaped into the Darién jungle, where they became known as Cimarróns, literally "wild, untamed." The term also applied to indigenous villagers who fled into the jungle to escape life on the missions—and is the source of the seafaring word "maroon." Cimarróns established jungle kingdoms who were happy to ally with anyone fighting against the Spanish. Their descendants still live in and around the Darién.

In 1698, several boatloads of Scottish settlers attempted to carve out a colony they called "New Caledonia" on the Darién coast. The unprepared Scots showed up with useless trade goods, like Scottish bonnets, hair buttons, tartan hose, and styled wigs—none of which held any appeal to the natives. The colonists picked a spot that receives up to seventeen *feet* of rain per year. There, they succumbed to tropical diseases, crop-destroying floods, and attacks by Spanish warships.

The first wave of settlers abandoned the colony before the second wave, who were already en route, could be notified. The second wave fared even worse. All told, only around 500 of the 2,500 Scots who set sail for New Caledonia survived the ordeal and return voyage. I shudder to think of my ancestral countrymen from cold, dreary Scotland, trying to make a go in one of the most inhospitable tropical climates on earth. Paradise not found.

In 1850, an Irish doctor named Edward Cullen published a fanciful description of a low pass through the Darién mountains that caused a sensation in Europe and America. In fact, the "Gap" in Darién Gap doesn't refer to the gap in the road, as one might assume. For more than a hundred years, the region was known by Europeans as "Cullen's Gap," for the pass he had supposedly discovered. Dr. Cullen didn't actually cross the isthmus but claimed to have seen both the Caribbean and the Pacific from a tall tree. A follow-up expedition purported to confirm Cullen's finding by spotting the end of a previous foray from the opposite side, again by climbing a tall tree.

Cullen's Gap led to a frenzy of surveys by French, British, and American groups looking to lay claim to Cullen's route and build a canal across the Darién. A twenty-seven-man expedition led by US Army Lieutenant Isaac Strain took one wrong turn and wound up lost in the jungle for nine weeks. Things went from serious to dire when someone broke the expedition's only fish hook. "Panama" is an indigenous word meaning "plenty of fish." But not if you can't catch them. Four men died of starvation before Strain could get help and make it back to his men. Three more succumbed after being rescued. Strain's ordeal, and a much less disastrous British expedition, proved Cullen's low gap was hogwash—at which point interest in building a canal shifted to central Panama, and the Darién was forgotten again.

The 1960s saw a brief revival in interest in the Darién when the US Atomic Energy Commission came up with a plan to blast a sea-level canal by setting off a series of 275 nuclear bombs in rapid succession. The venture, known as the Pan-Atomic Canal, fell under the auspices of Project Plowshare, a batshit crazy US initiative to find peacetime uses for nuclear bombs. Project Plowshare also worked up plans to blast a deep-water harbor in Alaska and carve out an alternative to the Suez Canal through Israel.

The Commission spent over $20 million planning the Pan-Atomic Canal and even shipped heavy equipment to the Darién in preparation. Strangely, local indigenous groups were not fully on board with the idea of blasting a giant radioactive trench through their territory. The project stalled and was finally scrapped in 1970.

From the 1960s until the mid-2000s, the Darién was a siren call for adventurers, missionaries, and the odd vehicular expedition. Then, drug runners and FARC showed up and spoiled the fun. Ever since, the Gap has fallen into a malaise of violent crime, smuggling, kidnapping, and migrant misery.

The homeless problem in Yaviza is rough—lots of sweaty, passed-out bikers with beer cans and trash strewn around them.

After the footbridge, the guys and I wandered over to an open area with a playground that seemed to function as the town square. I bought some fruit that looked like lychees but tasted like Lemon Pledge. Justin fiddled with his bike. Bob flew his drone. Dan took a nap in a puddle of sweat. Then, all three decided to call their loved ones for some reason.

I began to worry that the longer we lingered, the more we could become targets. According to Tony Bourdain, it takes three days to plan a kidnapping. I hoped it would take at least three hours to plan a mugging of four large dudes in broad daylight.

Once the guys' loved ones had all been debriefed on Yaviza, we got back on the road. The bikes sped ahead of me. I didn't try to keep up, remembering the guy in acid-washed jeans who had dressed us down on the way in. When I reached his little town, I thought I was going slow enough, but he still came running out of his hut to yell at me. The guys had blown through so fast he threatened to throw them all in jail, so he was already pre-angered when I showed up.

I didn't know this at the time, but tensions may have been running high in the area due to sprawling migrant collection camps that have sprung up around nearby indigenous villages. By all accounts, the border authorities would be less than enthusiastic if we made a surprise visit to one of these camps, where conditions are beyond appalling.

In *The Gap: Crossing the Deadliest Leg of the World's Greatest Migration*, author Barret Brewster chronicles a typical migrant passage in 2020. Unlike most documentaries and news pieces on the Darién crossing, Barret had no armed escorts and no special permission from the governments of Colombia or Panama, which means he and his group endured the authentic Darién migration experience. He was robbed along the way and incarcerated for weeks when his group reached Panama.

Migrants hail from underdeveloped countries as far-flung as Haiti, Congo, and Nepal. Some come to countries like Chile and Brazil to work but then decide their best chance for a future is to make a run for the US. Others arrive in South America through lax immigration policies, then immediately start working their way to the US, where they usually plan to seek asylum. The migrants almost universally seem to have no idea what they're getting into when they arrive at the Darién rendezvous point. Apparently, their guides, who work for Colombian cartels, don't advertise a life-threatening jungle trek in the brochure.

A family from Ghana struggles up a muddy embankment
(Carlos Villalon/Redux)

Migrants show up dressed in their Sunday best, sometimes lugging everything they own in a bulky suitcase or nothing more than a black trash bag. Their shoes are often flip-flops—which offer no protection against poisonous snakes and the Darién's notoriously sharp thorns—or tennis shoes, which are magnets for jungle rot. Colombian guides won't cross into Panama for fear of serious jail time, so they peel off and leave the migrants to find their own way for most of the crossing.

Haitian migrants ford the Parraganti River in 2019
(Carlos Villalon/Redux)

The Darién jungle is one of the hottest and wettest places on the planet. Somewhat counterintuitively, dehydration comes so quickly in the jungle that trekkers have died with water in their backpacks. The terrain is punishing. Those who are out of shape quickly fall back. Some stop to wait for the next group of migrants, which could be days or weeks. Some never get moving again.

Other than a Himalayan peak, the lawless Darién is one of the only places on earth where human bodies lie where they fall, never to be collected. Certain stretches toward the end of the journey seem to be bottlenecks for dead bodies—either deposited by the river or people who just gave up and died where they sat. Barret's group passed the heartbreaking scene of a recently deceased woman lying on the ground, still clutching her dead baby.

The skeleton of a man from India who reportedly spent the last two weeks of his life injured, trying to crawl along the trail (Carlos Villalon/Redux)

When Barret's group was robbed, the bandits took care to return passports—even as they kept everything else of value and threw food and family heirlooms in the river out of spite. This suggests some level of cooperation between the bandits and the Panamanian border authorities, since processing migrants without passports is a bureaucratic nightmare. While Barret's group was all men, he met other migrants who said that bandits raped women in their group.

Migrants stagger into rural collection camps after days or weeks in the jungle, some near death. While they wait to be processed, wounds and infections can become fatal due to the lack of a doctor and medical supplies. Barret's camp had no clean water, only a river with dead bodies floating by that everyone used as a toilet and a bathtub. Babies are particularly vulnerable to fatal bouts of diarrhea brought on by contaminated drinking water. Needless to say, indigenous villagers are not happy that their home has become a fetid death camp and have little sympathy for the migrants.

Migrants who survive the collection camps are brought to more established camps, where they're treated only slightly better. Once fully processed, they're transferred to yet another camp close to Panama's western border. Eventually, the migrants are released and encouraged on their way toward Costa Rica—like the classic small-town sheriff picking up a drifter at one end of town and dropping him off at the other.

Barrett and his friend standing in front of makeshift water filters (Barret Brewster)

After his release, Barrett stayed in Panama, where he raised funds to purchase medical supplies and then personally delivered them to his collection camp. He also designed, assembled, and delivered several industrial-sized water filters.

A tally of nationalities in the Barrett's camp (Barret Brewster)

By the time Barret published his account of the journey a year later, none of the migrants he stayed in contact with reported making it to the US. All had either been deported, dropped off the radar, or were still in Mexico, hoping to make it to the US. In 2021, an estimated 70,000 migrants attempted the Darién Gap death march. In 2023, that number could reach as high as half a million.

The guys and I arrived back at Saoul's hospedaje at dusk. By the lake in the parking lot, it was evident the area had been pummeled with rain while we were gone. Panama must have extremely localized weather patterns because we never got more than a sprinkle on the two-hour ride to Yaviza and back.

Saoul graciously served us carne asada and fries for dinner. I chatted with Saoul and his wife for a bit. As usual, once we established where everyone lived, what they did for a living, and the number and ages of their kids—we reached the limits of our translation capabilities and sat in awkward silence.

After dinner, we returned to the bar whose ditch I had dredged earlier in the day. Did they offer me a beer on the house in return for such a valuable service? No. Rude.

We didn't last long. The guys had a full day ahead. They had to deliver their bikes to the airline and crate them up for shipping to Colombia. I would be on my own again, and I needed to make a final decision on whether to head back to the States or come up with a different plan.

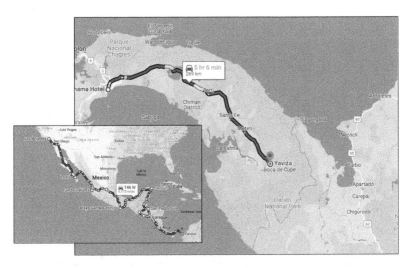

From Yaviza to Turbo, Colombia is about sixty-five miles as the crow flies.

CHAPTER 46

LOOSE ENDS AND FINAL DECISIONS

I WOKE up tangled in the Marriott's luxurious bedding with a blistering hangover. The guys and I decided to get **a** beer for their last night in town, which turned into shots, which turned into <blurry>. I was happy not to be on a plane back to Guam, like them, but annoyed that I'd be utterly useless on one of the waning days of my trip.

I reflexively grabbed my laptop and went online with no real purpose. I noticed someone had bumped a thread I created about Tony Bourdain many years earlier. Oh, let's see what that is...

Ugh.

Other than my parents, I've never had a mentor. Instead, I've accumulated a stable of public personalities, usually around a decade older than me, to serve as lodestars for how I want to be in the world.

Anthony Bourdain was far and away at the top of that list.

Tony taught me that it's okay to see a new place with childlike wonder, yet still let my snarky acerbic side out of its cage. That it's never too late to pursue a creative passion. That the best meals are eaten while sitting on little plastic stools on a bustling sidewalk in a developing country. That curiosity and humility are the most essential travel virtues. That sharing food with a cultural outsider might be the most life-affirming thing we do as human beings.

R.I.P. Tony. You're missed more than you could ever know.

CASCO VIEJO

When Dan left, so did my friends and family discount at the Marriott. So, I moved to Casco Viejo, Panama City's "old town." The neighborhood has a similar vibe to Antigua, with block after block of old colonial buildings either in ruins or enjoying second lives as mansions, boutique hotels, and trendy restaurants. While I would characterize Antigua as more of a shabby chic "rough restore," Casco Viejo is a gleaming, high-gloss callback to the city's heyday as the Istanbul of the New World. The neighborhood has come a long way from the '80s and '90s when it was by all accounts a crumbling, crime-ridden hellhole. In 1989, an adventurer bound for the Darién Gap claimed he was mugged three times in one day in Casco Viejo. Ironically, the Gap was relatively safe at the time.

A restored block in Casco Viejo

Casco Viejo is not the *oldest* Old Town. That honor goes to a city known as Portobelo, which was located about five miles up the coast. For over a century, gold and other treasures looted from the Incas were unloaded at Portobelo. To discourage pirates, Pizarro's Pacific fleet sailed from Peru once a year in a giant convoy. The King's cut—one-fifth of the total haul—was unloaded and transported across the Royal Road, where it was loaded onto waiting ships and escorted back to Spain by the Spanish Armada.

In 1671, the pirate Henry Morgan ransacked and razed the city, torturing anyone he came across to reveal the whereabouts of more gold. When it came time to rebuild, Portobelo's leaders chose the Casco Viejo site as a more defensible hilltop position.

As the flow of plunder from the Incas began to wane, the city remained the continental hub for the slavery and sugar trade for a time. But by the late 1700s, after centuries of economic prominence, the city had fallen into disrepair and became a backwater. In the early 1800s, the Royal Road lay in overgrown ruin, and Panama City was said to be harder to reach than Tibet.

The 1849 American gold rush reignited interest in crossing the isthmus as fast as possible. Sailing from the US East Coast to Panama, riding mules across the isthmus, and then sailing on to California was faster and less arduous than riding across the US in a covered wagon or sailing around the southern tip of South America. Only the route that crossed Lake Nicaragua on Cornelius Vanderbilt's expensive steamships was faster.

Within a few years, work began on the Panama Railroad. Conditions for the laborers were deplorable. The route had to negotiate a "bottomless" black swamp, later measured to a depth of 185 feet. Tropical disease ravaged the workforce. It was said at the time that the Panama Railroad cost one life for every railroad tie.

When the world's first interoceanic railroad was completed, Panama City again became one of the world's crossroads. Travelers could pay $25 to ride the train or $10 to walk the fifty miles of tracks.

BOQUETE

While I was staying in Casco Viejo, I made reservations to ship my car back to the US with a company called IVSS. I had ten days until I needed to deliver my car to the docks at Colón, so I decided to check out Boquete, a mountain town in western Panama. The drive took six hours, all through a "sky is broken" downpour, which added an extra layer of stress. At least the rain shooed away all the motorcycle cops with radar guns and all but one of the police checkpoints.

Boquete is a charming, lush mountain hamlet with an eternal spring climate, full of American and Canadian expats. The town has a selection of coffee shops, restaurants, and even a brewery. Unfortunately, I came down with a nasty sore throat soon after arrival, which tempered my enjoyment of the town's amenities. I spent my days in Boquete going to Spanish class, stopping at an Italian place for spaghetti, and then heading back to my rental to sleep. The cruelest irony was that beer instantly and significantly exacerbated the sore throat. I repeated this experiment a half-dozen times just to be rigorous. Hypothesis confirmed every time: spitting hot fire.

I even tried a Chinese medicine remedy my girlfriend's mom once prepared for me—gargling hot water mixed with salt and pepper. At the time, I was told that if the salt and pepper concoction didn't work, Mom had a more potent remedy, described as "hardcore," which I would need to **snort**. Over the years, I began to detect a pattern with Chinese medicine— if this remedy doesn't work, Mom's got something even more unpleasant waiting in the wings. I'm guessing the first remedy has a high success rate. Unfortunately, my own attempt at the potion did nothing.

When my week in Boquete was up, I headed back to Panama City. On my way, I stopped at the town of David *(pronounced dah-VEED)*, where I planned to give the decision to end the trip and go back to LA an honest mull. From David, I could turn left as planned, drive to Colón, and continue the process of shipping my car back to the States. Or I could turn right, head back to Costa Rica, and devise some kind of Plan B on the fly. By far, the most common regret I see on the expat forums is that they only wish they'd taken the plunge sooner.

The decision would have been a lot harder if my foot was healthy. Not being able to walk a new city for more than an hour, and having no chance of doing multi-day treks like the Inca Trail, really put a damper on the idea of taking up residence in San José or continuing on to South America. So I turned left toward Colón, hoping I'd made the right decision.

Author's note: *Five years later, I'm still not sure. Ask me on my deathbed.*

Colón

The city of Colón has been the neglected stepchild of the isthmus transit since the construction of the railroad. The town was originally built over a swamp, which became increasingly fetid as the population increased. One early US canal worker, thrilled to be going home alive, dubbed turn-of-the-century Colón: *Death's Nursery*.

I'd heard Colón was a bit gritty, to put it mildly, and the town lived up to that. Although I think some of the blogs may have exaggerated the actual danger, at least in the daytime. I didn't go wandering around at night.

A Colón neighborhood with potential, as a real estate agent might say

Having time to kill, I checked out the Agua Clara Visitor Center on the Caribbean side of the Canal. The Agua Clara expansion locks went live in 2016. The new locks can accommodate ships up to 180 feet wide—a 70-foot increase over the original 1913 locks. Ships built to the original 1913 size are known as *Panamax*. The new 180-foot-wide ships, which can hold up to 14,000 containers, are known as *New-Panamax*. Personally, I'd have gone with something more theatrical—like *Megamax*, *Gigamax*, or *Indominus Max*.

On my way to the visitor center, one of these behemoth container ships passed by, seemingly floating above the buildings in front of it. The mind struggles to process a structure the size of a skyscraper, lying on its side, moving along in a canal whose waterline is fifty feet above the surrounding landscape. It's easy to lose all sense of scale around the Canal, where everything is gigantic.

One of the most common topics on the international overlander forums is theft during RoRo (roll on, roll off) shipping. My strategy to avoid theft was to put the most valuable stuff in the locking trunk, then cram everything else into the rooftop cargo carrier. A thief could break into the cargo carrier by lightly pulling on it with their hand. But then it might be obvious that the carrier was broken into, which I hoped would deter ship and dock workers.

I cleaned every scrap of paper from the glove box and anywhere else a curious potential thief might look. The idea was to send a message that this car has been meticulously denuded of *everything*, so don't even bother. The only items I couldn't fit up top were my beat-up cooler and my still unopened yoga mat. If someone wanted to steal either of those, they could be my guest. I figured the Venn diagram of sticky-fingered dock workers and yoga aficionados is two non-contiguous circles.

On the morning I was to drop off my car, I hired local legend Boris for $75. Boris ran me around to handle all the paperwork between the shipping line, Wallenius Wilhelmsen, and the dock authorities. I probably could have figured it out myself, but I would have spent a great deal of time walking around the massive complex.

When it was time to get my car searched for contraband, I think it might have been the drug-sniffing dog's first day on the job. The skinny, hyperactive German Shepherd seemed young for a working dog. The inspector had me empty everything from my two locking containers and lay it on the tarmac in the drizzling rain. Hours of playing Tetris to fit everything in—down the drain. Boris said that level of inspection usually doesn't happen. I assumed the handler wanted to get some extra training in for his dog. Fortunately, I wasn't trying to smuggle any bricks of cocaine back to the US that day. I managed to stuff everything back in, although not as cleanly.

Handing off my car for shipping. Safe travels, buddy.

After everything we'd been through, I felt emotional and untethered leaving my car behind—like dropping your dog off at the vet for major surgery. We'd both be on our own until we could reunite in Galveston in a couple of weeks.

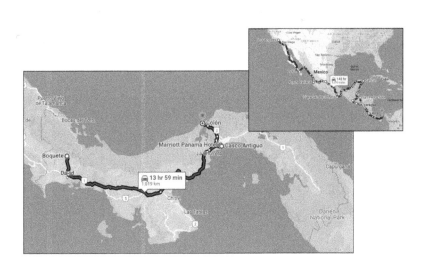

Chapter 47

The Big Ditch

Suddenly a pedestrian, I still had to find my way back to Panama City for my flight out in a few days. I could take an Uber or a taxi, which would be expensive and boring. I could take a bus, which would be cheap and boring. I could even take the train, which would be expensive and interesting. Or... I could hitch a ride through the Panama Canal, which would be free and exceedingly fascinating—at least for someone like me who still stops at construction sites to watch the big yellow machines move dirt around.

I connected online with a French couple named Wilma and Sebastien to volunteer as a line handler. They needed two more hands for their thirty-four-foot sailboat. I considered holding out for something more in line with the luxury catamaran I had wistfully envisioned when I first learned of this volunteer opportunity. But then it dawned on me that, duh, those multi-million-dollar yachts already have enough line handlers. And if not, they almost certainly don't have to go fishing online for some random weirdo like me. I had to accept there would be no air-conditioned cabin, no open bar, and no masseuse.

I posted on the Pan-Am Traveler forum asking if anyone might be interested in the second line handler spot. An Irish expat named Pat replied. We exchanged a few messages, and he seemed normal enough. So, I contacted Sebastien to let him know Pat and I would be happy to volunteer.

We all met up at an outdoor restaurant near my hotel, where Sebastien had about thirty minutes to ascertain whether one or both of us were psychopaths (see: *Dead Calm*, movie). Sebastien explained that he and Wilma were traveling the world on their sailboat, occasionally taking remote contract jobs as digital artists.

The next day, I met Wilma at the dock and rode their dinghy out to the boat, where I met Sebastien's father, Gerard, who had joined up for the canal crossing. Everyone referred to Gerard as Papa, always pronounced with an exaggerated lilting second syllable, like "Ah-HAHH!" A small, energetic, instantly charming man in his 60s, Papa constantly made Pat and I laugh, even though he didn't know a word of English and our French was effectively nil. The only relevant phrase I could remember from three years of high school French was "Où est Papa?" (Where is Papa?), which I entertained myself by blurting out in a silly French accent any time Papa dropped out of sight.

The boat was cluttered and extremely space-challenged for five people and Pat's and my luggage, but otherwise seemed in working order. As night fell, the cabin was still stuffy, so Pat and I had a beer out on the deck. Listening to little waves slap against the boat, surrounded by the lights and various clanging sounds of the harbor, we both agreed that from this vantage point, poor, ugly duckling Colón seemed tranquil, even charming.

My favorite thing about being on a boat is the change in perspective. When I'd take my little sailboat out in the bay, as the grid of my town got smaller and smaller, I'd get a sensation like I was hovering above the rat maze of my life. Whatever struggles I was mired in at the moment somehow seemed a little less relevant.

When it came time to sleep, there was only one fan between me and Pat. Since I was already lying close to the fan, I suggested that I take the fan the first night, and he could have it the second night—my reasoning being that if the boat sank during the canal crossing, I would come out ahead in the deal. I also remembered that sailing around the world on a small boat is decidedly **not** on my bucket list.

We were told to be ready to cross the canal the next day as early as dawn. This turned into a waiting game that dragged on well into the afternoon. Small sailboats don't get much priority. Pat and I occupied ourselves practicing the standard figure 8 knot we would need to use. The knot eventually came back to me from my boating days. Pat had no experience but was a quick learner.

Finally, we got word to be ready to cross at 3 p.m. An official harbor boat delivered our pilot, who would guide us through the transit, and a special set of heavy ropes that we'd use to tie off once inside the locks. The pilot explained that we'd link up with two other sailboats for the passage.

Our pilot was extremely knowledgeable about the canal and enjoyed answering our questions. He told us the gargantuan New-Panamax ships pay over a million dollars to cross, and about fifty ships cross daily. Not all are giants, but you get an idea of how much revenue the canal brings in for Panama. The record for the lowest toll goes to adventurer Richard Halliburton, who paid thirty-six cents, based on his weight, to *swim* the canal in 1928.

The pilot gave specific instructions on the figure 8 he wanted us to use. The knot has a crucial final step: before cinching the rope, you have to flip the loop upside down in a way that my brain struggled to wrap itself around. I'd get to the last step and say, "Okay, I remember I need to flip this thing some way. Is it that way? No. Okay, how about flipping it this way? Nope, not that either." In my spatial relations struggles, it slowly came back to me that this is **always** the correct figure 8. The lazy kind, which Pat and I had spent all day practicing, can be impossible to loosen under extreme tension. This doesn't typically pose a problem for a small sailboat sitting at a dock, but for reasons that would become clear, it's vitally important in the locks.

On the way to the locks, we passed under a gigantic suspension bridge still under construction, with only a small center section left to complete. Each side of the bridge loomed above us, literally suspended in mid-air. I could never get a good answer as to why this bridge was needed, since there's very little on that side of the canal other than a few villages. I did gather that the Pana- manian government required the Canal Authority to build the bridge as a condi- tion for approving the expansion locks.

Almost there! The Puente del Atlántico bridge under construction

As we approached the Gatun Locks, we met up with the other two sail- boats, which also had French crews—a feature that came in handy when anyone needed to communicate across the boats. We lashed all three boats together from the stern (rear) of each boat to the bow (front) of the adja- cent boat, a technique known as a "spring line." According to our pilot, lines from bow to bow or stern to stern are not a good idea since they can act like a slingshot and crash the boats together. The largest sailboat was placed in the middle, with the two smaller sailboats flanking each side. We all followed a giant tanker ship into the first lock.

Wilma gives thumbs up as we enter the first lock behind the
Blue Dragon

As we entered the lock, rope handlers walking along the top of the wall threw down feeder lines. After a few misses, we secured each feeder line, then tied it to the end of one of the heavy ropes that had come on board with our pilot. The workers then pulled up the heavy rope and tied it off on their end.

The center boat's captain was tasked with pushing our three-boat flotilla forward or backward, as directed by his pilot. As captain of our boat, Sebastien's job was to stay at the helm and do nothing unless instructed by our pilot. Since the center boat was flanked by a boat on each side, they had four line handlers with nothing to do. On the outer boats, we only had two lines to manage. All told, there were eight superfluous line handlers between the three boats. But you never know when your boat might have to go through the canal alone, hence the requirement that each boat have a captain and four line handlers.

Once we had entered the lock, the giant steel gates began to close behind us. The doors don't shut flat but form a shallow wedge facing the direction of higher water. This way, the water pushes the doors shut and distributes the force to the lock walls. The doors are also hollow inside, so they float, which puts less strain on the hinges.

The lock gates closing behind us

The scale of the walls and the giant ship in front of us was disorienting. It felt like an episode of *The Twilight Zone*, where we suddenly found ourselves on toy boats floating in a stadium-sized concrete bathtub. Only small boats like ours ever get this view, since the decks of the big ships are far above the water.

Soon after the gates clanged shut, the water around us started to roil and heave. Whirlpools sprang into existence for a few seconds, then disappeared. I wasn't sure what would happen if I fell in, but I knew I didn't want to find out. The water is fed from Gatun Lake by gravity, which means zero power is expended to raise the heaviest moving things on the planet. As an early canal engineer noted, "I could raise an aircraft carrier with a garden hose if you give me a big enough empty pool."

As our boats rose, I finally realized why line handlers were so important. I had been thinking our job was just to catch the feeder lines, tie off the boat with the heavy lines, and then wait. Four line handlers seemed like safety overkill just for that. But no. When the water starts to rise, the lines become slack. Roiling water doesn't make the most stable platform, so if the slack isn't constantly brought in, our convoy could drift to one side and crash into the lock walls. Wilma and Papa worked the stern line while Pat and I worked the bow. The pilots barked orders to pull in the ropes if our convoy drifted to either side. The process was stressful, but we kept up for the most part.

If you're wondering how the giant tanker in front of us handled all these gyrations—it didn't. Large ships are held in place by steel cables connected to automated cars, known as mules, which ride back and forth on rails along the top of the lock walls. Line handlers who work for the Canal Authority board the vessel and tie off the cables. A central computer simultaneously reels in or lets out each cable to keep the ship centered in the canal. The mules can hold a giant ship in position with as little as six inches of clearance between the hull and the lock walls. It's hard to fathom how this system worked in the days before computers. For the expansion locks, engineers chose to forgo mules for dedicated tugboats that attach to the ship's bow and stern during the lock passage.

Before the advent of computers, all controls for things like lock gates, valves to let in or release water, and safety mechanisms—such as a fender chain to prevent a runaway ship from ramming the gates—were operated by a scale model of the locks that looked something like a model train set. The genius of this model, which is still on display in the visitor center, was that it simply wouldn't *allow* the operator to do something out of sequence, like release the safety chain before the lock gates were fully open. As a software engineer who becomes instantly enraged by catastrophic mistakes that are *technically* the user's fault but could easily have been prevented by a smarter user interface, this design pleases me.

When we reached the top of the bathtub, the lock gates opened, and we all proceeded en masse to the next lock. The whole experience felt like some industrial amusement park ride, minus the forced whimsy and bored teenage attendants.

Once we had been raised to the top of the third lock, the gate opened, and we were released onto Gatun Lake—a massive expanse of blue-green water extending to the horizon in several directions, dotted with overgrown islands of various sizes.

Gatun was the largest artificial reservoir in the world when it was created in 1913. As the lake filled in, animals that couldn't swim or fly retreated to hilltops, which became islands (if they were lucky). Villages of various sizes had to be evacuated before they became part of the lake. Half-hearted attempts were made to relocate some of the larger villages, houses included, to new locations. But the magic of the original settlement was missing in the new location, and none thrived. A few years after the canal opened, the US government repeated this process with every settlement still residing inside the Canal Zone. Ultimately, the Canal Authority expelled some 40,000 people from their homes. It's not one of the more enthusiastically recounted chapters in Panama Canal history.

Our pilot guided our three-boat convoy to a buoy not far from the locks, where we were to tie up together for the night. The locks can run at night, but operators avoid doing so unless there's an emergency.

The lake looked refreshing. I asked our pilot if it was safe to swim. He pointed out a nearby fish processing plant whose effluent attracts crocodiles and said taking a dip probably wasn't a good idea. A few people on the center boat did jump in, but they were back out of the water in thirty seconds. The lake's freshwater kills barnacles, which captains of the big ships love. Although now I feel sad for the barnacles—an emotion I never thought I'd experience.

Everyone from the other two boats migrated to the big center boat, where they seemed to be having an impromptu party. One couple was dancing on the deck to the *Blues Brothers* soundtrack. I decided the man in the fun-loving couple was the Frenchest person on earth. Imagine Gerard Depardieu in *Castaway* instead of Tom Hanks—leathery burnt tan, long curly bleached hair, prodigious personality with a nose to match. He and his partner looked like they'd been living in a hut on a sunbaked island for decades.

A fun-loving couple dancing to the Blues Brothers soundtrack as the sun sets behind the center boat

The revelers invited us over, but Wilma and Sebastien declined. Apparently, we were the introvert boat. Pat and I would have been up for going over, but it didn't seem right to say, "So, uhhh... you guys are no fun. I think we're gonna go hang out on that other boat." Also, I don't think anyone over there spoke a lick of English.

So we watched them dance the sunset away while we ate our dinner in relatively glum silence. At least the food was delicious. Every meal was superb: tacos, pasta, stroganoff, charcuterie—all made from scratch. Even for snacks—there was a preparation phase, a communal eating phase, and a cleanup phase. There was no "just grab some Triscuits and aerosol cheese and shove it in your fat face" phase. From my limited experience, the French, much like Poblanos and Oaxacans, do not fuck around when it comes to food. If a meal is worth eating, it's worth sitting down and doing right.

Pat and I stayed out on the deck after sunset, watching a dazzling heat lighting show on the horizon. Giant tendrils of lightning fired off in all directions, like a tree with dozens of branches, each spawning smaller branches as the lightning climbed a third of the way up the sky. It was yet another one of those magical moments on a boat I'll never forget—this one tinged with a hint of danger, in that if the lightning made its way toward us, we were strapped to a giant metal buoy surrounded by crocodiles. Not ideal. Thankfully, the storm stayed put on the horizon.

We elected to sleep out on the deck, since it was more comfortable than the stuffy cabin. Hah! My fan gambit paid off after all.

Of course, karma had the last word. The next morning, I woke up with tiny welts covering every exposed patch of skin. For some reason, I was the only one who got them. The welts weren't intensely itchy, but they did take months to disappear. We saw no mosquitos, and noseeums usually live in sand or grass, so I had to wonder what critters rose from the lake to bite me.

We weren't allowed to untie from the buoy until our new pilot arrived in the morning. Our day two pilot was also full of information about the canal but not as jocular as the first pilot.

For the first four hours crossing Gatun Lake, everything we saw looked natural, just flooded. The scenery could have passed for Lake Mead in Nevada, except green instead of brown. Finally, the legendary Culebra Cut came into view.

I have to admit that after everything I'd read about this incredible engineering feat—which British academic Lord Bryce called "the greatest liberty man has ever taken with nature"—the final reveal was a little underwhelming. It looked like a hill that's been sliced through the middle to make a pass for a highway. I had to remind myself that scale is hard to process without a nearby reference object, and the bulk of the excavation work required to create the world's first artificial canyon is now underwater.

Before excavation, the highest point of the Culebra Cut was 325 feet above sea level. To create a ditch 300 feet wide at the base, engineers had to dig down as much as 500 feet from the original ground level. Along the nine-mile dig, they uncovered a layer of blue clay, which had a nasty habit of liquefying during the rainy season, causing devastating landslides. Major slides buried railroad tracks and equipment, setting the project back months each time.

The Culebra Cut under construction

The goal was to find the "angle of repose" from which the slope would hold its integrity, even under Panama's prodigious rains. After each slide, engineers scaled the walls back, widening the cut. A 20 percent grade, meaning one vertical foot for every five horizontal feet, still wasn't stable.

All told, excavators removed ninety-six million cubic yards of spoil—enough to fill a square city block nineteen miles high. After twenty-two major slides over the years, engineers finally found an angle that would hold, at least long enough to get the canal into operation.

On October 10th, 1913, newspaper reporters and Victorian-era tourists gathered on a nearby hill to watch water flood into the Culebra Cut. Explosives strapped to the last dike were detonated over telegraph wires by Woodrow Wilson from Washington, DC. Sporadic slides have continued ever since, sometimes blocking canal traffic for months. The true angle of repose has yet to be found.

Once through the Culebra Cut, we approached the Pedro Miguel Locks, where we lashed the three sailboats into the same configuration as the day before. Catching the rope was much easier this time, since we started at the top instead of the bottom.

The water began to churn again, but this time with even more sinister-looking whirlpools. I had an image of falling in and getting sucked into some exit valve letting out thousands of gallons of water a second.

The S.S. Ancon passes near the Culebra Cut at the official opening of the Panama Canal on August 15, 1914

Still beats falling off the crocodile bridge in Costa Rica.

It quickly became evident that the rope handling was more serious for this part. Instead of taking slack *in* as the boats rose, we'd need to ease tension *out* as the boats descended. Not too fast, or the boats might drift. Not too slow, or the ropes might become so tight that we couldn't pull them off the cleat.

A giant Panamax container ship, our lock mate for day two, looms over us

I jokingly asked our pilot, "If the ropes get stuck, will our boats just hang in midair like Wile E. Coyote?"—making a motion with my fingers like dangling legs to illustrate my point.

"No," he replied, "the metal cleat will come flying off and decapitate you."

Oh. That's not nearly as humorous of a visual gag. Like I said, our day two pilot was a bit of a Debbie Downer.

To keep from being decapitated, making the correct figure 8 knot became vitally important. With the extra stress of going down instead of up this time, Wilma and Papa felt more comfortable handling the ropes. This made sense on one level because they had more experience, and it was their boat. But Pat and I were bigger and could get more leverage trying to pull an already taut rope off a cleat. We did have to help pull a few times when Wilma and Papa couldn't get a rope loose. In the heat of the moment, I don't think they were always making the right knot. Papa cut a deep gash in his hand, and Wilma had her fingers smashed. Pat and I felt helpless watching. Again, everyone on the center boat chilled and took in the scenery.

After we moved into the final lock and tied off, I looked up and saw the Miraflores Visitor Center, where dozens of people looked down at us from the same observation deck I stood on with the End of All Roads guys a few weeks earlier. It felt cool to be part of the show this time instead of a spectator. We waved at the crowd, but no one seemed to notice. They didn't come to the Panama Canal to look at small sailboats. Understandable.

When we reached the bottom of the last lock, the doors eased open to reveal the Bay of Panama. As the gates widened, a few scattered islands came into view—the whole scene bathed in golden sun peeking under the rain clouds. Our pilot announced, "Welcome to the Pacific Ocean." A crowd-pleasing line for sure.

Welcome to the Pacific Ocean

We made our way to a small harbor, where Pat and I disembarked and grabbed a celebratory beer. The fun-loving, island-grizzled couple from the center boat stopped by to say hello. I got the impression they had little money and no idea where they were going to sleep that night, and they couldn't have had bigger smiles on their faces.

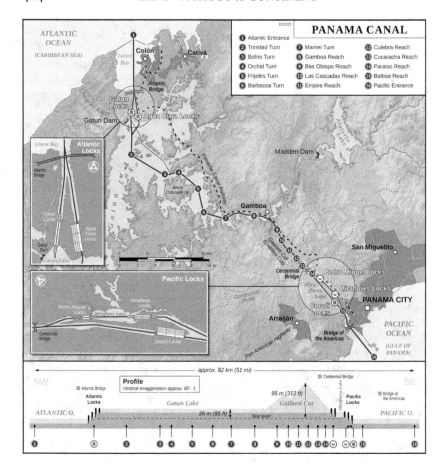

Chapter 48

Epilogue

> *It seems that the more places I see and experience, the bigger I realize the world to be. The more I become aware of, the more I realize how relatively little I know of it, how many places I have still to go, how much more there is to learn. Maybe that's enlightenment enough—to know that there is no final resting place of the mind, no moment of smug clarity. Perhaps wisdom, at least for me, means realizing how small I am, and unwise, and how far I have yet to go.*
>
> — Anthony Bourdain

During my stay in Boquete, just inside the doorway of my AirBnB, hung a life-size picture of a little indigenous girl of maybe three years old. She stood against a structure made from odd pieces of wood covered in various stages of peeling paint, which looked like it had been slapped together over generations. In juxtaposition to her surroundings, the girl wore a simple yet dazzlingly white dress with pink trim, fit for the preeminent special occasion in her young life. Instead of a smiling pose, she had the look and body posture that very young kids give off when they aren't quite sure what to think of you yet.

The striking portrait made me think of the girl I'd seen clipping her mother's toenails in Puebla, and all the mothers and daughters selling trinkets, or working together in the hundreds of tiendas and food stalls I'd seen on the trip. Every day, when I came back after Spanish class to nurse my sore throat, I was greeted by that little girl. Every day her mesmerizing gaze prompted me to think some version of "Politics be damned, that little girl deserves a good life."

The picture of the little girl in my AirBnB

I promised I would do something when I got back to the States to try to help people like her. That something became finishing this book.

If I pique the curiosity of a handful of readers, I'll be thrilled. The biggest compliment I could ever receive would be to hear that I inspired someone to overcome their misgivings, to go see some of the places in the book. I know they'll meet warm and gracious Latin Americans living their lives with dignity, and have their preconceptions about the region shattered, like I did. Hopefully, their empathy will move out of the realm of the abstract and into the gut, as mine did, and roam a little more freely across national borders, as human empathy should.

It's not much. But it's something.

And that, as they say in the movies, is a wrap.

I stayed true to my promise to revisit Antigua, laying over for a week while my car was on a slow boat to Galveston. I earned another Spanish certificate from Tecun Uman, which still hangs proudly on my refrigerator. I ran into Remus, the French vagabonder who worked at the Volcano Hostel, and otherwise spent the week watching World Cup games at Reilly's Pub. Poor England. The Cup was not, in fact, coming home.

I retrieved my vehicle from the port of Galveston and headed north to the Will Rogers Turnpike, listening to *Choctaw Bingo* by James McMurtry as I drove under the freeway-spanning Howard Johnsons-turned-McDonalds that nine-year-old Matt thought was just about the coolest thing he'd ever seen. I got to experience Kansas City in July for the first time in a few decades. I shared the drive across Kansas (which I actually enjoy for some sicko reason) with my sister/copy editor. And I pulled over to take a job interview somewhere outside of Barstow.

Then I plugged in my address and let Google Maps Lady guide me on home.

Fast-forward almost six years, my foot is better and I'm ready to finally erase the "bust" status in my blog ushuaiaorbust.com. So stay tuned for *[Working Title]: a Road Trip through South America.* I hope to cut the process down by a few years this time around. Lordy.

Che.' tza' ujtyi b'ajche' jiñi!

ACKNOWLEDGMENTS

All acknowledgments must start with my writing class teacher-turned-writing coach, Cole Kazdin, who steered me out of the dark woods of having no idea what I was doing. Cole, your energy is infectious, and your motivation, insights, and guidance were invaluable.

I have to thank my fact-checker, Professor Edwin Barnhart of the Maya Exploration Center. Ed, if I hadn't found your engaging and inspiring courses, and you hadn't agreed to come on board to corral my content, I'd simply have had to scrap the deep dive into Mesoamerica I had planned.

I took *Vagabonding* author Rolf Potts' travel writing workshop, looking for nuts and bolts tips to improve my prose. I learned plenty of those, but so much more about the philosophy, process, and soul of writing. "Where's the heat?" will forever ring in my ears when I sit down to write.

My friend Tommi went well above and beyond expectations as a beta reader. Tommi, your insights and contributions improved the book so much more than you know.

Finally, I have to thank my sister/copy editor, Jennifer. Your overwhelming generosity and Sisyphean patience with my comma struggles have touched me beyond words.

I cannot emphasize enough that I literally wouldn't have a book without the contributions of each of the people listed above. Thank you all from the bottom of my heart.

BIBLIOGRAPHY

Allen, William. *Green Phoenix: Restoring the Tropical Forests of Guanacaste, Costa Rica.* Oxford University Press, 2001.

Amaya, Rufina (video with her first-hand account of the El Mozote Massacre). S.I.T. Media Library, 2016. https://www.youtube.com/watch?v=X8E-RJxjYMo

Balf, Todd. *The Darkest Jungle.* Crown Publishers, 2003.

Barnhart, Ed. *Maya to Aztec: Ancient Mesoamerica Revealed.* The Great Courses, 2015. https://www.thegreatcourses.com/courses/maya-to-aztec-ancient-mesoamerica-revealed.html

Barnhart, Ed. *Exploring the Mayan World.* The Great Courses, 2020. https://www.thegreat courses.com/courses/the-mayan-world

Belli, Giaconda. *The Country Under My Skin: A Memoir of Love and War.* Anchor Books, 2002.

Biesanz, John & Mavis. *The People of Panama.* Columbia University Press, 1955.

Biesanz, Mavis, Richard & Karen. *The Ticos: Culture and Social Change in Costa Rica.* Lynne Rienner Publishers, 1999.

Boggs, Henrietta. *Married to a Legend: Don Pepe.* Henrietta Boggs-MacGuire, 2008.

Brewster, Barret. *The Gap: Crossing the Deadliest Leg of the World's Greatest Migration.* Barret Brewster, 2022.

Carlsen, William. *Jungle of Stone: The Extraordinary Journey of John L. Stephens and Frederick Catherwood and the Discovery of the Lost Civilization of the Maya.* HarperCollins Publishers, 2016.

Coe, Michael D. *Breaking the Maya Code.* Thames and Hudson Press, 2012.

Cowgill, George L. *Ancient Teotihuacan: Early Urbanism in Central Mexico.* Cambridge University Press, 2015.

Crosby, Harry W. *Californio Portraits: Baja California's Vanishing Culture.* University of Oklahoma Press, 2015.

Danner, Mark. *The Massacre at El Mozote.* Vintage Books, 1993.

Egan, Andrew Niall. *Crossing the Darien Gap.* Adventura Publishing, 2008.

Foster, Nelson & Cordell, Linda S. *Chiles to Chocolate: Food the Americas Gave the World.* University of Arizona Press, 1992.

Frank, Dana. *The Long Honduran Night.* Haymarket Books, 2018.

Goldman, Francisco. *The Art of Political Murder: Who Killed the Bishop?* Grove Press, 2007.

Kinzer, Stephen. *Blood of Brothers: Life and War in Nicaragua.* Harvard University Press, 2007.

Lapper, Richard & Painter, James. *Honduras: State for Sale.* Latin America Bureau, 1985.

Lasso, Marixa. *Erased: The Untold Story of the Panama Canal.* Harvard University Press, 2019.

Mann, Charles C., Dennis, Darrell, et al. *1491: New Revelations of the Americas Before Columbus.* Vintage Books, 2011.

Mitchinson, Martin. *The Darien Gap: Travels in the Rainforest of Panama.* Harbor Publishing, 2008.

McCafferty, Geoffrey G. *The Cholula Massacre: Factual Histories and Archaeology of the*

Spanish Conquest. University of Calgary, 2000. https://antharky.ucalgary.ca/mccafferty/sites/antharky.ucalgary.ca.mccafferty/files/CholulaMassacre_2000.pdf

McCullough, David, Runger, Nelson et al. *The Path Between the Seas: The Creation of the Panama Canal, 1870-1914.* Simon & Schuster, 1977.

Niemann, Greg. *Baja Legends.* Sunbelt Publications, 2002.

Peterson, Walt. *The Baja Adventure Book.* Wilderness Press, 1998.

Reichman, Daniel R. *The Broken Village: Coffee, Migration, and Globalization in Honduras.* Cornell University Press, 2011.

Rushdie, Salman. *The Jaguar Smile.* Random House, 1997.

Smith, Jack. *God and Mr. Gomez: Building a Dream House in Baja.* Reader's Digest Press, 1974.

Spence, Lewis. *The Myths of Mexico and Peru.* Cosimo, Inc., 1913.

Stephens, John Lloyd. *Incidents of Travel in Central America, Chiapas, and Yucatan.* Cosimo, Inc., 1841.

Wallace, David Rains. *The Quetzel and the Macaw: The Story of Costa Rica's National Parks.* Sierra Club Books, 1992.

About the Author

Matt Savino is a writer, traveler, software developer, avid photographer and one-time stand-up comedian and professional poker player originally from Kansas City, now living in parts unknown. His goal is to see the world in his beloved Toyota FJ Cruiser. This is his first book about that driving adventure.

Website: mattsavino.com

Travel Blog: ushuaiaorbust.com/blog

Instagram: instagram.com/ushuaia_or_bust